GCSE AQA

Chemistry

Complete Revision and Practice

Contents

How Science Works
Theories Come, Theories Go 1
Your Data's Got to Be Good 3
Bias and How to Spot it 5
Science Has Limits 6
Climate Change: A Modern Example 8

Chemistry 1a — Products From Rocks
Atoms and Elements 10
The Periodic Table 11
Compounds and Mixtures 12
Balancing Equations 14
Using Limestone 15
    Warm-Up and Exam Questions 18
    Exam Questions 19
Properties of Metals 20
Metals from Rocks 22
The Reactivity Series 24
Extraction of Metals 25
    Warm-Up and Exam Questions 26
    Exam Questions 27
Making Metals More Useful 28
Aluminium and Titanium 30
More About Metals 31
    Warm-Up and Exam Questions 32
Fractional Distillation of Crude Oil 33
Crude Oil — Alkanes 34
Using Crude Oil as Fuel 36
Environmental Problems 38
Environmental Problems (Alternative Fuels) 40
    Warm-Up and Exam Questions 41
    Exam Questions 42
Revision Summary for Chemistry 1a 43

Chemistry 1b — Oils, Earth and Atmosphere
Cracking Crude Oil 44
Alkenes 45
Ethanol 46
Using Alkenes to Make Polymers 47
    Warm-Up and Exam Questions 49
Extracting Plant Oils 50
Emulsions 51
Using Plant Oils for Fuels 52

Using Plant Oils in Food 53
Food Additives 54
    Warm-Up and Exam Questions 56
Plate Tectonics 57
The Earth's Structure 59
The Evolution of the Atmosphere 60
    Warm-Up and Exam Questions 62
    Exam Questions 63
Revision Summary for Chemistry 1b 64

Chemistry 2i — Bonding and Reactions
Atoms 65
Elements and Compounds 66
Isotopes 67
The Periodic Table 68
Electron Shells 69
Electron Configurations 70
    Warm-Up and Exam Questions 71
Ionic Bonding 72
Electron Shell and Ions 74
    Warm-Up and Exam Questions 75
Covalent Bonding 76
Covalent Substances: Giant Covalent 78
Covalent Substances: Simple Covalent 80
Metallic Structures 81
Nanomaterials 82
Nanomaterials and Smart Materials 83
    Warm-Up and Exam Questions 84
    Exam Questions 85
Relative Formula Mass 86
Formula Mass Calculations 87
Calculating Masses in Reactions 89
The Mole 90
    Warm-Up and Exam Questions 92
    Exam Questions 93
Atom Economy 94
Percentage Yield 96
    Warm-Up and Exam Questions 98
Revision Summary for Chemistry 2i 99

Chemistry 2ii — Rates of Reaction
Rates of Reaction 100
Measuring Rates of Reaction 101
Rate of Reaction Experiments 103
    Warm-Up and Exam Questions 107
Collision Theory 108
Catalysts 110
    Warm-Up and Exam Questions 112

Contents

Energy Transfer in Reactions 113
Reversible Reactions 115
Haber Process 117
    Warm-Up and Exam Questions 118
Revision Summary for Chemistry 2ii 119

Chemistry 2iii — Using Ions in Solution

Acids and Alkalis 120
Acids Reacting with Metals 121
Oxides and Hydroxides 122
Making Salts 123
    Warm-Up and Exam Questions 125
    Exam Questions 126
Electrolysis and the Half-Equations 127
Electrolysis of Salt Water 128
Purifying Copper by Electrolysis 129
    Warm-Up and Exam Questions 130
    Exam Questions 131
Revision Summary for Chemistry 2iii 132

Chemistry 3i — Elements, Acids and Water

History of the Periodic Table 133
The Modern Periodic Table 135
Group 1 — The Alkali Metals 137
Group VII — The Halogens 139
    Warm-Up and Exam Questions 141
    Exam Questions 142
Transition Elements 143
    Warm-Up and Exam Questions 145
Acids and Alkalis 146
    Warm-Up and Exam Questions 149
Concentration 150
Indicators 152
Titrations 153
Titration Calculations 154
    Warm-Up and Exam Questions 155
    Exam Questions 156
Water 157
Water Quality 159
    Warm-Up and Exam Questions 161
Solubility 162
Hard Water 164
    Warm-Up and Exam Questions 166
Revision Summary for Chemistry 3i 167

Chemistry 3ii — Energy and Chemical Tests

Energy 168
Energy and Fuels 170
Bond Energies 172
Energy and Food 174
    Warm-Up and Exam Questions 176
    Exam Questions 177
Tests for Cations 178
Tests for Anions 180
    Warm-Up and Exam Questions 182
    Exam Questions 183
Tests for Organic Compounds 184
Instrumental Methods 186
Identifying Unknown Substances 188
    Warm-Up and Exam Questions 190
Revision Summary for Chemistry 3ii 191

Exam Skills

Answering Experiment Questions 192

Practice Exams

Unit Chemistry 1 197
Unit Chemistry 2 211
Unit Chemistry 3 224

Answers 235

Index 250

Published by CGP

Editors:
Adam Moorhouse
Sharon Keeley-Holden
Simon Little

Contributors:
Michael Aicken, Mike Bossart, Mike Dagless, John Duffy, Max Fishel,
Gemma Hallam, Lucy Muncaster, Mike Thompson, Sophie Watkins.

With thanks to Katherine Craig for the proofreading.

ISBN: 978 1 84762 544 1

Website: www.cgpbooks.co.uk
Clipart source: CorelDRAW® and VECTOR
Printed by Elanders Ltd, Newcastle upon Tyne.

Graph to show trend in atmospheric CO_2 concentration and global temperature on page 9 based on data by
EPICA Community Members 2004 and Siegenthaler et al 2005

Based on the classic CGP style created by Richard Parsons.

Photocopying – it's dull, grey and sometimes a bit naughty. Luckily, it's dead cheap, easy and quick to
order more copies of this book from CGP – just call us on 0870 750 1242. Phew!
Text, design, layout and original illustrations © Coordination Group Publications Ltd. (CGP) 2010
All rights reserved.

How Science Works

Theories Come, Theories Go

SCIENTISTS ARE ALWAYS RIGHT — OR ARE THEY?

Well it'd be nice if that were so, but it just ain't — never has been and never will be. Increasing scientific knowledge involves making mistakes along the way. Let me explain...

Scientists come up with **hypotheses** — then **test** them

1) Scientists try and explain things. Everything.

2) They start by observing or thinking about something they don't understand — it could be anything, e.g. planets in the sky, a person suffering from an illness, what matter is made of... anything.

3) Then, using what they already know (plus a bit of insight), they come up with a hypothesis (a theory) that could explain what they've observed.

> Remember, a hypothesis is just a theory, a belief. And believing something is true doesn't make it true — not even if you're a scientist.

About 100 years ago, we thought atoms looked like this.

4) So the next step is to try and convince other scientists that the hypothesis is right — which involves using evidence. First, the hypothesis has to fit the evidence already available — if it doesn't, it'll convince no one.

5) Next, the scientist might use the hypothesis to make a prediction — a crucial step. If the hypothesis predicts something, and then evidence from experiments backs that up, that's pretty convincing.

> This doesn't mean the hypothesis is true (the 2nd prediction, or the 3rd, 4th or 25th one might turn out to be wrong) — but a hypothesis that correctly predicts something in the future deserves respect.

A hypothesis is a good place to start

You might have thought that science was all about facts... well, it's not as cut and dried as that — you also need to know about the process that theories go through to become accepted, and how those theories change over time. Remember, nothing is set in stone...

Theories Come, Theories Go

*Other scientists will **test** the hypotheses too*

1) Now then... <u>other</u> scientists will want to use the hypothesis to make their <u>own predictions</u>, and they'll carry out their <u>own experiments</u>. (They'll also try to <u>reproduce</u> earlier results.) And if all the experiments in all the world back up the hypothesis, then scientists start to have a lot of <u>faith</u> in it.

2) However, if a scientist somewhere in the world does an experiment that <u>doesn't</u> fit with the hypothesis (and other scientists can <u>reproduce</u> these results), then the hypothesis is in trouble. When this happens, scientists have to come up with a new hypothesis (maybe a <u>modification</u> of the old theory, or maybe a completely <u>new</u> one).

3) This process of testing a hypothesis to destruction is a vital part of the scientific process. Without the '<u>healthy scepticism</u>' of scientists everywhere, we'd still believe the first theories that people came up with — like thunder being the belchings of an angered god (or whatever).

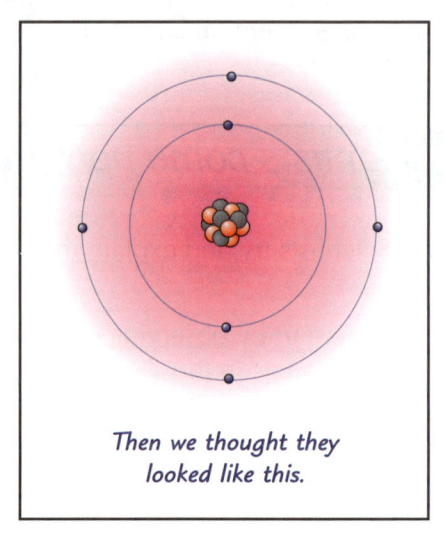

Then we thought they looked like this.

*If **evidence** supports a hypothesis, it's **accepted** — **for now***

1) If pretty much every scientist in the world believes a hypothesis to be true because experiments back it up, then it usually goes in the <u>textbooks</u> for students to learn.

2) Our <u>currently accepted</u> theories are the ones that have survived this 'trial by evidence' — they've been tested many, many times over the years and survived (while the less good ones have been ditched).

3) However... they never, <u>never</u> become hard and fast, totally indisputable <u>fact</u>.

Now we think it's more like this.

> You can never know... it'd only take <u>one</u> odd, totally inexplicable result, and the hypothesising and testing would start all over again.

You expect me to believe that — then show me the evidence...

If scientists think something is true, they need to produce evidence to convince others — it's all part of <u>testing a hypothesis</u>. One hypothesis might survive these tests, while others will be shown not to be true — this is progress. So, you see... not everything scientists say is true. <u>It's how science works</u>.

Your Data's Got to Be Good

Evidence is the key to science — but not all evidence is equally good.
The way that evidence is gathered can have a big effect on how trustworthy it is.

Lab experiments are better than rumour or small samples

1) Results from controlled experiments in laboratories are great. A lab is the easiest place to control variables so that they're all kept constant (except for the one you're investigating).

   This makes it easier to carry out a fair test.

   It's also the easiest way for different scientists around the world to carry out the same experiments. (There are things you can't study in a lab though, like climate.)

2) Old wives' tales, rumours, hearsay, 'what someone said', and so on, should be taken with a pinch of salt. They'd need to be tested in controlled conditions to be genuinely scientific.

3) Data based on samples that are too small don't have much more credibility than rumours do.

   A sample should be representative of the whole population (i.e. it should share as many of the various characteristics in the whole population as possible) — a small sample just can't do that.

Evidence is only reliable if other people can repeat it

Scientific evidence needs to be reliable (or reproducible). If it isn't, then it doesn't really help.

RELIABLE means that the data can be reproduced by others.

Example: Cold fusion

In 1989, two scientists claimed that they'd produced 'cold fusion' (the energy source of the Sun — but without the enormous temperatures).

It was huge news — if true, this could have meant energy from sea water — the ideal energy solution for the world... forever.

However, other scientists just couldn't get the same results — i.e. the results weren't reliable. And until they are, 'cold fusion' isn't going to be generally accepted as fact.

Reliability is really important in science
The scientific community won't accept someone's data if it can't be repeated by anyone else. It may sound like a really fantastic new theory, but if there's no other support for it, it just isn't reliable.

HOW SCIENCE WORKS

Your Data's Got to Be Good

Evidence also needs to be valid

To answer scientific questions scientists often try to link changes in one variable with changes in another. This is useful evidence, as long as it's valid.

VALID means that the data is reliable AND answers the original question.

Example: Do power lines cause cancer?

Some studies have found that children who live near overhead power lines are more likely to develop cancer. What they'd actually found was a correlation between the variables "presence of power lines" and "incidence of cancer" — they found that as one changed, so did the other.

But this evidence is not enough to say that the power lines cause cancer, as other explanations might be possible.

For example, power lines are often near busy roads, so the areas tested could contain different levels of pollution from traffic. Also, you need to look at types of neighbourhoods and lifestyles of people living in the tested areas (could diet be a factor... or something else you hadn't thought of...).

So these studies don't show a definite link and so don't answer the original question.

Controlling all the variables is really hard

In reality, it's very hard to control all the variables that might (just might) be having an effect.

You can do things to help — e.g. choose two groups of people (those near power lines and those far away) who are as similar as possible (same mix of ages, same mix of diets, etc).
But you can't easily rule out every possibility.

If you could do a properly controlled lab experiment, that'd be better — but you just can't do it without cloning people and exposing them to things that might cause cancer... hardly ethical.

Does the data really say that?

If it's so hard to be definite about anything, how does anybody ever get convinced about anything? Well, what usually happens is that you get a load of evidence that all points the same way.
If one study can't rule out a particular possibility, then maybe another one can. So you gradually build up a whole body of evidence, and it's this (rather than any single study) that convinces people.

Bias and How to Spot it

Scientific results are often used to make a point, but results are sometimes presented in a biased way.

You don't need to lie to make things biased

1) For something to be misleading, it doesn't have to be untrue. We tend to read scientific facts and assume that they're the 'truth', but there are many different sides to the truth. Look at this headline...

1 in 2 people are above average weight

Sounds like we're a nation of fatties. It's a scientific analysis of the facts and almost certainly true.

2) But an average is a kind of 'middle value' of all your data. Some readings are higher than average (about half of them, usually). Others will be lower than average (the other half).

So the above headline (which made it sound like we should all lose weight) could just as accurately say:

1 in 2 people are below average weight

3) The point is... both headlines sound quite worrying, even though they're not. That's the thing... you can easily make something sound really good or really bad — even if it isn't. You can...

① ...use only some of the data, rather than all of it:

"Many people lost weight using the new SlimAway diet. Buy it now!!"

"Many" could mean anything — e.g. 50 out of 5000 (i.e. 1%). But that could be ignoring most of the data.

② ...phrase things in a 'leading' way:

90% fat free!

Would you buy it if it were "90% cyanide free"? That 10% is the important bit, probably.

③ ...use a statistic that supports your point of view:

- The amount of energy wasted is increasing.
- Energy wasted per person is decreasing.
- The rate at which energy waste is increasing is slowing down.

These describe the same data. But two sound positive and one negative.

Think about why things might be biased

1) People who want to make a point can sometimes present data in a biased way to suit their own purposes (sometimes without knowing they're doing it).

2) And there are all sorts of reasons why people might want to do this — for example...

- Governments might want to persuade voters, other governments, journalists, etc. Evidence might be ignored if it could create political problems, or emphasised if it helps their cause.
- Companies might want to 'big up' their products. Or make impressive safety claims, maybe.
- Environmental campaigners might want to persuade people to behave differently.

3) People do it all the time. This is why any scientific evidence has to be looked at carefully. Are there any reasons for thinking the evidence is biased in some way?

- Does the experimenter (or the person writing about it) stand to gain (or lose) anything?
- Might someone have ignored some of the data for political or commercial reasons?
- Is someone using their reputation rather than evidence to help make their case?

Scientific data's not always misleading, you just need to be careful. The most credible argument will be the one that describes all the data that was found, and gives the most balanced view of it.

Science Has Limits

Science can give us amazing things — cures for diseases, space travel, heated toilet seats... But science has its limitations — there are questions that it just can't answer.

Some questions are *unanswered* by science — so far

1) We don't understand everything. And we never will. We'll find out more, for sure — as more hypotheses are suggested, and more experiments are done. But there'll always be stuff we don't know.

> For example, today we don't know as much as we'd like about climate change (global warming).
> Is climate change definitely happening? And to what extent is it caused by humans?

2) These are complicated questions (see page 8). At the moment scientists don't all agree on the answers. But eventually, we probably will be able to answer these questions once and for all.
3) But by then there'll be loads of new questions to answer.

Other questions are *unanswerable* by science

1) Then there's the other type... questions that all the experiments in the world won't help us answer — the "Should we be doing this at all?" type questions. There are always two sides...
2) Take embryo screening (which allows you to choose an embryo with particular characteristics). It's possible to do it — but does that mean we should?
3) Different people have different opinions. For example...

- Some people say it's good... couples whose existing child needs a bone marrow transplant, but who can't find a donor, will be able to have another child selected for its matching bone marrow. This would save the life of their first child — and if they want another child anyway... where's the harm?

- Other people say it's bad... they say it could have serious effects on the child. In the above example the new child might feel unwanted — thinking they were only brought into the world to help someone else. And would they have the right to refuse to donate their bone marrow (as anyone else would)?

4) This question of whether something is morally or ethically right or wrong can't be answered by more experiments — there is no "right" or "wrong" answer.
5) The best we can do is get a consensus from society — a judgement that most people are more or less happy to live by. Science can provide more information to help people make this judgement, and the judgement might change over time. But in the end it's up to people and their conscience.

Science Has Limits

*Loads of other **factors** can **influence decisions** too*

Here are some other factors that can influence decisions about science, and the way science is used:

Economic factors:

- Companies very often won't pay for research unless there's likely to be a profit in it.
- Society can't always afford to do things scientists recommend without cutting back elsewhere (e.g. investing heavily in alternative energy sources).

Social factors:

Decisions based on scientific evidence affect people — e.g. should fossil fuels be taxed more highly (to invest in alternative energy)?

Should alcohol be banned (to prevent health problems)? Would the effect on people's lifestyles be acceptable...

Environmental factors:

Genetically modified crops may help us produce more food — but some people say they could cause environmental problems.

Science is a "real-world" subject...

Science isn't just done by people in white coats in labs who have no effect on the outside world. Science has a massive effect on the real world every day, and so real-life things like money, morals and how people might react need to be considered. It's why a lot of issues are so difficult to solve.

HOW SCIENCE WORKS

Climate Change: A Modern Example

So if we're never quite sure of anything, why does anyone bother trying to find stuff out? Well, some scientific stuff is quite important — like avoiding planetary catastrophe, say. Yup, here's global warming...

Taking the temperature of a planet is hard

Years ago, a French scientist worked out that atmospheric gases, including CO_2, keep the Earth at a temperature that's just right. Later, a Swedish chemist, Arrhenius, predicted that as people burned more coal, the concentration of CO_2 in the atmosphere would rise, and the Earth would get warmer.

1) To test this hypothesis, you need reliable data for two variables — the CO_2 level and temperature. To be valid, the investigation has to cover the whole globe over hundreds of thousands of years (or we'd just discover that it was colder during the last ice age, which we know anyway).

2) To monitor global temperature, scientists often measure the temperature of the sea surface.

The first measurements were done from ships — some bloke would fling a bucket overboard, haul it up and stick a thermometer in it. Later, ships recorded the temperature of the water they took on board to cool their engines. Neither method was exactly great —

- Water samples weren't all taken from the same depth (and deeper water is usually colder).
- The sailors taking the readings were probably a bit slapdash — they were busy sailing. So if two samples were taken in the same place, at the same time, the results would quite possibly be different — in other words, not reproducible.
- Ships didn't go everywhere, so the records are a bit patchy. So, you might see that the North Atlantic ocean is getting warmer, but have no idea about the rest of the world. The original hypothesis was about global temperature, so the validity of these results is doubtful.

3) Today, things are much better — we can measure sea surface temperature from satellites, with modern, accurate instruments. These results are reliable, and they give us global coverage.

4) We also have very clever ways of finding temperatures and CO_2 levels from the distant past (before thermometers existed) — by examining air bubbles trapped deep in the ice in Antarctica, for example. There are similar tricks involving tree rings, sediments and pollen, so the results can be checked. Even so, these methods aren't perfect — there may be contamination problems, for instance.

Climate Change: A Modern Example

Interpreting the data is even harder...

1) This is a graph of the CO$_2$ and global temperature data. It shows temperature and CO$_2$ rising very rapidly from about 1850 (when the Industrial Revolution began).

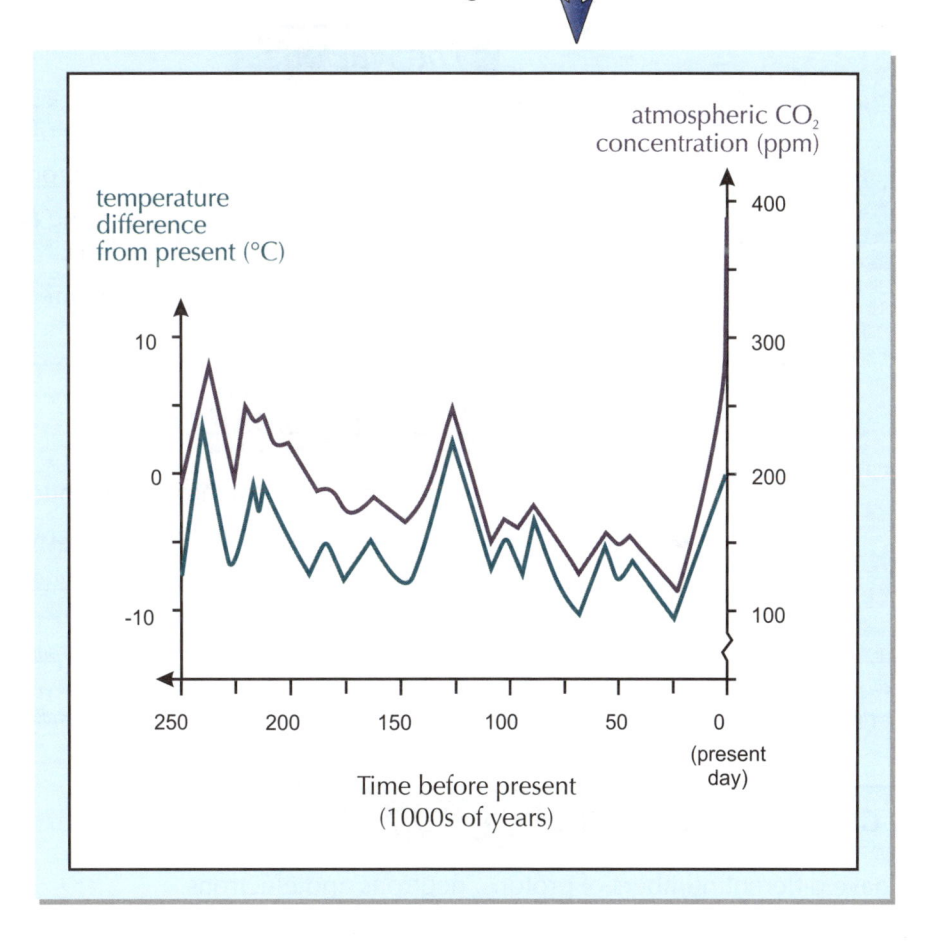

[Graph showing temperature difference from present (°C) on left y-axis ranging from -10 to 10, atmospheric CO$_2$ concentration (ppm) on right y-axis ranging from 100 to 400, and Time before present (1000s of years) on x-axis from 250 to 0 (present day).]

2) But the graph also shows that there have been huge changes in the climate before — you could argue that the recent warming is just part of that natural variability.

3) So from this graph you can't conclude that the increase in CO$_2$ since 1850 is causing the increase in global temperrature.

4) However, climate scientists have looked at lots of other sources of data as well, so there's now a scientific consensus that the recent warming isn't natural variation. Scientists now know that humans are causing it because we're emitting too much CO$_2$.

Anthropogenic warming — eh?
There's almost no argument about the 'more CO$_2$ is making us warmer' theory now (there was plenty of doubt previously, when the data was dodgy). And there's a consensus among climate scientists that the warming is 'anthropogenic' (our fault) instead of being down to natural variability in climate.

Atoms and Elements

Atoms are the building blocks of everything — and I mean everything.
They're amazingly tiny — you can only see them with an incredibly powerful microscope.

Atoms have a small nucleus surrounded by electrons

This is the model of the atom you have to know about — and it's really simple.
There's nothing to it. Just learn and enjoy.

The Nucleus

1) The nucleus is in the middle of the atom.
2) It contains protons and neutrons.
3) Almost the whole mass of the atom is concentrated in the nucleus.
4) But size-wise it's tiny compared to the atom as a whole.

The Electrons

1) Electrons move around the nucleus in shells.
2) They're tiny, but their paths cover a lot of space.
3) Electron shells explain the whole of Chemistry.

The most recent evidence about atoms actually suggest that atoms are made of lots of weird and wonderful subatomic particles — some of them are just very hard to 'see'. So the picture we've given here, with atoms made up from just protons, neutrons and electrons, is probably not quite 'right'... but it's a really useful way to think about atoms and can help explain loads of chemistry.

Elements consist of one type of atom only

1) Atoms can have different numbers of protons, neutrons and electrons.
   It's the number of protons in the nucleus that decides what type of atom it is though.
2) For example, an atom with one proton in its nucleus is hydrogen, an atom with two protons is helium.
3) If a substance only contains one type of atom it's called an element.
   Quite a lot of everyday substances are elements:

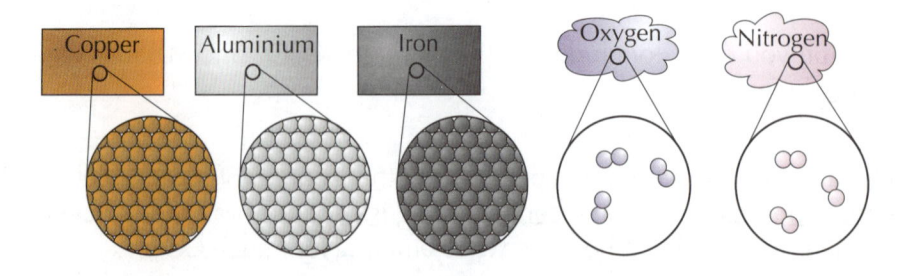

Copper   Aluminium   Iron   Oxygen   Nitrogen

This stuff's not too hard — in fact it's elementary...

Early last century, the theory was that atoms were solid balls. But in 1909, Ernest Rutherford tried firing helium nuclei at thin gold foil. Most of the nuclei went straight through and only the odd one bounced back. This surprised Ernest — but he was pretty smart, and realised it meant that most of the mass is concentrated in the nucleus and that most of the atom is empty space.
And that was that. The existing theory didn't fit with the new evidence, so it was adapted.

The Periodic Table

Chemistry would be really messy if it was all big lists of names and properties. So instead they've come up with a kind of shorthand for the names, and made a beautiful table to organise the elements — like a big filing system.

Atoms can be represented by symbols

Atoms of each element can be represented by a one or two letter symbol — it's a type of shorthand that saves you the bother of having to write the full name of the element.

Some make perfect sense, e.g.

> C = carbon   Li = lithium   Mg = magnesium

Others seem to make about as much sense as an apple with a handle. E.g.

> Na = sodium   Fe = iron   Pb = lead

Most of these odd symbols actually come from the Latin names of the elements.

The periodic table puts elements with similar properties together

1) The periodic table is laid out so that elements with similar properties form columns.
2) These vertical columns are called groups and Roman numerals are often used for them.
3) If you know the properties of one element, you can predict properties of other elements in that group.
4) For example the Group 1 elements are Li, Na, K, Rb, Cs and Fr. They're all metals and they react the same way. E.g. they all react with water to form an alkaline solution and hydrogen gas.
5) You can also make predictions about reactivity. E.g. in Group 1, the elements react more vigorously as you go down the group. And in Group 7, reactivity decreases as you go down the group.
6) There are 100ish elements, which all materials are made of. If it wasn't for the periodic table organising everything, you'd have a terrible job remembering all those properties.

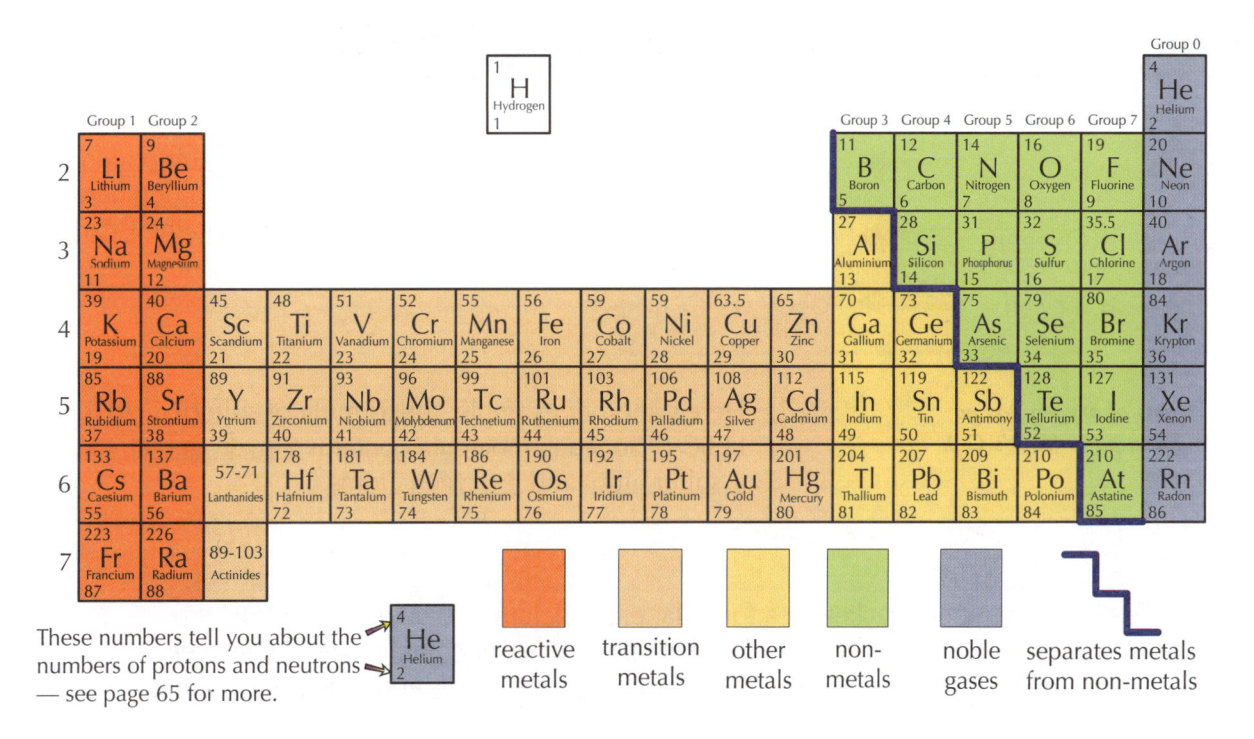

These numbers tell you about the numbers of protons and neutrons — see page 65 for more.

Colour key: reactive metals, transition metals, other metals, non-metals, noble gases, separates metals from non-metals

CHEMISTRY 1A — PRODUCTS FROM ROCKS

Compounds and Mixtures

Life'd be simple if you only had to worry about elements, even if there are a hundred or so of them. But you can mix and match elements to make lots of compounds, which complicates things no end.

Atoms *join together* to make *compounds*

1) When different elements react, atoms form chemical bonds with other atoms to form compounds. It's usually difficult to separate the two original elements out again.

2) Making bonds involves atoms giving away, taking or sharing electrons. Only the electrons are involved — it's nothing to do with the nuclei of the atoms at all.

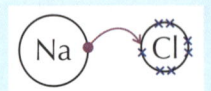

A sodium atom gives an electron to a chlorine atom to form an ionic bond.

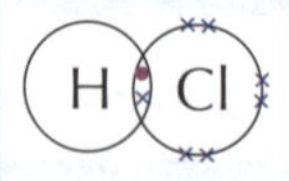

A hydrogen atom bonds with a chlorine atom by sharing an electron with it.

3) The properties of a compound are totally different from the properties of the original elements. For example, if iron (a lustrous magnetic metal) and sulfur (a nice yellow powder) react, the compound formed (iron sulfide) is a dull grey solid lump, and doesn't behave anything like either iron or sulfur.

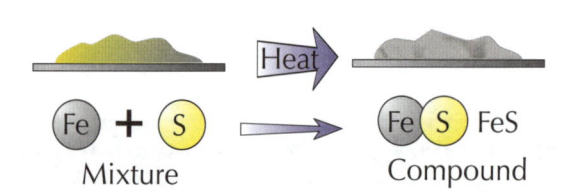

4) Compounds can be small molecules like water, or large lattices like sodium chloride.

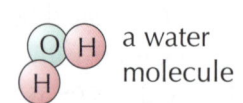

a water molecule

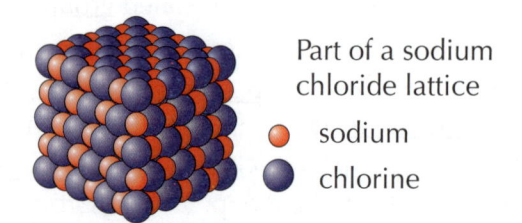

Part of a sodium chloride lattice
● sodium
● chlorine

A *formula* shows what *atoms* are in a *compound*

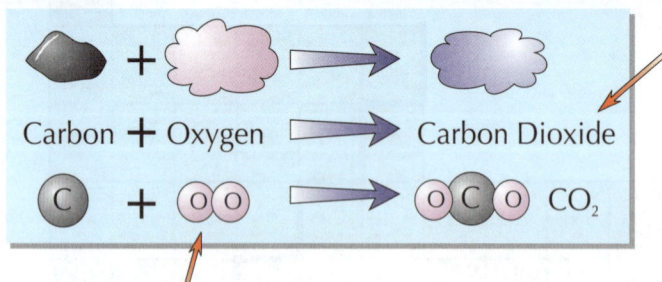

Carbon + Oxygen ⟹ Carbon Dioxide

C + OO ⟹ OCO CO_2

Atoms of oxygen gas go round in pairs (so it's O_2).

1) Carbon dioxide, CO_2, is a compound formed from a chemical reaction between carbon and oxygen. It contains 1 carbon atom and 2 oxygen atoms.

2) Here's another example: the formula of sulfuric acid is H_2SO_4. So, each molecule contains 2 hydrogen atoms, 1 sulfur atom and 4 oxygen atoms.

3) There might be brackets in a formula, e.g. calcium hydroxide is $Ca(OH)_2$. The little number outside the bracket applies to everything inside the brackets. So in $Ca(OH)_2$ there is 1 calcium atom, 2 oxygen atoms and 2 hydrogen atoms.

CHEMISTRY 1A — PRODUCTS FROM ROCKS

Compounds and Mixtures

Formulas can be used to write symbol equations for reactions

A chemical reaction can be described by the process <u>reactants</u> → <u>products</u>.
You can write the reaction as a <u>word equation</u> or <u>symbol equation</u>.

e.g. magnesium reacts with oxygen to produce magnesium oxide.

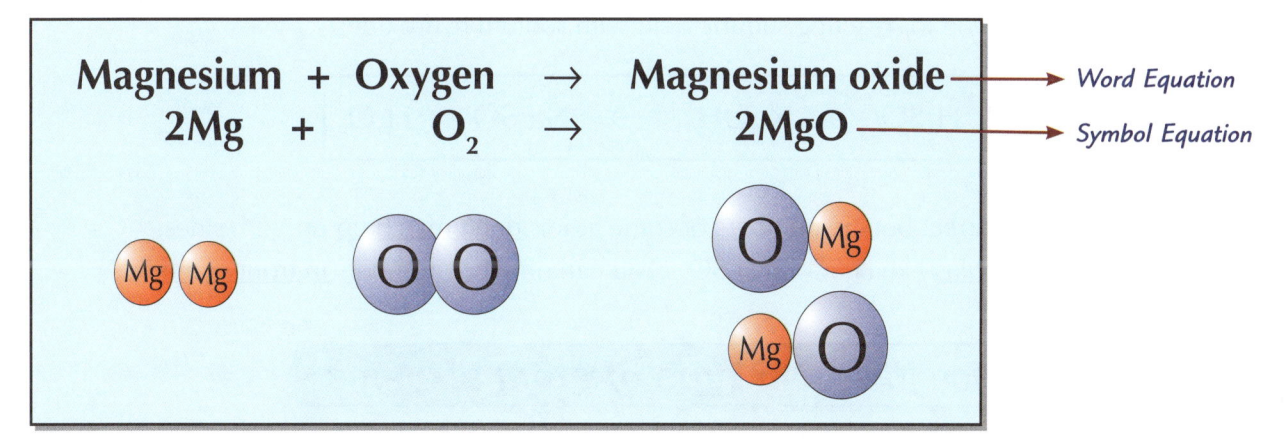

$$\text{Magnesium} + \text{Oxygen} \rightarrow \text{Magnesium oxide} \quad \text{— Word Equation}$$
$$2Mg + O_2 \rightarrow 2MgO \quad \text{— Symbol Equation}$$

In this reaction, two <u>elements</u> — Mg and O_2 — are combining to form a single compound.
Because atoms aren't gained or lost, the <u>mass</u> of the reactants <u>equals</u> the mass of the products.
So, if you react <u>6 g of magnesium</u> with <u>4 g of oxygen</u>, you'd end up with <u>10 g of magnesium oxide</u>.

Mixtures are easily separated — not like compounds

Mixtures are <u>completely different</u> to compounds — <u>don't confuse them</u>...

1) Unlike in a compound, there's <u>no chemical bond</u> between the different parts of a mixture. The parts can be separated out by <u>physical methods</u> such as distillation (see page 33).

2) <u>Air</u> is a <u>mixture</u> of gases, mainly nitrogen, oxygen, carbon dioxide and argon. The gases can all be <u>separated out</u> fairly easily.

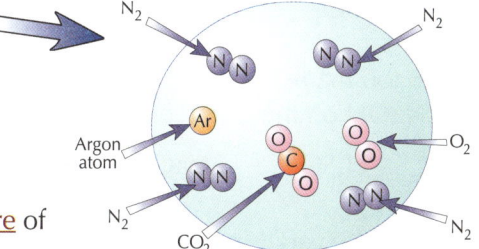

3) The <u>properties</u> of a mixture are just a <u>mixture</u> of the properties of the <u>separate parts</u>.

4) A <u>mixture</u> of <u>iron powder</u> and <u>sulfur powder</u> will show the properties of <u>both iron and sulfur</u>. It will contain grey magnetic bits of iron and bright yellow bits of sulfur.

Iron and sulfur mixed together, but unreacted.

5) <u>Crude oil</u> is a <u>mixture</u> of different length hydrocarbon molecules — see page 33.

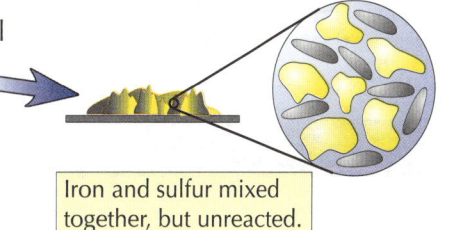

Not learning this stuff will only compound your problems...

Think of Lego bricks. You can have a bucket of individual different coloured bricks — this is a <u>mixture</u>. The individual bricks can be <u>separated</u> really easily. You can also have some different coloured Lego bricks stuck together — this'd be like a <u>compound</u>. It's a bit <u>harder</u> to separate these bricks.

CHEMISTRY 1A — PRODUCTS FROM ROCKS

Balancing Equations

Balancing equations is a pretty essential skill for any wannabe chemist. Here's how to do it...

Balancing the equation — match them up one by one

1) There must always be the same number of atoms on both sides — they can't just disappear.
2) You balance the equation by putting numbers in front of the formulas where needed.

Take this equation for reacting sulfuric acid with sodium hydroxide:

$$H_2SO_4 + NaOH \rightarrow Na_2SO_4 + H_2O$$

The formulas are all correct but the numbers of some atoms don't match up on both sides. You can't change formulas like H_2SO_4 to H_2SO_5. You can only put numbers in front of them:

Method: balance just ONE type of atom at a time

The more you practise, the quicker you get, but all you do is this:

1) Find an element that doesn't balance and pencil in a number to try and sort it out.
2) See where it gets you. It may create another imbalance, but pencil in another number and see where that gets you.
3) Carry on chasing unbalanced elements and it'll sort itself out pretty quickly.

I'll show you. In the equation above you soon notice we're short of H atoms on the RHS (Right-Hand Side).

1) The only thing you can do about that is make it $2H_2O$ instead of just H_2O:

$$H_2SO_4 + NaOH \rightarrow Na_2SO_4 + 2H_2O$$

2) But that now causes too many H atoms and O atoms on the RHS, so to balance that up you could try putting 2NaOH on the LHS (Left-Hand Side):

$$H_2SO_4 + 2NaOH \rightarrow Na_2SO_4 + 2H_2O$$

3) And suddenly there it is! Everything balances. And you'll notice the Na just sorted itself out.

State symbols tell you what physical state it's in

These are easy enough, so just make sure you know them — especially aq (aqueous).

(s) — Solid	(l) — Liquid	(g) — Gas	(aq) — Dissolved in water

E.g. $2Mg\,(s) + O_2\,(g) \rightarrow 2MgO\,(s)$

All this balancing — it's enough to make you dizzy...

Write balanced symbol equations for these, and put the state symbols in too:
1) Iron(III) oxide + hydrogen → iron + water
2) Dilute hydrochloric acid + aluminium → aluminium chloride solution + hydrogen

Using Limestone

The Mendip Hills and the Yorkshire Dales are mainly made of a rock called limestone. When limestone is dug out of the ground it's great for building stuff like houses and churches from. You need limestone to make mortar, cement, concrete and glass too.

Limestone is used as a building material

1) Limestone is a bit of a boring grey/white colour. It's often formed from sea shells and, although the original shells are mostly crushed, there are still quite a few fossilised shells remaining.
2) It's quarried out of the ground. This causes some environmental problems though — see the next page.
3) It's great for making into blocks for building with. Fine old buildings like cathedrals are often made purely from limestone blocks. It's also used for statues and fancy carved bits on nice buildings too.
4) Limestone's virtually insoluble in plain water. But acid rain is a big problem. The acid reacts with the limestone and dissolves it away.
5) Limestone can also be crushed up into chippings and used in road surfacing.

St Paul's Cathedral is made from limestone.

Limestone is mainly calcium carbonate

1) Limestone is mainly calcium carbonate — $CaCO_3$.
2) When it's heated it thermally decomposes (breaks down) to make calcium oxide (quicklime) and carbon dioxide.

> calcium carbonate → calcium oxide + carbon dioxide
> (quicklime)
> $CaCO_3(s)$ → $CaO(s)$ + $CO_2(g)$

Thermal decomposition is when one substance chemically changes into at least two new substances when it's heated.

3) When other carbonates are heated, they decompose in the same way (e.g. $Na_2CO_3 \rightarrow Na_2O + CO_2$).

Quicklime reacts with water to produce slaked lime

1) When you add water to quicklime you get slaked lime. Slaked lime is actually calcium hydroxide.

> quicklime + water → slaked lime   or $CaO + H_2O \rightarrow Ca(OH)_2$

2) Slaked lime is an alkali which can be used to neutralise acid soils in fields. Powdered limestone can be used for this too, but the advantage of slaked lime is that it works much faster.

CHEMISTRY 1A — PRODUCTS FROM ROCKS

Using Limestone

Limestone is really very handy. However, digging huge amounts of limestone out of the ground can have a quite a significant negative effect on the environment.

Limestone is used to make other building materials too

1) Powdered limestone is heated in a kiln with powdered clay to make cement.

2) Cement can be mixed with sand and water to make mortar. Mortar is the stuff you stick bricks together with. You can also use it to cover outside walls.

3) Or you can mix cement with sand, water and gravel to make concrete. And by including steel rods, you get reinforced concrete — a composite material with the hardness of concrete and the strength of steel.

4) And believe it or not — limestone is also used to make glass. You just heat it with sand and sodium carbonate until it melts.

Extracting rocks can cause environmental damage

1) Quarrying uses up land and destroys habitats. It costs money to make quarry sites look pretty again. And the waste materials from mines and quarries produce unsightly tips.

2) Transporting rock can cause noise and pollution, and the quarrying process itself produces dust and makes a lot of noise — they often use dynamite to blast the rock out of the ground.

3) Disused sites can be dangerous. Disused mines have been known to collapse. And quarries are sometimes turned into (very deep) lakes — people drown in them every year.

4) Quarries also destroy the habitats of animals and birds.

Limestone's amazingly useful

It sounds like you can achieve pretty much anything with limestone. Fred Flintstone even managed to make his car wheels and bowling balls out of rock (although I'm not 100% certain it was limestone).

Using Limestone

So using limestone ain't all hunky-dory — making stuff from it causes quite a few problems.

Making stuff from limestone causes pollution too

1) Cement factories make a lot of dust, which can cause breathing problems for some people.
2) Energy is needed to produce cement and quicklime. The energy is likely to come from burning fossil fuels, which causes pollution.

But on the plus side...

1) Limestone provides things that people want — like houses and roads. Chemicals used in making dyes, paints and medicines also come from limestone.
2) Limestone products are used to neutralise acidic soil. Acidity in lakes and rivers caused by acid rain is also neutralised by limestone products.
3) Limestone is also used in power station chimneys to neutralise sulfur dioxide, which is a cause of acid rain.
4) The quarry and associated businesses provide jobs for people and bring more money into the local economy. This can lead to local improvements in transport, roads, recreation facilities and health.
5) Once quarrying is complete, landscaping and restoration of the area is normally required as part of the planning permission.

Limestone products have advantages and disadvantages

1) Limestone, concrete (made from cement) and glass are used as building materials. In some cases they're perfect for the job, but in other cases they're a bit of a compromise.
2) Limestone is widely available and is cheaper than granite or marble. It's also a fairly easy rock to cut.
3) Some limestone is more hardwearing than marble, but it still looks attractive.
4) Concrete can be poured into moulds to make blocks or panels that can be joined together. It's a very quick and cheap way of constructing buildings — and it shows... — concrete has got to be the most hideously unattractive building material ever known.
5) Glass is transparent, making it useful for windows, etc. It easily breaks into sharp pieces though. It can be toughened, or made into safety glass which shatters into safer pieces. Clear plastic, such as perspex, is an alternative to glass. It's far lighter and won't shatter, but doesn't look quite as attractive.
6) Limestone, concrete, cement and glass don't rot when they get wet like wood does. They can't be gnawed away by insects or rodents either. And to top it off, they're fire-resistant too.
7) Concrete doesn't corrode like lots of metals do. It does have a fairly low tensile strength though, and can crack. If it's reinforced with steel bars it'll be much stronger.

Tough revision here — this stuff's rock hard...

There's a downside to everything, including using limestone — ripping open huge quarries definitely spoils the countryside. But you have to find a balance between the environmental and ecological factors and the economic and social factors — is it worth keeping the countryside pristine if it means loads of people have nowhere to live because there's no stuff available to build houses with?

Warm-Up and Exam Questions

It's easy to think you've learnt everything in the section until you try the warm-up questions. Don't panic if there are bits you've forgotten. Just go back over those bits until they're firmly fixed in your brain.

Warm-Up Questions

1) What is the definition of an element? Give two everyday substances that are elements.
2) Balance this equation for the reaction of glucose ($C_6H_{12}O_6$) and oxygen:
   $C_6H_{12}O_6 + O_2 \rightarrow CO_2 + H_2O$
3) List the four state symbols and say what they mean.
4) Give three major uses of limestone.
5) Give an example of environmental damage caused by quarrying.
6) Describe the difference between cement and mortar.

Exam Questions

1 Which of these statements about the structure of atoms is **not** true?

  A   The nucleus is in the middle of the atom.
  B   Electrons move around the nucleus in shells.
  C   The nucleus contains protons and electrons.
  D   Almost the whole mass of the atom is concentrated in the nucleus.

(1 mark)

2 The modern periodic table can be divided into metals and non-metals.
  The non-metals are:

  A   on the left of the periodic table.
  B   on the right of the periodic table.
  C   in the middle of the periodic table.
  D   in Group 2.

(1 mark)

3 Which of these statements about chemical reactions is **not** true?

  A   The mass of the reactants is always equal to the mass of the products.
  B   Atoms are neither created nor destroyed in a reaction.
  C   The mass of the products is always less than the mass of the reactants.
  D   In a written equation, the mass of all the atoms on the left of the arrow is equal to the mass of all the atoms on the right of the arrow.

(1 mark)

Exam Questions

4 Air is a mixture of gases, mainly nitrogen, oxygen, carbon dioxide and argon.

    (a) How is a compound different from a mixture?
(1 mark)

    (b) Name one gas found in air which is a compound.
(1 mark)

    (c) Oxygen gas, O_2, reacts with magnesium to form magnesium oxide, MgO. Write a balanced symbol equation for this reaction.
(2 marks)

5 Sulfuric acid, H_2SO_4, reacts with ammonia, NH_3, to form ammonium sulfate, $(NH_4)_2SO_4$.

    (a) Write the word equation for this reaction.
(1 mark)

    (b) Write a balanced symbol equation for this reaction.
(2 marks)

    (c) In the balanced equation, how many atoms are there in the reactants?
(1 mark)

6 Limestone is mainly calcium carbonate, $CaCO_3$. When heated, it thermally decomposes to produce calcium oxide and carbon dioxide.

    (a) Write a balanced symbol equation for this reaction.
(1 mark)

    (b) Calcium oxide is also known as quicklime. When water is added to quicklime, slaked lime is produced.
       (i) Write the chemical name and formula of slaked lime.
(2 marks)

       (ii) Give **one** use of slaked lime.
(1 mark)

7 Limestone is often used to make building materials.

    (a) How is cement made from limestone?
(2 marks)

    (b) How is glass made from limestone?
(2 marks)

Properties of Metals

Metals are all similar but slightly different. They have some basic properties in common, but each has its own specific combination of properties, which means you use different ones for different purposes.

Metals are on the left and middle of the periodic table

Most of the elements are metals — so they cover most of the periodic table.
In fact, only the elements on the far right are non-metals.
The so-called transition metals are found in the centre block of the periodic table.
Many of the metals in everyday use are transition metals — such as titanium, iron and nickel.

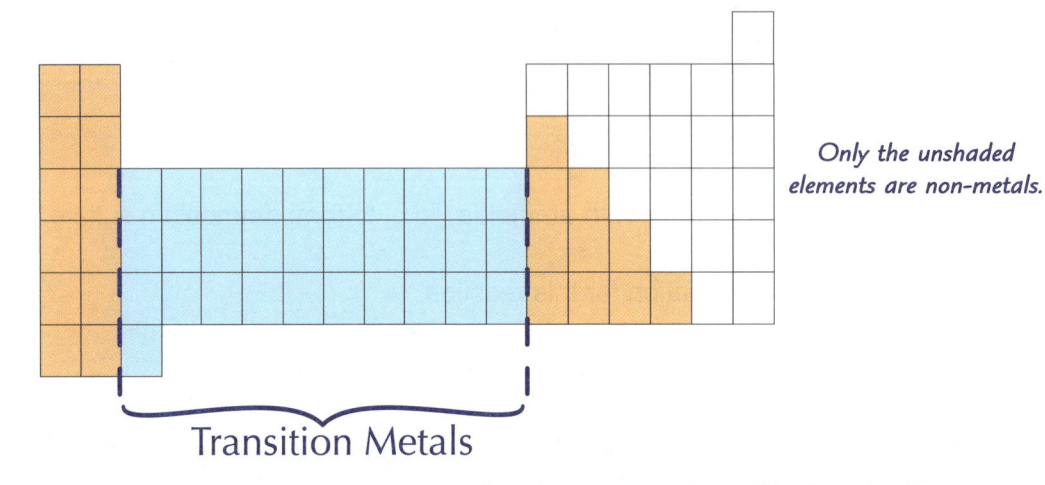

Only the unshaded elements are non-metals.

Transition Metals

Metals are strong and bendy, and they're great conductors

All metals have some fairly similar basic properties.
1) Metals are strong (hard to break), but they can be bent or hammered into different shapes.
2) They're great at conducting heat.
3) They conduct electricity well.

Metals (and especially transition metals) have loads of everyday uses because of these properties...

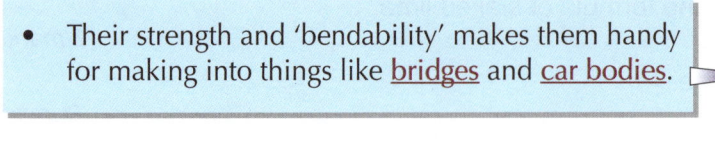

- Their strength and 'bendability' makes them handy for making into things like bridges and car bodies.

- Metals are ideal if you want to make something that heat needs to travel through, like a saucepan base.

- And their conductivity makes them great for making things like electrical wires.

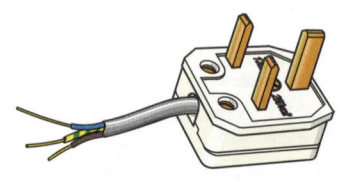

Transition metals have loads of everyday uses — partly because they're not crazily reactive like, say, potassium (which would catch fire if it got rained on).

CHEMISTRY 1A — PRODUCTS FROM ROCKS

Properties of Metals

The reason all metals have the same basic properties is because of the bonding in metals. It's their exact properties which are used to match metals to their uses.

It's the structure of metals that gives them their properties

1) All metals have the same basic properties. These are due to the special type of bonding in metals.

2) Metals consist of a giant structure of atoms held together with metallic bonds.

3) These special bonds allow the outer electron(s) of each atom to move freely.

4) This creates a "sea" of free electrons throughout the metal, which is what gives rise to many of the properties of metals.

5) This includes their conduction of heat and electricity.

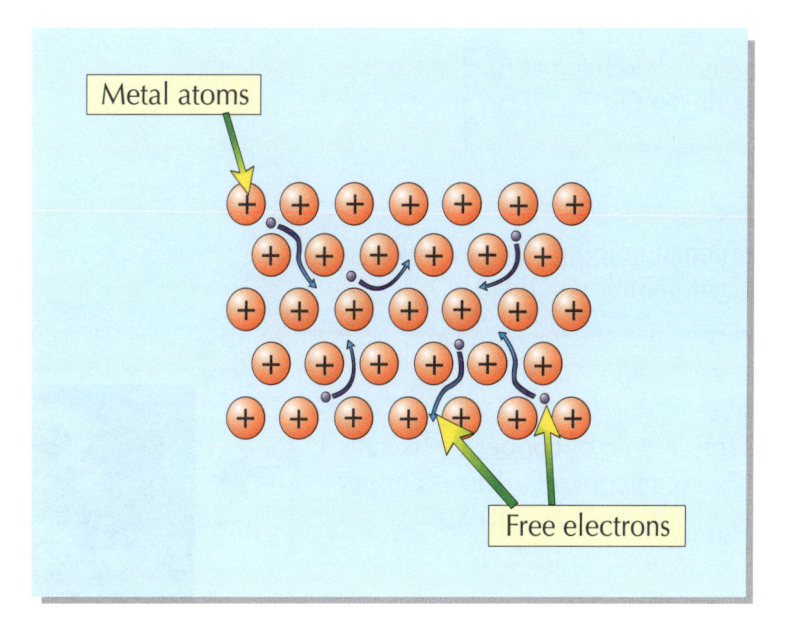

A metal's exact properties decide how it's best used

1) The properties above are typical properties of metals.
Not all metals are the same though — their exact properties determine how they're used.

2) If you wanted to make an aeroplane, you'd probably use metal as it's strong and can be bent into shape, but you'd also need it to have a low density — so aluminium would be a good choice.

3) And if you were making replacement hips, you'd pick a metal that won't corrode when it comes in contact with water — it'd also have to have a low density too, and not be too bendy. Titanium has all of these properties so it's used for this.

Properties of metals are all due to the "sea" of free electrons

So, all metals conduct electricity and heat and can be bent into shape. But lots of them have special properties too. You have to decide what properties you need and use a metal with those properties.

Metals from Rocks

You don't tend to find big lumps of pure metal in the ground — the metal atoms tend to be joined to other atoms in compounds. It can be a bit of a tricky, expensive process to separate the metal out.

Ores contain enough metal to make extraction worthwhile

1) Rocks are made of minerals. (Minerals are just solid elements and compounds.)

2) A metal ore is a mineral which contains enough metal to make it worthwhile extracting the metal from it.

3) In many cases the ore is an oxide of the metal. Here are a few examples:

As technology improves, it becomes possible to extract more metal from a sample of rock than previously. So it might now be worth extracting metal that wasn't worth extracting in the past.

a) A type of iron ore is called haematite. This is iron(III) oxide (Fe_2O_3).

b) The main aluminium ore is called bauxite. This is aluminium oxide (Al_2O_3).

c) A type of copper ore is called chalcopyrite. This is copper iron sulfide ($CuFeS_2$).

Chalcopyrite — a copper ore

4) There's a limited amount of ores — they're "finite resources".

5) People have to balance the social, economic and environmental effects of mining the ores. Most of the issues are exactly the same as those to do with quarrying limestone on page 16.

6) So mining metal ores is good because it means that useful products can be made. It also provides local people with jobs and brings money into the area. This means services such as transport and health can be improved.

7) But mining ores is bad for the environment as it causes noise, scarring of the landscape and loss of habitats. Deep mine shafts can also be dangerous for a long time after the mine has been abandoned.

CHEMISTRY 1A — PRODUCTS FROM ROCKS

Metals from Rocks

Copper has some important uses. So it's useful to know how to extract it as efficiently as possible.

Copper is purified by *electrolysis*

1) Copper is a transition metal. It is hard, strong and has a high melting point.
2) It is a good conductor of electricity, so it's ideal for drawing out into electrical wires.

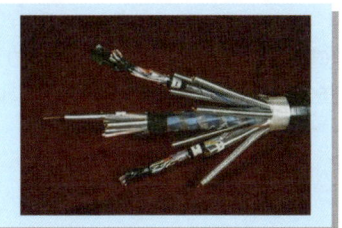

3) It can also be made into pipes, and as it's below hydrogen in the reactivity series (see p.24), it doesn't react with water. This makes it great for using in plumbing.

4) If you look on page 25 you'll see that copper can be easily extracted by reduction with carbon. But the copper produced this way is impure — and impure copper doesn't conduct electricity very well.
5) So electrolysis is used to purify it (see p.129), even though it's expensive. This produces very pure copper, which is a much better conductor.

Electrolysis uses electricity to separate the metal from the ore. Aluminium is another metal separated from its ore in this way.

Copper-rich ores are in *short supply*

1) The supply of copper-rich ores is limited, so it's important to recycle as much copper as possible.
2) The demand for copper is growing and this may lead to shortages in the future.
3) Scientists are looking into new ways of extracting copper from low-grade ores (ores that only contain small amounts of copper) or from the waste that is currently produced when copper is extracted.
4) One way is to use bacteria to separate copper from copper sulfide. The bacteria get energy from the bond between copper and sulfur, separating out the copper from the ore in the process.
5) This process is slow but it's more environmentally friendly than other methods, which need lots of energy and release sulfur dioxide gas which causes acid rain.

Copper is a really useful metal

The skin of the Statue of Liberty is made of copper — about 80 tonnes of it in fact. Its surface reacts with gases in the air to form copper carbonate — which is why it's that pretty shade of green. It was a present from France to the United States — I wonder if they found any wrapping paper big enough?

The Reactivity Series

How easy it is to get a metal out of its ore all comes down to the metal's position in the reactivity series.

More reactive metals are harder to get

1) A few unreactive metals like gold are found in the Earth as the metal itself, rather than as a compound.

2) But most metals need to be extracted from their ores using a chemical reaction.

3) More reactive metals, like sodium, are harder to extract — that's why it took longer to discover them.

A more reactive metal displaces a less reactive metal

1) More reactive metals react more strongly than less reactive metals.

2) This means that a metal can be extracted from its oxide by any more reactive metal. The more reactive metal bonds more strongly to the oxygen and pushes out the less reactive metal.

   E.g. tin could be extracted from tin oxide by more reactive iron.

   $$\text{tin oxide} + \text{iron} \rightarrow \text{iron oxide} + \text{tin}$$

3) And if you put a more reactive metal into the solution of a dissolved metal compound, the more reactive metal will replace the less reactive metal in the compound.

   E.g. put an iron nail in a solution of copper sulfate and the more reactive iron will "kick out" the less reactive copper from the solution. You end up with iron sulfate solution and copper metal.

   $$\text{copper sulfate} + \text{iron} \rightarrow \text{iron sulfate} + \text{copper}$$

4) But if a piece of silver metal is put into a solution of copper sulfate, nothing happens. The more reactive metal (copper) is already in the solution.

Extraction of Metals

Some metals can be *extracted* by *reduction* with *carbon*

1) Electrolysis (splitting with electricity) is one way of extracting a metal from its ore.

2) The other common way is chemical reduction using carbon or carbon monoxide.

3) When an ore is reduced, oxygen is removed from it, e.g.

$$Fe_2O_3 + 3CO \rightarrow 2Fe + 3CO_2$$

iron(III) oxide + carbon monoxide → iron + carbon dioxide

Position in the *reactivity series* is important for extraction

1) Metals higher than carbon in the reactivity series have to be extracted using electrolysis, which is expensive.

2) Metals below carbon in the reactivity series can be extracted by reduction using carbon. For example, iron oxide is reduced in a blast furnace to make iron.

3) This is because carbon can only take the oxygen away from metals which are less reactive than carbon itself is.

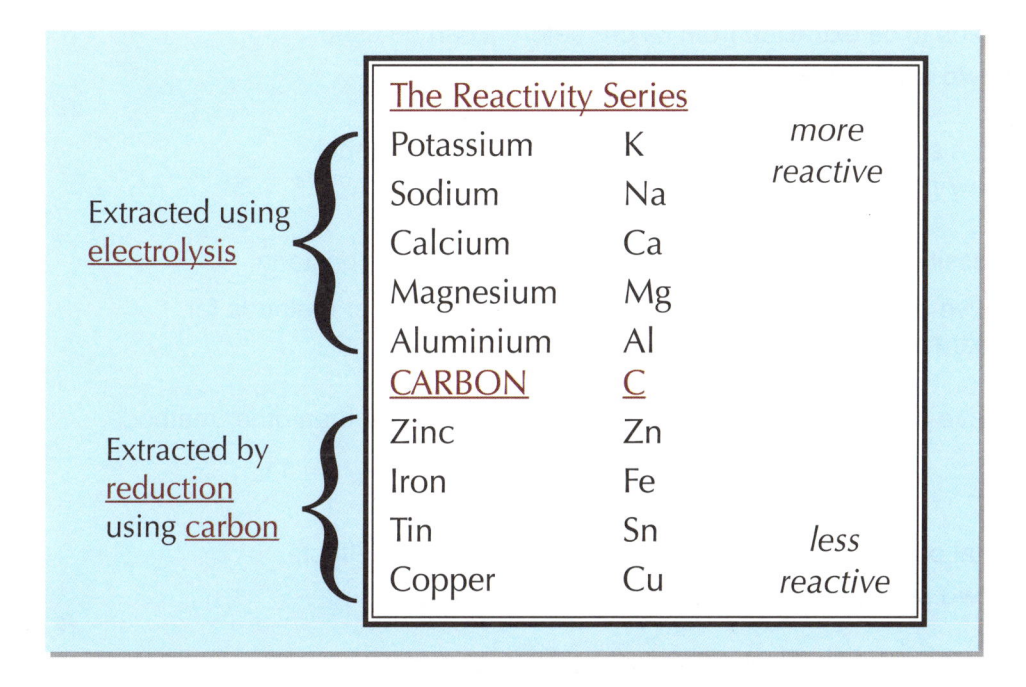

	The Reactivity Series		
	Potassium	K	*more reactive*
	Sodium	Na	
Extracted using electrolysis	Calcium	Ca	
	Magnesium	Mg	
	Aluminium	Al	
	CARBON	C	
	Zinc	Zn	
Extracted by reduction using carbon	Iron	Fe	
	Tin	Sn	*less reactive*
	Copper	Cu	

Extraction of metals is difficult

Extracting metals isn't cheap. You have to pay for special equipment, energy and labour. Then there's the cost of getting the ore to the extraction plant. If there's a choice of extraction methods, a company always picks the cheapest, unless there's a good reason not to — they're not extracting it for fun.

CHEMISTRY 1A — PRODUCTS FROM ROCKS

Warm-Up and Exam Questions

You've arrived at the next set of warm-up and exam questions. It's really important to find out what you know (as well as what you think you know but actually don't). So give them a go.

Warm-Up Questions

1) Give three useful physical properties of most metals.
2) What type of bonding do metals contain?
3) Name a metal ore.
4) Explain why copper used in electrical wires needs to be purified by electrolysis.
5) Name a metal which can be extracted from its ore by reduction with carbon.

Exam Questions

1 Which of the following statements does **not** describe copper?

   A A hard, strong transition metal.
   B The main product extracted from the ore bauxite.
   C A metal that is less reactive than iron.
   D A material used to make electrical wires.
   (1 mark)

2 Copper needs to be extracted from its ore before it can be used.
   (a) Give **two** uses of copper.
   (2 marks)

   (b) Why are scientists trying to find new ways to extract copper from low-grade ores?
   (1 mark)

   (c) It is possible to obtain copper from copper sulfide using bacteria.
      (i) Give **one** advantage of using this method over other methods for extracting copper from copper sulfide.
      (1 mark)

      (ii) Give **one** disadvantage of using this method rather than other methods.
      (1 mark)

3 Mining metal ores has social, economic and environmental effects.
   (a) Give **two** positive effects of mining metal ores.
   (2 marks)

   (b) Give **two** negative effects of mining metal ores.
   (2 marks)

CHEMISTRY 1A — PRODUCTS FROM ROCKS

Exam Questions

4   The diagram shows part of the reactivity series of metals, together with carbon.

Potassium	K	*more*
Sodium	Na	*reactive*
Calcium	Ca	
Magnesium	Mg	
Aluminium	Al	
<u>CARBON</u>	<u>C</u>	
Zinc	Zn	
Iron	Fe	
Tin	Sn	*less*
Copper	Cu	*reactive*

(a) Name one metal which is extracted from its ore using electrolysis.
(1 mark)

(b) Some metals can be extracted from their ores by reduction with carbon, producing the metal and carbon dioxide.

   (i) Explain the meaning of reduction.
   (1 mark)

   (ii) Write a word equation for the reduction of zinc oxide by carbon.
   (1 mark)

(c) Iron can be extracted by the reduction of iron(III) oxide (Fe_2O_3) with carbon monoxide (CO), to produce iron and carbon dioxide.
Write a balanced symbol equation for this reaction, including state symbols.
(3 marks)

(d) In which of these test tubes will a reaction occur?
(1 mark)

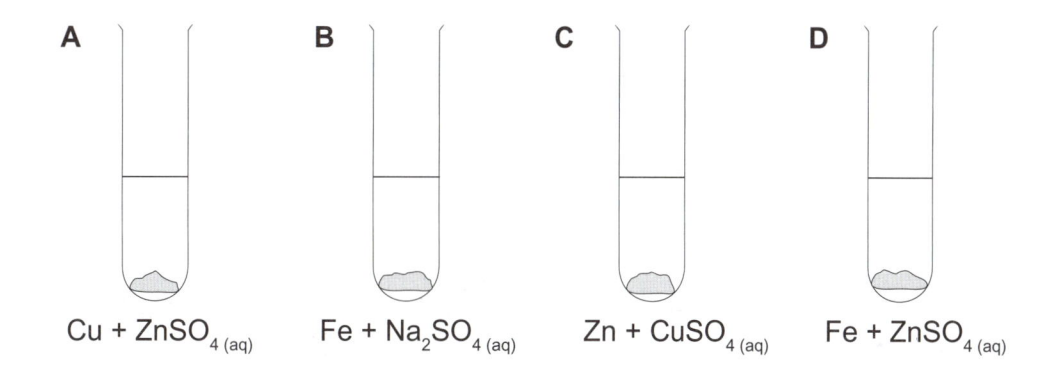

A $Cu + ZnSO_{4\,(aq)}$ **B** $Fe + Na_2SO_{4\,(aq)}$ **C** $Zn + CuSO_{4\,(aq)}$ **D** $Fe + ZnSO_{4\,(aq)}$

5   All metals have the same basic properties.

(a) Describe how the structure of a metal allows it to carry an electric current.
(2 marks)

(b) Why are metals good conductors of heat?
(1 mark)

Making Metals More Useful

Pure metals often aren't quite right for certain jobs. Instead of just making do with what they've got, scientists mix stuff in with the metals to make them exactly how they want.

Pure iron tends to be a bit too bendy

1) 'Iron' straight from the blast furnace is only 96% iron. The other 4% is impurities such as carbon.
2) This impure iron is brittle. It's used for ornamental railings but it doesn't have many other uses.
3) So all the impurities are removed from most of the blast furnace iron. This pure iron has a regular arrangement of identical atoms. The layers of atoms can slide over each other, which makes the iron soft and easily shaped. This iron is far too bendy for most uses.

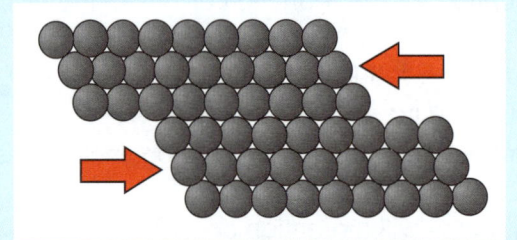

Most iron is converted into steel — an alloy

Most of the pure iron is changed into alloys called steels. Steels are formed by adding small amounts of carbon and sometimes other metals to the iron.

An alloy is a mixture of two or more metals, or a mixture of a metal and a non-metal.

TYPE OF STEEL	PROPERTIES	USES
Low carbon steel (0.1% carbon)	easily shaped	car bodies
High carbon steel (1.5% carbon)	very hard, inflexible	blades for cutting tools, bridges
Stainless steel (chromium added, and sometimes nickel)	rust-resistant	cutlery, containers for corrosive substances

Most iron is changed into steel, otherwise it's too bendy or too brittle

The Eiffel Tower is made of iron — but the problem with iron is, it goes rusty if air and water get to it. So the Eiffel Tower has to be painted every seven years to make sure that it doesn't rust. This is quite a job and takes an entire year for a team of 25 painters. Too bad they didn't use stainless steel.

Making Metals More Useful

Alloys are harder than pure metals

1) Different elements have <u>different sized atoms</u>. So when an element such as carbon is added to pure iron, the <u>smaller</u> carbon atom will <u>upset</u> the layers of pure iron atoms, making it more difficult for them to slide over each other. So alloys are <u>harder</u>.

2) Many metals in use today are actually <u>alloys</u>. For example:

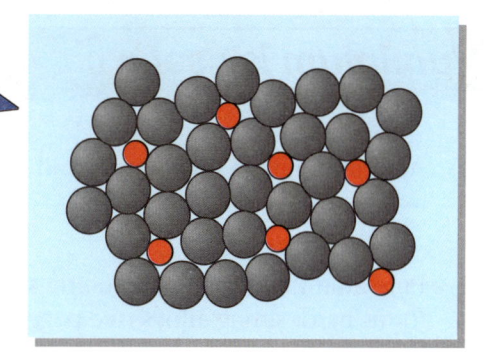

> **BRONZE = COPPER + TIN**
> Bronze is <u>harder</u> than copper.
> It's good for making medals and statues from.

> **CUPRONICKEL = COPPER + NICKEL**
> This is <u>hard</u> and <u>corrosion resistant</u>.
> It's used to make "silver" coins.

> **GOLD ALLOYS ARE USED TO MAKE JEWELLERY**
> Pure gold is <u>too soft</u>. Metals such as zinc, copper, silver, palladium and nickel are used to harden the "gold".

> **ALUMINIUM ALLOYS ARE USED TO MAKE AIRCRAFT**
> Aluminium has a <u>low density</u>, but it's <u>alloyed</u> with small amounts of other metals to make it <u>stronger</u>.

3) In the past, the development of alloys was by <u>trial and error</u>. But nowadays we understand much more about the properties of metals, so alloys can be <u>designed</u> for specific uses.

Smart alloys return to their original shape

1) <u>Smart alloys</u> have a <u>shape memory</u> property.

2) If you <u>bend</u> a wire made of a smart alloy, it'll go back to its <u>original shape</u> when it's <u>heated</u>.

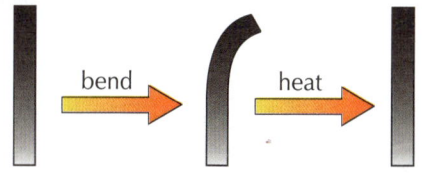

3) The possibility of using shape memory alloys to <u>control aeroplane movements</u> is being explored. At the moment the turning of aeroplanes is controlled by hydraulic flap systems which are <u>big and heavy</u>. If smart alloys could be used instead then <u>less fuel</u> would be needed.

4) At the moment, <u>metal fatigue</u> (see page 31) in smart alloys is a lot <u>worse</u> than in normal alloys. Smart alloys are also <u>more expensive</u> than steel or aluminium.

Alloys are really important in industry

If the properties of a metal aren't quite suited to a job, an alloy is often used instead. To make an alloy you mix one metal with another metal or non-metal. The finished alloy can be a lot harder, or less brittle — the properties can be varied and they can be made to suit a particular job really well.

Aluminium and Titanium

Aluminium and titanium are both low density metals, and a lot of their uses rely on this fact.

Aluminium is useful but expensive to extract...

1) Aluminium has a low density and is corrosion-resistant.

It seems a bit odd that aluminium is corrosion-resistant because it's a reactive metal. What happens is that the aluminium reacts quickly with the oxygen in the air to form aluminium oxide. This sticks firmly to the aluminium below and stops any further reaction taking place.

2) Pure aluminium isn't particularly strong, but it forms hard, strong alloys (see page 28).

3) These properties make aluminium a very useful structural material. It can be used for loads of things from window frames to electricity cables and aircraft.

4) You can't extract aluminium from its oxide by the cheap method of reduction with carbon.

5) It has to be extracted by electrolysis (see page 127). A high temperature is needed to melt the oxide — this requires lots of energy, which makes it an expensive process.

...and so is titanium

1) Titanium is another low density metal. Unlike aluminium it's very strong.

2) It has a low chemical reactivity which makes it resistant to corrosion.

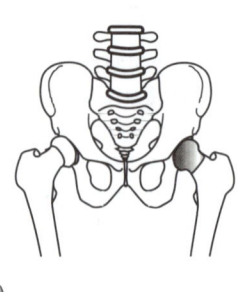

3) These properties mean that titanium is used in spacecraft, jet engines and hip replacements.

4) Like with aluminium, extracting titanium needs lots of energy, so it's expensive. The cost is increased further still by the fact that it's a long-winded process, with lots of little stages.

CHEMISTRY 1A — PRODUCTS FROM ROCKS

More About Metals

Metals are definitely a big part of modern life. Once they're finished with, it's far better to recycle them than to dig up more ore and extract fresh metal.

Metals are *good* — but *not perfect*

1) Metals, especially transition metals, tend to be strong and hard, so they're useful as structural materials. They can be mixed with other elements to make stronger and harder alloys.

2) Metals are often shiny, so they look attractive.

3) Metals do have problems though. Some corrode when exposed to air and water, so they need to be protected, e.g. by painting. If metals corrode, they lose their strength and hardness.

4) Metals can get 'tired' when stresses and strains are repeatedly put on them over time. This is known as metal fatigue and leads to metals breaking, which can be very dangerous, e.g. in planes.

Recycling metals is *important*

1) Mining and extracting metals takes lots of energy, most of which comes from burning fossil fuels.
2) Fossil fuels are running out so it's important to conserve them. Not only this, but burning them causes acid rain, global dimming and climate change (see pages 38 and 39).
3) Recycling metals only uses a small fraction of the energy needed to mine and extract new metal. E.g. recycling copper only takes 15% of the energy that's needed to mine and extract new copper.
4) Energy doesn't come cheap, so recycling saves money too.
5) Also, there's a finite amount of each metal in the Earth. Recycling conserves these resources.
6) Recycling metal cuts down on the amount of rubbish that gets sent to landfill. Landfill takes up space and pollutes the surroundings. If all the aluminium cans in the UK were recycled, there'd be 14 million fewer dustbins each year.

A titanium hip is nothing — my Granny's got a wooden chest...

Recycling metals saves natural resources and money and reduces environmental problems. It's great. There's no limit to the number of times metals like aluminium, copper and steel can be recycled. So your humble little drink can may one day form part of a powerful robot who takes over the galaxy.

Warm-Up and Exam Questions

The warm-up questions run quickly over the basic facts you'll need in the exam. Unless you've learnt the facts first you'll find the exam questions pretty difficult.

Warm-Up Questions

1) What is the main impurity in blast furnace iron?
2) What is an alloy? Give two examples, with a use for each.
3) What is a smart alloy?
4) Give two disadvantages of smart alloys compared to ordinary alloys.
5) Why does aluminium not corrode?
6) What is metal fatigue?

Exam Questions

1 Which of these statements best describes aluminium?
   A   A high density, corrosion-resistant metal.
   B   One of the main components in steel.
   C   A very tough, completely unreactive, dense metal.
   D   A low density, versatile metal that can't be extracted by reduction with carbon.
   (1 mark)

2 Alloys are often used instead of pure metals because
   A   they are more plentiful.
   B   their properties make them more suitable for the application.
   C   their melting points are higher.
   D   they are completely inert.
   (1 mark)

3 Match words **A**, **B**, **C** and **D** with the numbers **1 - 4** in the sentences below.
   A   titanium
   B   tin
   C   iron
   D   gold

   Pure ...**1**... is a soft metal, so metals such as nickel are alloyed with it to make it harder.
   ...**2**... is used for making replacement hips as it has a low density and does not corrode.
   ...**3**... is added to copper to make bronze.
   Carbon is added to ...**4**... to make steel.
   (4 marks)

CHEMISTRY 1A — PRODUCTS FROM ROCKS

Fractional Distillation of Crude Oil

Crude oil is formed from the buried remains of plants and animals — it's a fossil fuel. Over millions of years, with high temperature and pressure, the remains turn to crude oil, which can be drilled up.

Crude oil can be split into separate hydrocarbons

1) Crude oil is a mixture of hydrocarbons — molecules which are made of just carbon and hydrogen.

2) Fractional distillation splits crude oil into fractions (groups of compounds with carbon chains of similar length).

3) Heated crude oil is piped in at the bottom of a fractionating column. The various fractions are constantly tapped off at the different levels where they condense.

4) Because it's a mixture, the different hydrocarbon molecules aren't chemically bonded to one another — so they keep all their original properties, such as their condensing points.

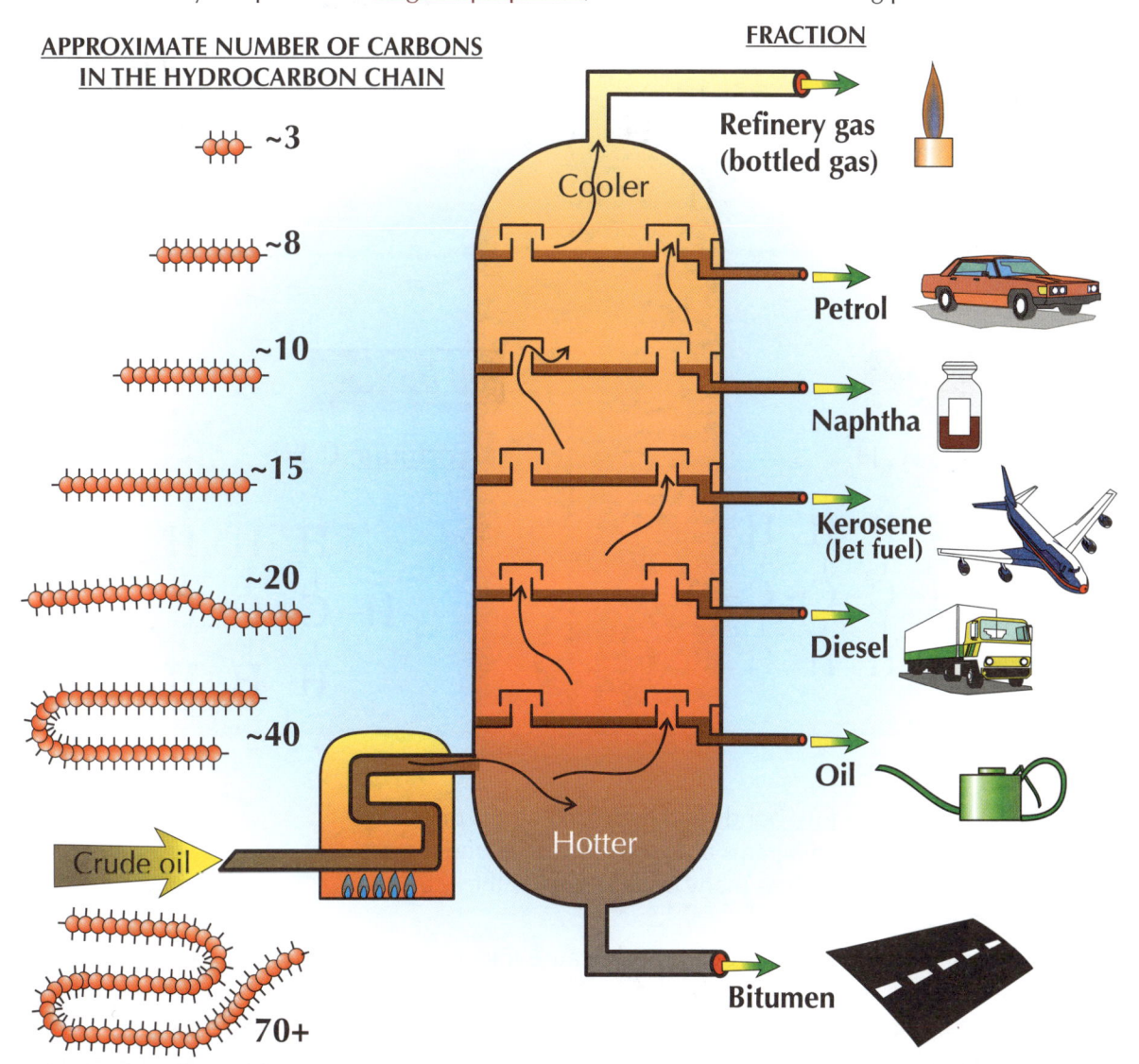

APPROXIMATE NUMBER OF CARBONS IN THE HYDROCARBON CHAIN

- ~3
- ~8
- ~10
- ~15
- ~20
- ~40
- 70+

FRACTION
- Refinery gas (bottled gas)
- Petrol
- Naphtha
- Kerosene (Jet fuel)
- Diesel
- Oil
- Bitumen

All this from buried dead stuff

But it has had a few hundred million years to get into the useful state it's in now. So if we use it all, we're going to have to wait an awful long time for more to form. No one knows exactly when oil will run out, but some scientists reckon that it'll only last about another 30 years. The thing is, technology is advancing all the time, so one day it's likely that we'll be able to extract oil that's too difficult and expensive to extract at the moment.

CHEMISTRY 1A — PRODUCTS FROM ROCKS

Crude Oil — Alkanes

Crude oil contains lots of alkanes and some alkenes (see page 45). They have different properties, and it's all down to their structure.

Crude oil is mostly alkanes

1) All the fractions of crude oil contain hydrocarbons called alkanes.
2) Alkanes are made up of chains of carbon atoms surrounded by hydrogen atoms.
3) Different alkanes have chains of different lengths.
4) The first four alkanes are methane (natural gas), ethane, propane and butane.

1) Methane
Formula: CH_4
(natural gas)

2) Ethane
Formula: C_2H_6

3) Propane
Formula: C_3H_8

4) Butane
Formula: C_4H_{10}

5) Carbon atoms form four bonds and hydrogen atoms only form one bond. The diagrams above show that all the atoms have formed bonds with as many other atoms as they can — this means they're saturated.
6) They're called saturated hydrocarbons because they have no spare bonds left (i.e. no double bonds that can open up and have things join onto them). This contrasts with alkenes (see p.45) which are unsaturated as they contain double bonds.
7) They burn cleanly, producing carbon dioxide and water.
8) Alkanes all have the general formula C_nH_{2n+2}. So if an alkane has 4 carbons, it's got to have (2×4)+2 = 10 hydrogens.

Alkanes = C_nH_{2n+2}

Crude Oil — Alkanes

The different fractions of crude oil have different properties, and it's all down to their alkane structure. You need to know a few trends about how the structure of alkanes affects the fraction's properties.

Learn the basic trends:

1) The longer the molecules, the less runny the hydrocarbon is — that is, the more viscous (gloopy) it is.

2) The shorter the molecules, the more volatile they are. "More volatile" means they turn into a gas at a lower temperature.

3) So, the shorter the molecules, the lower the temperature at which that fraction vaporises or condenses.

The uses of hydrocarbons depend on their properties

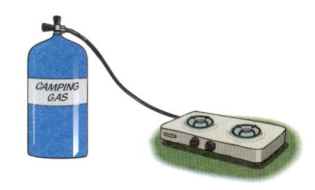

1) The volatility helps decide what the fraction is used for. The refinery gas fraction has the shortest molecules, so it has the lowest boiling point — in fact it's a gas at room temperature. This makes it ideal for using as bottled gas. It's stored under pressure as liquid in 'bottles'. When the tap on the bottle is opened, the fuel vaporises and flows to the burner where it's ignited.

2) The petrol fraction has longer molecules, so it has a higher boiling point. Petrol is a liquid which is ideal for storing in the fuel tank of a car. It can flow to the engine where it's easily vaporised to mix with the air before it is ignited.

3) The viscosity also helps decide how the hydrocarbons are used. The really gloopy, viscous hydrocarbons are used for lubricating engine parts and for covering roads.

Alkane ya if you don't learn this...

So long-chain hydrocarbons are viscous and non-volatile. Shorter-chain hydrocarbons are less viscous and more volatile — they're more likely to be gases at room temperature. These properties decide how they're used. In the real world there's more demand for stuff like petrol than there is for long gloopy hydrocarbons like bitumen — I guess there's only so many roads that need covering. Luckily, the long hydrocarbons can be "cracked" into the more valuable short hydrocarbons — see page 44.

Using Crude Oil as Fuel

Nothing as amazingly useful as crude oil would be without its problems.
No, that'd be too good to be true.

Crude oil provides an important *fuel* for modern life

1) Crude oil fractions burn cleanly so they make good fuels. Most modern transport is fuelled by a crude oil fraction, e.g. cars, boats, trains and planes. Parts of crude oil are also burned in central heating systems in homes and in power stations to generate electricity.

2) There's a massive industry with scientists working to find oil reserves, take it out of the ground, and turn it into useful products. As well as fuels, crude oil also provides the raw materials for making various chemicals, including plastics. There's more on this on pages 47 and 48.

3) Often, alternatives to using crude oil fractions as fuel are possible. E.g. electricity can be generated by nuclear power or wind power, solar energy can be used to heat water, and there are ethanol-powered cars.

4) But things tend to be set up for using oil fractions. For example, cars are designed for petrol or diesel and it's readily available. There are filling stations all over the country, with storage facilities and pumps specifically designed for these crude oil fractions. So crude oil fractions are often the easiest and cheapest thing to use.

5) Crude oil fractions are often more reliable too — e.g. solar and wind power won't work without the right weather conditions. Nuclear energy is reliable, but there are lots of concerns about its safety and the storage of radioactive waste.

CHEMISTRY 1A — PRODUCTS FROM ROCKS

Using Crude Oil as Fuel

Crude oil is a really useful fuel that we use every day — there is a possibility that it might run out.

Crude oil might run out one day... eeek

1) Most scientists think that oil will run out. But no one knows exactly when.

2) There have been heaps of different predictions — e.g. about 40 years ago, scientists predicted that it'd all be gone by the year 2000.

3) New oil reserves are discovered from time to time — e.g. a major new oil field was found in southern Oman in the Middle East in 2002. No one knows how much oil will be discovered in the future though.

4) Also, technology is constantly improving, so it's now possible to extract oil that was once too difficult or expensive to extract. It's likely that technology will improve further — but who knows how much?

5) In the worst-case scenario, oil may be pretty much gone in about 25 years — and that's not far off.

6) Some people think we should immediately stop using oil for things like transport, for which there are alternatives, and keep it for things that it's absolutely essential for, like some chemicals and medicines.

7) It will take time to develop alternative fuels that will satisfy all our energy needs (see page 40 for more info). It'll also take time to adapt things so that the fuels can be used on a wide scale. E.g. we might need different kinds of car engines, or special storage tanks built.

8) So however long oil does last for, it's a good idea to start conserving it and finding alternatives now.

Crude oil is not the environment's best friend

1) Oil spills can happen as the oil is being transported by tanker — this spells disaster for the local environment. Birds get covered in the stuff and are poisoned as they try to clean themselves. Other creatures, like sea otters and whales, are poisoned too. In 2010, an oil rig explosion in the gulf of Mexico caused a massive oil spill which had a huge enviromental impact.

2) You have to burn oil to release the energy from it. But burning oil is thought to be a major cause of global warming (p.39), acid rain (p.38) and global dimming (p.39).

If oil alternatives aren't developed, we might get caught short

Crude oil is really important to our lives. Take petrol for instance — at the first whisper of a shortage, there's mayhem. Loads of people dash to the petrol station and start filling up their tanks. This causes a queue, which starts everyone else panicking. I don't know what they'll do when it runs out totally.

Environmental Problems

90% of crude oil is used as fuel. It's burnt to release the energy stored inside it.

Burning fuels releases gases and particles

1) Power stations burn huge amounts of fossil fuels to make electricity.
   Cars are also a major culprit in burning fossil fuels.
2) When fossil fuels are burnt, carbon dioxide and water vapour are always released into the atmosphere.

$$\text{hydrocarbon} + \text{oxygen} \rightarrow \text{carbon dioxide} + \text{water vapour}$$

3) Sulfur impurities are found in petrol and diesel so sulfur dioxide is also put into the air.
4) If there's not enough oxygen for the fuel to burn properly, particles of soot (carbon) and carbon monoxide (a poisonous gas) are also released.

Sulfur dioxide causes acid rain

1) Sulfur dioxide is one of the gases that causes acid rain.
2) When the sulfur dioxide mixes with clouds it forms dilute sulfuric acid. This then falls as acid rain.

3) Acid rain causes lakes to become acidic and many plants and animals die as a result.
4) Acid rain kills trees and damages limestone buildings and ruins stone statues. It's shocking.
5) Links between acid rain and human health problems have been suggested.
6) The benefits of electricity and travel have to be balanced against the environmental impacts. Governments have recognised the importance of this and international agreements have been put in place to reduce emissions of air pollutants such as sulfur dioxide.

Sulfur can be removed from fuels before they're burned

1) Most of the sulfur can be removed from fuels before they are burnt, but it costs more to do it.
2) Also, removing sulfur from fuels takes more energy. This usually comes from burning more fuel, which releases more of the greenhouse gas carbon dioxide.
3) However, petrol and diesel are starting to be replaced by low-sulfur versions.

Acid rain is prevented by cleaning up emissions

1) Power stations now have Acid Gas Scrubbers to take the harmful gases out before they release their fumes into the atmosphere.
2) Cars are fitted with catalytic converters to clean up their exhaust gases.
3) The other way of reducing acid rain is simply to reduce our usage of fossil fuels.

Environmental Problems

More doom and gloom on this page I'm afraid... You've got to know it all though.

Increasing carbon dioxide levels contribute to climate change

1) The level of carbon dioxide in the atmosphere is increasing because of the large amounts of fossil fuels humans burn.
2) There's a scientific consensus that this extra carbon dioxide has led to the average surface temperature of the Earth increasing.
3) This warming could cause changes in climate and weather patterns all over the world. Flooding due to the polar ice caps melting might happen too.
4) This problem is explained in more depth on pages 8, 9 and 61.

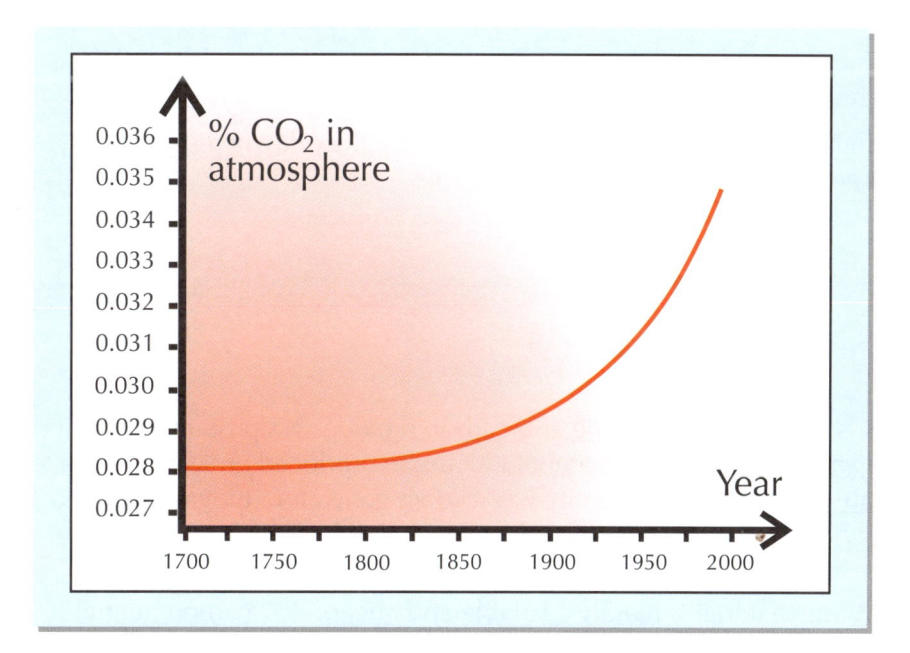

Particles cause global dimming

1) In the last few years, some scientists have been measuring how much sunlight is reaching the surface of the Earth and comparing it to records from the last 50 years.
2) They have been amazed to find that in some areas nearly 25% less sunlight has been reaching the surface compared to 50 years ago. They have called this global dimming.
3) They think that it is caused by particles of soot and ash that are produced when fossil fuels are burnt. These particles reflect sunlight back into space, or they can help to produce more clouds that reflect the sunlight back into space.
4) There are many scientists who don't believe that the change is real and blame it on inaccurate recording equipment.

London by day — if global dimming gets really bad.

Global dimming — romantic lighting all day...

On a cold winter's day, I often think that a bit of global warming would be nice — but it seems that it does mess things up. There have been lots of other times in the past when the climate has changed — volcanic eruptions, changes in the Earth's orbit and the movements of tectonic plates (see page 59) have all had effects. But this is the first time we've had the technology and knowledge to investigate it.

Environmental Problems (Alternative Fuels)

As the demand on resources increases it's important to develop new, alternative fuels.

Alternative fuels are being developed

Some alternative fuels have already been developed, and there are others in the pipeline (so to speak). None of them are perfect — they all have pros and cons. For example:

Ethanol

ETHANOL can be produced by fermentation of plants and is used to power cars in some places. It's often mixed with petrol to make a better fuel.

PROS: The CO_2 released when it's burnt was taken in by the plant as it grew, so it's 'carbon neutral'. The only other product is water.

CONS: Engines need to be converted before they'll work with ethanol fuels. And ethanol fuel isn't widely available.

Biogas

BIOGAS is a mixture of methane and carbon dioxide. It's produced when microorganisms digest waste material. It can be produced on a large scale, or on a small scale where each family has its own generator. Biogas is burned and the energy can be used for cooking, heating or lighting.

PROS: Waste material is readily available and cheap. It's 'carbon neutral'.
CONS: Biogas production is slow in cool weather.

Hydrogen gas

HYDROGEN GAS can also be used to power vehicles. You get the hydrogen from the electrolysis of water — there's plenty of water about but it takes electrical energy to split it up. This energy can come from a renewable source, e.g. solar.

PROS: Hydrogen combines with oxygen in the air to form just water — so it's very clean.
CONS: You need a special, expensive engine and hydrogen isn't widely available. You still need to use energy from another source to make it. Also, hydrogen's hard to store because it's explosive.

We should probably be using alternative fuels already...

You may have heard about these fuels in the news. Some of the big car manufacturers are spending loads of money trying to make hydrogen-powered cars a reality. These are the fuels of the future...

Warm-Up and Exam Questions

Give these questions your best shot. If they highlight areas where your knowledge falls short, it's time to re-revise those sections so you can boost you confidence for the exam.

Warm-Up Questions

1) Name three fractions obtained from crude oil.
2) What are hydrocarbons?
3) What are alkanes?
4) List three modern-day activities that depend on crude oil and its fractions.
5) Describe the process which produces acid rain.
6) What is global dimming and what causes it?

Exam Questions

1   The bonds in alkanes are best described as

   A   carbon-carbon single bonds and carbon-hydrogen single bonds.
   B   carbon-carbon single bonds and carbon-hydrogen double bonds.
   C   carbon-carbon double bonds and carbon-hydrogen single bonds.
   D   carbon-carbon double bonds and carbon-hydrogen double bonds.

   (1 mark)

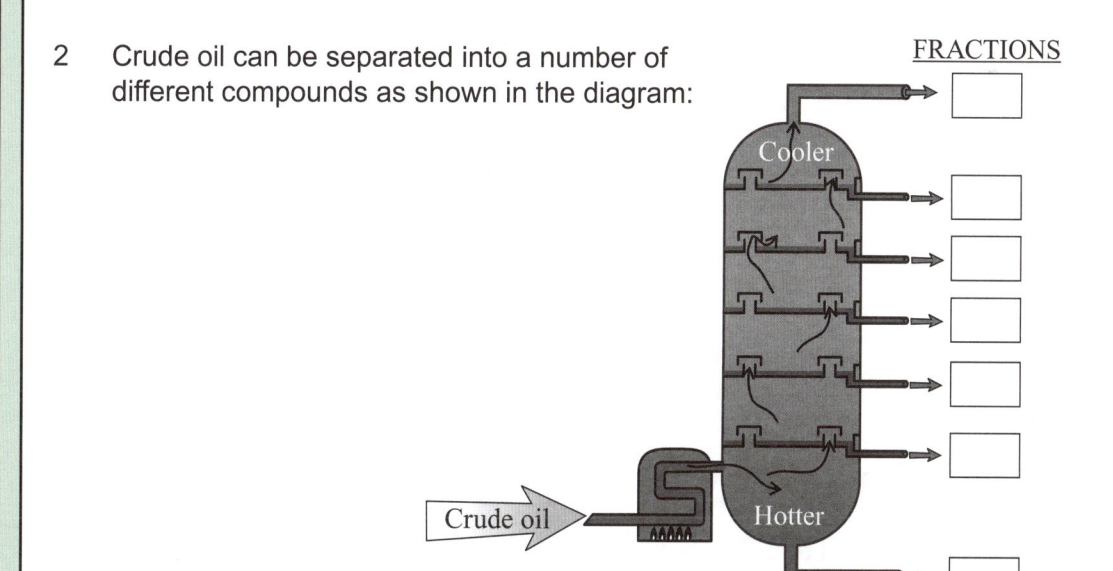

2   Crude oil can be separated into a number of different compounds as shown in the diagram:

   (a) (i)   Put an **M** in the box of the fraction with the largest hydrocarbon molecules.
   (1 mark)

   (ii)   Put a **B** in the box of the fraction with the lowest boiling point.
   (1 mark)

   (b)   Give **one** use for the kerosene fraction.
   (1 mark)

   (c)   Briefly explain how the separation process works.
   (3 marks)

Exam Questions

3   Even though there are many environmental problems caused by using crude oil fractions, we continue to use them mainly because
   A   they are a renewable resource.
   B   technology is always improving.
   C   they are a readily available and concentrated energy source.
   D   global warming is only a theory.
   (1 mark)

4   When diesel is burnt, it produces carbon dioxide, sulfur dioxide and particulate matter.
   (a)   Briefly describe the environmental problems caused by each of these pollutants.
   (3 marks)

   (b)   One advantage of burning ethanol is that it produces no sulfur. Describe one **disadvantage** of ethanol as a fuel compared to diesel.
   (1 mark)

5   Currently, fossil fuels provide about 60-70% of the world's electricity.
   Since fossils fuels will eventually run out, it is important to find alternative energy sources for the future.

   (a)   Biogas is one fuel that may be more widely used in the future.
      (i)   What are the main constituents of biogas?
      (1 mark)

      (ii)   How is biogas produced and what could it be used for?
      (2 marks)

      (iii)   Give **one** advantage and **one** disadvantage of using biogas.
      (2 marks)

   (b)   Another 'fuel for the future' could be hydrogen.
      (i)   Describe how hydrogen is produced on a large scale.
      (1 mark)

      (ii)   Why is hydrogen difficult to store?
      (1 mark)

      (iii)   Give **one** other disadvantage of using hydrogen as a fuel in a car compared with using petrol or diesel.
      (1 mark)

Revision Summary for Chemistry 1a

There wasn't anything too ghastly in this section, and a few bits were even quite interesting I reckon. But you've got to make sure the facts are all firmly embedded in your brain and that you really understand the issues. These questions will let you see what you know and what you don't. If you get stuck on any, you need to look at that stuff again. Keep going till you can do them all without coming up for air.

1) Sketch an atom. Label the nucleus and the electrons.
2) What are the symbols for: a) calcium, b) carbon, c) sodium?
3)* Which element's properties are more similar to magnesium's: calcium or iron?
4)* What atoms make up a molecule of Na_2CO_3?
5)* Say which of the diagrams on the right show:
   a) a mixture of compounds,   b) a mixture of elements,
   c) an element,   d) a compound
   Suggest what elements or compounds could be in each. 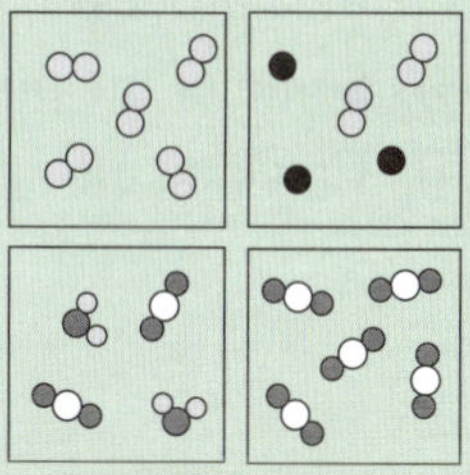
6) Compounds and mixtures are both equally difficult to separate out — true or false?
7)* Balance these equations: a) $CaCO_3 + HCl \rightarrow CaCl_2 + H_2O + CO_2$ b) $Ca + H_2O \rightarrow Ca(OH)_2 + H_2$
8) Write down the symbol equation showing the thermal decomposition of limestone.
9) What is slaked lime used for? What is its chemical name and how is it made?
10) Name three building materials made from limestone.
11) Plans to develop a limestone quarry and a cement factory on some hills next to your town are announced. Describe the views that the following might have:
    a) dog owners   b) a mother of young children
    c) the owner of a cafe   d) a beetle
12) Describe how the structure of a metal allows it to carry an electric current.
13) What's the definition of an ore? If something is not an ore now, will it ever be an ore?
14) What method is used to purify copper once extracted from its ore? Why is this method used?
15) Explain why zinc can be extracted by reduction with carbon but magnesium can't.
16) What happens if you put: a) a piece of magnesium in a solution of zinc sulfate?
                              b) a copper bracelet in a solution of iron chloride?
17) What is the problem with using a) iron straight from the blast furnace, b) very pure iron?
18) Why are alloys harder than pure metals? Give two examples of alloys and say what's in them.
19) What's so clever about smart alloys?
20) Why is stuff made from titanium likely to be more expensive than stuff made from steel?
21) Give three reasons why it's good to recycle metal.
22) What does crude oil consist of? What does fractional distillation do to crude oil?
23) Is a short-chain hydrocarbon more viscous than a long-chain hydrocarbon? Is it more volatile?
24) What's the general formula for an alkane? What's the formula for a 5-carbon alkane?
25)* You're going on holiday to a very cold place. The temperature will be about −10 °C. Which of the fuels shown on the right do you think will work best in your camping stove? Explain your answer.

Fuel	Boiling point (°C)
Propane	−42
Butane	−0.4
Pentane	36.2

26) Name three pollutants released into the atmosphere when fuels are burned. What environmental problems are associated with each?
27) List three ways of reducing acid rain.
28) What problems does the burning of fossil fuels cause?
29) Has the theory of global dimming been proven? If not, can it ever be proved? Explain your answer.
30) List three alternative ways of powering cars. What are the pros and cons of each?

*Answers on page 236

CHEMISTRY 1A — PRODUCTS FROM ROCKS

Cracking Crude Oil

After the distillation of crude oil, you've still got both short and long hydrocarbons, just not all mixed together. But there's more demand for some products, like petrol, than for others.

Cracking means splitting up long-chain hydrocarbons...

1) Long-chain hydrocarbons form thick gloopy liquids like tar which aren't all that useful, so...
2) ... a lot of the longer molecules produced from fractional distillation are turned into smaller ones by a process called cracking.
3) Some of the products of cracking are useful as fuels, e.g. petrol for cars and paraffin for jet fuel.
4) Cracking also produces short alkenes like ethene, which are needed for making plastics (see p.47).

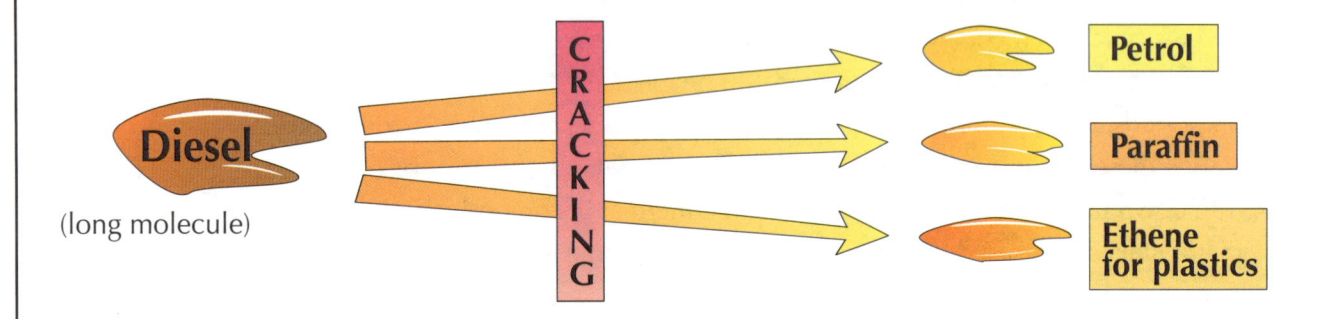

...by passing vapour over a hot catalyst

1) Cracking is a thermal decomposition reaction — breaking molecules down by heating them.
2) The first step is to heat the long-chain hydrocarbon to vaporise it (turn it into a gas).
3) Then the vapour is passed over a powdered catalyst at a temperature of about 400 °C – 700 °C.
4) Aluminium oxide is the catalyst used.
5) The long-chain molecules split apart or "crack" on the surface of the specks of catalyst.

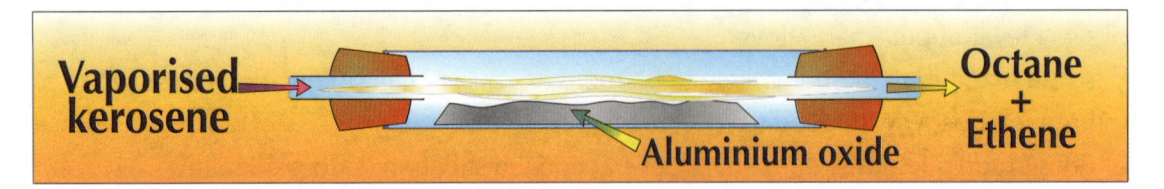

6) Most of the products of cracking are alkanes (see p.34) and alkenes (see p.45).

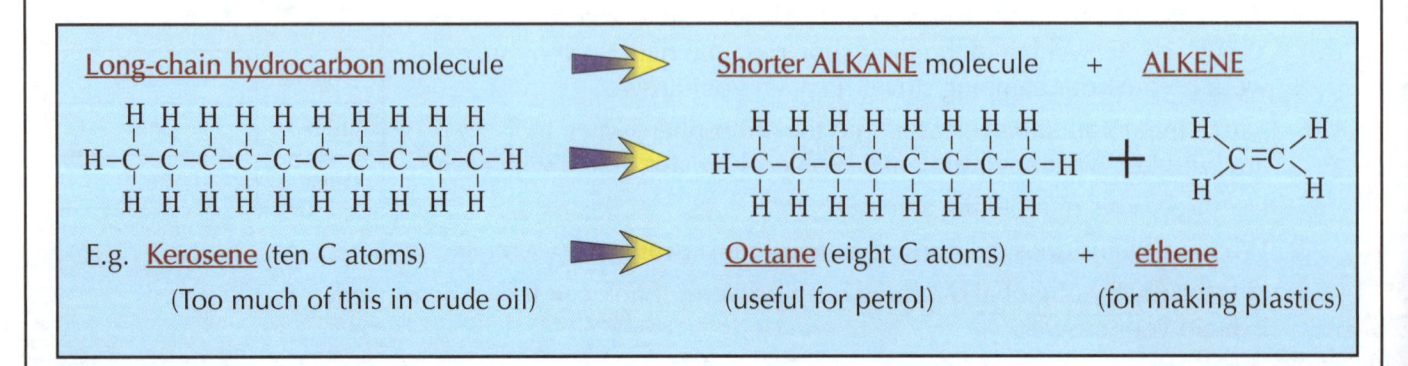

Long-chain hydrocarbon molecule ➡ Shorter ALKANE molecule + ALKENE

E.g. Kerosene (ten C atoms) ➡ Octane (eight C atoms) + ethene
(Too much of this in crude oil)   (useful for petrol)   (for making plastics)

Alkenes

Alkenes are very useful. Here are the basics for you to learn.

Alkenes have a C=C double bond

1) Alkenes are hydrocarbons which have a double bond between two of the carbon atoms in their chain.

2) They are known as unsaturated because they can make more bonds — the double bond can open up, allowing the two carbon atoms to bond with other atoms.

3) The first three alkenes are ethene (with two carbon atoms) propene (three Cs) and butene (four Cs).

4) All alkenes have the formula: C_nH_{2n} — they have twice as many hydrogens as carbons.

1) Ethene

Formula: C_2H_4

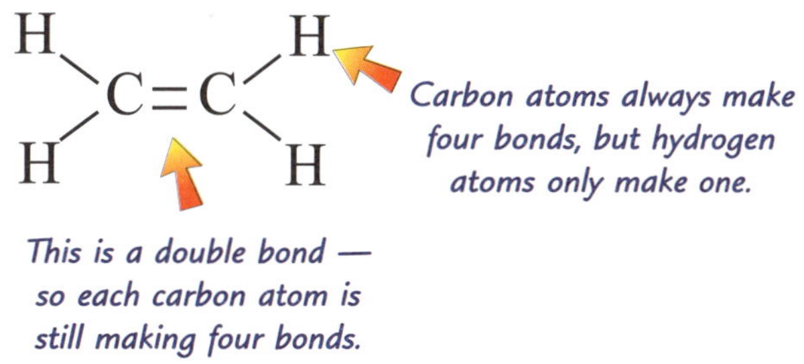

Carbon atoms always make four bonds, but hydrogen atoms only make one.

This is a double bond — so each carbon atom is still making four bonds.

2) Propene

Formula: C_3H_6

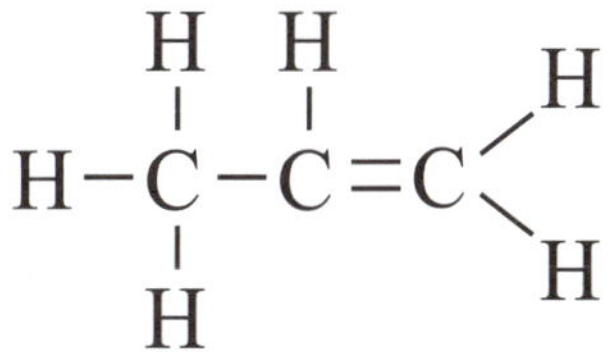

3) Butene

Formula: C_4H_8

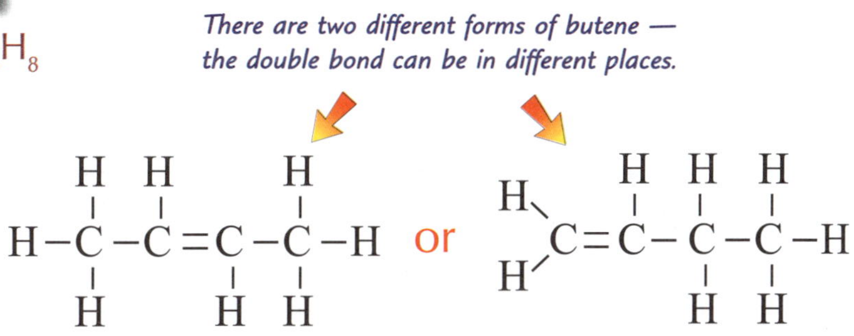

There are two different forms of butene — the double bond can be in different places.

CHEMISTRY 1B — OILS, EARTH AND ATMOSPHERE

Ethanol

Ethene can be used to produce ethanol

1) Ethene (C_2H_4) will react with steam (H_2O) to make ethanol.

$$H_2C=CH_2 + H_2O \longrightarrow H_3C-CH_2-OH$$

2) The reaction needs a temperature of 300 °C and a pressure of 70 atmospheres.
3) Phosphoric acid is used as a catalyst (see p.110-111).
4) At the moment this is a cheap process, because ethene's fairly cheap and not much of it is wasted.
5) The trouble is that ethene's produced from crude oil, which is a non-renewable resource and which will start running out fairly soon. This means using ethene to make ethanol will become very expensive.

Ethanol can also be produced from renewable resources

1) The alcohol in beer and wine etc. isn't made from ethene — it's made by fermentation.
2) The raw material for fermentation is sugar. This is converted into ethanol using yeast.
3) This process needs a lower temperature (30-40 °C) and simpler equipment than when using ethene.
4) Another advantage is that the raw materials are all renewable resources. Sugar is grown as a major crop in several parts of the world, including many poorer countries. Yeast is also easy to grow.
5) The ethanol produced this way can also be used as quite a cheap fuel in countries which don't have oil reserves for making petrol.
6) There are disadvantages though. The ethanol you get from this process isn't very concentrated, so it needs to be distilled to increase its strength (as in whisky distilleries). It also needs to be purified.

Make ethanol — not war...

Don't get alkenes confused with alkanes — that one letter makes all the difference. Alkenes have a C=C bond, alkanes don't. The first part of their names is the same though. "Meth-" means "one carbon atom", "eth-" means "two C atoms", "prop-" means "three C atoms", "but-" means "four C atoms", etc.

Using Alkenes to Make Polymers

Before we knew how to make polymers, there were no polythene bags. Everyone used string bags for their shopping. Now we have plastic bags that hurt your hands and split halfway home.

Alkenes can be used to make polymers

1) Probably the most useful thing you can do with alkenes is polymerisation. This means joining together lots of monomers (small molecules, e.g. alkenes) to form very large molecules — these long-chain molecules are called polymers.

Polymers are often written without the brackets — e.g. polyethene.

2) For instance, many ethene molecules can be joined up to produce poly(ethene) or "polythene".

Many monomers → Pressure and Catalyst → Polymer

$n \begin{pmatrix} | & | \\ C=C \\ | & | \end{pmatrix}$ → $\begin{pmatrix} | & | \\ C-C \\ | & | \end{pmatrix}_n$

Many single ethenes → poly(ethene)

3) In the same way, if you join lots of propene molecules together, you've got poly(propene).

Different polymers have different physical properties

1) The physical properties of a polymer depend on what it's made from. Polyamides are usually stronger than poly(ethene), for example.
2) A polymer's physical properties are also affected by the temperature and pressure of polymerisation. Poly(ethene) made at 200 °C and 2000 atmospheres pressure is flexible, and has low density. But poly(ethene) made at 60 °C and a few atmospheres pressure with a catalyst is rigid and dense.
3) And poly(ethenol) forms slime when it's mixed with different concentrations of sodium tetraborate. The more concentrated the sodium tetraborate, the more viscous and gungy the slime is.

Polymers are really important...

...so it's really important that you know the basics. Monomers are often alkenes that contain double bonds. When they are put under pressure in the presence of a catalyst, they join together to form really big, long-chain molecules called polymers. So remember monomers form polymers...

CHEMISTRY 1B — OILS, EARTH AND ATMOSPHERE

Using Alkenes to Make Polymers

Polymers are suitable for various different *uses*

1) Light, stretchable polymers such as low density poly(ethene) are used to make plastic bags. Elastic polymer fibres are used to make super-stretchy spandex fibre for tights.

2) New uses are developed all the time. Waterproof coatings for fabrics are made of polymers. Dental polymers are used in resin tooth fillings. Polymer hydrogel wound dressings keep wounds moist.

3) Memory foam is an example of a smart material. It's a polymer that gets softer as it gets warmer. Mattresses can be made of memory foam — they mould to your body shape when you lie on them.

Polymers are cheap, but most **don't rot**
— they're hard to get rid of

1) Most polymers aren't "biodegradable" — they're not broken down by microorganisms, so they don't rot.

2) It's difficult to get rid of them — if you bury them in a landfill site, they'll still be there years later. The best thing is to reuse them as many times as possible and then recycle them if you can.

3) Things made from polymers are usually cheaper than things made from metal. However, as crude oil resources get used up, the price of crude oil will rise. Crude oil products like polymers will get dearer.

4) It may be that one day there won't be enough oil for fuel AND plastics AND all the other uses. Choosing how to use the oil that's left means weighing up advantages and disadvantages on all sides.

Revision's like a polymer — you join lots of little facts up...

Polymers are all over the place — and I don't just mean all those plastic bags stuck in trees. There are naturally occurring polymers, like rubber and silk. That's quite a few clothing options, even without synthetic polymers like polyester and PVC. You've even got polymers on the inside — DNA's a polymer.

Warm-Up and Exam Questions

These warm-up questions should ease you in gently before you move onto the exam questions. Unless you've learnt the facts you'll find the exam questions tougher than leather sandwiches.

Warm-Up Questions

1) What sort of hydrocarbon molecules are cracked, and why are they cracked?
2) Describe the conditions used for cracking hydrocarbons.
3) Why are alkenes described as unsaturated hydrocarbons?
4) How is ethanol produced from ethene?
5) How is poly(ethene) made?

Exam Questions

1 (a) Complete this equation for the formation of polypropene.

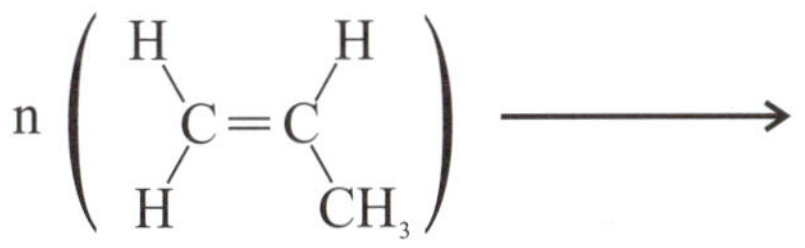

$$n \left(\begin{array}{c} H \\ | \\ H \end{array} C=C \begin{array}{c} H \\ | \\ CH_3 \end{array} \right) \longrightarrow$$

(1 mark)

(b) The structural formula of polystyrene is shown below. Draw the structural formula of its monomer.

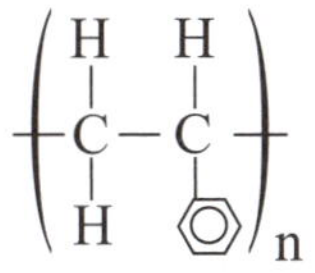

$$\left(\begin{array}{cc} H & H \\ | & | \\ -C - C - \\ | & | \\ H & \phi \end{array} \right)_n$$

(1 mark)

2 The symbol equation shows the reaction of ethene with steam.

$$C_2H_4 + H_2O \rightarrow C_2H_5OH$$

(a) Name the product with the formula C_2H_5OH.

(1 mark)

(b) What is the catalyst used in this reaction?

(1 mark)

CHEMISTRY 1B — OILS, EARTH AND ATMOSPHERE

Extracting Plant Oils

Plant oils come from plants. I know it's tricky, but just do your best to remember.

We can *extract oils* from *plants*

1) Some fruits and seeds contain a lot of oil. For example, avocados and olives are oily fruits. Brazil nuts, peanuts and sesame seeds are oily seeds (a nut is just a big seed really).

2) These oils can be extracted and used for food or for fuel.

3) To get the oil out, the plant material is crushed. The next step is to press the crushed plant material between metal plates and squash the oil out. This is the traditional method of producing olive oil.

4) Oil can be separated from crushed plant material by a centrifuge — rather like using a spin-dryer to get water out of wet clothes. Or solvents can be used to get the oil from the plant material.

5) Distillation is used to refine the oil — it removes water, solvents and impurities.

Vegetable oils are used in *food*

1) Vegetable oils provide a lot of energy.

2) There are other nutrients in vegetable oils too — for example, oils from seeds contain vitamin E.

3) Vegetable oils contain essential fatty acids, which the body needs for many metabolic processes.

Emulsions

Emulsions can be made from oil and water

1) Oils don't dissolve in water. So far so good...
2) However, you can mix an oil with water to make an emulsion. Emulsions are made up of lots of droplets of one liquid suspended in another liquid. E.g. you can have an oil-in-water emulsion (oil droplets suspended in water) or a water-in-oil emulsion (water droplets suspended in oil).

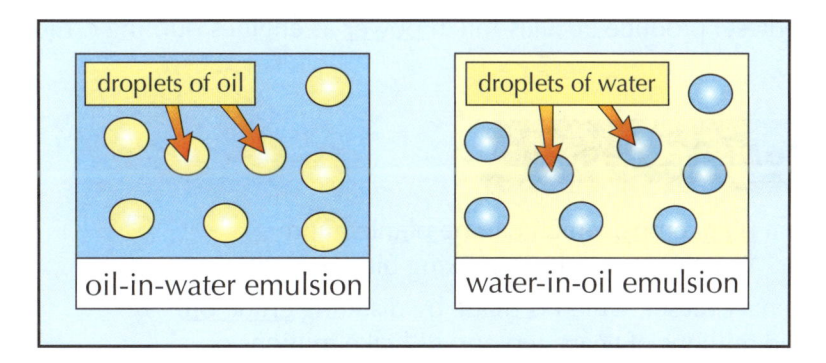

3) Emulsions are thicker than either oil or water. For example, mayonnaise is an emulsion of sunflower oil (or olive oil) and vinegar — it's an awful lot thicker than either.
4) The physical properties of emulsions make them suited to lots of uses in food — e.g. as salad dressings and in sauces. For instance, a salad dressing made by shaking olive oil and vinegar together forms an emulsion that coats salad better than plain oil or plain vinegar.
5) Generally, the more oil you've got in an oil-in-water emulsion, the thicker it is. Milk is an oil-in-water emulsion with not much oil and a lot of water — there's about 3% oil in full-fat milk. Single cream has a bit more oil — about 18%. Double cream has lots of oil — nearly 50%.

6) Whipped cream and ice cream are oil-in-water emulsions with an extra ingredient — air. Air is whipped into cream to give it a fluffy, frothy consistency for use as a topping. Whipping air into ice cream gives it a softer texture, which makes it easier to scoop out of the tub.
7) Emulsions also have non-food uses. Most moisturising lotions are oil-in-water emulsions. The smooth texture of an emulsion makes it easy to rub into the skin.

Emulsion paint — spread mayonnaise all over the walls...

Before fancy stuff from abroad like olive oil, we fried our bacon and eggs in lard. Lard wouldn't be so good for making salad cream though. Emulsions like salad cream have to be made from shaking up two liquids — tiny droplets of one liquid are 'suspended' (NOT dissolved) in the other liquid.

Using Plant Oils for Fuels

Clean fuel from vegetable oil sounds great — but as always, you have to weigh up the pros and cons.

Vegetable oils can be used to produce fuels

1) Vegetable oils such as rapeseed oil and soybean oil can be processed and turned into fuels.
2) Vegetable oil provides a lot of energy — that's why it's suitable for use as a fuel.
3) A particularly useful fuel made from vegetable oils is called biodiesel. Biodiesel has similar properties to ordinary diesel fuel — it burns in the same way, so you can use it to fuel a diesel engine.
4) Most diesel engines can burn 100% biodiesel, but usually biodiesel is mixed with ordinary diesel.
5) Engines burning biodiesel produce 90% as much power as engines burning ordinary diesel.

Biodiesel is a renewable fuel

1) Biodiesel comes from plant crops, which can be planted and harvested every year. You can always keep making biodiesel.
2) Compare this to ordinary diesel, which is made by distilling crude oil. Crude oil was formed millions of years ago and it'll take millions of years to make more — once it runs low that's it.

Biodiesel releases less pollution than ordinary diesel

1) Engines burning biodiesel produce much less sulfur dioxide pollution than engines burning diesel or petrol.
2) Burning biodiesel doesn't release as many "particulates" as burning diesel or petrol.

Particulates are little pieces of solid that you get in smoke and car exhausts.

3) Biodiesel is also biodegradable and it's less toxic than regular diesel.
4) Biodiesel engines do release the same amount of carbon dioxide (CO_2) as ordinary diesel engines. BUT biodiesel comes from recently grown plants. The plants took in carbon dioxide from the air when they were alive, and it's this same carbon which is released again when the biodiesel is burned. So net increase in carbon dioxide in the atmosphere: nil.
5) Regular diesel, on the other hand, comes from crude oil, which has been under the ground for millions of years. The carbon in crude oil was taken out of the atmosphere millions of years ago. Burning regular diesel does create a net increase in carbon dioxide in the atmosphere.

Biodiesel is expensive and it's difficult to make enough

1) We can't make enough biodiesel to replace regular diesel — there aren't enough veg oil crops. Biodiesel can be made from used vegetable oil, but there isn't enough of that either.
2) Because of this, biodiesel is expensive. Most people won't want to use it until it's cheaper.
3) Biodiesel has fewer drawbacks than some other "green" car fuels like biogas or electricity, though. Car engines need modification to run on gas — most diesel cars run on biodiesel without any tinkering. And biodiesel could use the same filling stations and pumps as diesel. (Compare this with electric cars, which would need a new network of recharging stations.)

Using Plant Oils in Food

Oils are usually quite runny at room temperature. That's fine for salad dressing, say, but not so good for spreading in your sandwiches. For that, you could hydrogenate the oil to make margarine...

Unsaturated oils contain C=C double bonds

1) Oils and fats contain long-chain molecules with lots of carbon atoms.
2) Oils and fats are either saturated or unsaturated.
3) Unsaturated oils contain double bonds between some of the carbon atoms in their carbon chains.
4) C=C double bonds can be detected by reacting with bromine or iodine. An unsaturated oil will decolourise bromine water or iodine water (as the bromine or iodine opens up the double bond and joins on).
5) Monounsaturated fats contain one C=C double bond somewhere in their carbon chains. Polyunsaturated fats contain more than one C=C double bond.

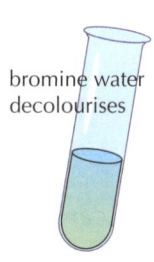

Unsaturated oils can be hydrogenated

1) Unsaturated vegetable oils are liquid at room temperature.
2) They can be hardened by reacting them with hydrogen in the presence of a nickel catalyst at about 60 °C. This is called hydrogenation. The hydrogen reacts with the double-bonded carbons and opens out the double bonds.
3) Hydrogenated oils have higher melting points than unsaturated oils, so they're more solid at room temperature. This makes them useful as spreads and for baking cakes.
4) Margarine is usually made from partially hydrogenated vegetable oil — turning all the double bonds in vegetable oil to single bonds would make margarine too hard and difficult to spread. Hydrogenating most of them gives margarine a nice, buttery, spreadable consistency.
5) Partially hydrogenated vegetable oils are often used instead of butter in processed foods, e.g. biscuits. These oils are a lot cheaper than butter and they keep longer. This makes biscuits cheaper and gives them a long shelf life.
6) But partially hydrogenating vegetable oils means you end up with a lot of so-called trans fats. And there's evidence to suggest that trans fats are very bad for you.

Vegetable oils in foods can affect health

1) Vegetable oils tend to be unsaturated, while animal fats tend to be saturated.
2) In general, saturated fats are less healthy than unsaturated fats (as saturated fats increase the amount of cholesterol in the blood, which can block up the arteries and increase the risk of heart disease).
3) Natural unsaturated fats such as olive oil and sunflower oil reduce the amount of blood cholesterol.

But because of the trans fats, partially hydrogenated vegetable oil increases the amount of "bad" cholesterol in the blood, and decreases the amount of "good" cholesterol. So eating a lot of foods made with partially hydrogenated vegetable oils can actually increase the risk of heart disease.

Cholesterol is carried in the blood by high density lipoproteins (HDLs) and low density lipoproteins (LDLs). HDLs are called 'good cholesterol' and LDLs are 'bad cholesterol' — so ideally you want more HDLs than LDLs in your blood.

Food Additives

Humans have been adding stuff to food for years. Before fridges were invented, we added salt to meat to stop it going off. Now we use additives not just to preserve food, but to make it look or taste different.

Processed foods often contain additives

1) Food manufacturers add various chemical compounds to food to improve its appearance, taste, texture and shelf life. These additives must be listed in the ingredients list on the back of the packet.
2) Most additives used in the UK have E-numbers — e.g. E127 is erythrosine (a red dye) and E201 is sodium sorbate (a preservative). Additives with E-numbers have passed safety tests and can be used in Europe.

Food additives have benefits and drawbacks

1) Preservatives help food stay fresh. Without them, more food would go off and need throwing away.

2) Colourings and flavourings make food look and taste better.

3) Emulsifiers and stabilisers stop emulsions like mayonnaise (see page 51) from separating out.

4) Sweeteners can replace sugar in some processed foods — helpful to diabetics and dieters.

5) Some food additives are of natural origin, e.g. lecithin from soya beans. And some synthetic additives are identical to natural substances, e.g. citric acid. Others are completely new synthetic substances.

6) Some people think that some synthetic food colourings (e.g. sunset yellow) make children hyperactive. Many scientific studies haven't found any connection between additives and hyperactivity at all.

7) A small number of people are allergic to some additives, for example the food dye tartrazine.

8) Some additives aren't suitable for vegetarians. For example, the food colouring cochineal comes from crushed insects. And gelatin from animal bones is used to thicken and set some foods.

Food Additives

Now time for some proper chemistry. You can sometimes tell what substances are present in a mixture using chromatography.

Artificial colours can be detected by chromatography

To identify different colourings in a food sample, you can use chromatography.

Paper chromatography uses the fact that different dyes wash through wet filter paper at different rates — the more soluble the dye, the faster it travels through the wet paper.

Here's how you'd analyse food colourings...

1) Extract the colour from each food sample by placing it in a small cup with a few drops of solvent (can be water, ethanol, salt water, etc). Use a different cup for each different food sample.
2) Put spots of each coloured solution on a pencil baseline on filter paper. (Label them in pencil — don't use pen because it might dissolve in the solvent and confuse everything.)
3) Roll up the sheet and put it in a beaker with some solvent — but keep the baseline above the level of the solvent.
4) The solvent seeps up the paper, taking the food dyes with it. Different dyes form spots in different places.

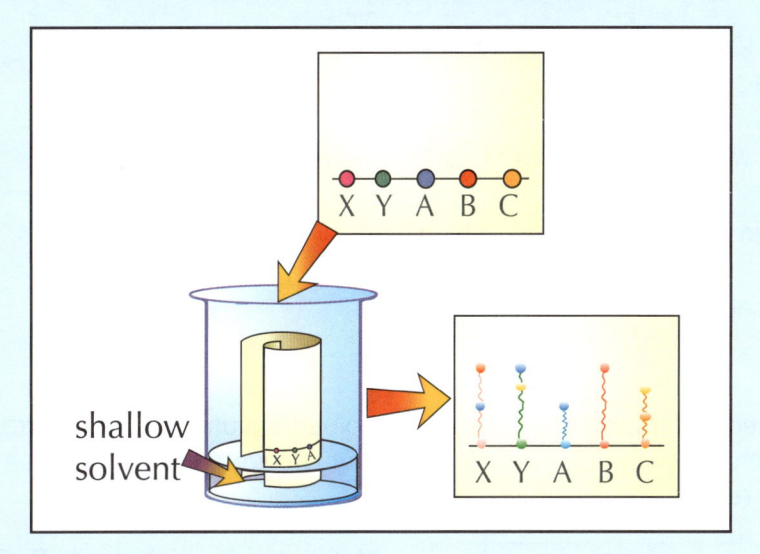

shallow solvent

X Y A B C

5) Watch out though — a chromatogram with four spots means at least four dyes, not exactly four dyes. There could be five dyes, with two of them making a spot in the same place. It can't be three dyes though, because one dye can't split into two spots.

Make sure your solvent level is lower than the spots...

Chromatography is used all the time in industry — it can separate accurately even dead complex mixtures if you choose the right solvent, "filter paper" and conditions. On a different note, there's a lot of talk about food additives in newspapers and so on. Some statements are based on facts, but some are based on rumour and prejudice. Without evidence to support a claim, it's not worth a bean.

Warm-Up and Exam Questions

Warm-Up Questions

1) Describe the process used to extract and refine oil from plants.
2) What is an emulsion?
3) What conditions are used for the hydrogenation of unsaturated vegetable oils?
4) Give three examples of types of food additive.

Exam Questions

1   Match words **A**, **B**, **C** and **D** with the numbers **1 - 4** in the sentences below.

   A   saturated
   B   unsaturated
   C   polyunsaturated
   D   monounsaturated

   Animal fats tend to be ...**1**....   Vegetable oils are usually ...**2**....
   ...**3**... oils have only one C=C double bond in their carbon chains,
   whereas ...**4**... oils contain more than one C=C double bond.

   (4 marks)

2   Biodiesel can be used in diesel engines.
   (a) What is biodiesel made from?
   (1 mark)

   (b) (i) Explain why biodiesel doesn't add to the greenhouse effect.
   (2 marks)

       (ii) Give **two** other advantages of biodiesel.
   (2 marks)

   (c) Give **two** disadvantages of biodiesel.
   (2 marks)

3   Scientists analysed the composition of six food colourings using chromatography. Four of the colourings were unknown (**1 – 4**), and the other two were known, Sunrise yellow and Sunset red. The results are shown below.

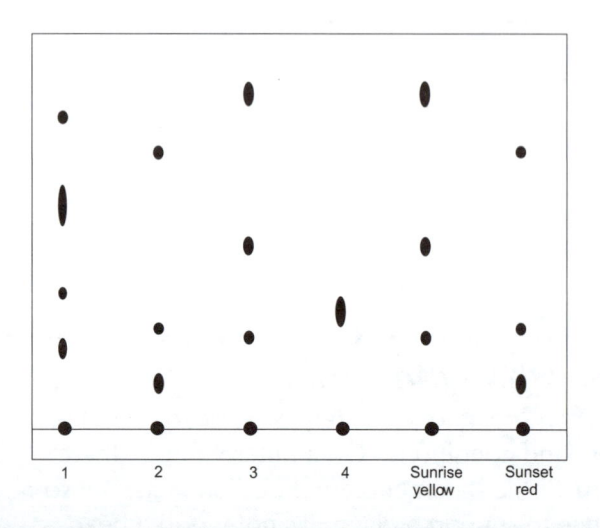

   Match the descriptions **A**, **B**, **C** and **D** to the correct food colouring **1 – 4**.

   A   The food colouring that is most likely to be a pure compound.

   B   The food colouring that contains at least four different compounds.

   C   The food colouring that contains the same compounds as sunrise yellow.

   D   The food colouring that contains the same compounds as sunset red.

   (4 marks)

CHEMISTRY 1B — OILS, EARTH AND ATMOSPHERE

Plate Tectonics

The Earth's surface is very crinkly — lots of mountains and valleys. Scientists used to think that these 'wrinkles' were caused by the shrinkage of the surface as it cooled down after the Earth was formed. This theory has now been replaced by one that fits the facts better, but most people took a lot of persuading...

Wegener's theory describes continental drift

1) Alfred Wegener came across some work listing the fossils of very similar plants and animals which had been found on opposite sides of the Atlantic Ocean.

2) He investigated further, and found other cases of very similar fossils on opposite sides of oceans.

3) Other people had probably noticed this too. The accepted explanation was that there had once been land bridges linking the continents — so animals had been able to cross. The bridges had 'sunk' or been covered over since then.

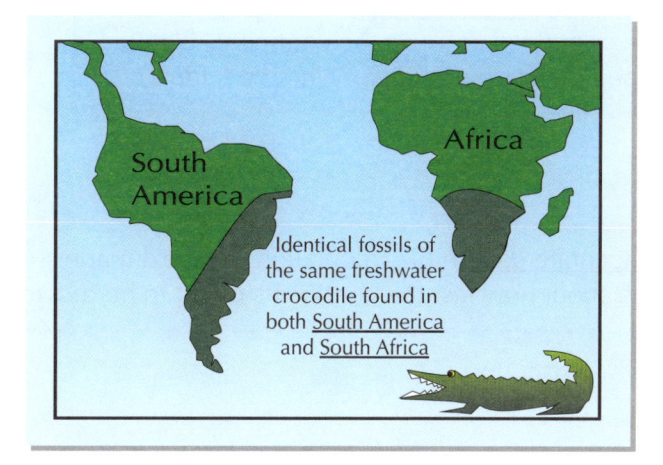

Identical fossils of the same freshwater crocodile found in both South America and South Africa

4) But Wegener had also noticed that the coastlines of Africa and South America seemed to 'match' like the pieces of a jigsaw. He wondered if these two continents had previously been one continent which then split. He started to look for more evidence, and found it...

5) There were matching layers in the rocks in different continents.

6) Fossils had been found in the 'wrong' places — e.g. fossils of tropical plants had been discovered on Arctic islands, where the present climate would clearly have killed them off.

7) In 1915, Wegener felt he had enough evidence. He published his theory of "continental drift".

8) Wegener said that about 300 million years ago, there had been just one 'supercontinent'. This landmass, Pangaea, broke into smaller chunks which moved apart. He claimed that these chunks — our modern-day continents — were still slowly 'drifting' apart.

CHEMISTRY 1B — OILS, EARTH AND ATMOSPHERE

Plate Tectonics

Wegener's theory wasn't accepted for many years

The reaction from other scientists was mostly very hostile. The main problem was that Wegener's explanation of how the 'drifting' happened wasn't very convincing.

1) Wegener thought that the continents were 'ploughing through' the sea bed, and that their movement was caused by tidal forces and the earth's rotation.

2) Other geologists said this was impossible. One scientist calculated that the forces needed to move the continents like this would also have stopped the Earth rotating. (Which it hadn't.)

3) Wegener had used inaccurate data in his calculations, so he'd made some rather wild predictions about how fast the continents ought to be moving apart.

4) A few scientists supported Wegener, but most of them didn't see any reason to believe such a strange theory. It probably didn't help that he wasn't a 'proper' geologist — his PhD was in astronomy.

5) Then in the 1950s, scientists were able to investigate the ocean floor and found new evidence to support Wegener's theory. He wasn't right about everything, but his main idea was correct.

6) By the 1960s, geologists were convinced. We now think the Earth's crust is made of several chunks which move about and that colliding chunks push the land up to create mountains.

I told you so — but no one ever believes me...

Sadly, Wegener died before his theory was accepted (when hundreds of geologists had to rewrite their textbooks). His story is a classic example of how science progresses — someone puts forward an idea, everyone else points out why it's nonsense, and eventually the really good ideas are accepted.

The Earth's Structure

No one accepted the theory of plate tectonics for ages. Almost everyone does now. How times change.

The earth has a crust, mantle, outer and inner core

The Earth is almost spherical and it has a layered structure, a bit like a scotch egg. Or a peach.

1) The bit we live on, the crust, is very thin (about 20 km).
2) Below that is the mantle. The mantle has all the properties of a solid, except that it can flow very slowly.
3) Within the mantle, radioactive decay takes place. This produces a lot of heat, which causes the mantle to flow in convection currents.
4) At the centre of the Earth is the core, which we think is made of iron and nickel.

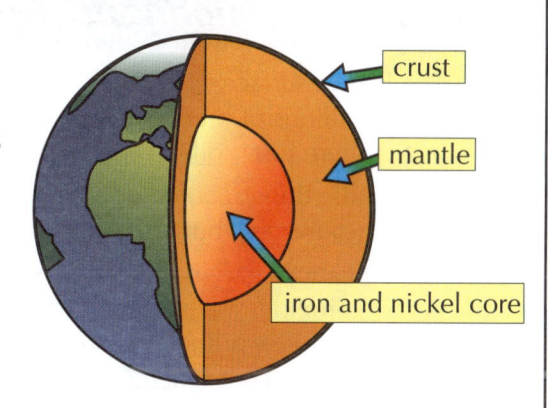

The earth's surface is made up of tectonic plates

1) The crust and the upper part of the mantle are cracked into a number of large pieces called tectonic plates. These plates are a bit like big rafts that 'float' on the mantle.
2) The plates don't stay in one place though. That's because the convection currents in the mantle cause the plates to drift.
3) The map shows the edges of the plates as they are now, and the directions they're moving in (red arrows).
4) Most of the plates are moving at speeds of a few cm per year relative to each other.
5) Occasionally, the plates move very suddenly, causing an earthquake.
6) Volcanoes often form at the boundaries between two tectonic plates.

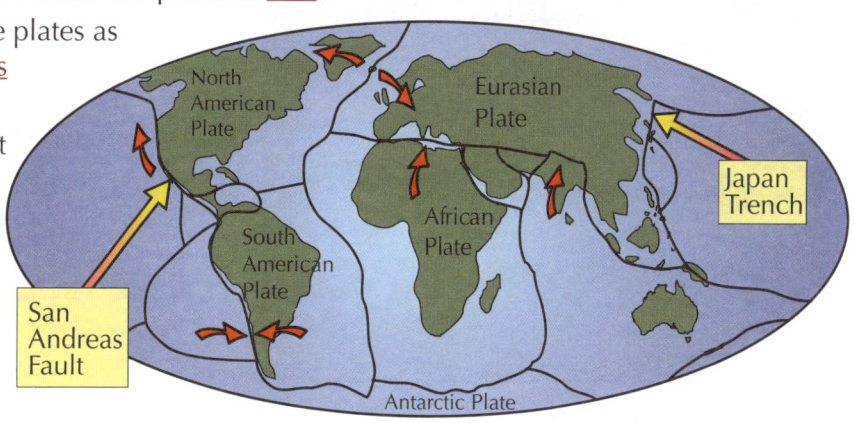

Scientists can't predict earthquakes and volcanic eruptions

1) Tectonic plates can stay more or less put for a while and then suddenly lurch forwards. It's impossible to predict exactly when they'll move.
2) Scientists are trying to find out if there are any clues that an earthquake might happen soon — things like strain in underground rocks. Even with these clues they'll only be able to say an earthquake's likely to happen, not exactly when it'll happen.
3) There are some clues that say a volcanic eruption might happen soon. Before an eruption, molten rock rises up into chambers near the surface, causing the ground surface to bulge slightly. This causes mini-earthquakes near the volcano.
4) But sometimes molten rock cools down instead of erupting, so mini-earthquakes can be a false alarm.

CHEMISTRY 1B — OILS, EARTH AND ATMOSPHERE

The Evolution of the Atmosphere

For 200 million years or so, the atmosphere has been about how it is now: 78% nitrogen, 21% oxygen, and small amounts of other gases, mainly CO_2 and noble gases. There can be a lot of water vapour too. But it wasn't always like this. Here's how the past 4.5 billion years may have gone:

Phase 1 — *Volcanoes* gave out *gases*

1) The Earth's surface was originally molten for many millions of years. It was so hot that any atmosphere just 'boiled away' into space.
2) Eventually things cooled down a bit and a thin crust formed, but volcanoes kept erupting.
3) The volcanoes gave out lots of gas — including carbon dioxide, water vapour and nitrogen. We think this was how the oceans and atmosphere were formed.
4) According to this theory, the early atmosphere was probably mostly CO_2, with virtually no oxygen. This is quite like the atmospheres of Mars and Venus today.
5) The oceans formed when the water vapour condensed.

The First Two Billion Years

Holiday report: Not a nice place to be. Take strong walking boots and a good coat.

Phase 2 — *Green plants* evolved and produced *oxygen*

The Next Two Billion Years

1) Green plants evolved over most of the Earth. They were quite happy in the CO_2 atmosphere.
2) A lot of the early CO_2 dissolved into the oceans. The green plants also removed CO_2 from the air and produced O_2 by photosynthesis.
3) When plants died and were buried under layers of sediment, the carbon they had removed from the air (as CO_2) became 'locked up' in sedimentary rocks as insoluble carbonates and fossil fuels.
4) When we burn fossil fuels today, this 'locked-up' carbon is released and the concentration of CO_2 in the atmosphere rises.

Holiday report: A bit slimy underfoot. Take wellies and a lot of suncream.

Phase 3 — *Ozone layer* allows evolution of *complex animals*

1) The build-up of oxygen in the atmosphere killed off some early organisms that couldn't tolerate it, but allowed other, more complex organisms to evolve and flourish.
2) The oxygen also created the ozone layer (O_3) which blocked harmful rays from the Sun and enabled even more complex organisms to evolve — us, eventually.
3) There is virtually no CO_2 left now.

The Last Billion Years or so

Nice safe OZONE, O_3

Holiday report: A nice place to be. Visit before the crowds ruin it.

The Evolution of the Atmosphere

Evidence for how the atmosphere evolved has been found in rocks and other sources. But no one was actually there, billions of years ago, to record the changes as they happened. So our theories about how today's atmosphere came about are just that — theories.

About 1% of the atmosphere is noble gases

1) Helium, neon, argon, krypton, xenon and radon are the noble gases, Group 0 of the periodic table.
2) They're all chemically unreactive. In fact, they're sometimes called the inert gases — inert means "doesn't react". They exist as separate atoms.
3) Argon's used in filament lamps (light bulbs) — it's the atmosphere's most common noble gas (0.93%).
   Neon is used in electric discharge tubes — when a current is passed through neon it gives out a bright light.
   Helium is much less dense than air. It's used in party balloons and airships.

There are competing theories about atmospheric change

1) As well as the theories on page 60, there are other theories about how the Earth's atmosphere changed millions of years ago. Ultimately, all the theories have to be judged on the evidence.
2) For example, one theory says that the water on Earth came mainly from comets rather than volcanoes. Comets contain ice and dust, so a comet hitting the Earth would release water into the atmosphere. When this theory was first suggested, it seemed far-fetched. But space science research suggested that lots of small icy comets really are hitting the Earth every day. So far so good.
   However, studies of comets found that the water in comets isn't the same as the water on Earth. The water in comets contains much more of a form of water called "heavy water" than Earth's water. So current thinking is that most of Earth's water probably didn't come from comets.

The atmosphere is still changing

Levels of CO_2 in the atmosphere have increased by about 25% since 1750...
1) Burning fossil fuels releases CO_2 — so as the world's become more industrialised, more fossil fuels have been burnt in power stations and in car engines.
2) Deforestation also contributes to the increase in CO_2 levels. Plants take in CO_2 from the atmosphere, so getting rid of a whole load of plants means there's more CO_2 left in the atmosphere.
3) Carbon dioxide is a greenhouse gas — it traps heat from the Sun. (See p.8 and p.39 for more info.)

Over the last 50 years, the amount of ozone in the ozone layer has decreased...
1) Currently, holes in the Earth's ozone layer form over Antarctica each year (and also the Arctic to a lesser extent).
2) Ozone is broken down by man-made gases called CFCs, widely used as aerosol propellants and fridge coolants between the 1930s and the 1980s. CFCs were phased out in the 1990s.
3) The ozone layer protects us from the harmful UV radiation which can cause skin cancer. It's difficult to test whether changes in the ozone layer are to blame for increases in skin cancer, though. Other factors affect skin cancer — people sunbathe more and have more beach holidays abroad, so they expose themselves to more UV radiation anyway.

Warm-Up and Exam Questions

If you still think the Earth is flat, you may want to re-read the last few pages. If you think you know otherwise, and also know more interesting facts about the Earth's structure, test yourself with these...

Warm-Up Questions

1) What was 'Pangaea'?
2) Give an example of a visible clue that a volcano might be about to erupt.
3) State one geological feature often seen at the boundary of two tectonic plates.
4) How did the formation of the ozone layer enable the evolution of complex organisms?
5) Give three common uses of noble gases.

Exam Questions

1 The existence of animal fossils of the same species in both South Africa and Brazil suggests that:

   A these continents are moving towards each other.
   B South America and Africa were once joined together.
   C South America and Africa were never joined together.
   D South America and Africa have changed places.

   (1 mark)

2 Alfred Wegener came up with the theory of continental drift.

   (a) Describe two pieces of evidence to support his theory.
   (2 marks)

   (b) Give one reason why it wasn't accepted at the time.
   (1 mark)

3 Tectonic plates generally move at speeds of:

   A several metres per year.
   B between 5 and 10 kilometres per hour.
   C a few centimetres per year.
   D 1 or 2 millimetres per century.

   (1 mark)

CHEMISTRY 1B — OILS, EARTH AND ATMOSPHERE

Exam Questions

4   The following diagram shows the internal structure of the Earth.

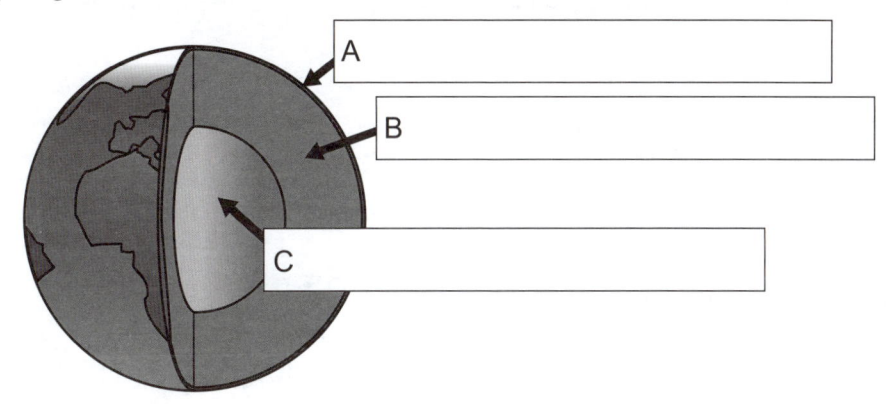

   A
   B
   C

   (a) Label the diagram.
   (3 marks)

   (b) What **two** elements do scientists believe part **C** is largely made from? Circle the correct answers.

   cadmium   nickel   silicon   aluminium   iron
   (2 marks)

5   The following graph shows how atmospheric CO_2 concentration and global temperature have varied over the last 250 000 years.

   (a) Describe what the graph shows about temperature and CO_2 levels.
   (2 marks)

   (b) Mark with an X on the graph the time when the temperature was most different from its present value.
   (1 mark)

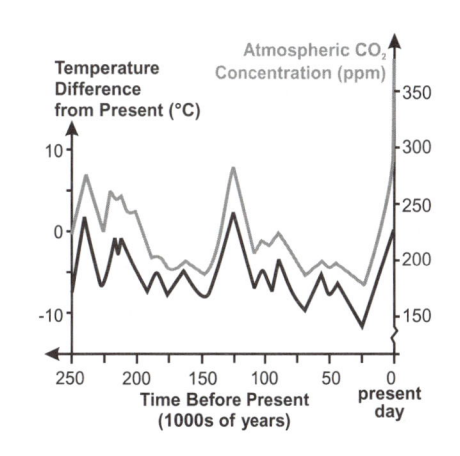

6   Match the words for **A**, **B**, **C** and **D** with the numbers **1 - 4** in the sentences below.

   A   photosynthesis
   B   oxygen
   C   carbon
   D   carbon dioxide

   Once green plants had evolved, they thrived in an atmosphere rich in ...**1**....
   These plants produced ...**2**... by the process of ...**3**....
   ...**4**... from dead plants eventually became 'locked up' in fossil fuels.
   (4 marks)

CHEMISTRY 1B — OILS, EARTH AND ATMOSPHERE

Revision Summary for Chemistry 1b

Cracking alkanes, making mayonnaise, food additives and earthquakes — can they really belong in the same section, I almost hear you ask. Whether you find the topics easy or hard, interesting or dull, you need to learn it all before the exam. Try these questions and see how much you really know:

1) What is "cracking"? Why is it done?
2) Give a typical example of a substance that is cracked, and the products that you get from cracking it.
3) What kind of carbon-carbon bond do alkenes have?
4) Pentene is an alkene with five carbon atoms. What is pentene's chemical formula?
5) Draw the chemical structure of ethene.
6) When ethene reacts with steam, what substance is formed?
7) What are polymers? What kinds of substance can form polymers?
8) Give two factors which affect the physical properties of a polymer.
9) List four uses of polymers.
10) Give an example of a "smart material" polymer.
11) Describe how olive oil is extracted from olives.
12) Why do some oils need to be distilled?
13) Give an example of a nutrient that is found in vegetable oil.
14) What is an emulsion?
15) List three foods that are emulsions.
16) What is biodiesel made from?
17) State one advantage and one disadvantage of biodiesel compared to ordinary diesel.
18) What kind of carbon-carbon bond do unsaturated oils contain?
19) Why are unsaturated oils hardened by reacting them with hydrogen?
20) What are the industrial conditions for the hydrogenation of unsaturated vegetable oil?
21) What is an E-number?
22) Describe how chromatography can be used to separate the different colours in a sweet.
23) Give two advantages and two disadvantages of using food additives.
24) A geologist places a very heavy marker on the seabed in the middle of the Atlantic ocean. She records the marker's position over a period of four years. The geologist finds that the marker moves in a straight-line away from its original position. Her measurements are shown in the graph on the right.
    a) Explain the process that has caused the marker to move.
    b)* What is the marker's average movement each year?
    c)* On average, how many years will it take for the marker to move 7 cm?
25)* The gases in Earth's early atmosphere came mostly from volcanic eruptions. The data table shows the compounds emitted by a typical volcanic eruption.
    a) What proportion of the emissions from the volcanic eruption is carbon dioxide?
    b) What compound makes up the greatest proportion of volcanic emissions?

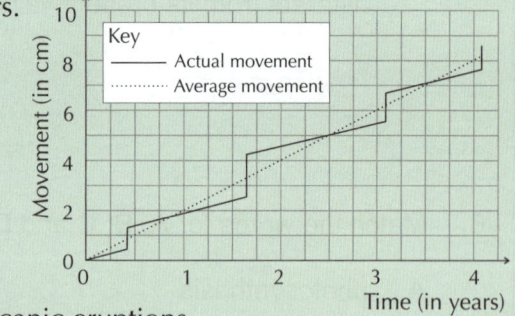

Compounds	H_2O	CO_2	SO_2	Other
Proportion	96%	2%	1.5%	0.5%

26) Name the two main gases that make up the Earth's atmosphere today.
27) Explain why today's atmosphere is different from the Earth's early atmosphere.
28) Describe three ways that human activity is changing the atmosphere. What are the effects of these changes?

* Answers on page 237

CHEMISTRY 21 — BONDING AND REACTIONS

Atoms

There are quite a few different (and equally useful) models of the atom — but chemists tend to like this nuclear model best. You can use it to explain pretty much the whole of Chemistry... which is nice.

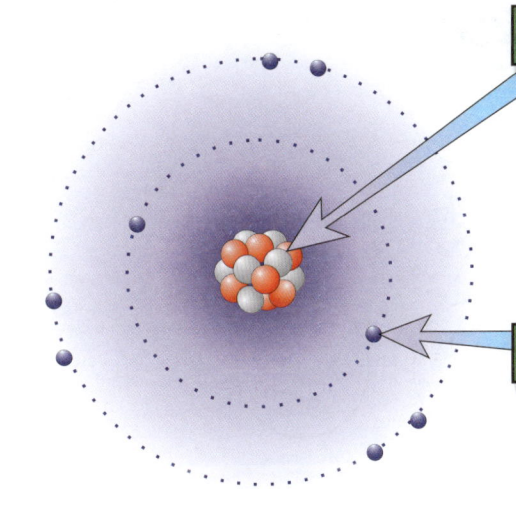

The Nucleus

1) It's in the middle of the atom.
2) It contains protons and neutrons.
3) It has a positive charge because of the protons.
4) Almost the whole mass of the atom is concentrated in the nucleus.
5) But size-wise it's tiny compared to the rest of the atom.

The Electrons

1) Move around the nucleus.
2) They're negatively charged.
3) They're tiny, but they cover a lot of space.
4) The volume of their orbits determines how big the atom is.
5) They have virtually no mass.
6) They occupy shells around the nucleus.
7) These shells explain the whole of Chemistry.

Atoms are really tiny, don't forget. They're too small to see, even with a microscope.

PARTICLE	MASS	CHARGE
Proton	1	+1
Neutron	1	0
Electron	very small	−1

Protons are heavy and positively charged
Neutrons are heavy and neutral
Electrons are tiny and negatively charged

(Electron mass is often taken as zero.)

Number of protons equals number of electrons

1) Neutral atoms have no charge overall.
2) The charge on the electrons is the same size as the charge on the protons — but opposite.
3) This means the number of protons always equals the number of electrons in a neutral atom.
4) If some electrons are added or removed, the atom becomes charged and is then an ion.

Atomic number and mass number describe an atom

These two numbers tell you how many of each kind of particle an atom has.

The Mass Number ➔ 23
— Total of protons and neutrons

The Atomic Number ➔ 11
— Number of protons

Na

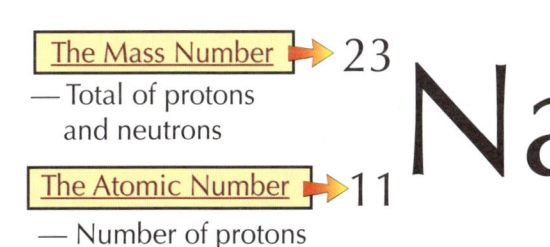

1) The atomic (proton) number tells you how many protons there are.
2) Atoms of the same element all have the same number of protons — so atoms of different elements will have different numbers of protons.

3) To get the number of neutrons, just subtract the atomic number from the mass number.
4) The mass number is always the biggest number. On a periodic table, the mass number is actually the relative atomic mass.
5) The mass number tends to be roughly double the proton number.
6) Which means there's about the same number of protons as neutrons in any nucleus.

Elements and Compounds

Because elements and compounds are so important, here's a quick reminder of these important type of substance.

Elements consist of one type of atom only

Quite a lot of everyday substances are elements:

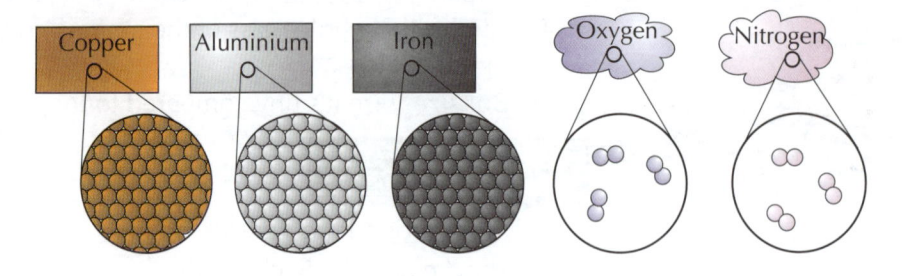

Copper   Aluminium   Iron   Oxygen   Nitrogen

Compounds are chemically bonded

1) Compounds are formed when two or more elements chemically react together. For example, carbon dioxide is a compound formed from a chemical reaction between carbon and oxygen.

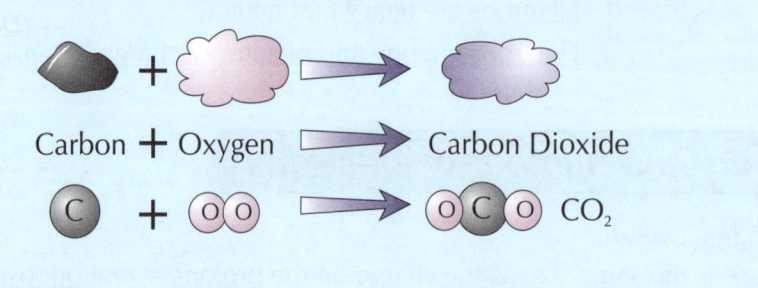

Carbon + Oxygen ⟶ Carbon Dioxide

C + O O ⟶ O C O CO_2

2) It's difficult to separate the two original elements out again.

3) The properties of a compound are totally different from the properties of the original elements.

4) If iron and sulfur react to form iron sulfide, the compound formed is a grey solid lump, and doesn't behave anything like either iron or sulfur.

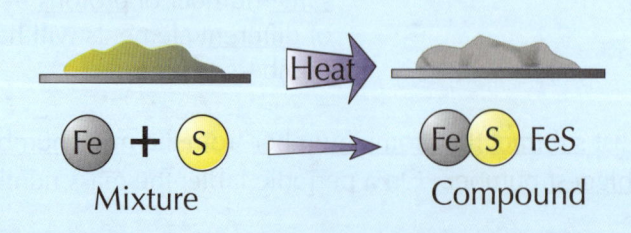

Fe + S ⟶ Fe S   FeS
Mixture   Compound

Isotopes

This page is all to do with the stuff inside the nucleus...

Isotopes *are the same except for an extra* neutron *or two*

A favourite trick exam question: "Explain what is meant by the term isotope".
The trick is that it's impossible to explain what one isotope is. Nice of them that, isn't it.
You have to outsmart them and always start your answer "Isotopes are..."
LEARN the definition:

> Isotopes are: different atomic forms of the same element, which have the
> SAME number of PROTONS but DIFFERENT numbers of NEUTRONS.

1) The upshot is: isotopes must have the same proton number but different mass numbers.

2) If they had different proton numbers, they'd be different elements altogether.

3) A very popular pair of isotopes are carbon-12 and carbon-14, used for carbon dating.

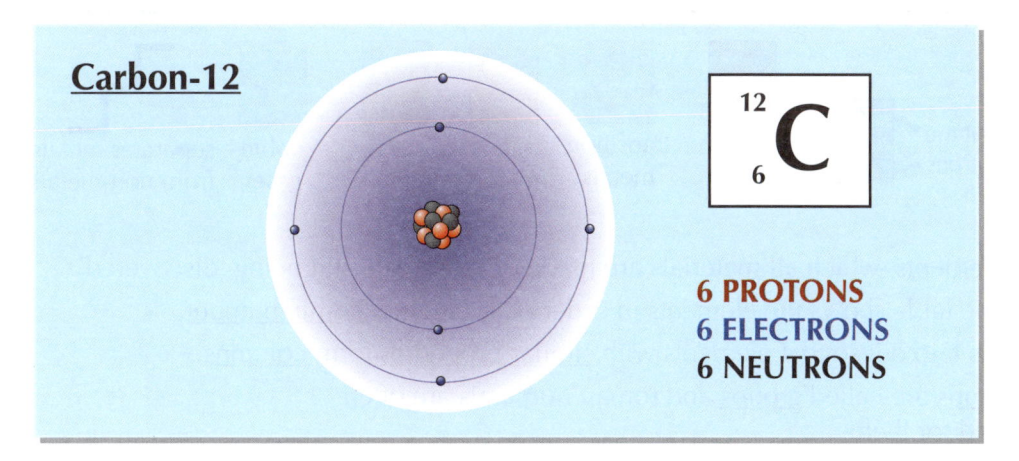

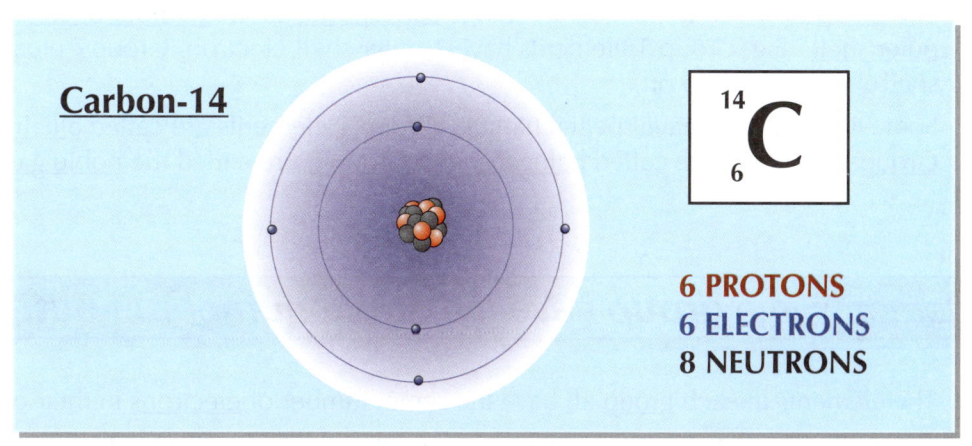

See page 65 for more about atomic structure.

Carbon-12

$^{12}_{6}C$

6 PROTONS
6 ELECTRONS
6 NEUTRONS

Carbon-14

$^{14}_{6}C$

6 PROTONS
6 ELECTRONS
8 NEUTRONS

The number of electrons decides the chemistry of the element. If the atomic number (that is, the number of protons) is the same, then the number of electrons must be the same, so the chemistry is the same. The different number of neutrons in the nucleus doesn't affect the chemical behaviour at all.

Will this be in your exam — isotope so...

Carbon-14 is unstable. It makes up about one ten-millionth of the carbon in living things. When things die, the C-14 is trapped inside the dead material, and it gradually decays into nitrogen. So by measuring the proportion of C-14 found in some old wood you can calculate how long ago it was living wood.

The Periodic Table

The periodic table is a chemist's best friend — start getting to know it now... seriously...

The **periodic table** is a table of all known **elements**

[Periodic table diagram with colour key: reactive metals, transition metals, other metals, non-metals, noble gases, and a line that separates metals from non-metals. A helium box is labelled: "These numbers tell you about the numbers of protons and neutrons — see page 65 for more."]

1) There are 100ish elements, which all materials are made of. More are still being 'discovered'.
2) The modern periodic table shows the elements in order of ascending atomic number.
3) The periodic table is laid out so that elements with similar properties form columns.
4) These vertical columns are called groups and roman numerals are often (but not always) used for them.
5) The group to which the element belongs corresponds to the number of electrons it has in its outer shell. E.g. Group 1 elements have 1 outer shell electron, Group 7 elements have 7 outer shell electrons and so on.
6) Some of the groups have special names. Group 1 elements are called alkali metals. Group 7 elements are called halogens, and Group 0 are called the noble gases.

Elements in a **group** have the **same number** of **outer electrons**

1) The elements in each group all have the same number of electrons in their outer shell.
2) That's why they have similar properties. And that's why we arrange them in this way.
3) When only a handful of elements were known, the periodic table was made by looking at the properties of the elements and arranging them in groups — the same groups that they are in today.
4) This idea is extremely important to chemistry — so make sure you understand it.
5) The properties of the elements are decided entirely by how many electrons they have. Atomic number is therefore very significant because it is equal to the number of electrons each atom has. But it's the number of electrons in the outer shell which is the really important thing.

Electron Shells

Electron shells are what chemistry is **all about**

The fact that electrons form shells around atoms is the basis for the whole of chemistry. If they just whizzed round the nucleus any old how and didn't care about shells, there'd be no chemical reactions. No nothing in fact — because nothing would happen. The atoms would just sit there.

But amazingly, they do form shells (if they didn't, we wouldn't even be here to wonder about it), and the electron arrangement of each atom determines the whole of its chemical behaviour.

Electron arrangements explain practically the whole Universe. Pretty amazing.

Electrons always follow the *same pattern* when *filling shells*

It's really important that you know these electron shell rules:

Electron shell rules:

1) Electrons always occupy shells (sometimes called energy levels).

2) The lowest energy levels are always filled first — these are the ones closest to the nucleus.

3) Only a certain number of electrons are allowed in each shell:

   - 1st shell — 2
   - 2nd shell — 8
   - 3rd shell — 8

   (This isn't strictly true, but it works for the first 20 elements so it's all you need to know for now.)

4) Atoms are much happier when they have full electron shells — like the noble gases in Group 0.

5) In most atoms the outer shell is not full and this makes the atom want to react to fill it.

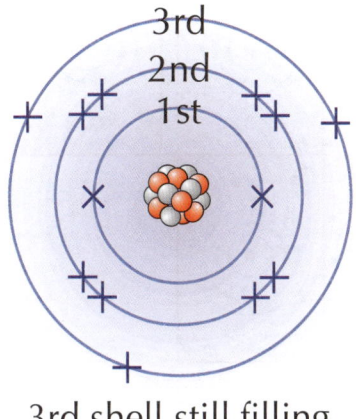

3rd shell still filling

Electron shells — probably the most important thing in chemistry...

It's really important to learn the rules for filling electron shells. It's so important I'll just leave this page with a quick reminder. Energy of the shells increases with increasing number (so shell one is the lowest). Fill the shell with lowest energy first. And the 1st shell can only hold a maximum of 2 electrons, but the 2nd and 3rd shells can both hold 8 electrons. Practise following these rules on the next page.

Electron Configurations

You need to know the electron configurations for the first twenty elements (things get a bit more complicated after that — luckily you don't have to worry about it).

Follow the rules to **work out** electron configurations

Electron configurations are not hard to work out.
For a quick example, take nitrogen:

1) The periodic table tells you nitrogen has seven protons... so it must have seven electrons.

2) Follow the 'Electron Shell Rules' from the last page. The first shell can only take 2 electrons and the second shell can take a maximum of 8 electrons.

3) So the electron configuration for nitrogen must be 2, 5.

The best way to get better at working these out is to practise, so now you try it for argon.

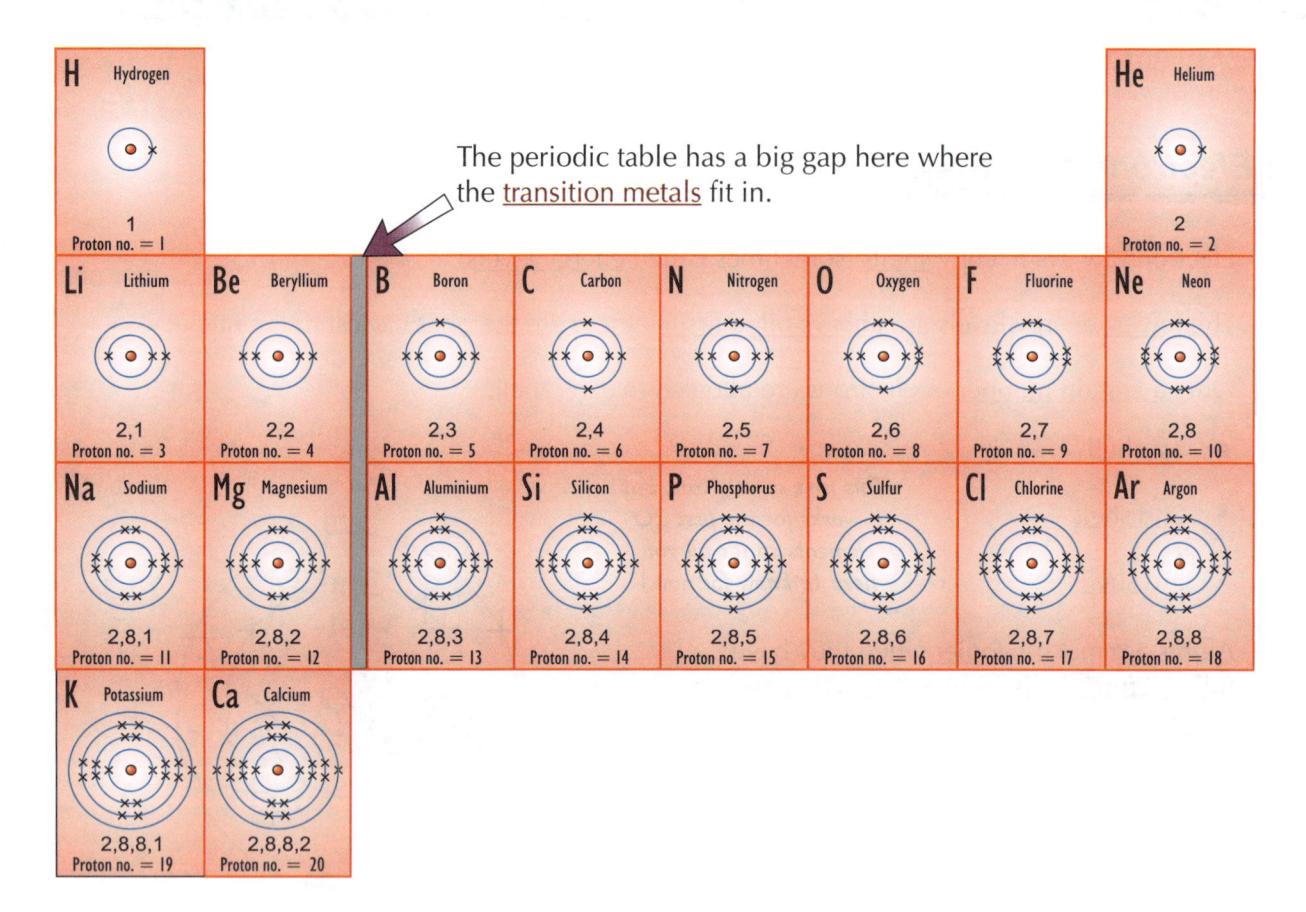

The periodic table has a big gap here where the transition metals fit in.

Element	Configuration	Proton no.
H Hydrogen	1	1
He Helium	2	2
Li Lithium	2,1	3
Be Beryllium	2,2	4
B Boron	2,3	5
C Carbon	2,4	6
N Nitrogen	2,5	7
O Oxygen	2,6	8
F Fluorine	2,7	9
Ne Neon	2,8	10
Na Sodium	2,8,1	11
Mg Magnesium	2,8,2	12
Al Aluminium	2,8,3	13
Si Silicon	2,8,4	14
P Phosphorus	2,8,5	15
S Sulfur	2,8,6	16
Cl Chlorine	2,8,7	17
Ar Argon	2,8,8	18
K Potassium	2,8,8,1	19
Ca Calcium	2,8,8,2	20

Answer:
To calculate the electron configuration of argon, follow the rules. It's got 18 protons, so it must have 18 electrons. The first shell must have 2 electrons, the second shell must have 8, and so the third shell must have 8 as well. It's as easy as 2, 8, 8.

Warm-Up and Exam Questions

These questions will help you find out if you've learnt all the basics about the structure of atoms and the arrangement of elements in the periodic table. Have a look back through the last few pages if you're unsure about any of these questions. It's really important to get these basics right.

Warm-Up Questions

1) In a neutral atom, which particles are always equal in number?
2) Explain the difference between mass number and atomic number.
3) What is the name given to the neutral particle in the nucleus?
4) What is the name given to atoms of the same element with different mass numbers?
5) How many electrons can be held in: a) the first shell, and b) the second shell?

Exam Questions

1   The proton has a relative mass of 1. What is the relative mass of a neutron?

   A   2000
   B   1
   C   1/2000
   D   2

   (1 mark)

2   Which two of the following substances are elements?

   A   water
   B   oxygen
   C   sulfur
   D   carbon dioxide

   (2 marks)

3   The electron arrangement of an element, Z, is shown in the diagram:

   (a) What is the atomic number of element Z?

   (1 mark)

   (b) Which group does Z belong to in the periodic table? Explain how you can tell.

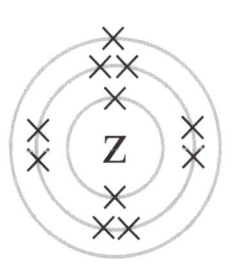

   (2 marks)

Ionic Bonding

In ionic bonding, atoms lose or gain electrons to form charged particles (called ions) which are then strongly attracted to one another (because of the attraction of opposite charges, + and –).

A shell with just *one or two* electrons is *well keen to get rid*...

1) All the atoms over at the left-hand side of the periodic table, e.g. sodium, potassium, calcium, etc. have just one or two electrons in their outer shell.

2) They're pretty keen to lose these electrons, because then they'll only have full shells left, which is how they like it.

3) So given half a chance they do lose them, and that leaves the atom as an ion instead.

4) Now ions aren't the kind of things that sit around quietly watching the world go by. They tend to leap at the first passing ion with an opposite charge and stick to it like glue...

A *nearly full* shell *wants* to get that *extra electron*...

1) On the other side of the periodic table, the elements in Group 6 and Group 7, such as oxygen and chlorine, have outer shells which are nearly full.

2) They're obviously pretty keen to gain that extra one or two electrons to fill the shell up.

3) When they do, of course, they become ions and before you know it, pop, they've latched onto the atom (ion) that gave up the electron a moment earlier.

The reaction of sodium and chlorine is a classic case:

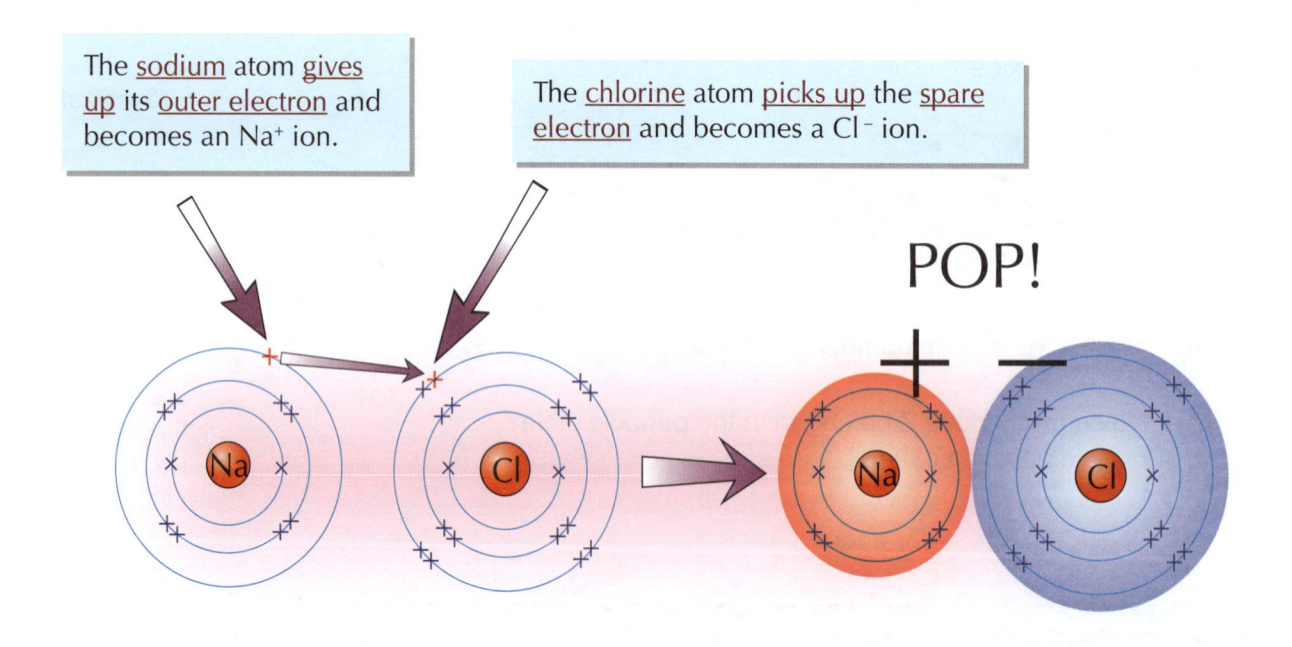

The sodium atom gives up its outer electron and becomes an Na$^+$ ion.

The chlorine atom picks up the spare electron and becomes a Cl$^-$ ion.

POP!

CHEMISTRY 21 — BONDING AND REACTIONS

Ionic Bonding

Ionic bonds produce giant ionic structures.

Giant ionic structures don't melt easily — but when they do...

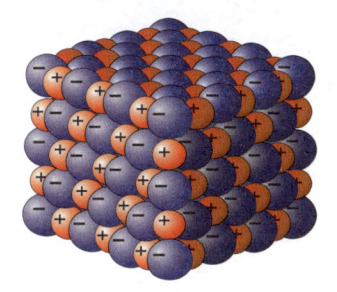

1) Ionic bonds always produce giant ionic structures.
2) The ions form a closely packed regular lattice arrangement.
3) There are very strong chemical bonds between all the ions.
4) A single crystal of salt is one giant ionic lattice, which is why salt crystals tend to be cuboid in shape.

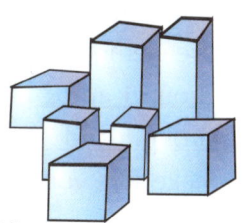

1) They have **high melting points** and **boiling points**

This is due to the very strong chemical bonds between all the ions in the giant structure.

2) They **dissolve** to form solutions that **conduct electricity**

When dissolved, the ions separate and are all free to move in the solution. These free-moving charged particles allow the solution to carry electric current.

Dissolved lithium salts are used to make rechargeable batteries.

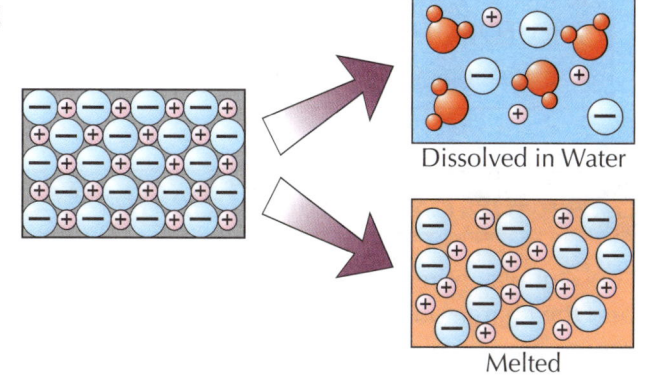

Dissolved in Water

Melted

3) They **conduct** electricity when **molten**

When the substance melts, the ions are free to move and so they'll carry electric current.

Batteries need to contain a conducting solution

Because they conduct electricity when they're dissolved in water, ionic compounds are used to make some types of battery. In the olden days, most batteries had actual liquid in, so they tended to leak all over the place. Now they've come up with a sort of paste that doesn't leak but still conducts. Clever.

Electron Shell and Ions

Atoms in Groups 1, 2, 6 and 7 always form ions with the same charges.
You need to know what these are.

Groups *1 & 2* and *6 & 7* are the most likely to form **ions**

1) Remember, atoms that have lost or gained an electron (or electrons) are ions.
2) The elements that most readily form ions are those in Groups 1, 2, 6 and 7.
3) Group 1 and 2 elements are metals and they lose electrons to form +ve ions or cations.
4) Group 6 and 7 elements are non-metals. They gain electrons to form –ve ions or anions.
5) Make sure you know these easy ones:

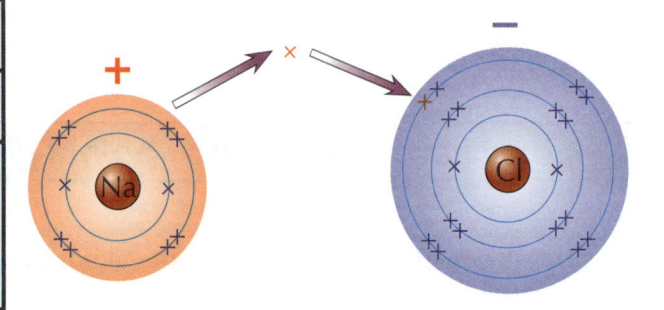

CATIONS		ANIONS	
Group 1	Group 2	Group 6	Group 7
Li^+	Be^{2+}	O^{2-}	F^-
Na^+	Mg^{2+}		Cl^-
K^+	Ca^{2+}		Br^-

6) When any of the above cations react with the anions, they form ionic bonds.
7) Only elements at opposite sides of the periodic table will form ionic bonds, e.g. Na and Cl, where one of them becomes a cation (+ve) and one becomes an anion (–ve).

Remember, the + and – charges, e.g. Na^+ for sodium, just tell you what type of ion the atom WILL FORM in a chemical reaction. In sodium metal there are only neutral sodium atoms, Na. The Na^+ ions will only appear if the sodium metal reacts with something like water or chlorine.

Show the Electronic Structure of *Simple* Ions With *Brackets* [ ]

A useful way of representing ions is by specifying the ion's name, followed by its electron configuration and the charge on the ion. For example, the electronic structure of the sodium ion Na^+ can be represented by Na [2, 8]$^+$. That's the electron configuration followed by the charge on the ion. Simple enough. A few ions and the ionic compounds they form are shown below.

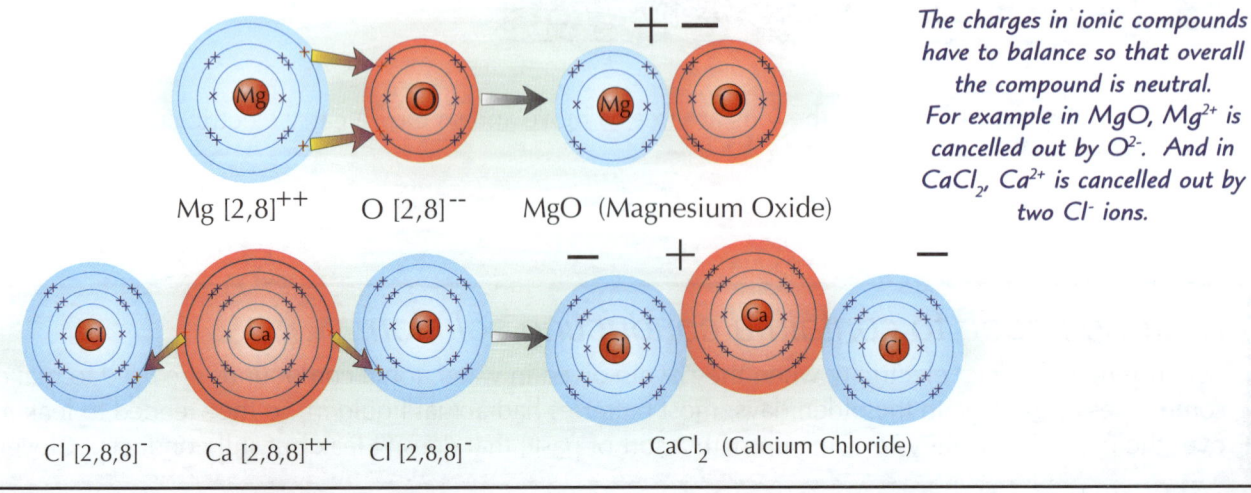

Mg [2,8]$^{++}$ O [2,8]$^{--}$ MgO (Magnesium Oxide)

Cl [2,8,8]$^-$ Ca [2,8,8]$^{++}$ Cl [2,8,8]$^-$ $CaCl_2$ (Calcium Chloride)

The charges in ionic compounds have to balance so that overall the compound is neutral. For example in MgO, Mg^{2+} is cancelled out by O^{2-}. And in $CaCl_2$, Ca^{2+} is cancelled out by two Cl^- ions.

CHEMISTRY 2I — BONDING AND REACTIONS

Warm-Up and Exam Questions

Without a good warm-up you're likely to strain a brain cell or two. So take the time to run through these simple questions before tackling the exam questions.

Warm-Up Questions

1) Sodium chloride has a giant ionic structure. Does it have a high or a low boiling point?
2) Why do giant ionic solids conduct electricity when dissolved?
3) Do elements from Group 1 form cations or anions?
4) Do elements from Group 7 form cations or anions?
5) What is the formula of the compound containing Al^{3+} and OH^- ions only?

Exam Questions

1   Magnesium (atomic number 12) and fluorine (atomic number 9) combine vigorously to form magnesium fluoride, an ionic compound.

   (a) Draw dot and cross diagrams to show the electron arrangement of each atom.
(2 marks)

   (b) Give the symbol (including the charge) for each of the ions formed.
(2 marks)

   (c) Using your answer to (b), work out the formula of magnesium fluoride.
(1 mark)

   (d) Once formed, explain why the ions remain together in a compound.
(1 mark)

   (e) Magnesium fluoride has a giant ionic structure. Explain why:
      (i) it doesn't melt easily.
(2 marks)
      (ii) it conducts electricity when molten.
(1 mark)

2   Potassium and chlorine react to form potassium chloride.

   (a) Complete the following table.
(3 marks)

	Potassium atom, K	Potassium ion, K^+	Chlorine atom, Cl	Chloride ion, Cl^-
Number of electrons	19			
Electron arrangement	2, 8, 8, 1			

   (b) Draw a dot and cross diagram to show the formation of potassium chloride.
(2 marks)

Covalent Bonding

Ionic bonding isn't the only way for an atom to get a nice full shell of electrons...

Covalent bonds — sharing electrons

1) Sometimes atoms prefer to make covalent bonds by sharing electrons with other atoms.
2) This way both atoms feel that they have a full outer shell, and that makes them happy.
3) Each covalent bond provides one extra shared electron for each atom.
4) Each atom involved has to make enough covalent bonds to fill up its outer shell.
5) Learn these seven important examples:

1) Hydrogen, H_2

Hydrogen atoms have just one electron. They only need one more to complete their first shell, so they often form single covalent bonds to achieve this.

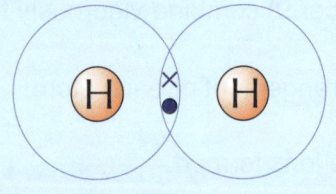

H ⊗• H   or   H—H

2) Chlorine, Cl_2

Chlorine atoms also need only one more electron to complete their outer shell, so they also form single covalent bonds.

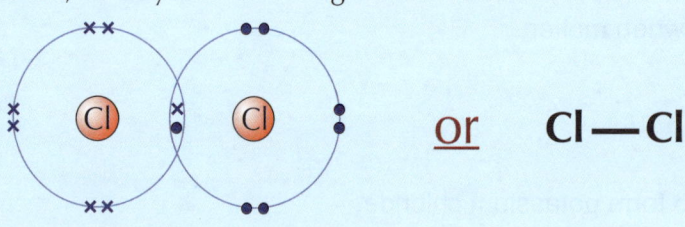

Cl ⊗• Cl   or   Cl—Cl

You only have to draw the outer shell of electrons.

3) Hydrogen chloride, HCl

This is very similar to H_2 and Cl_2. Again, both atoms only need one more electron to complete their outer shells.

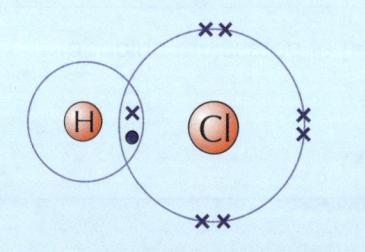

H ⊗• Cl   or   H—Cl

CHEMISTRY 21 — BONDING AND REACTIONS

Covalent Bonding

4) Ammonia, NH_3

Nitrogen has <u>five</u> outer electrons, so it needs to form <u>three covalent bonds</u> to make up the extra <u>three</u> electrons needed.

5) Methane, CH_4

Carbon has <u>four outer electrons</u>, which is <u>half a full</u> shell.

To become a 4^+ or a 4^- ion is hard work, so it forms <u>four covalent bonds</u> to make up its outer shell.

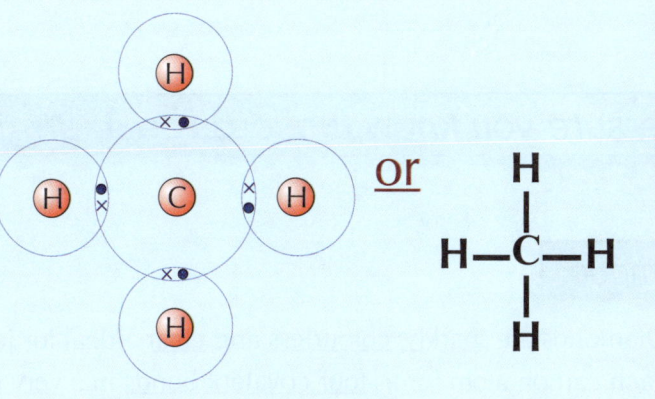

6) Water, H_2O

7) Oxygen, O_2

<u>Oxygen</u> atoms have <u>six</u> outer electrons. They sometimes form <u>ionic</u> bonds by <u>taking</u> two electrons to complete their outer shell.

However, they'll also cheerfully form <u>covalent bonds</u> and <u>share</u> two electrons instead. In <u>water molecules</u>, the oxygen <u>shares</u> electrons with the H atoms and in oxygen gas it shares with another oxygen atom.

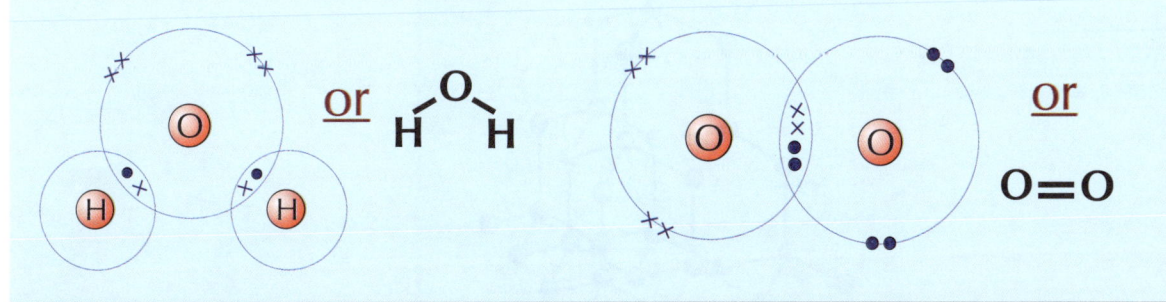

Covalent bonding involves sharing rather than giving electrons

Make sure you learn these seven really basic examples and <u>why they work</u>. Every atom wants a full outer shell, and they can get that either by becoming an <u>ion</u> (p.74) or by <u>sharing electrons</u>. Once you understand that, you should be able to apply it to any example they give you in the exam.

CHEMISTRY 2I — BONDING AND REACTIONS

Covalent Substances: Giant Covalent

Substances formed from covalent bonds can either be simple molecules (see p.80) or giant structures. The next two pages are all about the giant structures, and there are three examples to learn.

Giant covalent structures

1) These are similar to giant ionic structures except that there are no charged ions.

2) All the atoms are bonded to each other by strong covalent bonds.

3) They have very high melting and boiling points.

4) They don't conduct electricity — not even when molten (except for graphite that is — see next page).

5) They're usually insoluble in water.

6) Important examples are diamond and graphite, which are both made only from carbon atoms.

Make sure you know these three examples

Diamond

1) Diamonds are sparkly, colourless and clear. Ideal for jewellery.
2) Each carbon atom forms four covalent bonds in a very rigid giant covalent structure, which makes diamond the hardest natural substance. This makes diamonds ideal as cutting tools.
3) All those strong covalent bonds give diamond a very high melting point.
4) It doesn't conduct electricity because it has no free electrons.

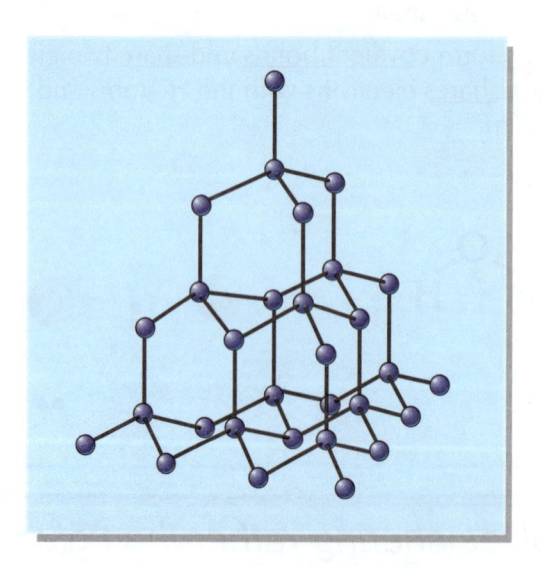

CHEMISTRY 21 — BONDING AND REACTIONS

Covalent Substances: Giant Covalent

Here are the other two examples of giant covalent structures that you need to learn.

Graphite

1) Graphite is black and opaque, but still kind of shiny.
2) Each carbon atom only forms three covalent bonds, creating sheets of carbon atoms which are free to slide over each other. This makes graphite slippery, so it's useful as a lubricant.
3) The layers are held together so loosely that they can be rubbed off onto paper to leave a black mark — that's how pencils work.
4) Graphite has a high melting point — the covalent bonds need lots of energy before they break.
5) Only three out of each carbon's four outer electrons are used in bonds, so there are lots of spare electrons. This means graphite conducts electricity — it's used for electrodes.

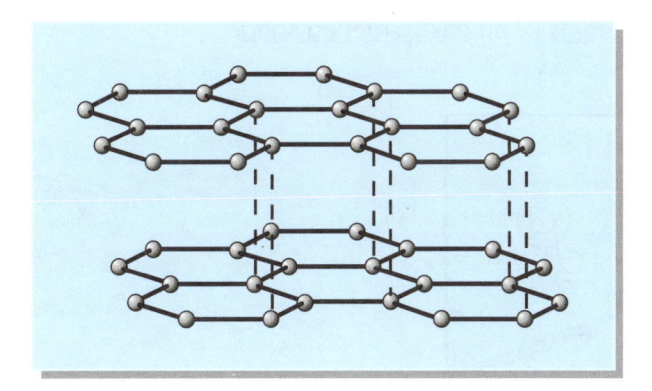

Silicon dioxide (silica)

1) Sometimes called silica, this is what sand is made of.
2) Each grain of sand is one giant structure of silicon and oxygen.
3) Silica can be melted down with sodium carbonate (Na_2CO_3) and limestone ($CaCO_3$) to make glass.

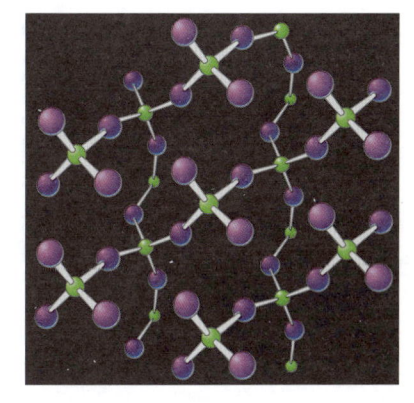

Graphite and diamond contain exactly the same atoms

Graphite and diamond are both made purely from carbon — there's no difference at all in their atoms. The difference in properties (and price) of the two substances is all down to the way the atoms are held together. Different structural forms of the same element like this are called allotropes.

CHEMISTRY 21 — BONDING AND REACTIONS

Covalent Substances: Simple Covalent

Atoms that bond covalently don't all form giant structures.
Some form simple covalent substances.

Simple *covalent* substances

1) The atoms form very strong covalent bonds to form small molecules of two or more atoms.

2) By contrast, the forces of attraction between these molecules are very weak.

3) The result of these feeble inter-molecular forces is that the melting and boiling points are very low, because the molecules are easily parted from each other.

4) Most molecular substances are gases or liquids at room temperature.

5) Molecular substances don't conduct electricity, simply because there are no ions.

6) You can usually tell a simple molecular substance just from its physical state, which is always kind of 'mushy' — i.e. liquid or gas or an easily-melted solid.

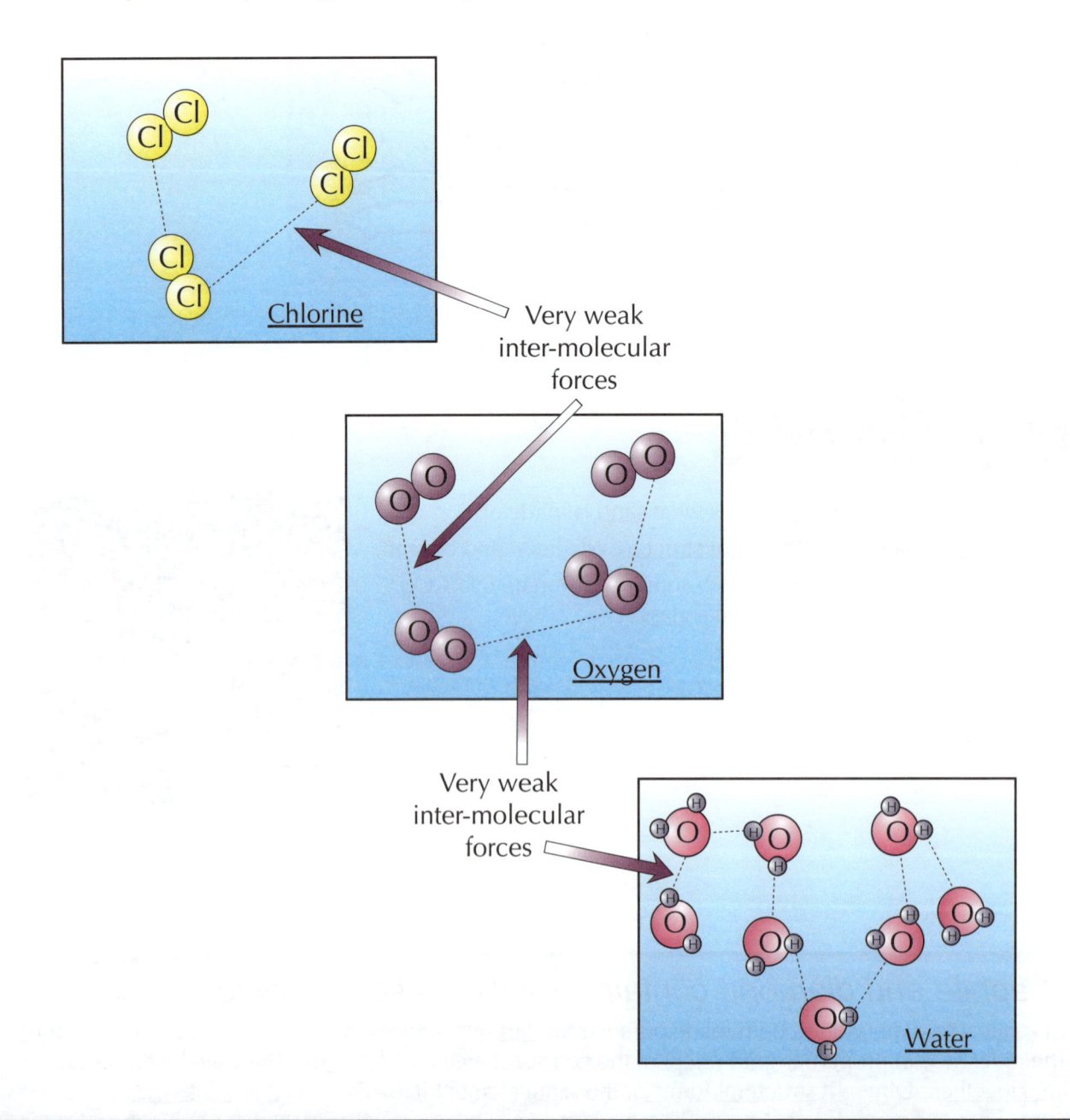

Chlorine

Very weak inter-molecular forces

Oxygen

Very weak inter-molecular forces

Water

CHEMISTRY 21 — BONDING AND REACTIONS

Metallic Structures

Metal properties are all due to the sea of free electrons

1) <u>Metals</u> also consist of a <u>giant structure</u>.
2) <u>Metallic bonds</u> involve the all-important '<u>free electrons</u>', which produce <u>all</u> the properties of metals. These free electrons come from the <u>outer shell</u> of <u>every</u> metal atom in the structure.
3) These electrons are <u>free to move</u> and so metals are good conductors of <u>heat and electricity</u>.
4) These electrons also <u>hold</u> the atoms together in a regular structure.

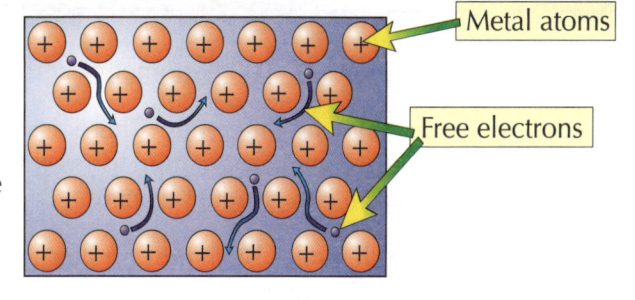

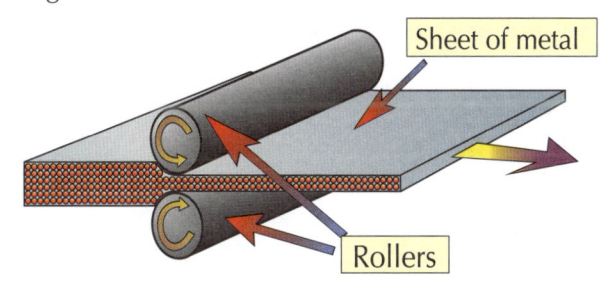

5) And they allow the atoms to <u>slide</u> over each other, causing metals to be <u>malleable</u>.

Identifying the bonding in a substance by its properties

If you've learnt the properties of the <u>four types</u> of substance properly, together with their <u>names</u> of course, then you should be able to easily <u>identify</u> most substances just by the way they <u>behave</u> as either:

- <u>ionic</u>,
- <u>giant covalent</u>,
- <u>simple covalent</u>,
- or <u>metallic</u>.

The way they're likely to test you in the Exam is by describing the <u>physical properties</u> of a substance and asking you to decide <u>which type of bonding</u> it has and therefore what type of material it is.

If you know your onions you'll have no trouble at all. If not, you're gonna struggle. Try this one:

<u>Example</u>: Four substances were tested for various properties with the results below:

Identify the type of bonding in each substance. (Answers at bottom of page.)

Substance	Melting point (°C)	Boiling point (°C)	Good electrical conductor?
A	−218.4	−182.96	No
B	1535	2750	Yes
C	1410	2355	No
D	801	1413	When molten

Answers: A is simple molecular, B is metal, C is giant covalent, D is ionic.

Nanomaterials

Hmm, nanomaterials. Very useful but, let's face it, pretty bizarre.

Nanomaterials are really really really really tiny   ...in fact, they're smaller than that.

1) Really tiny particles, 1–100 nanometres across, are called 'nanoparticles' (1 nm = 0.000 000 001 m).

2) Nanoparticles include fullerenes. These are molecules of carbon, shaped like hollow balls or closed tubes. Each carbon atom forms three covalent bonds with its neighbours, leaving free electrons that can conduct electricity.

3) The smallest fullerene is buckminsterfullerene, which has 60 carbon atoms joined in a ball — its molecular formula is C_{60}.

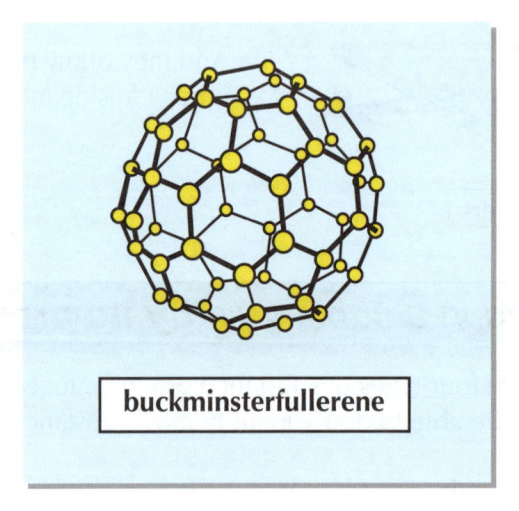

buckminsterfullerene

Fullerenes can be joined together to form nanotubes — teeny tiny hollow carbon tubes, a few nanometers across:

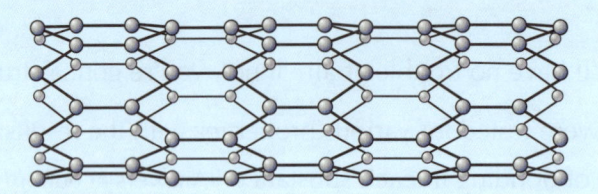

A nanoparticle has very different properties from the 'bulk' chemical that it's made from — e.g. fullerenes have different properties from big lumps of carbon.

a) All those covalent bonds make carbon nanotubes very strong. They can be used to reinforce graphite in tennis rackets and to make stronger, lighter building materials.

b) Nanotubes conduct electricity, so they can be used in tiny electric circuits for computer chips.

Nanomaterials and Smart Materials

Nanomaterials are becoming more and more widely used

1) Nanoparticles have some very useful properties:

    a) They have a huge surface area, so they could help make great industrial catalysts (see pages 110-111) — individual catalyst molecules could be attached to carbon nanotubes.
    b) With nanoparticles, you can build surfaces with very specific properties. That means you can use them to make sensors to detect one type of molecule and nothing else. These highly specific sensors are already being used to test water purity.

2) Nanoparticles can be made by molecular engineering but this is really hard. Molecular engineering is building a product molecule-by-molecule to a specific design — either by positioning each molecule exactly where you want it or by starting with a bigger structure and taking bits off it.

If you're not freaked out by nanomaterials, there are also smart materials. Which can be surprising.

Smart materials have some really weird properties

1) Smart materials behave differently depending on the conditions, e.g. temperature.

2) A good example is nitinol — a "shape memory alloy". It's a metal, but when it's cool you can bend it and twist it like rubber. Bend it too far, though, and it stays bent. But here's the really clever bit — if you heat it above a certain temperature, it goes back to a "remembered" shape (hence the name). It's really handy for glasses frames. If you accidentally bend them, you can just pop them into a bowl of hot water and they'll jump back into shape. Nitinol is made from about half nickel, half titanium.

3) Other examples of smart materials include dyes that change colour depending on temperature or light intensity, liquids that turn solid when you put them in a magnetic field, and materials that expand or contract when you put an electric current through them.

Bendy specs, tennis rackets and computer chips — cool...

Some nanoparticles have really unexpected properties. Silver's normally very unreactive, but silver nanoparticles can kill bacteria. Gold nanoparticles aren't gold-coloured — they're either red or purple.

Warm-Up and Exam Questions

Warm-Up Questions

1) How is covalent bonding different from ionic bonding?
2) Describe the differences in the physical properties of diamond and graphite.
3) Give another example of a substance that has a giant covalent structure.
4) Why does chlorine have a very low boiling point?

Exam Questions

1   Carbon dioxide is a covalently bonded molecule with the formula CO_2.
    Draw a dot and cross diagram for the carbon dioxide molecule,
    showing only the outer electrons.

(2 marks)

2   The table compares some physical properties of silicon dioxide, bromine and graphite.

Property	silicon dioxide	bromine	graphite
Melting point (°C)	1610	−7	3657
Electrical conductivity	poor	poor	good
Solubility in water	insoluble	slightly soluble	insoluble

(a) What is the structure and type of bonding in:
   (i) silicon dioxide?

(1 mark)

   (ii) graphite?

(1 mark)

   (iii) bromine?

(1 mark)

(b) Why does silicon dioxide have poor electrical conductivity?

(1 mark)

(c) Why does graphite have good electrical conductivity?

(1 mark)

(d) Bromine is a liquid at room temperature (20 °C).
    Explain why bromine has such a low melting point compared with
    silicon dioxide and graphite.

(2 marks)

CHEMISTRY 21 — BONDING AND REACTIONS

Exam Questions

3 Scientists have developed new materials using nanoparticles, which show different properties from the same materials in bulk.

(a) Use words from the box to help you complete the sentences below.

volume   mm   catalysts   surface   nm   area   circuits

(i) Nanoparticles are up to 100 .... in size.
(1 mark)

(ii) Nanoparticles have a large ....

to .... ratio.
(2 marks)

(b) Floyd Landis used a bike in the Tour de France with a frame weighing about 1 kg. Carbon nanotubes (CNT) were used in the manufacture of the frame of the bike.

Suggest two properties of a material made using CNTs that make it suitable for use in a bike frame.
(2 marks)

(c) Give one other application of nanoparticles.
(1 mark)

4 Carbon nanotubes have a tube-like structure based on the covalent bonding between carbon atoms, as shown in the diagram. They can be used to make tiny electrical circuits.

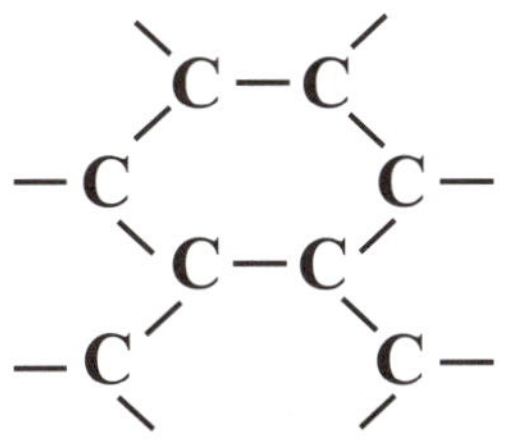

Consider the number of bonds carbon normally forms, and use this to help explain why nanotubes conduct electricity.

(3 marks)

Relative Formula Mass

The biggest trouble with relative atomic mass and relative formula mass is that they sound so blood-curdling. Take a few deep breaths and just enjoy, as the mists slowly clear...

Relative atomic mass, A_r, is dead easy

1) This is just a way of saying how heavy different atoms are compared with the mass of an atom of carbon-12. So carbon-12 has an A_r of exactly 12.

2) It turns out that the relative atomic mass A_r is nothing more than the mass number of the element (to the nearest whole number).

3) In the periodic table, the elements all have two numbers. The smaller one is the atomic number (how many protons it has). But the bigger one is the mass number (how many protons and neutrons an atom has), which is also the relative atomic mass. See? Dead easy.

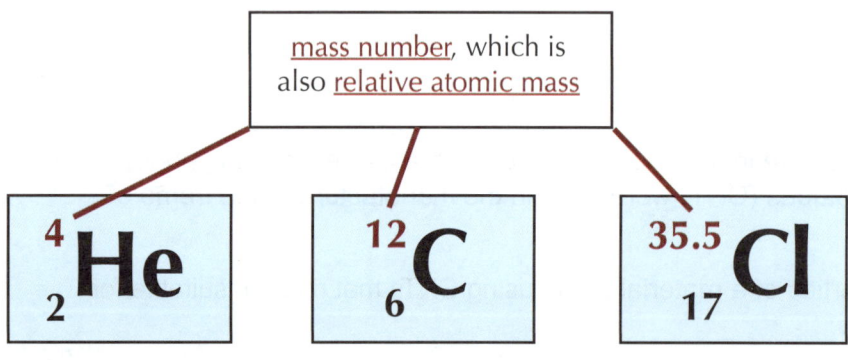

mass number, which is also relative atomic mass

$^{4}_{2}He$ $^{12}_{6}C$ $^{35.5}_{17}Cl$

Helium has $A_r = 4$. Carbon has $A_r = 12$. Chlorine has $A_r = 35.5$.

You may have noticed that the relative atomic mass of chlorine isn't a whole number like the others. That's because it has more than one stable isotope (which have different mass numbers) and the relative atomic mass is the average of the mass numbers of the different isotopes based on their relative abundance.

Relative formula mass, M_r, is also dead easy

If you have a compound like $MgCl_2$ then it has a relative formula mass, M_r, which is just all the relative atomic masses added together.

For $MgCl_2$ it would be:

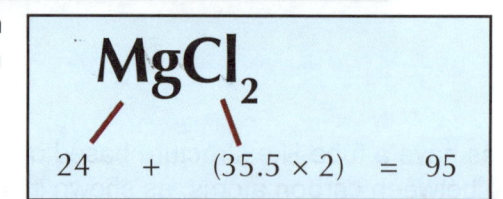

$MgCl_2$

$24 + (35.5 \times 2) = 95$

So M_r for $MgCl_2$ is simply 95.

You can easily get A_r for any element from the periodic table (see inside front cover), but in a lot of questions they give you them anyway. Since it's nearly Christmas I'll run through another example:

Example:

Find the relative formula mass for calcium carbonate, $CaCO_3$, using the given data:
A_r for Ca = 40 A_r for C = 12 A_r for O = 16

ANSWER:

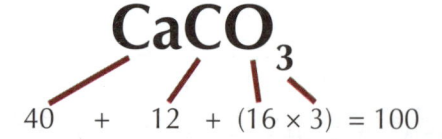

$CaCO_3$

$40 + 12 + (16 \times 3) = 100$

So the M_r for $CaCO_3$ is 100.

And that's it. Big fancy name like relative formula mass and all it means is "add up the mass numbers".

Formula Mass Calculations

Although relative atomic mass and relative formula mass are <u>easy enough</u>, it can get just a tad <u>trickier</u> when you start getting into other calculations which use them. It depends on how good your maths is basically, because it's all to do with ratios and percentages.

Calculating % mass of an element in a compound

This is actually dead easy — so long as you've learnt <u>this formula</u>:

$$\text{Percentage mass of an element in a compound} = \frac{A_r \times \text{no. of atoms (of that element)}}{M_r \text{ (of whole compound)}} \times 100$$

If you don't learn the formula then you'd better be pretty smart — or you'll struggle. Here's an <u>example</u> of how you'd use it:

Example:

Find the percentage mass of nitrogen in ammonium sulfate fertiliser, $(NH_4)_2SO_4$, using the following:

- A_r for H = 1
- A_r for N = 14
- A_r for O = 16
- A_r for S = 32

<u>ANSWER</u>: M_r of $(NH_4)_2SO_4$ = 2 × [14 + (1 × 4)] + 32 + (16 × 4)
= 132

Now use the formula:

$$\text{Percentage mass} = \frac{A_r \times n}{M_r} \times 100$$

$$= \frac{14 \times 2}{132} \times 100 = \mathbf{21.2\%}$$

So there you have it. Nitrogen represents <u>21.2%</u> of the mass of ammonium sulfate.

As usual with these calculations, <u>practice makes perfect</u>. You'll find some to do on the bottom of the next page. Don't skip it, you'll be glad you're perfect when it comes to exam day.

Formula Mass Calculations

Finding the empirical formula (from masses or percentages)

This also sounds a lot worse than it really is. Try this for a nice simple stepwise method:

1) List all the elements in the compound (there's usually only two or three).

2) Underneath them, write their experimental masses or percentages.

3) Divide each mass or percentage by the A_r for that particular element.

4) Turn the numbers you get into a nice simple ratio by multiplying and/or dividing them by well-chosen numbers.

5) Get the ratio in its simplest form, and that tells you the empirical formula of the compound.

Here's a nice example to give you a better idea of what I'm on about:

Example:

Find the empirical formula of the iron oxide produced when 44.8 g of iron react with 19.2 g of oxygen.
(A_r for iron = 56, A_r for oxygen = 16)

METHOD:

1) List the two elements: **Fe**   **O**

2) Write in the experimental masses: 44.8   19.2

3) Divide by the A_r for each element: 44.8/56 = 0.8   19.2/16 = 1.2

4) Multiply by 10...   8   12

   ...then divide by 4:   2   3

5) So the simplest formula is 2 atoms of Fe to 3 atoms of O, i.e. **Fe_2O_3**.

You need to realise (for the exam) that this empirical method (i.e. based on experiment) is the only way of finding out the formula of a compound. Rust is iron oxide, sure, but is it FeO, or Fe_2O_3? Only an experiment to determine the empirical formula will tell you for certain.

Don't learn that list of instructions — practise using it (it's much quicker)

These sort of questions are the backbone of chemistry. They're really common exam questions as well. If you find them a bit scary, just keep practising using the stepwise method until you've mastered it.
Try these: 1) Find the percentage mass of oxygen in each of these: a) Fe_2O_3 b) H_2O c) H_2SO_4
2) Find the empirical formula of the compound formed from 2.4 g of carbon and 0.8 g of hydrogen.

CHEMISTRY 21 — BONDING AND REACTIONS   Answers on page 238.

Calculating Masses in Reactions

You can also work out masses of reactants (starting materials) and products in reactions.

The three important steps — not to be missed...

1) Write out the balanced equation.

2) Work out M_r — just for the two bits you want.

3) Apply the rule: Divide to get one, then multiply to get all.
(First for the substance they give info about, then for the other one!)

Don't worry — these steps should all make sense when you look at the example below.

Example:

What mass of magnesium oxide is produced when 60 g of magnesium is burned in air?

METHOD:

1) Write out the balanced equation: $\quad 2Mg + O_2 \rightarrow 2MgO$

2) Work out the relative formula masses: $\quad 2 \times 24 \rightarrow 2 \times (24 + 16)$
(don't do the oxygen — you don't need it) $\quad\quad 48 \rightarrow 80$

3) Apply the rule: Divide to get one, then multiply to get all:

**The two numbers, 48 and 80, tell you 48 g of Mg react to give 80 g of MgO.
Here's the tricky bit. You've now got to be able to write this down:**

> 48 g of Mg ...... reacts to give ...... 80g of MgO
> 1 g of Mg ...... reacts to give ......
> 60 g of Mg ...... reacts to give ......

The big clue is that they've said you want to burn "60 g of magnesium", i.e. they've told you how much Mg to have, and that's how you know to write down the left-hand side of it first, because:
You'll first need to ÷ by 48 to get 1 g of Mg, and then need to × by 60 to get 60 g of Mg.

Then you can work out the numbers on the other side (shown in blue below) by realising that you must divide both sides by 48 and then multiply both sides by 60.

÷ 48
× 60

> 48 g of Mg .... 80 g of MgO   ÷ 48
> 1 g of Mg .... 1.67 g of MgO
> 60 g of Mg .... 100 g of MgO   × 60

The mass of product is called the yield of a reaction. You should realise that in practice you never get 100% of the yield, so the amount of product will be slightly less than calculated (see p.96).

This finally tells us that 60 g of magnesium will produce 100 g of magnesium oxide.
If the question had said, "Find how much magnesium gives 500 g of magnesium oxide", you'd fill in the MgO side first, because that's the one you'd have the information about.

You can't just read these pages — work through the examples too

The only way to get good at these is to practise. So have a go at this question (answer on p.238):

1) Find the mass of calcium which gives 30 g of calcium oxide (CaO) when burnt in air.

CHEMISTRY 21 — BONDING AND REACTIONS

The Mole

The mole can be really confusing. I think it's the word that puts people off. It's very difficult to see the relevance of the word "mole" to different-sized piles of brightly coloured powders.

"THE MOLE" is simply the name given to a certain number

Just like 'a million' is this many: 1 000 000,

or 'a billion' is this many: 1 000 000 000,

so 'a mole' is this many: 602 300 000 000 000 000 000 000 or 6.023×10^{23}.

1) And that's all it is. Just a number. The burning question, of course, is why is it such a silly long one like that, and with a six at the front?

2) The answer is that when you get precisely that number of atoms of carbon-12, it weighs exactly 12 g.

3) So, get that number of atoms or molecules, of any element or compound, and conveniently, they weigh exactly the same number of grams as the relative atomic mass, A_r (or M_r) of the element (or compound).

4) This is arranged on purpose of course, to make things easier.

Here's the definition of a mole written out nicely so you can learn it:

One mole of atoms or molecules of any substance will have a mass in grams equal to the relative formula mass (A_r or M_r) for that substance.

And here are a few more examples to really drive the point home:

Iron has an A_r of 56.   So one mole of iron weighs exactly 56 g

Nitrogen gas, N_2, has an M_r of 28 (2×14).   So one mole of N_2 weighs exactly 28 g

Carbon dioxide, CO_2, has an M_r of 44.   So one mole of CO_2 weighs exactly 44 g

This means that 12 g of carbon, or 56 g of iron, or 28 g of N_2, or 44 g of CO_2, all contain the same number of particles, namely one mole or 6×10^{23} atoms or molecules.

CHEMISTRY 21 — BONDING AND REACTIONS

The Mole

Of course, we can't leave you just knowing <u>what</u> a mole <u>is</u>. It's no fun without a few <u>formulas</u>...

Here's a formula for finding **the number of moles** in a **given mass**

NUMBER OF MOLES = mass in g (of element or compound) / M_r (of element or compound)

Example:

How many moles are there in 42 g of carbon?

ANSWER:
No. of moles = mass (g) ÷ M_r = 42 ÷ 12 = <u>3.5 moles</u>.

'Relative formula mass' is also 'molar mass'

1) You've been quite happy using the <u>relative formula mass</u>, M_r, all through the calculations so far.
2) In fact, that was already using the idea of moles because M_r is actually the mass of one mole in grams, or as it's sometimes called, the <u>molar mass</u>.
3) <u>The volume of one mole of any gas</u> at room temperature and pressure is <u>24 litres</u> — <u>the molar volume</u>.

A '1M solution' contains 'one mole per litre'

The 'moles per litre' of a solution is sometimes called its 'molarity'.

This is pretty easy. So a <u>2 M solution</u> of NaOH contains <u>2 moles</u> of NaOH per litre of solution.
You need to know how many moles there'll be in a given volume:

NUMBER OF MOLES = volume in litres × moles per litre of solution

Example:

How many moles in 185 cm^3 of a 2 M solution?

ANSWER:
No. of moles = vol (l) × molarity = 0.185 × 2 = <u>0.37 moles</u>

The M_r or A_r of a substance is the mass of one mole of it in grams

It's possible to do <u>all</u> the calculations on the previous pages without ever talking about <u>moles</u>.
You just concentrate on M_r and A_r instead — M_r and A_r represent <u>the mass of one mole</u> anyway.
Learn both the equations above. They'll make your life more complete (and they're useful in the exam).

CHEMISTRY 2i — BONDING AND REACTIONS

Warm-Up and Exam Questions

Lots to remember on those 6 pages. Try these and see how good your understanding really is.

Warm-Up Questions

1) What name is given to the sum of the number of protons and neutrons in an atom?
2) What name is given to the average mass of isotopes of an element?
3) What name is given to the sum of the relative atomic masses of the atoms in a molecule?
4) Write down the definition of a mole.
5) What is the mass of one mole of oxygen gas?
6) How many moles are there in 500 cm³ of a 0.5 M solution?

Exam Questions

1 (a) Boron has two main isotopes, $^{11}_{5}B$ and $^{10}_{5}B$. Its A_r value is 10.8.

   (i)   What does A_r stand for?
   (1 mark)

   (ii) What is the difference between the two boron isotopes?
   (1 mark)

   (iii) Which isotope is the most abundant? Explain your reasoning.
   (2 marks)

   (b) Use the A_r values B = 11, O = 16, F = 19 and H = 1 to calculate the relative formula masses of these boron compounds:

   (i) BF_3
   (1 mark)

   (ii) $B(OH)_3$.
   (1 mark)

2 The nucleus of the most common hydrogen isotope consists of a single proton. Deuterium is an isotope of hydrogen with one neutron and one proton in its nucleus.

   (a) Draw a labelled diagram to show the atomic particles in a deuterium atom.
   (2 marks)

   (b) Water molecules containing deuterium instead of hydrogen are written as D_2O. 'Heavy water', as D_2O is known, was used in the early development of nuclear weapons during World War II.

   (i)   What is the relative formula mass of deuterium oxide, D_2O?
        (A_r of oxygen = 16.)
   (1 mark)

   (ii) Why do you think D_2O is known as 'heavy water'?
   (1 mark)

CHEMISTRY 21 — BONDING AND REACTIONS

Exam Questions

3. Nitrogen is good for plant growth. An agricultural scientist needs to compare the amount of nitrogen in each of the three different fertilisers listed below to find out which has the highest amount of nitrogen by percentage mass.

Fertiliser	Formula
urea	$CO(NH_2)_2$
potassium nitrate	KNO_3
ammonium nitrate	NH_4NO_3

    (A_r values: C = 12, O = 16, N = 14, H = 1, K = 39.)

    (a) Work out the percentage mass of nitrogen in each of the three fertilisers.
    (6 marks)

    (b) Using your answers to part (a), explain which one of the three you would expect to make the best fertiliser.
    (2 marks)

4. Analysis of an oxide of sulfur shows that it contains 60% oxygen by mass.
    (A_r values: S = 32, O = 16.)

    (a) What is the percentage mass of sulfur in the oxide?
    (1 mark)

    (b) Work out the formula of the oxide.
    (2 marks)

5. Heating a test tube containing 2 g of calcium carbonate produced 1.08 g of calcium oxide when it was reweighed. The equation for the reaction is:

    $$CaCO_3(s) \rightarrow CaO(s) + CO_2(g)$$

    (M_r values: $CaCO_3$ = 100, CaO = 56.)

    (a) Calculate the amount of calcium oxide you would expect to be formed from 2 g of calcium carbonate.
    (1 mark)

    (b) Compare the value to the amount obtained in the experiment. Suggest a possible reason for the difference.
    (1 mark)

Atom Economy

It's important in industrial reactions that as much of the reactants as possible get turned into useful products. This depends on the atom economy and the percentage yield (see page 96) of the reaction.

'Atom economy' — % of reactants changed to useful products

1) A lot of reactions make more than one product.

2) Some of them will be useful, but others will just be waste, e.g. when you make quicklime from limestone, you also get CO_2 as a waste product.

3) The atom economy of a reaction tells you how much of the mass of the reactants ends up as useful products.

Learn the equation:

$$\text{atom economy} = \frac{\text{total } M_r \text{ of useful products}}{\text{total } M_r \text{ of reactants}} \times 100$$

Example:

> Hydrogen gas is made on a large scale by reacting natural gas (methane) with steam.
> $CH_4(g) + H_2O(g) \rightarrow CO(g) + 3H_2(g)$
> Calculate the atom economy of this reaction.

METHOD:
1) Identify the useful product — **that's the hydrogen gas**.

2) Work out the M_r of the reactants and of the useful product:

   CH_4: $12 + (4 \times 1) = 16$

   H_2O: $(2 \times 1) + 16 = 18$

   $3H_2$: $3 \times (2 \times 1) = 6$

   So M_r of useful products = 6, and M_r of reactants = 16 + 18 = 34

3) Use the formula to calculate the atom economy:

   $$\text{atom economy} = \frac{6}{34} \times 100 = \underline{17.6\%}$$

So in this reaction, over 80% of the starting materials are wasted.

In industry, the waste CO is reacted with more steam to make CO_2 (and a bit more H_2). That brings the overall atom economy down to only 15% — but the final waste product is much less nasty that way.

Atom Economy

As you may have guessed already, a <u>high</u> atom economy is <u>good</u>, and a <u>low</u> atom economy is <u>not so good</u>. Make sure you know all the reasons why.

High atom economy is better for **profits** and the **environment**

1) Pretty obviously, if you're making <u>lots of waste</u>, that's a <u>problem</u>.

2) Reactions with low atom economy <u>use up resources</u> very quickly.

3) At the same time, they produce loads of <u>waste</u> materials that have to be <u>disposed</u> of somehow.

4) That tends to make these reactions <u>unsustainable</u> — the raw materials will run out and the waste has to go somewhere.

5) For the same reasons, low atom economy reactions aren't usually <u>profitable</u>.

6) Raw materials are <u>expensive to buy</u>, and waste products can be expensive to <u>remove</u> and dispose of <u>responsibly</u>.

7) The best way around the problem is to find a <u>use</u> for the waste products rather than just <u>throwing them away</u>.

8) There's often <u>more than one way</u> to make the product you want, so the trick is to come up with a reaction that gives <u>useful "by-products"</u> rather than useless ones.

9) The reactions with the <u>highest</u> atom economy are the ones that only have <u>one product</u> — like the Haber process (see page 117).

10) Those reactions have an atom economy of <u>100%</u>.

So why do they make <u>hydrogen</u> in that nasty, <u>inefficient</u> way you saw on the last page? Well, currently it's the best of a bad bunch. The other ways to make hydrogen on an industrial scale (like the electrolysis of brine, see page 128) use up huge amounts of <u>energy</u> and are <u>too expensive</u> to be worthwhile.

Atom economy — important, but not the whole story...

Atom economy isn't the only thing that affects profits — there are other costs besides buying raw materials and disposing of waste. There are <u>energy</u> and <u>equipment</u> costs, as well as the cost of <u>paying people</u> to work at the plant. You need to think about the <u>percentage yield</u> of the reaction too (p.96).

Percentage Yield

Percentage yield tells you about the overall success of an experiment. It compares what you think you should get (predicted yield) with what you get in practice (actual yield).

The *higher* the *percentage* yield — the *better* the reaction

The more reactants you start with, the higher the actual yield will be — that's pretty obvious. But the percentage yield doesn't depend on the amount of reactants you started with — it's a percentage.

1) The predicted yield of a reaction can be calculated from the balanced reaction equation (see page 14).

2) Percentage yield is given by the formula:

$$\text{percentage yield} = \frac{\text{actual yield (grams)}}{\text{predicted yield (grams)}} \times 100$$

3) Percentage yield is always somewhere between 0 and 100%.

4) A 100% percentage yield means that you got all the product you expected to get.

5) A 0% yield means that no reactants were converted into product, i.e. no product at all was made.

Yields are always *less than 100%*

1) In real life, you never get a 100% percentage yield.

2) Some product or reactant always gets lost along the way — and that goes for big industrial processes as well as school lab experiments.

3) How this happens depends on what sort of reaction it is and what apparatus is being used.

Lots of things can go wrong, but you can find the four you need to know about conveniently located on the next page.

Even with the best equipment, you can't get the maximum product

A high percentage yield means there's not much waste — which is good for preserving resources and keeping production costs down. If a reaction's going to be worth doing commercially, it generally has to have a high percentage yield or recyclable reactants, e.g. the Haber process (see p.117).

CHEMISTRY 21 — BONDING AND REACTIONS

Percentage Yield

Learn these **four reasons** why yields **can't** be 100%

1) The reaction is **reversible**

In reversible reactions (like the Haber process, see page 117), not all the reactants change into product.

Instead, you get reactants and products in equilibrium. Increasing the temperature moves the equilibrium position (see pages 115-116), so heating the reaction to speed it up might mean a lower yield.

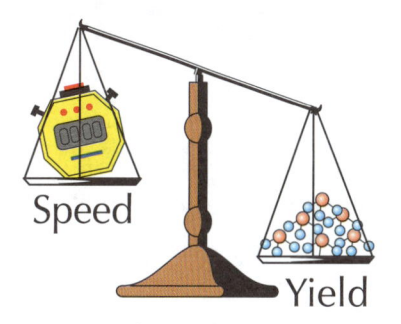

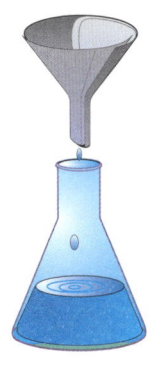

Speed

Yield

2) *Filtration*

When you filter a liquid to remove solid particles, you nearly always lose a bit of liquid or a bit of solid.

1) If you want to keep the liquid, you lose the bit that remains with the solid and filter paper (as they always stay a bit wet).

2) If you want to keep the solid, some of it usually gets left behind when you scrape it off the filter paper — even if you're really careful.

3) *Transferring* liquids

You always lose a bit of liquid when you transfer it from one container to another — even if you manage not to spill it.

Some of it always gets left behind on the inside surface of the old container. Think about it — it's always wet when you finish.

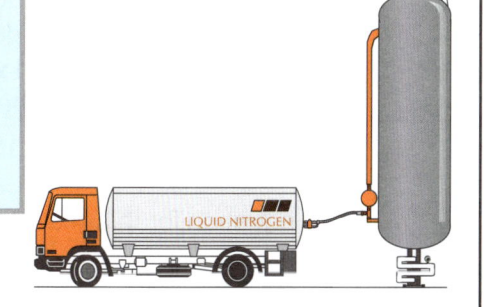

4) *Unexpected reactions*

Things don't always go exactly to plan.

Sometimes you get unexpected reactions happening, so the yield of the intended product goes down. These can be caused by impurities in the reactants, but sometimes just changing the reaction conditions affects what products you make.

Warm-Up and Exam Questions

This is all about trying to judge how much useful product you're actually getting from a reaction. Try these questions to help make sure you won't get stuck in the exam. First a (fairly) gentle warm-up, and then some more exam-like questions to give you an idea of what you can expect.

Warm-Up Questions

1) What effect does a waste by-product have on the atom economy of a reaction?
2) What is the atom economy of the reaction shown? $2SO_2 + O_2 \rightarrow 2SO_3$
3) Why might a reaction with a low atom economy be bad for the environment?
4) Why might a reaction with a low atom economy not be profitable?
5) What is the percentage yield of a reaction which produced 4 g of product if the predicted yield was 5 g?

Exam Questions

1 Ethanol produced by the fermentation of sugar can be converted into ethene, as shown below. The ethene can then be used to make polythene.

   $C_2H_6O\ (g) \rightarrow C_2H_4\ (g) + H_2O\ (g)$

   Calculate the atom economy of this reaction.
   (A_r values: C = 12, O = 16, H = 1.)

   (3 marks)

2 A sample of copper was made by reducing 4 g of copper oxide with methane gas. When the black copper oxide turned orange-red, the sample was scraped out into a beaker. Sulfuric acid was added to dissolve any copper oxide that remained. The sample was then washed, filtered and dried. 2.8 g of copper was obtained.
   (A_r values: Cu = 63.5, O = 16.)

   The equation for this reaction is: $CH_4 + 4CuO \rightarrow 4Cu + 2H_2O + CO_2$

   (a) Use the equation to calculate the maximum mass of copper which could be obtained from the reaction (the predicted yield).

   (3 marks)

   (b) Calculate the percentage yield of the reaction.

   (2 marks)

   (c) Suggest three different reasons why the yield of the reaction was less than 100%.

   (3 marks)

Revision Summary for Chemistry 2i

Make sure you don't skip these pages, because what's the point in reading that great big section if you're not going to check if you really know it or not? Look, just read the first ten questions, and I guarantee there'll be an answer you'll have to look up. And when it comes up in the exam, you'll be so glad you did.

1) Sketch the nuclear model of an atom.
   Give five details about the nucleus and five details about the electrons.
2) Draw a table showing the relative masses and charges of the three types of particle in an atom.
3) What do the mass number and atomic number represent?
4) Explain the difference between an element and a compound. Give an example of each.
5) Define the term isotope.
6) What feature of atoms determines the order of the modern periodic table?
7) What are groups in the periodic table? Explain their significance in terms of electrons.
8) Describe how you would work out the electron configuration of an atom given its atomic number.
   Find the electron configuration of potassium (using the periodic table at the front of the book).
9) Describe the process of ionic bonding.
10) List the main properties of ionic compounds.
11) What is covalent bonding?
12) What are the two types of covalent substance? Give three examples of each.
13) Industrial diamonds are used in drill tips and precision cutting tools. What property of diamond makes it suitable for this use? Explain how the bonding in diamond causes its physical properties.
14) List three properties of metals and explain how metallic bonding causes these properties.
15)* a) Identify the type of bonding in each of the substances in the table:

Substance	Melting point (°C)	Electrical conductivity	Hardness [scale of 0 – 10 (10 being diamond)]
A	3410	Very high	7.5
B	2072	Zero	9
C	605	Zero in solid form High when molten	Low

   b) Suggest which substance from the table would be most suitable for the following applications:
   i) a light-bulb filament
   ii) abrasive paper
   iii) a rechargeable battery
16) Give an example of a "smart" material and describe how it behaves.
17) What are nanoparticles? Describe two different applications of nanoparticles.
18)* Write balanced symbol equations for the following reactions:
   a) calcium carbonate + hydrochloric acid → calcium chloride + water + carbon dioxide
   b) sulfuric acid + potassium hydroxide → potassium sulfate + water
19) Define relative atomic mass and relative formula mass.
20)* Find A_r or M_r for these (use the periodic table at the front of the book):
   a) Ca   b) Ag   c) CO_2 d) $MgCO_3$ e) Na_2CO_3 f) ZnO   g) KOH   h) NH_3
21)* a) Calculate the percentage mass of carbon in: i) $CaCO_3$ ii) CO_2 iii) CH_4
   b) Calculate the percentage mass of metal in: i) Na_2O ii) Fe_2O_3 iii) Al_2O_3
22)* What is an empirical formula? Find the empirical formula of the compound formed when 21.9 g of magnesium, 29.3 g of sulfur and 58.4 g of oxygen react.
23)* What mass of sodium is needed to produce 108.2 g of sodium oxide (Na_2O)?
24) What is a mole? Why is it that precise number?
25)* How many moles of HCl are there sin 230 cm³ of 2M hydrochloric acid?
26) Explain why it is important, both economically and environmentally, to use industrial reactions with a high atom economy.
27) Describe four factors that can reduce the percentage yield of a reaction.

*Answers on page 239

Rates of Reaction

This section is all about how fast chemical reactions go and the energy changes involved.

Reactions can go at all sorts of different rates

1) One of the slowest is the rusting of iron.
2) A moderate speed reaction is a metal (like magnesium) reacting with acid to produce a gentle stream of bubbles.
3) A really fast reaction is an explosion, where it's all over in a fraction of a second.

The rate of a reaction depends on four things

Make sure you learn them:

1) Temperature
2) Concentration — (or pressure for gases)
3) Catalyst
4) Size of particles — (or surface area)

Typical graphs for rate of reaction

The plot below shows how the speed of a particular reaction varies under different conditions. The quickest reaction is shown by the line that becomes flat in the least time. The line that flattens out first must have the steepest slope compared to the others, so you can spot the slowest and fastest reactions.

1) Graph 1 represents the original fairly slow reaction. The graph is not very steep.

2) Graphs 2 and 3 represent the reaction happening more quickly but with the same initial amounts of reactants. The slope of the graphs gets steeper.

3) The increased rate could be due to any of these:

   a) increase in temperature
   b) increase in concentration (or pressure)
   c) catalyst added
   d) solid reactant crushed into smaller bits

4) Graph 4 produces more product as well as going faster. This can only happen if more reactant(s) are added at the start. Graphs 1, 2 and 3 all converge at the same level, showing that they all produce the same amount of product, although they take different times to get there.

It's really important that you understand the graph above

Industrial reactions generally use a catalyst and are done at high temperature and pressure. Time is money, so the faster an industrial reaction goes the better... but only up to a point. Chemical plants are quite expensive to rebuild if they get blown into lots and lots of teeny tiny pieces.

Measuring Rates of Reaction

You need to know some examples of how reaction rates are measured.

There are three ways to measure the speed of a reaction

The speed of a reaction can be observed either by how quickly the reactants are used up or by how quickly the products are formed. It's usually a lot easier to measure products forming.

You can calculate the rate of a reaction using the following equation:

$$\text{Rate of reaction} = \frac{\text{amount of reactant used or amount of product formed}}{\text{time}}$$

There are different ways that the speed of a reaction can be measured.

Below and on the next page are three ways to measure the rate of a reaction. Learn them.

1) Precipitation

1) This is when the product of the reaction is a precipitate which clouds the solution.

2) Observe a marker through the solution and measure how long it takes for it to disappear.

3) The quicker the marker disappears, the quicker the reaction.

4) This only works for reactions where the initial solution is rather see-through.

5) The result is very subjective — different people might not agree over the exact point when the mark 'disappears'.

CHEMISTRY 2II — RATES OF REACTION

Measuring Rates of Reaction

2) *Change in mass* (usually gas given off)

1) Measuring the speed of a reaction that produces a gas can be done using a mass balance.

2) As the gas is released the mass disappearing is measured on the balance.

3) The quicker the reading on the balance drops, the faster the reaction.

4) Rate of reaction graphs are particularly easy to plot using the results from this method.

5) This is the most accurate of the three methods described because the mass balance is very accurate. But it has the disadvantage of releasing the gas straight into the room.

3) The *volume* of gas given off

1) This involves the use of a gas syringe to measure the volume of gas given off.

2) The more gas there is given off during a given time interval, the faster the reaction.

3) A graph of gas volume against time elapsed could be plotted to give a rate of reaction graph.

4) Gas syringes usually give volumes accurate to the nearest millilitre, so they're quite accurate. But if the reaction is too vigorous, you can blow the plunger out of the end of the syringe.

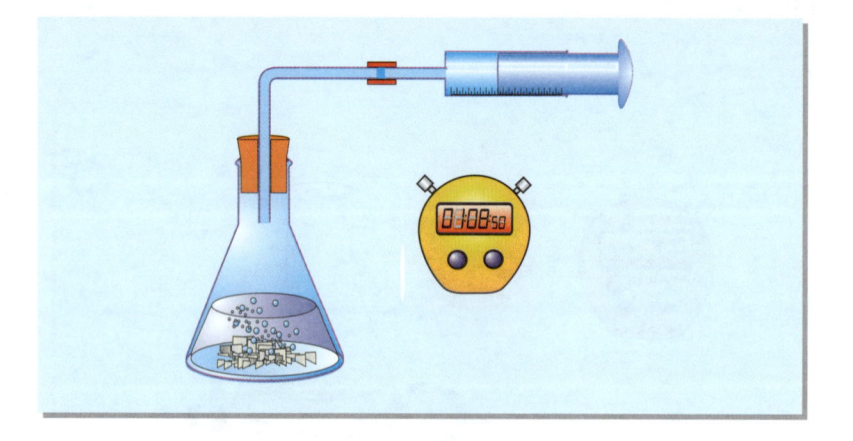

Each of these methods has pros and cons

The mass balance method is only accurate as long as the flask isn't too hot, otherwise you lose mass by evaporation as well as in the reaction. The first method isn't very accurate, but if you're not producing a gas you can't use either of the other two. Ah well.

CHEMISTRY 2II — RATES OF REACTION

Rate of Reaction Experiments

Remember: <u>Any reaction</u> can be used to investigate <u>any</u> of the four factors that affect the <u>rate</u>. The next four pages illustrate <u>four important reactions</u>, but only <u>one factor</u> is considered for each. But we could just as easily use, say, the marble chips/acid reaction to test the effect of <u>temperature</u> instead.

1) Reaction of **hydrochloric acid** and **marble chips**

This experiment is often used to demonstrate the effect of <u>breaking</u> the solid up into <u>small bits</u>.

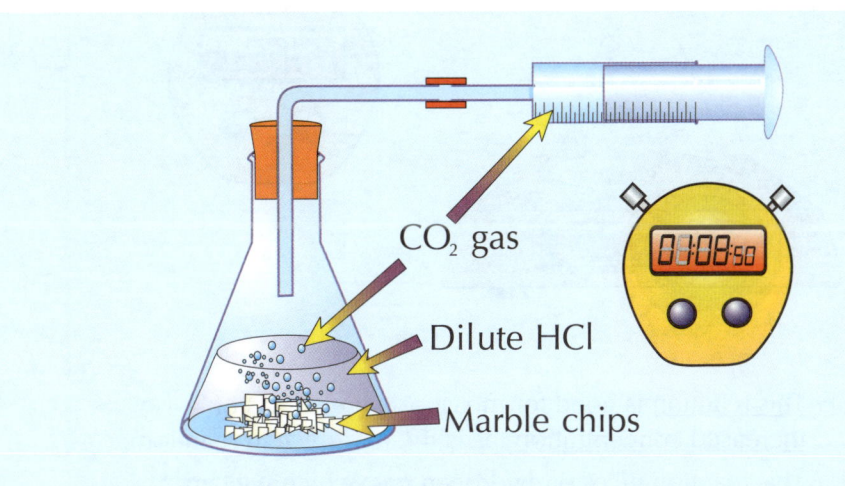

- CO_2 gas
- Dilute HCl
- Marble chips

1) Measure the <u>volume</u> of gas evolved with a <u>gas syringe</u> and take readings at <u>regular intervals</u>.
2) Make a <u>table of readings</u> and plot them as a <u>graph</u>. You <u>choose</u> regular time intervals, so <u>time</u> is the <u>independent variable</u> (x) and <u>volume</u> is the <u>dependent variable</u> (y) — see page 192 for the definitions of these.
3) <u>Repeat</u> the experiment with <u>exactly the same</u> volume of <u>acid</u>, and <u>exactly the same</u> mass of <u>marble</u> chips, but with the marble <u>more crunched up</u>.
4) Then <u>repeat</u> with the same mass of <u>powdered chalk</u> instead of marble chips.

This graph shows the effect of using **finer particles of solid**

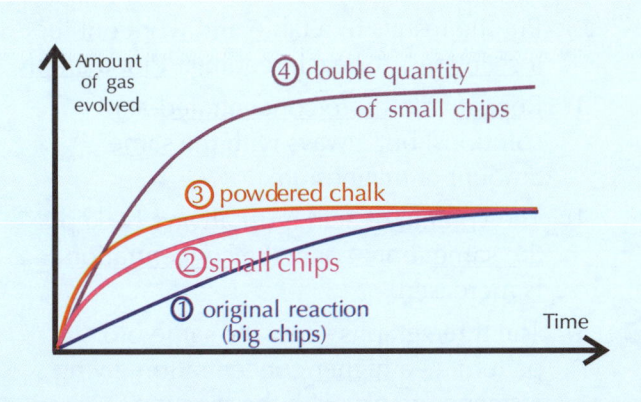

Amount of gas evolved vs Time:
- ① original reaction (big chips)
- ② small chips
- ③ powdered chalk
- ④ double quantity of small chips

1) An increase in <u>surface area</u> causes <u>more collisions</u>, so the rate of reaction is <u>faster</u>.
2) <u>Line 4</u> shows the reaction if a <u>greater mass</u> of small marble chips is added.
3) The <u>extra surface area</u> gives a <u>quicker reaction</u> and there is also <u>more gas evolved</u> overall.

Rate of Reaction Experiments

The reaction of magnesium metal with dilute HCl is often used to determine the effect of concentration.

2) Reaction of **magnesium metal** with **dilute HCl**

1) <u>This reaction</u> is good for measuring the effects of <u>increased concentration</u> (as is the marble/acid reaction).
2) This reaction gives off <u>hydrogen gas</u>, which we can measure with a <u>mass balance</u>, as shown.
3) In this experiment, <u>time</u> is again the <u>independent variable</u> and <u>mass loss</u> is the <u>dependent variable</u>. (The other method is to use a gas syringe, as above.)

This graph shows the effect of using **more concentrated acid solutions**

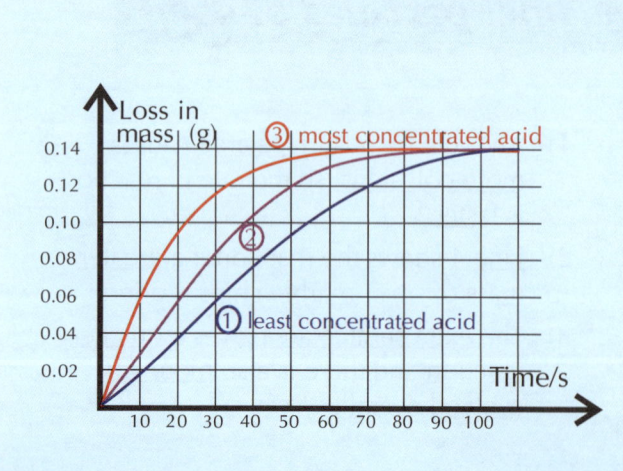

1) Take <u>readings</u> of mass at <u>regular</u> time intervals.
2) Put the results in a <u>table</u> and work out the <u>loss in mass</u> for each reading. <u>Plot a graph</u>.
3) <u>Repeat</u> with <u>more concentrated</u> acid solutions, but always with the <u>same</u> amount of magnesium.
4) The <u>volume</u> of acid must always be kept <u>the same</u> too — only the <u>concentration</u> is increased.
5) The three graphs show the <u>same</u> old pattern — a <u>higher</u> concentration giving a <u>steeper graph</u>, with the reaction <u>finishing</u> much quicker.

Rate of Reaction Experiments

3) Sodium thiosulfate and HCl produce a cloudy precipitate

1) These two chemicals are both clear solutions.

2) They react together to form a yellow precipitate of sulfur.

3) The experiment involves watching a black mark disappear through the cloudy sulfur and timing how long it takes to go.

4) The reaction can be repeated for solutions at different temperatures. In practice, that's quite hard to do accurately and safely (it's not a good idea to heat an acid directly). The best way to do it is to use a water bath to heat both solutions to the right temperature before you mix them.

5) The depth of liquid must be kept the same each time, of course.

6) The results will of course show that the higher the temperature the quicker the reaction and therefore the less time it takes for the mark to disappear. These are typical results:

Temperature (°C)	20	25	30	35	40	independent variable
Time taken for mark to disappear (s)	193	151	112	87	52	dependent variable

This reaction can also be used to test the effects of concentration.
One sad thing about this reaction is it doesn't give a set of graphs.
All you get is a set of readings of how long it took till the mark disappeared for each temperature.

CHEMISTRY 2II — RATES OF REACTION

Rate of Reaction Experiments

4) The Decomposition of Hydrogen Peroxide

This is a *good* reaction for showing the effect of different *catalysts*.
The decomposition of hydrogen peroxide is:

$$2H_2O_{2\,(aq)} \rightleftharpoons 2H_2O_{(l)} + O_{2\,(g)}$$

1) This is normally quite *slow* but a sprinkle of *manganese(IV) oxide catalyst* speeds it up no end. Other catalysts which work are found in:
   a) *potato peel* and b) *blood*.
2) *Oxygen gas* is given off, which provides an *ideal way* to measure the rate of reaction using the good ol' *gas syringe* method.

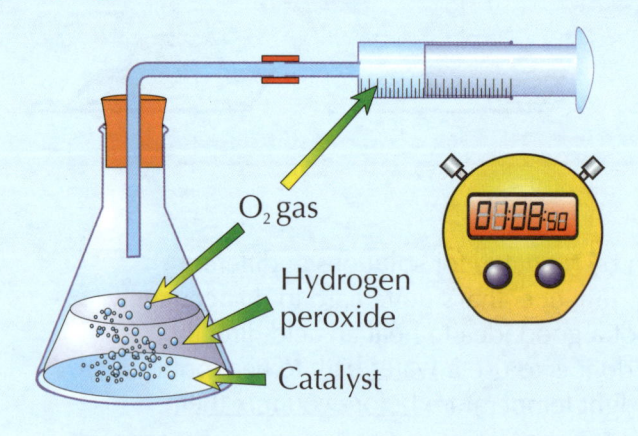

O₂ gas
Hydrogen peroxide
Catalyst

1) Same old graphs of course.
2) *Better* catalysts give a *quicker reaction*, which is shown by a *steeper graph* which levels off quickly.
3) This reaction can also be used to measure the effects of *temperature*, or of *concentration* of the H₂O₂ solution. The graphs will look just the same.

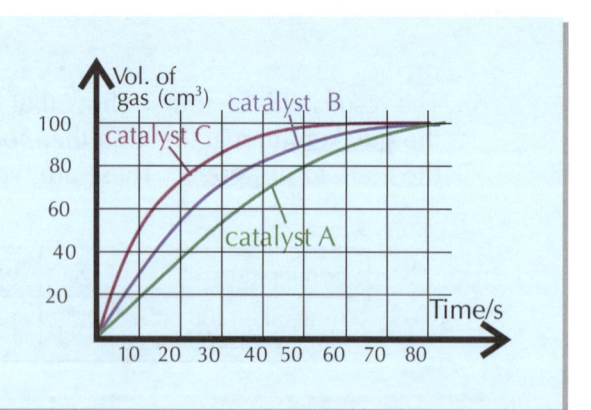

BLOOD is a catalyst? — eeurgh...

You don't need to know all the details of these specific reactions on the last four pages — it's the experimental methods you need to learn. If you understand how all this works, you should be able to apply it to any reaction.

CHEMISTRY 2ll — RATES OF REACTIONS

Warm-Up and Exam Questions

Time to test your knowledge again. This time on the rates of chemical reactions. If you struggle with these questions and you don't feel up to speed, it's time to have another look at the last few pages.

Warm-Up Questions

1) Give three ways of increasing the rate of a reaction between magnesium and sulfuric acid.
2) How would adding water to an acid alter the time taken for a piece of zinc to react with it?
3) Oxidation of lactose in milk makes it go 'sour'. How could this reaction be slowed down?
4) Give an example of a reaction that happens very slowly, and one that is very fast.
5) Describe one way of monitoring a reaction in which a gas is given off.

Exam Questions

1. Set volumes of sodium thiosulfate and hydrochloric acid were reacted at different temperatures. The time taken for a black cross to be obscured by the sulfur precipitated was measured at each temperature. The results are shown in the table.

Time (s)	Temperature (°C)
6	55
11	36
17	24
27	16
40	9
51	5

    (a) Give two things that should be kept constant in this experiment.
    (2 marks)

    (b) Plot the results on a graph (with time on the x-axis) and draw a best-fit curve.
    (2 marks)

    (c) Explain the relationship illustrated by your graph.
    (2 marks)

    (d) How might the results change if the sodium thiosulfate concentration was reduced?
    (2 marks)

2. The table shows the results of reactions between excess marble and 50 cm^3 of 1 M hydrochloric acid.

Time (min)	Mass of flask A (g)	Mass of flask B (g)
0	121.6	121.6
1	120.3	119.8
2	119.7	119.2
3	119.4	119.1
4	119.2	119
5	119.1	119
6	119	119
7	119	

    (a) Why did the mass of the contents of the flasks decrease during the reaction?
    (1 mark)

    (b) Why did the mass of each flask and its contents fall by the same total amount?
    (1 mark)

    (c) (i) Suggest what conditions may have been different inside flask B.
    (1 mark)

    (ii) Explain how this difference could lead to a change in the rate of the reaction.
    (1 mark)

    (d) In both reactions, the rate is fastest at the beginning. Explain why.
    (1 mark)

Collision Theory

Reaction rates are explained perfectly by collision theory. It's really simple.

Collision theory shows why certain things increase reaction rates

1) Collision theory just says that the rate of a reaction depends on how often and how hard the reacting particles collide with each other.

2) The basic idea is that particles have to collide in order to react, and they have to collide hard enough (with enough energy).

More collisions increases the rate of reaction

All four methods of increasing the rate of reactions (see also next page) can be explained in terms of increasing the number of successful collisions between the reacting particles:

1) HIGHER TEMPERATURE increases collisions

When the temperature is increased the particles all move more quickly. If they're moving quicker, they're going to have more collisions.

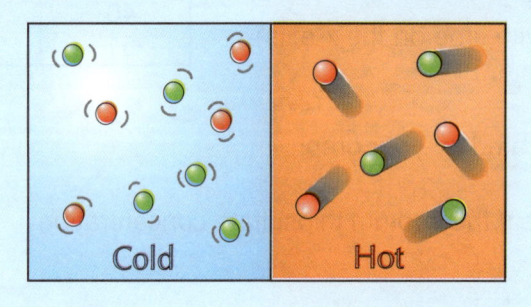

Cold   Hot

2) HIGHER CONCENTRATION increases collisions

If a solution is made more concentrated it means there are more particles of reactant knocking about between the water molecules, which makes collisions between the important particles more likely.
In a gas, increasing the pressure means the particles are more squashed up together so there are going to be more collisions.

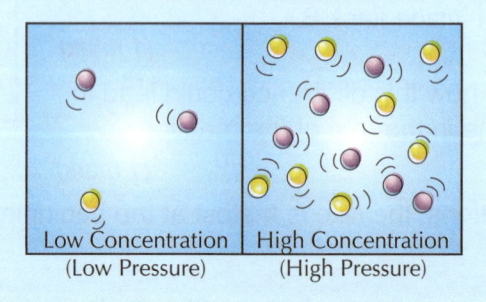

Low Concentration (Low Pressure)   High Concentration (High Pressure)

CHEMISTRY 2II — RATES OF REACTION

Collision Theory

3) LARGER SURFACE AREA increases collisions

If one of the reactants is a solid then breaking it into smaller pieces will increase its surface area. This means the particles around it in the solution will have more area to work on, so there'll be more useful collisions.

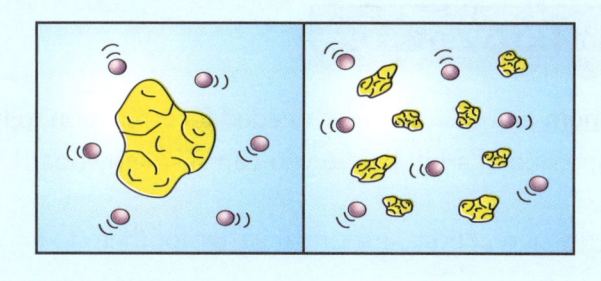

4) CATALYSTS increase the SUCCESSFUL collisions

A solid catalyst works by giving the reacting particles a surface to stick to. They increase the number of SUCCESSFUL collisions by lowering the activation energy (see next page).

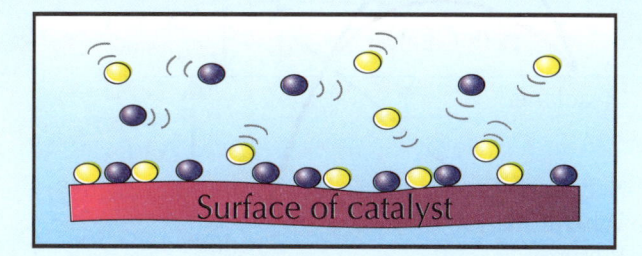

Faster collisions increase the rate of reaction

Faster collisions are only caused by increasing the temperature

Reactions only happen if the particles collide with enough energy. At higher temperatures there are more particles colliding with enough energy to make the reaction happen.

This initial energy is known as the activation energy, and it's needed to break the original bonds.

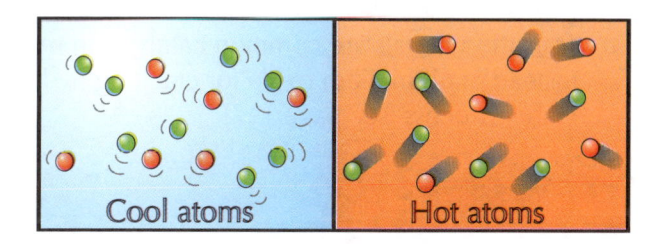

It's easier to learn stuff when you know the reasons for it

Once you've learnt everything on these last two pages, the rates of reaction stuff should start making a lot more sense to you. The concept's fairly simple — the more often particles bump into each other, and the harder they hit when they do, the faster the reaction happens.

CHEMISTRY 2ll — RATES OF REACTION

Catalysts

Many reactions can be speeded up by adding a catalyst.

> A catalyst is a substance which changes the speed of a reaction, without being changed or used up in the reaction.

Catalysts *lower* the *activation energy*

1) The activation energy is the minimum amount of energy needed for a reaction to happen.
2) It's a bit like having to climb up one side of a hill before you can ski / snowboard / sledge / fall down the other side.
3) Catalysts lower the activation energy of reactions, making it easier for them to happen.
4) This means a lower temperature can be used.

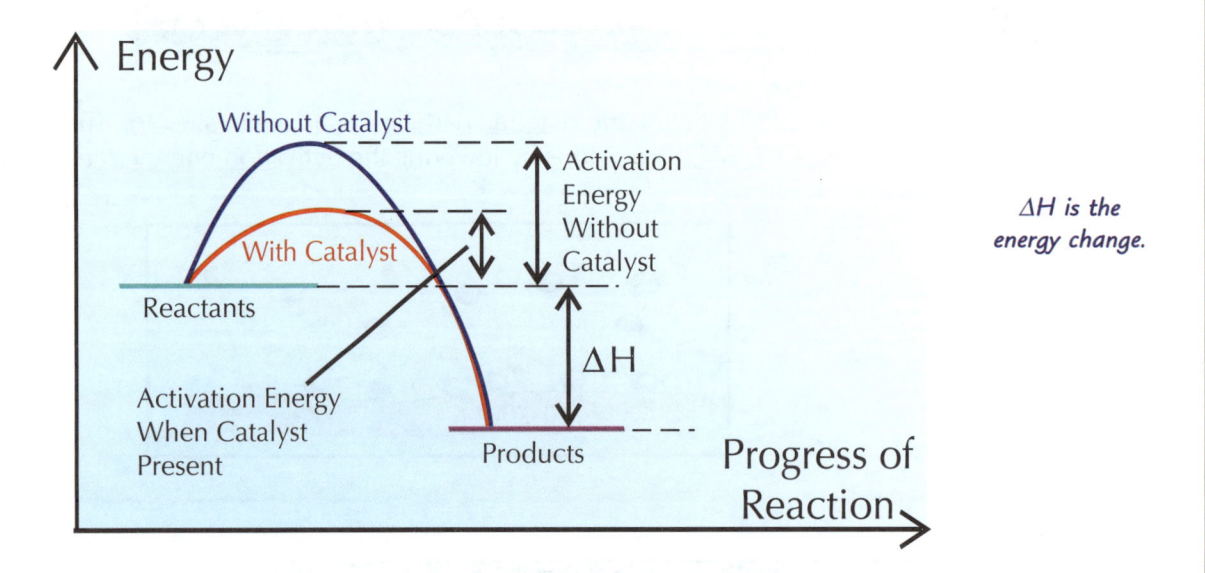

ΔH is the energy change.

Solid catalysts *work best* when they have a *big surface area*

1) Catalysts are usually used as a powder or pellets or a fine gauze.
2) This gives them a very large surface area to enable the reacting particles to meet up and react.
3) Transition metals are common catalysts in many industrial reactions, e.g. nickel can be used instead of aluminium oxide for cracking hydrocarbons (see page 44) and iron catalyses the Haber process (see page 117).

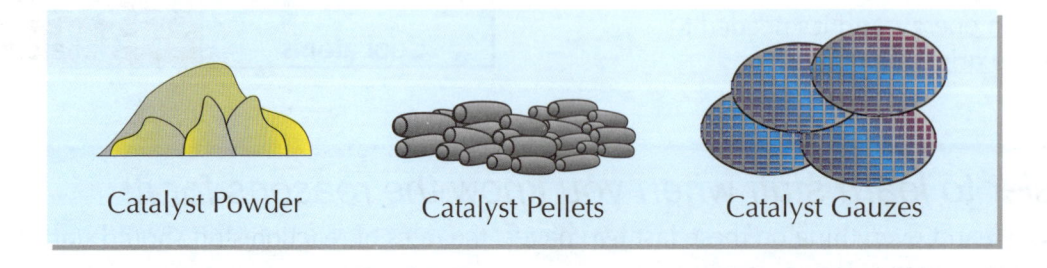

Catalyst Powder   Catalyst Pellets   Catalyst Gauzes

Catalysts

In industrial reactions, the main thing they're interested in is making a nice profit. Catalysts are helpful for this — they can reduce costs and increase the amount of product.

Catalysts help to **reduce costs** in industrial reactions

1) Catalysts are very important for commercial reasons — most industrial reactions use them.

2) Catalysts increase the rate of the reaction, which saves a lot of money simply because the plant doesn't need to operate for as long to produce the same amount of stuff.

3) Alternatively, a catalyst will allow the reaction to work at a much lower temperature. That reduces the energy used up in the reaction (the energy cost), which is good for sustainable development and can save a lot of money too.

Catalysts do sometimes have their **drawbacks** too

1) Nothing's perfect of course, and there are disadvantages to using catalysts. For starters, they can be very expensive to buy.

2) They often need to be removed from the product and cleaned each time the reaction is finished. They never get used up in the reaction though, so once you've got them you can use them over and over again.

3) Different reactions use different catalysts, so if you make more than one product at your plant you'll probably need to buy different catalysts for each of them.

4) Catalysts can be 'poisoned' by impurities, so they stop working — for example, sulfur can poison the iron catalyst used in the Haber process. That means you have to keep your reaction mixture very clean.

A big advantage of catalysts is that they can be used over and over

And they're not only used in industry... every useful chemical reaction in the human body is catalysed by a biological catalyst (an enzyme). If the reactions in the body were just left to their own devices, they'd take so long to happen, we couldn't exist. Quite handy then, these catalysts.

Warm-Up and Exam Questions

Think you've got to grips with activation energy. Then see how fast you can react to these questions.

Warm-Up Questions

1) According to the collision theory, what must happen in order for two particles to react?
2) What can you do to a reaction mixture to ensure more frequent collisions between particles?
3) Why does an increase in gas pressure increase the rate of a reaction between two gases?
4) Give a definition of a catalyst.
5) What is meant by the activation energy of a reaction?

Exam Questions

1. Hydrogen peroxide decomposes into water and oxygen. When lumps of a catalyst are dropped into a solution of hydrogen peroxide, bubbles of oxygen immediately start to form on the surface. Heating the solution increases the rate at which bubbles are formed.

    (a) Use the collision theory to explain how heating increases the rate of the reaction.
    (3 marks)

    (b) Breaking the catalyst into smaller pieces also increases the rate. Explain why.
    (2 marks)

    (c) How else could the rate of the reaction be increased?
    (1 mark)

2. Hydrocarbons can be cracked by passing their hot vapour over a nickel catalyst. The nickel used is in the form of small, hollow, cylindrical pellets. Using a catalyst reduces the operating temperature needed.

    (a) Why do you think that the pellets used are hollow?
    (1 mark)

    (b) Why is it an advantage that a lower temperature can be used?
    (2 marks)

    (c) Suggest two possible drawbacks of using catalysts.
    (2 marks)

    (d) Copy and complete the diagram on the right and label it to show how the activation energy is different for catalysed and uncatalysed cracking of hydrocarbons.
    (3 marks)

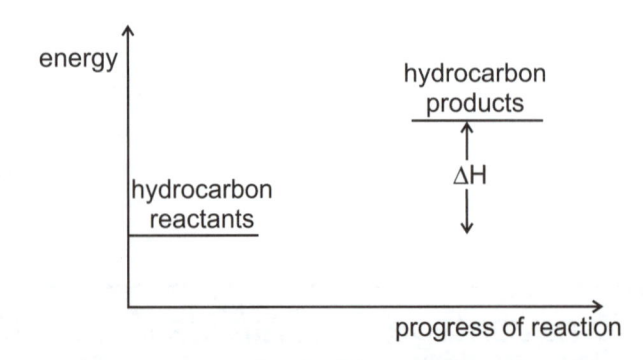

Energy Transfer in Reactions

Whenever chemical reactions occur energy is usually transferred to or from the surroundings.

In an *exothermic* reaction, heat is *given out*

An EXOTHERMIC reaction is one which gives out energy to the surroundings, usually in the form of heat and usually shown by a rise in temperature.

1) *Burning* Fuels

The best example of an exothermic reaction is burning fuels — also called COMBUSTION.
This gives out a lot of heat — it's very exothermic.

2) *Neutralisation* Reactions

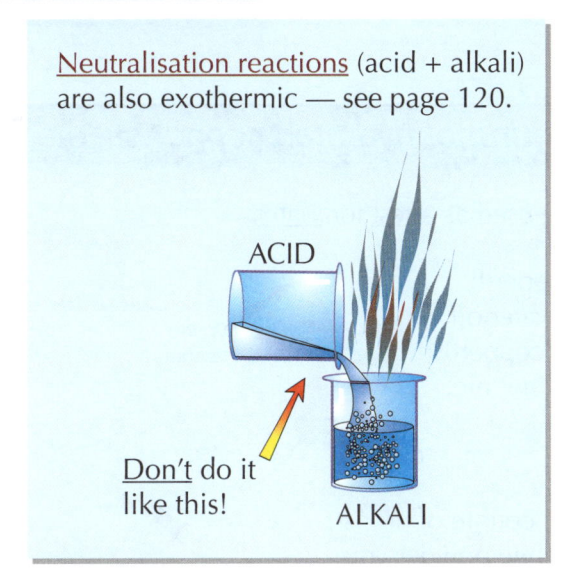

Neutralisation reactions (acid + alkali) are also exothermic — see page 120.

ACID

Don't do it like this!

ALKALI

3) *Oxidation* Reactions

Many oxidation reactions are exothermic...

Addition of sodium to water produces heat, so it must be exothermic.

The sodium emits heat and moves about on the surface of the water as it is oxidised.

CHEMISTRY 2II — RATES OF REACTION

Energy Transfer in Reactions

In an *endothermic* reaction, heat is *taken in*

An ENDOTHERMIC reaction is one which takes in energy from the surroundings, usually in the form of heat and usually shown by a fall in temperature.

Endothermic reactions are much less common. Thermal decompositions are a good example:

THERMAL DECOMPOSITION OF CALCIUM CARBONATE:

Heat must be supplied to make the compound decompose to make quicklime.

$$CaCO_3 \rightarrow CaO + CO_2$$

A lot of heat energy is needed to make this happen. In fact the calcium carbonate has to be heated in a kiln and kept at about 800 °C. It takes almost 18 000 kJ of heat to make 10 kg of calcium carbonate decompose. That's pretty endothermic I'd say.

The *thermal decomposition* of hydrated copper sulfate

Copper(II) sulfate crystals can be used as a test for water.

1) If you heat blue hydrated copper(II) sulfate crystals it drives the water off and leaves white anhydrous copper(II) sulfate powder. This is endothermic.

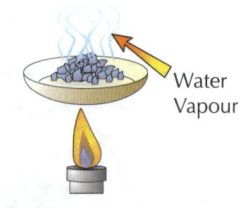

2) If you then add a couple of drops of water to the white powder you get the blue crystals back again. This is exothermic.

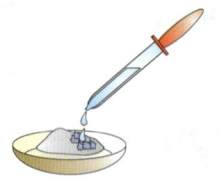

This is a reversible reaction (see next page). In reversible reactions, if the reaction is endothermic in one direction, it will be exothermic in the other direction. The energy absorbed by the endothermic reaction is equal to the energy released during the exothermic reaction.

Right, so burning gives out heat — really...

This whole energy transfer thing is a fairly simple idea — don't be put off by the long words. Remember, "exo-" = exit, "-thermic" = heat, so an exothermic reaction is one that gives out heat. And "endo-" = erm... the other one. Okay, so there's no easy way to remember that one. Tough.

Reversible Reactions

In most of the reactions covered so far in this book, you mix some reactants and after a while you get the products. Makes sense. But of course, real life isn't always so simple.

Reversible reactions go in *both directions*

A reversible reaction is one where the products of the reaction can react with each other and convert back into the original reactants. In other words, it can go both ways.

> **A reversible reaction is one where the products of the reaction can themselves react to produce the original reactants**
> $$A + B \rightleftharpoons C + D$$

Reversible reactions will reach **dynamic equilibrium**

1) If a reversible reaction happens in a closed system then a state of equilibrium will always be reached.

2) Equilibrium means that the relative (%) quantities of reactants and products will reach a certain balance and then stay there. (A 'closed system' just means that none of the reactants or products are able to escape.)

3) It is in fact a DYNAMIC EQUILIBRIUM, which means that the reactions are still taking place in both directions, but the overall effect is nil because the forward and reverse reactions cancel each other out. The reactions are taking place at exactly the same rate in both directions.

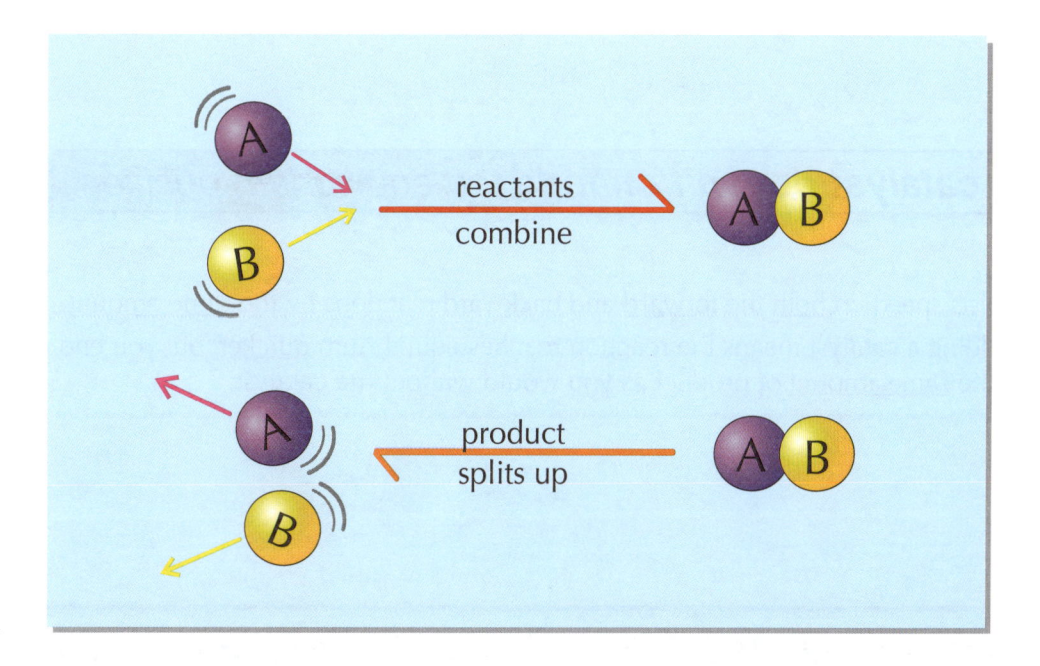

CHEMISTRY 2II — RATES OF REACTION

Reversible Reactions

Reversible reactions always reach equilibrium eventually, but by changing the conditions you can change the position of the equilibrium — i.e. shift it over so you end up with more products.

You can change *temperature* and *pressure* to get *more product*

1) In a reversible reaction the 'position of equilibrium' (the relative amounts of reactants and products) depends very strongly on the temperature and pressure surrounding the reaction.

2) If you deliberately alter the temperature and pressure you can move the 'position of equilibrium' to give more products and fewer reactants.

Temperature

All reactions are exothermic in one direction and endothermic in the other.

- If you raise the temperature, the endothermic reaction will increase to use up the extra heat.
- If you reduce the temperature, the exothermic reaction will increase to give out more heat.

Pressure

Many reactions have a greater volume on one side, either of products or reactants (greater volume means there are more molecules and less volume means there are fewer molecules).

- If you raise the pressure it will encourage the reaction which produces less volume.
- If you lower the pressure it will encourage the reaction which produces more volume.

Adding a *catalyst doesn't change* the equilibrium position

1) Catalysts speed up both the forward and backward reactions by the same amount.
2) So, adding a catalyst means the reaction reaches equilibrium quicker, but you end up with the same amount of product as you would without the catalyst.

Remember — catalysts DON'T affect the equilibrium position...

Changing the temperature always changes the equilibrium position, but that's not true of pressure. If your reaction has the same number of molecules on each side of the equation, changing the pressure won't make any difference at all to the equilibrium position (it still affects the rate of reaction though).

Haber Process

This is an important industrial process. It produces ammonia (NH_3), which is used to make fertilisers.

Nitrogen and hydrogen are needed to make ammonia

$$N_2(g) + 3H_2(g) \rightleftharpoons 2NH_3(g) \quad (+ \text{ heat})$$

1) The nitrogen is obtained easily from the air, which is 78% nitrogen (and 21% oxygen).
2) The hydrogen comes from natural gas or from other sources like crude oil.
3) Because the reaction is reversible — it occurs in both directions — not all of the nitrogen and hydrogen will convert to ammonia. The reaction reaches a dynamic equilibrium.

Industrial conditions: pressure = 200 atmospheres; temperature = 450 °C; catalyst: iron.

The reaction is reversible, so there's a compromise to be made

1) Higher pressures favour the forward reaction (since there are four moles of gas on the left-hand side for every two moles on the right).
2) So the pressure is set as high as possible to give the best percentage yield, without making the plant too expensive to build (it'd be too expensive to build a plant that'd stand pressures of over 1000 atmospheres, for example). Hence the 200 atmospheres operating pressure.
3) The forward reaction is exothermic, which means increasing the temperature will move the equilibrium the wrong way — away from ammonia and towards N_2 and H_2. So the yield of ammonia would be greater at lower temperatures.
4) The trouble is, lower temperatures mean a slower rate of reaction. So what they do is increase the temperature anyway, to get a much faster rate of reaction.
5) The 450 °C is a compromise between maximum yield and speed of reaction. It's better to wait just 20 seconds for a 10% yield than to have to wait 60 seconds for a 20% yield.
6) The ammonia is formed as a gas but as it cools in the condenser it liquefies and is removed.
7) The unused hydrogen, H_2, and nitrogen, N_2, are recycled so nothing is wasted.

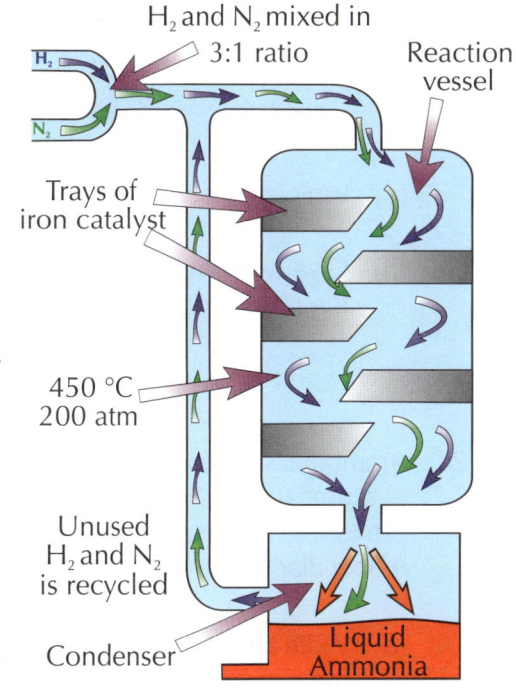

The iron catalyst speeds up the reaction and keeps costs down

1) The iron catalyst makes the reaction go faster, which gets it to the equilibrium proportions more quickly. But remember, the catalyst doesn't affect the position of equilibrium (i.e. the % yield).
2) Without the catalyst the temperature would have to be raised even further to get a quick enough reaction, and that would reduce the % yield even further. So the catalyst is very important.

Warm-Up and Exam Questions

Warm-Up Questions

1) What word is used to describe a reaction that gives out heat?
2) An endothermic reaction happens when ammonium nitrate is dissolved in water. Predict how the temperature of the solution will change during the reaction.
3) What could you do to speed up a reaction without changing the position of equilibrium?
4) What can you say about the forward and backward reaction rates at dynamic equilibrium?
5) How does increasing the pressure alter the equilibrium position of a reaction which produces fewer moles of gas molecules in the forward direction?
6) Name the catalyst used in the Haber process.
7) What happens to leftover reactants that are not converted to product in the Haber process?

Exam Questions

1   When calcium carbonate is heated to a high temperature in a closed system, an equilibrium is reached:

$$CaCO_3 \text{ (s)} \rightleftharpoons CaO \text{ (s)} + CO_2 \text{ (g)} \quad (\Delta H \text{ is +ve})$$

(a) Why is a closed system needed for this reaction to reach equilibrium?

(1 mark)

(b) Give two ways in which the equilibrium could be changed to increase the proportion of products present.

(2 marks)

2   Ammonia, NH_3, is made by combining nitrogen and hydrogen at a pressure of 200 atm, a temperature of 450 °C and in the presence of a catalyst.
A flow diagram is shown for the reaction:

(a) Write labels for boxes (i) and (ii) to show the sources of nitrogen and hydrogen.

(2 marks)

(b) Write an equation with state symbols for the reaction between nitrogen and hydrogen.

(3 marks)

(c) Write a label for box (iii) to show what ammonia is used to make.

(1 mark)

(d) The reaction is exothermic. Explain why a high temperature is still used.

(2 marks)

Revision Summary for Chemistry 2ii

Well, I don't think that was too bad, was it. Four things affect the rate of reactions, there are loads of ways to measure reaction rates and it's all explained by collision theory. Reactions can be endothermic or exothermic, and quite a few of them are reversible. Well here are some more of those nice questions that you enjoy so much. If there are any you can't answer, go back to the appropriate page, do a bit more learning, then try again.

1) What are the four factors that affect the rate of a reaction?
2) Describe three different ways of measuring the rate of a reaction. List one advantage and one disadvantage of each method.
3) A student carries out an experiment to measure the effect of surface area on the reaction between marble and hydrochloric acid. He measures the amount of gas given off at regular intervals.
   a) What factors must he keep constant for it to be a fair test?
   b)* He uses four samples for his experiment:
      Sample A – 10 g of powdered marble
      Sample B – 10 g of small marble chips
      Sample C – 10 g of large marble chips
      Sample D – 5 g of powdered marble
   Sketch a typical set of graphs for this experiment.
4) Explain how each of the four factors which affect reaction rates increases the number of successful collisions between particles.
5) What is the other aspect of collision theory which determines the rate of reaction?
6) Which is the only physical factor which affects this other aspect of collision theory?
7) What is the definition of a catalyst? What does a catalyst do to the activation energy of a reaction?
8) Discuss the advantages and disadvantages of using catalysts in industrial processes.
9) What is an exothermic reaction? Give three examples.
10) The reaction to split ammonium chloride into ammonia and hydrogen chloride is endothermic. What can you say for certain about the reverse reaction?
11) What is a reversible reaction? Explain what is meant by a dynamic equilibrium.
12) How does changing the temperature and pressure of a reversible reaction alter the equilibrium position?
13) How does this influence the choice of pressure for the Haber process?
14) What determines the choice of operating temperature for the Haber process?
15) What effect does the iron catalyst have on the reaction between nitrogen and hydrogen?

* Answer on page 241

CHEMISTRY 2III — Using Ions in Solution

Acids and Alkalis

The pH scale and universal indicator

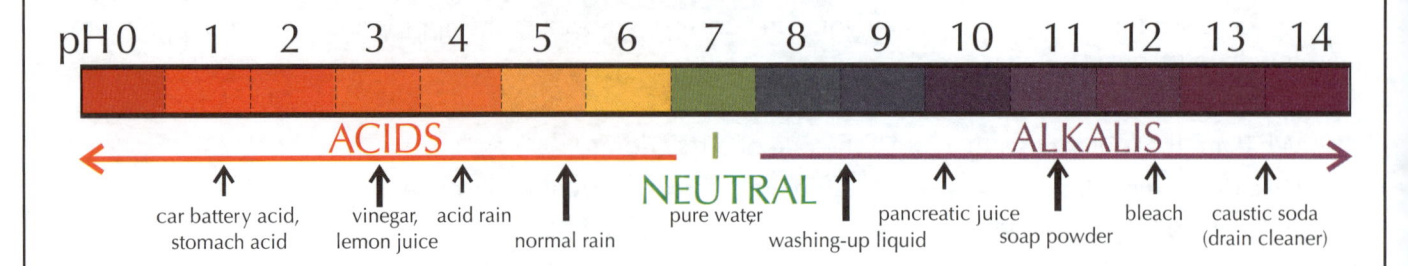

pH 0 1 2 3 4 5 6 7 8 9 10 11 12 13 14

← ACIDS | ALKALIS →

NEUTRAL

- car battery acid, stomach acid
- vinegar, lemon juice
- acid rain
- normal rain
- pure water
- washing-up liquid
- pancreatic juice
- soap powder
- bleach
- caustic soda (drain cleaner)

The pH scale goes from 0 to 14

1) The strongest acid has pH 0. The strongest alkali has pH 14.
2) A neutral substance has pH 7 (e.g. pure water).

An indicator is just a dye that changes colour

The dye in the indicator changes colour depending on whether it's above or below a certain pH. Universal indicator is a very useful combination of dyes which gives the colours shown above. It's very useful for estimating the pH of a solution.

Acids and bases neutralise each other

An ACID is a substance with a pH of less than 7. Acids form $H^+_{(aq)}$ ions in water.
A BASE is a substance with a pH of greater than 7.
An ALKALI is a base that dissolves in water. Alkalis form $OH^-_{(aq)}$ ions in water.

The reaction between acids and bases is called neutralisation. Make sure you learn it:

$$\text{acid} + \text{base} \rightarrow \text{salt} + \text{water}$$

Neutralisation can also be seen in terms of H^+ and OH^- ions like this, so learn it too:

$$H^+_{(aq)} + OH^-_{(aq)} \rightarrow H_2O_{(l)}$$

When an acid neutralises a base (or vice versa), the products are neutral, i.e. they have a pH of 7.

Three "real-life" examples of neutralisation:

1) Indigestion is caused by too much hydrochloric acid in the stomach. Indigestion tablets contain bases such as magnesium oxide, which neutralise the excess HCl (see page 122).
2) Fields with acidic soils can be improved no end by adding lime (see page 15). The lime added to fields is calcium hydroxide $Ca(OH)_2$ which is of course an alkali.
3) Lakes affected by acid rain can also be neutralised by adding lime. This saves the fish.

Acids Reacting with Metals

$$\text{acid} + \text{metal} \rightarrow \text{salt} + \text{hydrogen}$$

That's written big because it's really worth remembering. Here's the typical experiment:

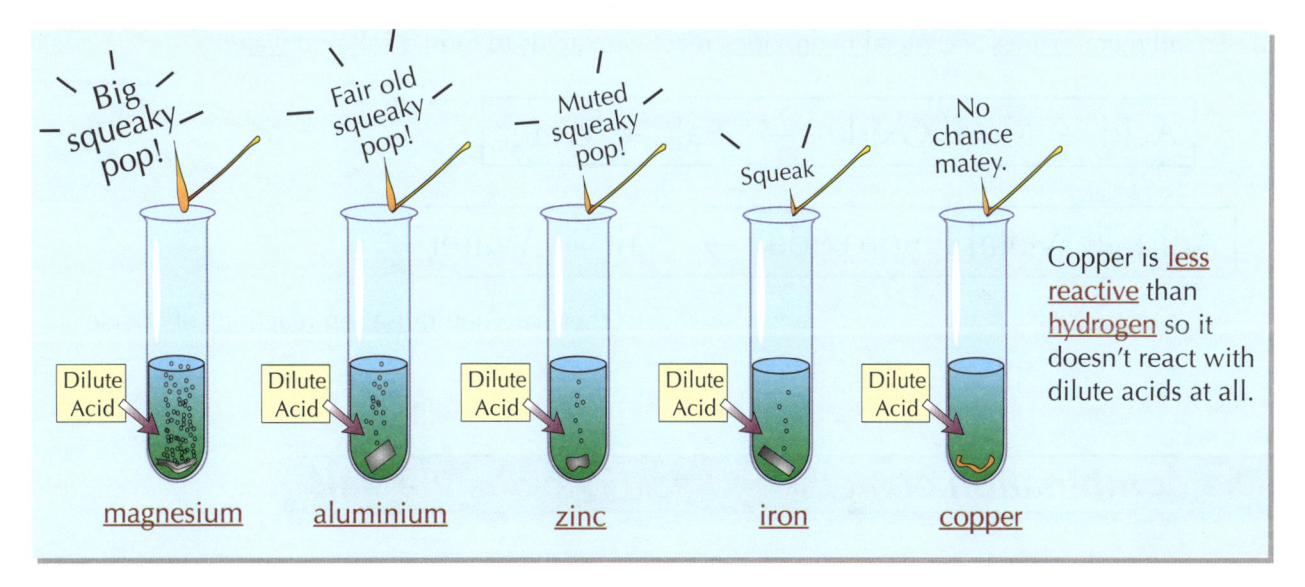

Big squeaky pop! — magnesium
Fair old squeaky pop! — aluminium
Muted squeaky pop! — zinc
Squeak — iron
No chance matey. — copper

Copper is less reactive than hydrogen so it doesn't react with dilute acids at all.

1) The more reactive the metal, the faster the reaction will go — very reactive metals (e.g. sodium) react explosively.
2) Copper does not react with dilute acids at all — because it's less reactive than hydrogen.
3) The speed of the reaction is indicated by the rate at which the bubbles of hydrogen are given off.
4) The hydrogen is confirmed by the burning splint test giving the notorious 'squeaky pop'.
5) The name of the salt produced depends on which metal is used, and which acid is used:

Hydrochloric acid will always produce chloride salts

$2HCl + Mg \rightarrow MgCl_2 + H_2$ (magnesium chloride)
$6HCl + 2Al \rightarrow 2AlCl_3 + 3H_2$ (aluminium chloride)
$2HCl + Zn \rightarrow ZnCl_2 + H_2$ (zinc chloride)

Chloride and sulfate salts are generally soluble in water (the main exceptions are lead chloride, lead sulfate and silver chloride, which are insoluble).

Sulfuric acid will always produce sulfate salts

$H_2SO_4 + Mg \rightarrow MgSO_4 + H_2$ (magnesium sulfate)
$3H_2SO_4 + 2Al \rightarrow Al_2(SO_4)_3 + 3H_2$ (aluminium sulfate)
$H_2SO_4 + Zn \rightarrow ZnSO_4 + H_2$ (zinc sulfate)

Nitric acid produces nitrate salts when NEUTRALISED, but...

Nitric acid reacts fine with alkalis to produce nitrates, but it can play silly devils with metals and produce nitrogen oxides instead, so we'll ignore it here.

Oxides and Hydroxides

Metal *oxides* and metal *hydroxides* are *bases*

1) Some metal oxides and metal hydroxides dissolve in water. These soluble compounds are alkalis.
2) Even bases that won't dissolve in water will still react with acids.
3) So, all metal oxides and metal hydroxides react with acids to form a salt and water.

> Acid + Metal Oxide → Salt + Water

> Acid + Metal Hydroxide → Salt + Water

(These are neutralisation reactions of course)

The *combination* of metal and acid decides the *salt*

This isn't exactly exciting but it's pretty easy, so try and get the hang of it:

Hydrochloric acid	+	Copper oxide	→ Copper chloride	+ water
Hydrochloric acid	+	Sodium hydroxide	→ Sodium chloride	+ water

Sulfuric acid	+	Zinc oxide	→ Zinc sulfate	+ water
Sulfuric acid	+	Calcium hydroxide	→ Calcium sulfate	+ water

Nitric acid	+	Magnesium oxide	→ Magnesium nitrate	+ water
Nitric acid	+	Potassium hydroxide	→ Potassium nitrate	+ water

The symbol equations are all pretty much the same. Here are two of them:

$$H_2SO_{4\,(aq)} + ZnO_{(s)} \rightarrow ZnSO_{4\,(aq)} + H_2O_{(l)}$$

$$HNO_{3\,(aq)} + KOH_{(aq)} \rightarrow KNO_{3\,(aq)} + H_2O_{(l)}$$

CHEMISTRY 2III — USING IONS IN SOLUTION

Making Salts

Ammonia can be neutralised with HNO₃ to make fertiliser

Ammonia dissolves in water to make an alkaline solution.
When it reacts with nitric acid, you get a neutral salt — ammonium nitrate:

$$NH_{3\,(g)} + HNO_{3\,(aq)} \rightarrow NH_4NO_{3\,(aq)}$$
Ammonia + Nitric acid → Ammonium nitrate

This is a bit different from most neutralisation reactions because there's NO WATER produced — just the ammonium salt.

Ammonium nitrate is an especially good fertiliser because it has nitrogen from two sources, the ammonia and the nitric acid. Kind of a double dose. Plants need nitrogen to make proteins.

Making soluble salts from insoluble bases

Most chlorides, sulfates and nitrates are soluble in water (the main exceptions are lead chloride, lead sulfate and silver chloride). Most oxides, hydroxides and carbonates are insoluble in water.

1) You need to pick the right acid, plus a metal carbonate or metal hydroxide, as long as it's insoluble. You can't use sodium, potassium or ammonium carbonates or hydroxides, as they're soluble (so you can't tell whether the reaction has finished).

2) You add the carbonate or hydroxide to the acid until all the acid is neutralised. (The excess carbonate or hydroxide will just sink to the bottom of the flask when all the acid has reacted.)

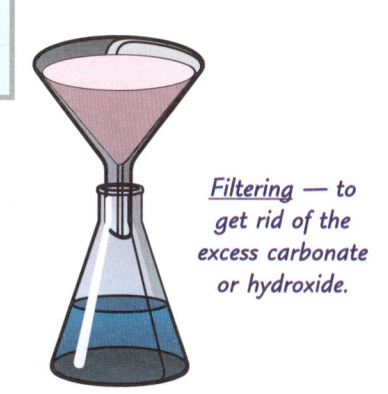

Filtering — to get rid of the excess carbonate or hydroxide.

3) Then filter out the excess carbonate, and evaporate off the water — and you should be left with a pure, dry salt.

E.g. you can use copper carbonate and nitric acid to make copper nitrate:

$$CuCO_{3\,(s)} + 2HNO_{3\,(aq)} \rightarrow Cu(NO_3)_{2\,(aq)} + CO_{2\,(g)} + H_2O_{(l)}$$

Making Salts

Making *insoluble* salts — *precipitation* reactions

Just mix an acid and a nitrate — simple as that.

1) If the salt you want to make is insoluble, you can use a precipitation reaction.

2) You just need to pick the right acid and nitrate, then mix them together. E.g. if you want to make lead chloride (which is insoluble), mix hydrochloric acid and lead nitrate.

3) Once the salt has precipitated out (and is lying at the bottom of your flask), all you have to do is filter it from the solution, wash it and then dry it on filter paper.

$$\text{E.g.} \quad Pb(NO_3)_{2\,(aq)} + 2HCl_{(aq)} \rightarrow PbCl_{2\,(s)} + 2HNO_{3\,(aq)}$$

4) Precipitation reactions can be used to remove poisonous ions (e.g. lead) from drinking water. Calcium and magnesium ions can also be removed from water this way — they make water "hard", which stops soap lathering properly.

> If both the base and the salt are SOLUBLE, things get a bit trickier. You can't just add an excess of base and filter out what's left — you have to add exactly the right amount of base to just neutralise the acid. You need to use an indicator to show when the reaction's finished. Then repeat using exactly the same volumes of base and acid so the salt isn't contaminated with indicator. All this is quite fiddly.

Making salts by *displacement*

1) If you put a more reactive metal like magnesium into a salt solution of a less reactive metal, like copper sulfate, then the magnesium will take the place of the copper — and make magnesium sulfate.

2) The "kicked-out" (or displaced) metal then coats itself onto the more reactive metal.

3) Once the magnesium has been completely coated with copper, the reaction stops, so this isn't a very practical way to make a salt.

Get two beakers, mix them together...

It's hard to find the precise neutral point using universal indicator. There's quite a wide range of "green"s between blue and yellow. There are more accurate indicators, but you don't need to know them.

Warm-Up and Exam Questions

Now try these questions — you're less likely to get a nasty surprise in the exam if you do.

Warm-Up Questions

1) What name is given to the type of reaction in which an acid reacts with a base?
2) Which two substances are formed when an acid reacts with a metal such as zinc?
3) Which two substances are formed when nitric acid reacts with copper oxide?
4) Explain what you would do to make a dry sample of a soluble salt from an insoluble base.
5) Why couldn't you make an iron salt from an aluminium salt by displacement?

Exam Questions

1   The table shows the results when five solutions, A–E, were tested with universal indicator.

Solution	Colour	pH
A		1
B	pale green	
C	orange	5
D	dark blue	
E		14

(a) Complete the blanks in the table.
(2 marks)

(b) Which solution is a weak acid?
(1 mark)

(c) Which solution is a strong alkali?
(1 mark)

(d) Which solution contains sodium chloride?
(1 mark)

(e) Which solution is battery acid?
(1 mark)

2   An experiment was carried out in which sodium hydroxide solution was added, 2 cm^3 at a time, to 10 cm^3 of sulfuric acid. The pH was estimated after each addition using universal indicator paper.
The results are shown in the table.

Volume of sodium hydroxide added (cm^3)	pH
0	1
2	1
4	2
6	4
8	12
10	13
12	13

(a) Plot the results on a graph, with pH on the vertical axis and volume of sodium hydroxide added on the horizontal axis.
Draw a best fit curve.
(2 marks)

(b) Estimate the volume of sodium hydroxide needed to neutralise the acid.
(1 mark)

(c) How do the results show that sulfuric acid is a strong acid?
(1 mark)

(d) Name the salt formed in the reaction.
(1 mark)

Exam Questions

3. An excess of different substances were added to a solution of hydrochloric acid containing universal indicator. The results are shown in the table below.

Substance	Formula	Observations during the reaction	Observations after excess added	Final pH
zinc oxide	ZnO	ZnO dissolves	ZnO settles out	7
potassium hydroxide	KOH	KOH dissolves	KOH stays in solution	14
ammonia	NH_3	NH_3 dissolves	NH_3 stays in solution	11
sodium chloride	NaCl	NaCl dissolves	NaCl stays in solution	1
magnesium metal	Mg	Mg dissolves, bubbling	Mg settles out	7

(a) Which substance didn't neutralise the acid?
(1 mark)

(b) Which two substances are alkalis?
(1 mark)

(c) Which substance is an insoluble base?
(1 mark)

(d) Complete the symbol equations for the following reactions. The ions involved are shown below to help you work out the formulas of the salts formed.

Ions: Mg^{2+}, Zn^{2+}, NH_4^+, K^+, Cl^-

(i) $Mg + 2HCl \rightarrow$
(1 mark)

(ii) $NH_3 + HCl \rightarrow$
(1 mark)

(iii) $ZnO + 2HCl \rightarrow$
(1 mark)

(iv) $KOH + HCl \rightarrow$
(1 mark)

4. Jenny wanted to make a dry sample of silver chloride, AgCl, by precipitation.

(a) What property must a salt have to be made by precipitation?
(1 mark)

(b) Jenny looked up the solubilities of some compounds she might use.
Write down one reaction using substances from the table that she could use to make silver chloride by precipitation.

Compound	Formula	Solubility
silver oxide	Ag_2O	insoluble
silver nitrate	$AgNO_3$	soluble
silver carbonate	$AgCO_3$	insoluble
sulfuric acid	H_2SO_4	soluble
nitric acid	HNO_3	soluble
hydrochloric acid	HCl	soluble

(1 mark)

(c) Outline the steps needed to give a pure dry sample of silver chloride after mixing the solutions.
(3 marks)

CHEMISTRY 2III — USING IONS IN SOLUTION

Electrolysis and the Half-Equations

You need to know about the electrolysis of salt solutions and copper solutions (p.129).

Electrolysis means "splitting up with electricity"

1) <u>Electrolysis</u> is the <u>breaking down</u> of a substance using <u>electricity</u>.
2) It requires a <u>liquid</u> to <u>conduct</u> the <u>electricity</u>, called the <u>electrolyte</u>.
3) Electrolytes are usually <u>free ions dissolved in water</u>, e.g. <u>dissolved salts</u>, and molten ionic substances.
4) In either case it's the <u>free ions</u> which <u>conduct</u> the electricity and allow the whole thing to work.
5) For an electrical circuit to be complete, there's got to be a <u>flow of electrons</u>. <u>Electrons</u> are taken <u>away from</u> ions at the <u>positive anode</u> and <u>given to</u> other ions at the <u>negative cathode</u>. As ions gain or lose electrons they become atoms or molecules and are released.

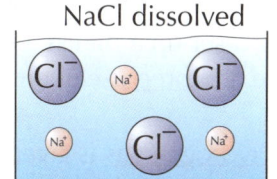

NaCl dissolved

Molten NaCl

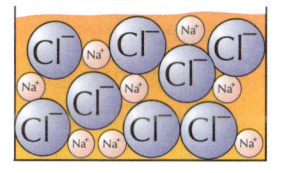

The electrolysis of a salt solution

When common salt (sodium chloride) is electrolysed, it produces three very useful products.

Cathode (-ve) ← flow of electrons   flow of electrons ← Anode (+ve)

+ve ions are called CATIONS because they're attracted to the –ve cathode.

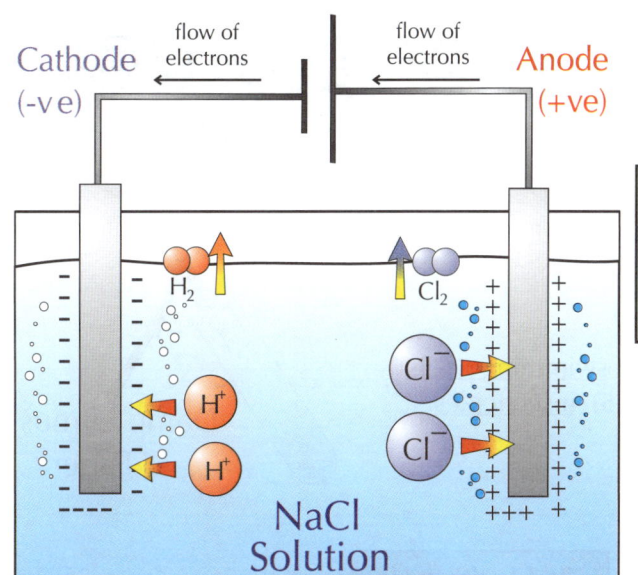

–ve ions are called ANIONS because they're attracted to the +ve anode.

<u>Hydrogen</u> is produced at the <u>–ve cathode</u>.

<u>Chlorine</u> is produced at the <u>+ve anode</u>.

NaCl Solution

1) At the <u>cathode</u>, two hydrogen ions accept two electrons to become <u>one hydrogen molecule</u>.
2) At the <u>anode</u>, two chloride (Cl^-) ions lose their electrons and become <u>one chlorine molecule</u>.
3) <u>NaOH</u> is left in the solution.

The half-equations — make sure the electrons balance

The main thing is to make sure the <u>number of electrons</u> is the <u>same</u> for <u>both half-equations</u>. For the above cell the half-equations are:

$$\text{Cathode:} \quad 2H^+ + 2e^- \rightarrow H_2$$
$$\text{Anode:} \quad 2Cl^- \rightarrow Cl_2 + 2e^-$$

CHEMISTRY 2III — USING IONS IN SOLUTION

Electrolysis of Salt Water

Electrolysis of salt gives hydrogen, chlorine and NaOH

Concentrated brine (sodium chloride solution) is electrolysed industrially using a set-up a bit like this one. There are three useful products:

a) Hydrogen gas is given off at the cathode.
b) Chlorine gas is given off at the anode.
c) Sodium hydroxide is left in solution.

These are collected, and then used in all sorts of industries to make various products as detailed below.

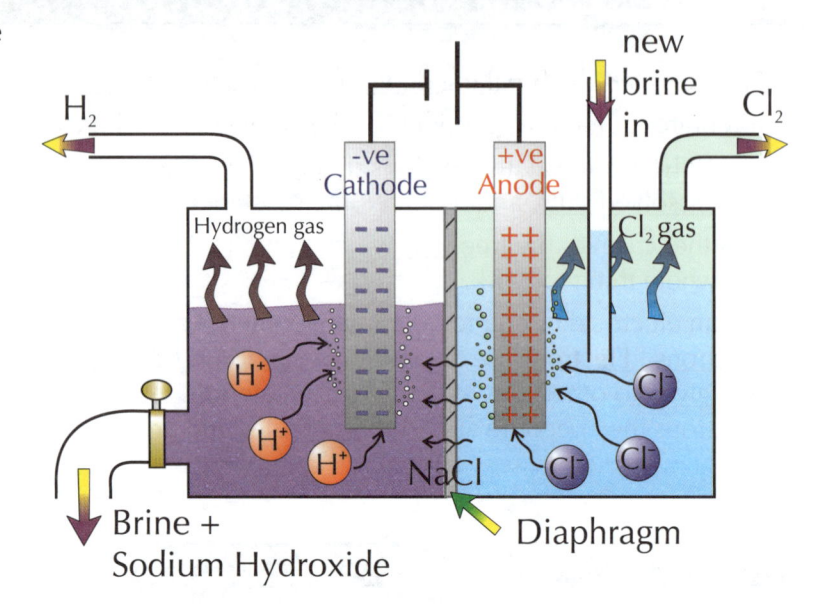

Useful products from the electrolysis of brine

With all that effort and expense going into the electrolysis of brine, there'd better be some pretty useful stuff coming out of it — and so there is... and you have to learn it all too. Ace.

1) Chlorine

Used in: 1) disinfectants
2) killing bacteria (e.g. in swimming pools)
3) plastics   4) HCl   5) insecticides.

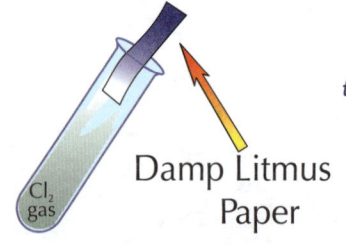

(Don't forget the simple lab test for chlorine — it bleaches damp litmus paper.)

2) Hydrogen

1) Used in the Haber process to make ammonia (see p.117).
2) Used to change oils into fats for making margarine (p.53) ("hydrogenated vegetable oil"). Think about that when you spread it on your toast in the morning.

3) Sodium hydroxide

Sodium hydroxide is a very strong alkali and is used widely in the chemical industry,
e.g.   1) soap   2) ceramics
3) organic chemicals
4) paper pulp   5) oven cleaner.

CHEMISTRY 2III — USING IONS IN SOLUTION

Purifying Copper by Electrolysis

1) <u>Copper</u> is a very <u>unreactive</u> metal. Not only is it below carbon in the reactivity series, it's also below <u>hydrogen</u>, which means that copper doesn't even react with <u>water</u>.
2) So copper can be obtained <u>very easily</u> from its ore by <u>reduction</u> with <u>carbon</u>.

Very pure copper is needed for *electrical conductors*

1) The copper produced by reduction with carbon <u>isn't pure enough</u> for use in <u>electrical conductors</u>.
2) The <u>purer</u> it is, the better it <u>conducts</u>.
3) <u>Electrolysis</u> is used to obtain <u>very pure copper</u>.

Cathode (−ve) — Copper(II) sulfate solution containing $Cu^{2+}_{(aq)}$ ions. — **Anode (+ve)**

The <u>cathode</u> starts as a <u>thin</u> piece of <u>pure copper</u> and more pure copper <u>adds</u> to it.

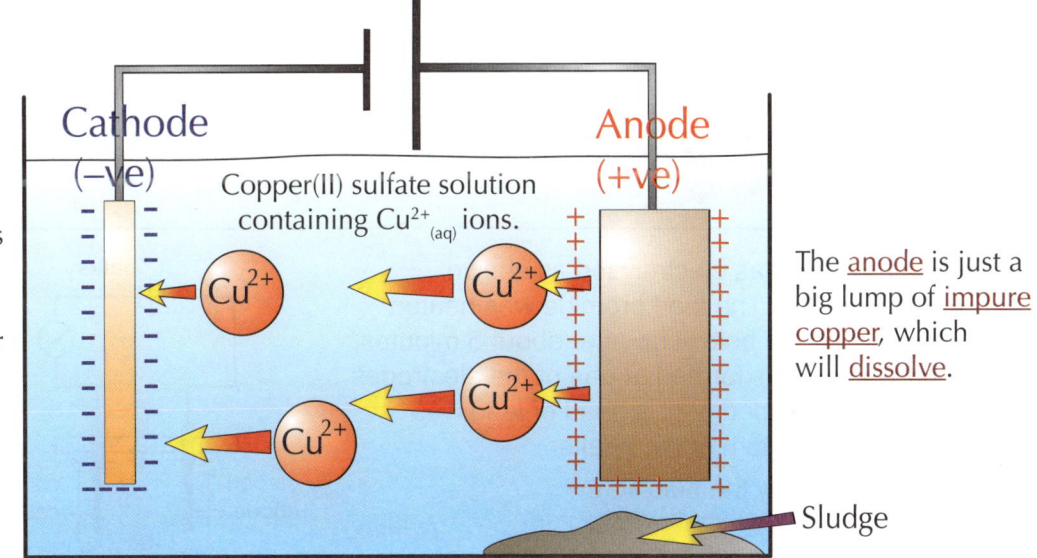

The <u>anode</u> is just a big lump of <u>impure copper</u>, which will <u>dissolve</u>.

Sludge

The <u>electrical supply</u> acts by:
1) <u>Pulling electrons off</u> copper atoms at the <u>anode</u>, causing them to go into solution as Cu^{2+} <u>ions</u>.
2) Then <u>offering electrons</u> at the <u>cathode</u> to nearby Cu^{2+} <u>ions</u> to turn them back into <u>copper atoms</u>.
3) The <u>impurities</u> are dropped at the <u>anode</u> as a <u>sludge</u>, whilst <u>pure copper atoms</u> bond to the <u>cathode</u>.
4) The electrolysis can go on for <u>weeks</u> and the cathode is often <u>twenty times bigger</u> at the end of it.

Pure copper is deposited on the pure cathode (−ve)	Copper dissolves from the impure anode (+ve)
The reaction at the <u>cathode</u> is: $Cu^{2+}_{(aq)} + 2e^- \rightarrow Cu_{(s)}$ The copper ions have been <u>converted</u> to copper atoms by <u>gaining</u> electrons.	The reaction at the <u>anode</u> is: $Cu_{(s)} \rightarrow Cu^{2+}_{(aq)} + 2e^-$ Copper atoms have been <u>converted</u> into copper ions by <u>losing</u> electrons.

You do the same thing to purify recycled copper...

Impure copper, like the stuff you get from reducing the ore or from recycling, is okay for most things. It's fine for pipes and pans and decorative stuff. It's only copper in wires and circuit boards that needs to be this pure. Which is handy, because <u>electrolysis</u> is really <u>expensive</u> and uses up <u>lots of energy</u>.

Warm-Up and Exam Questions

It's question time again. You know the drill. Off you go...

Warm-Up Questions

1) What state must an ionic compound be in if it's to be used as an electrolyte?
2) At which electrode are metals deposited during electrolysis?
3) Name the three products obtained from the electrolysis of salt (NaCl) solution.
4) If dilute sodium chloride solution is electrolysed, what two gases are produced?
5) Why is it necessary to purify copper?

Exam Questions

1 Lead bromide was electrolysed as shown in the diagram. The lead bromide was heated strongly and the bulb lit up after about 5 minutes. A brown gas was formed at one of the electrodes and after the experiment a bead of lead was found at the bottom of the beaker.

   (a) Explain why the bulb lit up?
   (1 mark)

   (b) At which electrode was the brown gas produced?
   (1 mark)

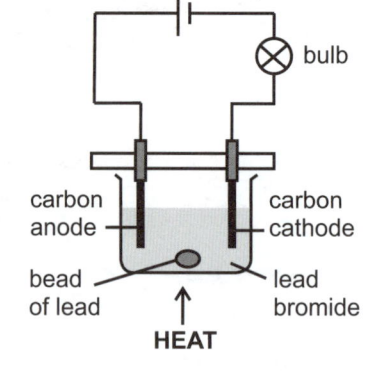

   (c) Explain fully why the bead of lead appeared on the bottom of the beaker.
   (2 marks)

   (d) Copy and complete the half-equations for the electrolysis of lead bromide:

   (i) Pb^{2+} + _____ → _____   (ii) ___ Br^- → _____ + ___ e^-

   (1 mark)   *(1 mark)*

2 When sodium chloride solution is electrolysed a gas is produced at each electrode. Gas A produced a squeaky pop when tested with a lighted splint and gas B bleached a piece of damp litmus paper.

   (a) (i) What is gas A?
   (1 mark)

   (ii) Which ion, present in water, is discharged when this gas is formed?
   (1 mark)

   (b) (i) What is gas B?
   (1 mark)

   (ii) Explain how this gas is formed at the electrode.
   (2 marks)

Exam Questions

3. The diagram shows a cell used for the electrolysis of brine.
   (a) Chlorine is produced at the anode.
       Copy and complete the half-equation:

       _____ – 2e⁻ → _____

       (2 marks)

   (b) Give one important industrial use of:
       (i) hydrogen   (ii) chlorine

       (2 marks)

   (c) If the electrolysis is done with molten sodium chloride, what will the products be?

       (2 marks)

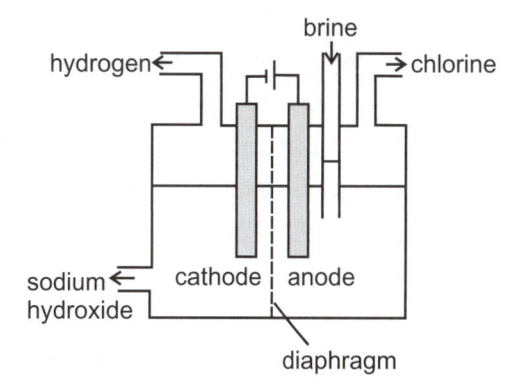

4. Potassium bromide can be electrolysed if it is in solution.

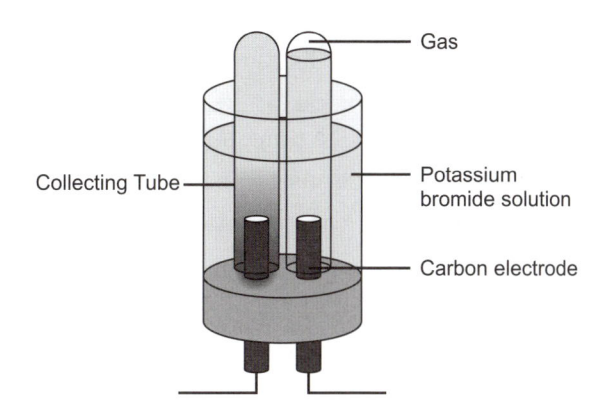

   (a) Explain why potassium bromide cannot be electrolysed when solid.

       (1 mark)

   (b) (i) The bromide ions are attracted to which electrode, the positive or the negative?

       (1 mark)

       (ii) Are the bromide ions oxidised or reduced at this electrode?

       (1 mark)

Revision Summary for Chemistry 2(iii)

There are two bits to this section — making salts (by various methods) and electrolysis. Don't try to remember all the individual reactions, just learn the rules. The salt produced depends on the acid and the metal. Have a go at these questions and see how much you can remember.

1) Describe fully the colour of universal indicator for every pH value from 0 to 14.
2) What type of ions are always present in a) acids and b) alkalis?
3) What is neutralisation? Write down the general equation for neutralisation in terms of ions.
4) Give three real-life examples of neutralisation reactions.
5) What is the general equation for reacting an acid with a metal?
6) Which metal(s) don't react at all with acid?
7) Why would you not make a potassium compound by reacting potassium metal with an acid?
8) What type of salts do hydrochloric acid and sulfuric acid produce?
9)* Name the salts formed and write balanced symbol equations for the following reactions:
    a) hydrochloric acid with: i) magnesium, ii) aluminium and iii) zinc,
    b) sulfuric acid with: i) magnesium, ii) aluminium and iii) zinc.
10) What type of reaction is "acid + metal oxide", or "acid + metal hydroxide"?
11)* Suggest a suitable acid and a suitable metal oxide/hydroxide to mix to form the following salts. Write out a balanced symbol equation for each reaction.
    a) copper(II) chloride   b) calcium nitrate   c) zinc sulfate
    d) magnesium nitrate   e) sodium sulfate   f) potassium chloride
12) Write a balanced symbol equation for the reaction between ammonia and nitric acid. What is the product of this reaction useful for? Explain why.
13) Iron chloride can made by mixing iron hydroxide (an insoluble base) with hydrochloric acid. Describe the method you would use to produce pure, solid iron chloride in the lab.
14) Describe a practical use of precipitation reactions.
15) How can you tell when a neutralisation reaction is complete if both the base and the salt are soluble in water?
16) What is electrolysis? Explain why only liquids can be electrolysed.
17) What are positive ions called in electrolysis? Why?
18) Write balanced half-equations for the reactions at the anode and the cathode during the electrolysis of sodium chloride solution.
19) Draw a detailed diagram showing how sodium chloride solution (brine) is electrolysed in industry.
20) Give uses for the three products from the electrolysis of brine.
21) Describe the process of purifying copper by electrolysis.

* Answers on page 242.

CHEMISTRY 3I — ELEMENTS, ACIDS AND WATER

History of the Periodic Table

We haven't always known as much about Chemistry as we do now. No sirree. Early chemists looked to try and understand <u>patterns</u> in the elements' properties to get a bit of understanding.

In the early 1800s they could only go on atomic mass

Until quite recently, there were <u>two</u> obvious ways to categorise elements:

> 1) Their <u>physical</u> and <u>chemical</u> <u>properties</u>   2) Their <u>Relative Atomic Mass</u>

1) Remember, they had <u>no idea</u> of <u>atomic structure</u> or of <u>protons</u> or <u>electrons,</u> so there was no such thing as <u>atomic number</u> to them. (It was only in the 20th century after protons and electrons were discovered that it was realised the elements were best arranged in order of <u>atomic number</u>.)

2) <u>Back then</u>, the only thing they could measure was <u>relative atomic mass</u>, and so the <u>known</u> elements were arranged <u>in order of atomic mass</u>. When this was done, a <u>periodic pattern</u> was noticed in the <u>properties</u> of the elements...

Newlands' law of octaves was the first good effort

A chap called <u>Newlands</u> had the first good stab at arranging things more usefully in <u>1864</u>. He noticed that every <u>eighth</u> element had similar properties, and so he listed some of the known elements in rows of seven:

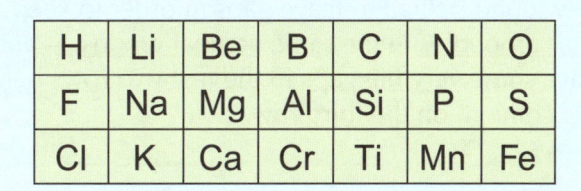

H	Li	Be	B	C	N	O
F	Na	Mg	Al	Si	P	S
Cl	K	Ca	Cr	Ti	Mn	Fe

These sets of eight were called <u>Newlands' Octaves</u>.
Unfortunately the pattern <u>broke down</u> on the <u>third row</u>, with <u>transition metals</u> like titanium (Ti) and iron (Fe) messing it up.
It was because he left <u>no gaps</u> that his work was <u>ignored</u>.
But he was getting <u>pretty close</u>, as you can see.

Newlands presented his ideas to the Chemical Society in 1865. But his work was criticised because:

1) His groups contained elements that didn't have <u>similar properties</u>, e.g. <u>carbon</u> and <u>titanium</u>.

2) He <u>mixed up metals and non-metals</u> e.g. <u>oxygen</u> and <u>iron</u>.

3) He <u>didn't leave any gaps</u> for elements that hadn't been discovered yet.

History of the Periodic Table

Dmitri Mendeleev left gaps and predicted new elements

1) In 1869, Dmitri Mendeleev in Russia, armed with about 50 known elements, arranged them into his Table of Elements — with various gaps as shown.

Mendeleev's Table of the Elements

H																
Li	Be											B	C	N	O	F
Na	Mg											Al	Si	P	S	Cl
K	Ca	*	Ti	V	Cr	Mn	Fe	Co	Ni	Cu	Zn	*	*	As	Se	Br
Rb	Sr	Y	Zr	Nb	Mo	*	Ru	Rh	Pd	Ag	Cd	In	Sn	Sb	Te	I
Cs	Ba	*	*	Ta	W	*	Os	Ir	Pt	Au	Hg	Tl	Pb	Bi		

2) Mendeleev put the elements in order of atomic mass (like Newlands did). But Mendeleev found he had to leave gaps in order to keep elements with similar properties in the same vertical groups — and he was prepared to leave some very big gaps in the first two rows before the transition metals come in on the third row.

3) The gaps were the really clever bit because they predicted the properties of so far undiscovered elements.

4) Since then new elements have been found which fit into the gaps in Mendeleev's table. Over the last hundred years or so the table has been refined to produce the periodic table we know (and love) today...

Elementary my dear Mendeleev

Even though its not the periodic table we use today, its important to know how much of an influence Mendeleev's periodic table has been on our modern periodic table. Make sure you know how Mendeleev arranged his table and how it came to look like the one we're used to using today.

The Modern Periodic Table

Chemists were getting pretty close to producing something useful.
The big breakthrough came when the structure of the atom was understood a bit better.

Not all scientists thought the periodic table was important

1) When the periodic table was first released, many scientists thought it was just a bit of fun. At that time, there wasn't all that much evidence to suggest that the elements really did fit together in that way — ideas don't get the scientific stamp of approval without evidence.

2) After Mendeleev released his work, newly discovered elements fitted into the gaps he left. This was convincing evidence in favour of the periodic table.

3) Once there was more evidence, many more scientists realised that the periodic table could be a useful tool for predicting properties of elements. It really worked.

4) In the late 19th century, scientists discovered protons, neutrons and electrons. The periodic table matches up very well to what's been discovered about the structure of the atom. Scientists now accept that it's a very important and useful summary of atomic structure.

The modern periodic table is based on electronic structure

When electrons, protons and neutrons were discovered, the periodic table was arranged in order of atomic (proton) numbers. All elements were put into groups.

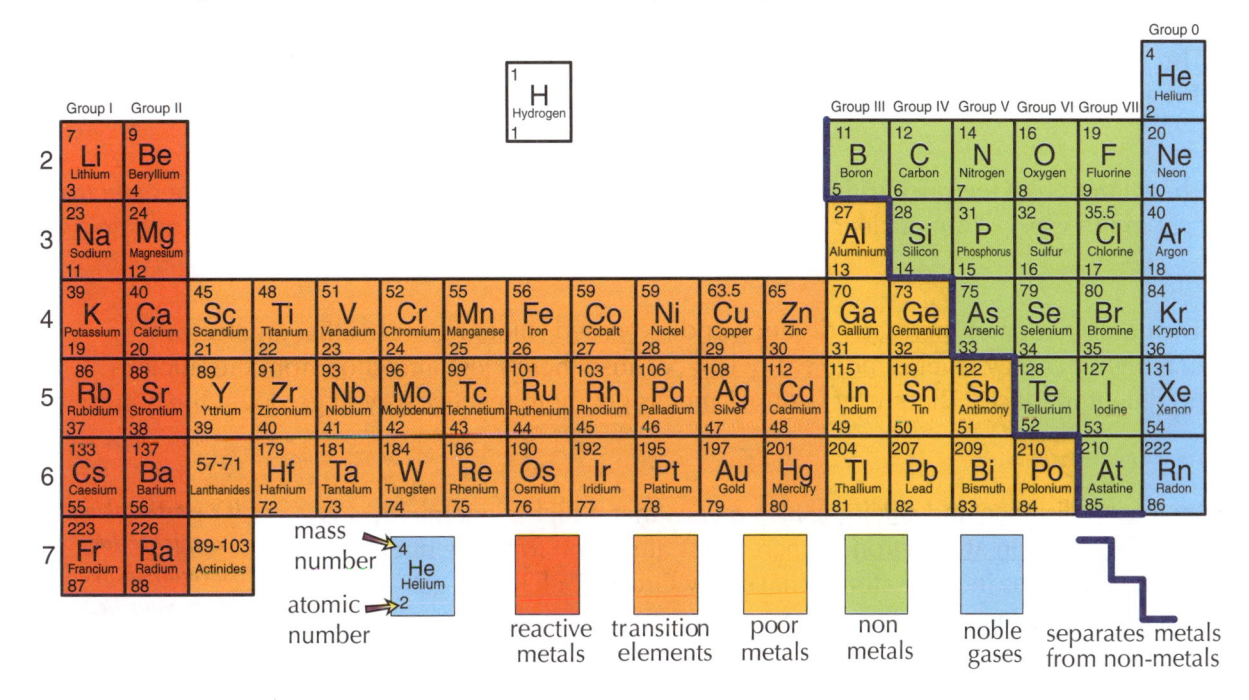

Ahh, finally, the nice colourful periodic table in full...

This is a good example of how science often progresses — even now. A scientist has a basically good (though incomplete) idea. Other scientists laugh and mock and generally deride. Eventually, the idea is modified a bit to take account of the available evidence, and voilà — into the textbooks it goes.

The Modern Periodic Table

You can find **electron configurations** from the periodic table

1) You can use the periodic table to work out the detailed arrangement of electrons in an atom of any element. Once you know the electron arrangement, you can predict the element's chemical properties.

2) Electrons in an atom are set out in shells which each correspond to an energy level.

3) The maximum number of electrons that can occupy each energy level is given by the simple formula $2 \times n^2$, where n is the number of the energy level.

> Energy level 1 has a maximum of 2×1^2 = 2 electrons
> Energy level 2 has a maximum of 2×2^2 = 8 electrons
> Energy level 3 has a maximum of 2×3^2 = 18 electrons

4) Apart from the transition metals, elements in the same group have the same number of electrons in their highest occupied energy level — e.g. Group 6 all have 6 electrons in the highest energy level. The transition metals fill up their electron shells in their own slightly peculiar way — see p.144.

The periodic table shows **reactivity patterns**

1) The positive charge of the nucleus attracts electrons and holds them in place. The further from the nucleus the electron is, the less the attraction.

2) The attraction of the nucleus is even less when there are a lot of inner electrons. Inner electrons "get in the way" of the nuclear charge, reducing the attraction. This effect is known as shielding.

3) The combination of increased distance and increased shielding means that an electron in a higher energy level is more easily lost because there's less attraction from the nucleus holding it in place. That's why Group 1 metals get more reactive as you go down the group.

4) Increased distance and shielding also means that a higher energy level is less likely to gain an electron — there's less attraction from the nucleus pulling electrons into the atom. That's why Group 7 elements get less reactive going down the group.

It's worth taking a minute (or several) to get this in your head.

The periodic table — surprisingly useful

In the exam, you can be asked factual questions like "Use electron structure to explain why Cs is more reactive than Na" or ideas questions like "Why did scientists accept the periodic table as important?", or both. So there's no excuse for not learning this stuff. Even though there is rather a lot of it...

Group 1 — The Alkali Metals

They're all silvery solids. And they're called 'alkali metals' because their hydroxides dissolve in water to give an alkaline solution. Simple.

Learn these trends:

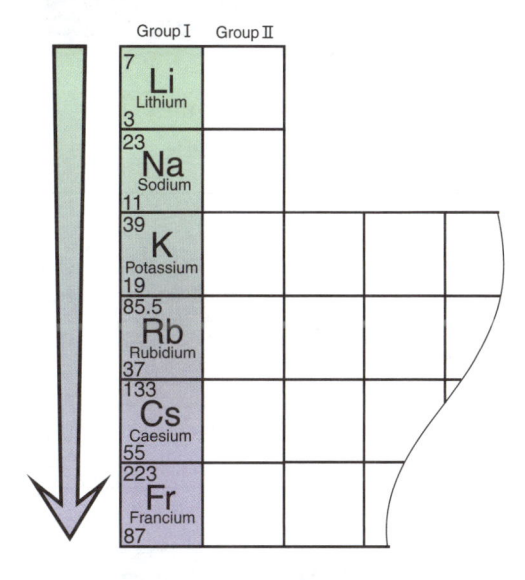

	Group I	Group II
7	Li Lithium 3	
23	Na Sodium 11	
39	K Potassium 19	
85.5	Rb Rubidium 37	
133	Cs Caesium 55	
223	Fr Francium 87	

As you go DOWN Group I, the alkali metals become:

1) **BIGGER ATOMS**
   ...because there's one extra full shell of electrons for each row you go down.
2) **MORE REACTIVE**
   ...because the outer electron is more easily lost, because it's further from the nucleus.
3) **HIGHER DENSITY**
   ...because the atoms have more mass.
   The three at the top are less dense than water.
4) **LOWER MELTING POINT**
5) **LOWER BOILING POINT**

1) The alkali metals are very reactive

They have to be stored in oil and handled with forceps (they burn the skin).

2) They are: lithium, sodium, potassium and a couple more

Know those three names real well. They may also mention rubidium and caesium.

3) The alkali metals all have ONE outer electron

This makes them very reactive and gives them all similar properties.

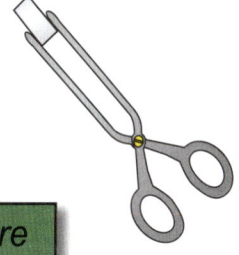

CHEMISTRY 31 — ELEMENTS, ACIDS AND WATER

Group 1 — The Alkali Metals

4) The alkali metals all form 1⁺ ions

They are <u>keen to lose</u> their one outer electron to form a <u>1⁺ ion</u>:

5) The alkali metals always form ionic compounds

They are so keen to lose the outer electron there's <u>no way</u> they'd consider <u>sharing</u>, so covalent bonding is <u>out of the question</u>.

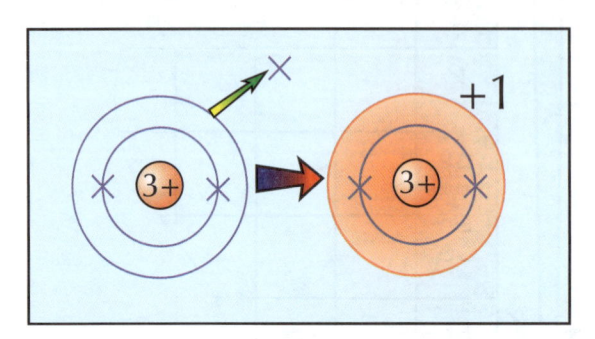

6) Reaction with water produces hydrogen gas

1) When <u>lithium</u>, <u>sodium</u> or <u>potassium</u> are put in <u>water</u>, they react very <u>vigorously</u>.
2) They <u>move</u> around the surface, <u>fizzing</u> furiously.
3) They produce <u>hydrogen</u>. Potassium gets hot enough to <u>ignite</u> it.
   A lighted splint will <u>indicate</u> hydrogen by producing the notorious "<u>squeaky pop</u>" as the H_2 ignites.
4) They form a <u>hydroxide</u> in solution, i.e. <u>aqueous OH⁻ ions</u>.

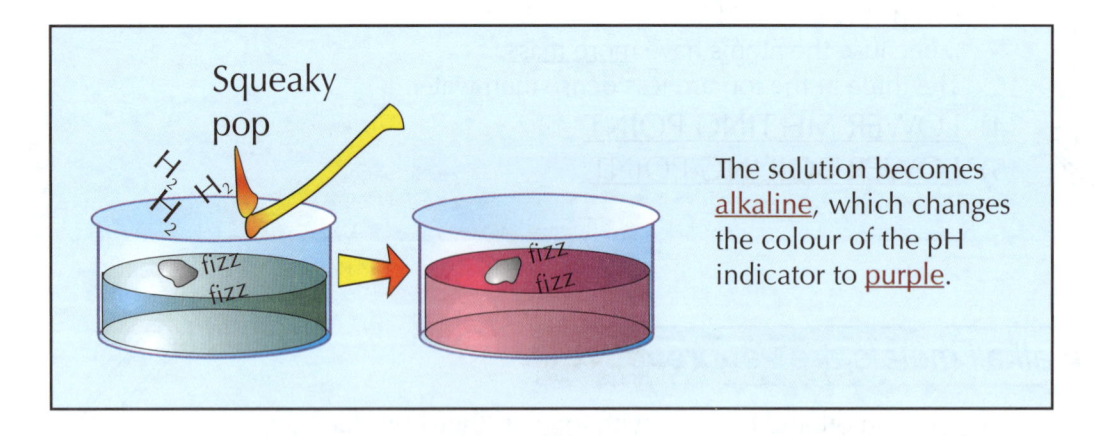

The solution becomes <u>alkaline</u>, which changes the colour of the pH indicator to <u>purple</u>.

$$2Na_{(s)} + 2H_2O_{(l)} \rightarrow 2NaOH_{(aq)} + H_{2\,(g)}$$
$$2K_{(s)} + 2H_2O_{(l)} \rightarrow 2KOH_{(aq)} + H_{2\,(g)}$$

---

5 trends and 6 properties — not much to learn at all...

I'm no gambler, but I'd put money on a question like this in the exam: "Using your knowledge of the Group I metals, describe what would happen if a piece of caesium were put into water." Just use what you know about the <u>other</u> Group I metals... you're going to get H_2, and a pretty violent reaction.

Group VII — The Halogens

The 'trend thing' happens in Group VII as well — that shouldn't come as a surprise.
But some of the trends are kind of the opposite of the Group I trends. Remember that.

Learn these trends:

As you go DOWN Group VII, the HALOGENS have the following properties:

1) LESS REACTIVE
2) HIGHER MELTING POINT
3) HIGHER BOILING POINT

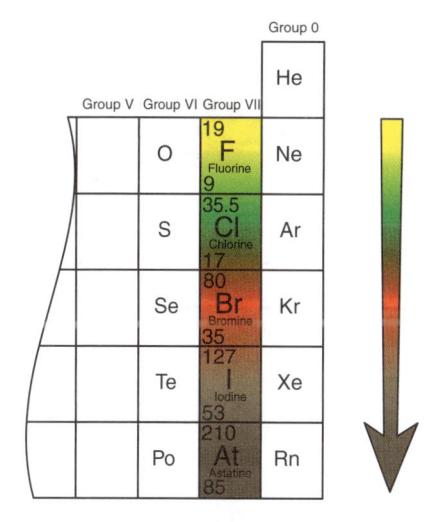

1) The halogens are all non-metals with coloured vapours

Fluorine is a very reactive, poisonous yellow gas.
Chlorine is a fairly reactive, poisonous dense green gas.
Bromine is a dense, poisonous, red-brown volatile liquid.
Iodine is a dark grey crystalline solid or a purple vapour.

2) They all form molecules which are pairs of atoms:

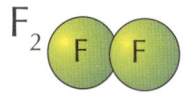

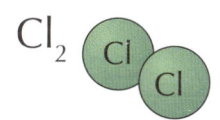

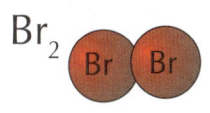

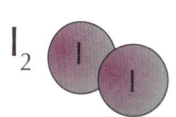

F_2 Cl_2 Br_2 I_2

3) The halogens do both ionic and covalent bonding

The halogens form 1⁻ ions when they bond with metals: F^-, Cl^-, Br^- and I^- (as in Na^+Cl^- or $Fe^{3+}Br_3^-$).
But they form covalent bonds with non-metals to form molecules like these:

Carbon tetrachloride: (CCl_4)

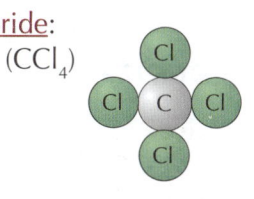

Hydrogen chloride: (HCl)

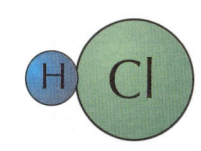

CHEMISTRY 31 — ELEMENTS, ACIDS AND WATER

Group VII — The Halogens

4) The halogens react with metals to form salts

They react with most metals, including iron and aluminium, to form salts (or 'metal halides').

Chlorine gas → [Heat, Aluminium] → Aluminium chloride

Best done in a fume cupboard — remember, chlorine is poisonous.

$$2Al_{(s)} + 3Cl_{2(g)} \rightarrow 2AlCl_{3(s)}$$
(Aluminium chloride)

$$2Fe_{(s)} + 3Br_{2(g)} \rightarrow 2FeBr_{3(s)}$$
(Iron(III) bromide)

5) More reactive halogens will displace less reactive ones

Chlorine can displace bromine and iodine from a solution of bromide or iodide. Bromine will also displace iodine because of the trend in reactivity.

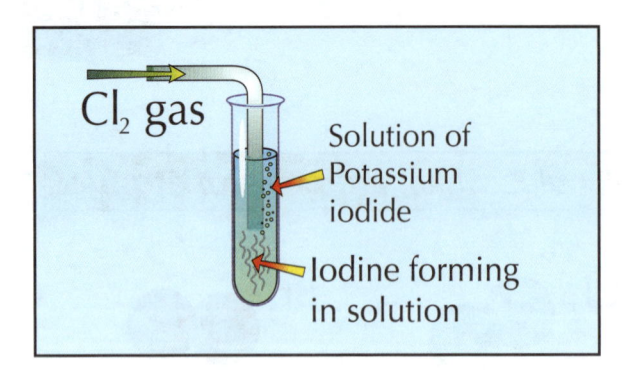

Cl_2 gas → Solution of Potassium iodide — Iodine forming in solution

$$Cl_{2(g)} + 2KI_{(aq)} \rightarrow I_{2(aq)} + 2KCl_{(aq)}$$

$$Cl_{2(g)} + 2KBr_{(aq)} \rightarrow Br_{2(aq)} + 2KCl_{(aq)}$$

Oooh, only 3 trends and 5 properties — even easier...

Once more, you don't have to be a mind-reader to be able to guess the kind of thing they're going to ask you in the exam. My money's on something to do with displacement reactions — will iodine displace bromine from some compound or other, for instance. Learn the facts... just learn the facts.

CHEMISTRY 3I — ELEMENTS, ACIDS AND WATER

Warm-Up and Exam Questions

Question time again. Sit down at a table for a short period, and try these...

Warm-Up Questions

1) In Group 1, as you go down the periodic table, does the reactivity increase or decrease?
2) In Group 7, what is the trend in physical state as you go down the group?
3) Which gas is produced when an alkali metal reacts with water?
4) Give an example of a salt produced when a Group 1 metal reacts with a Group 7 element.

Exam Questions

1 Which of the following statements about Mendeleev's periodic table is **not** true?
   A Elements with similar chemical properties were placed in vertical groups.
   B Gaps were left which helped in predicting the properties of undiscovered elements.
   C The elements were arranged in order of atomic mass.
   D Mendeleev's periodic table contained over 100 elements.
   (1 mark)

2 The table shows some of the physical properties of four of the halogens.

Halogen	Atomic number	Colour	Physical state at room temperature	Boiling point
Fluorine	9	yellow		−188 °C
Chlorine	17	green		−34 °C
Bromine	35	red-brown		59 °C
Iodine	53	dark grey		185 °C

(a) Give the physical state at room temperature of all four halogens.
(4 marks)

(b) Draw an arrow next to the left hand side of the table to show the direction of increasing reactivity in the halogens.
(1 mark)

(c) This equation shows a reaction between chlorine and potassium iodide.

   $Cl_2(g) + 2KI(aq) \rightarrow I_2(aq) + 2KCl(aq)$

   (i) What type of reaction is this?
   (1 mark)

   (ii) Which is the less reactive halogen in this reaction?
   (1 mark)

Chemistry 31 — Elements, Acids and Water

Exam Questions

3   Match the words labelled A, B, C and D, with the numbers 1 - 4 in the sentences below.
    A   electron
    B   rate
    C   reaction
    D   hydrogen

    All the alkali metals have a vigorous ...1... with water.
    This is because they all have an outer ...2... which is easily lost.
    Each metal reacts at a different ...3....
    ...4... is always produced in these reactions.

    (4 marks)

4   Chlorine is a Group 7 element used in water purification. Its electron arrangement is shown in the diagram below.

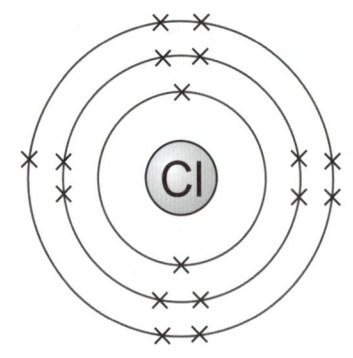

    (a) Chlorine is very reactive and forms compounds with both metals and non-metals. Describe the differences in the types of compound formed.
    (2 marks)

    (b) Chlorine is more reactive than bromine. When chlorine is bubbled through potassium bromide solution a reaction occurs.

        (i)   What colour change would be seen in the potassium bromide solution?
        (1 mark)

        (ii) Write a word equation for the reaction.
        (1 mark)

        (iii) Explain why chlorine atoms are more reactive than bromine atoms (electron arrangement 2, 8, 18, 7).
        (2 marks)

CHEMISTRY 31 — ELEMENTS, ACIDS AND WATER

Transition Elements

Transition elements make up the big clump of metals in the middle of the periodic table.

Transition elements tend to have the properties of a typical metal

Transition metals are typical metals and generally have the properties you'd expect of a 'proper' metal:

1) They're good conductors of heat and electricity.

2) They're very dense, strong and shiny.

3) Transition metals are much less reactive than Group 1 metals — they don't react very much with water or oxygen, for example.

4) They're also much denser, stronger and harder than the Group 1 metals, and have much higher melting points (except for mercury, which is a liquid at room temperature). For example, iron melts at 1500 °C, copper at 1100 °C and zinc at 400 °C.

Here they are, right in the middle of Group 2 and Group 3

Transition metals often have more than one ion, e.g. Fe^{2+}, Fe^{3+}

1) Two other examples are: copper: Cu^+ and Cu^{2+}
   chromium: Cr^{2+}, Cr^{3+} and Cr^{6+}

2) The different ions usually form different-coloured compounds too:
   Fe^{2+} ions usually give green compounds.
   Fe^{3+} ions usually form red/brown compounds (e.g. rust).

CHEMISTRY 31 — ELEMENTS, ACIDS AND WATER

Transition Elements

The compounds are very colourful

1) The compounds are colourful due to the transition metal ion they contain — for example:
   Potassium chromate(VI) is yellow.
   Potassium manganate(VII) is purple.
   Copper(II) sulfate is blue.

2) Transition metals are responsible for the colours in:
   People's hair.
   Gemstones, like blue sapphires and green emeralds.
   Some pottery glazes.
   And weathered (oxidised) copper is a lovely colourful green.

Transition metals and their compounds make good catalysts

1) Iron is the catalyst used in the Haber process for making ammonia.

2) Manganese(IV) oxide is a good catalyst for the decomposition of hydrogen peroxide.

3) Nickel is useful for turning oils into fats for making margarine.

Their properties are due to the way their electron shells fill

1) In an atom, as you get further from the nucleus, energy levels get closer together until they start to overlap. This first happens between energy levels 3 and 4. It affects the way the electron shells fill.

2) Potassium has 19 electrons — but the 19th electron goes into the 4th energy level, not the 3rd. The electron arrangement's 2, 8, 8, 1. Same thing with the next element, calcium — which is 2, 8, 8, 2.

3) The next ten elements (the transition metals) put their electrons into the overlapping third energy level until it's full.

You don't need to know how this causes their various properties, just that it does.

Sc	Ti	V	Cr	Mn	Fe	Co	Ni	Cu	Zn
2,8,9,2	2,8,10,2	2,8,11,2	2,8,13,1	2,8,13,2	2,8,14,2	2,8,15,2	2,8,16,2	2,8,18,1	2,8,18,2

(Chromium (Cr) and copper (Cu) fill up a bit differently. The reason's complicated (A2-level), so for now just learn the numbers.)

Shiny metals, pretty colours, electrons — these elements have it all...

Most common everyday metals are transition elements — for example, iron, nickel, copper, silver, gold, and so on. There are a lot of facts to learn here about colour and melting points. Learn the weird fact about electron shells and impress the examiners.

Warm-Up and Exam Questions

You know the drill — first get limbered up on the warm-ups, and then have a bash at the exam questions.

Warm-Up Questions

1) In an atom, what is the maximum number of electrons that the third energy level can hold?
2) Give three typical properties of transition metals.

Exam Questions

1 (a) These are the electronic configurations of five elements in the periodic table:
   Element A: 2.8.18.5   Element B: 2.8.8.2   Element C: 2.8.9.2
   Element D: 2.8.8.1   Element E: 2.8.16.2
   Which element(s) are transition metals?
   (2 marks)

   (b) Iron is a transition metal. Sodium is a Group I metal (alkali metal).
   (i) Give two differences between the physical properties of iron and sodium.
   (2 marks)

   (ii) Give one difference in the chemical properties of iron and sodium.
   (1 mark)

   (c) Copper can exist as two ions, Cu^+ and Cu^{2+}.
   (i) Which copper ion is present in copper sulfate solution, $CuSO_4$(aq)?
   (1 mark)

   (ii) What feature of the appearance of copper sulfate solution, $CuSO_4$(aq), is characteristic of transition metal compounds?
   (1 mark)

2 The table below shows some of the properties of four common metals.

Metal	Melting point (°C)	Density (g/cm³)	Effect of heating in air	Electron arrangement	Ions formed
Magnesium	650	1.74	Burns very brightly	2, 8, 2	Mg^{2+}
Iron	1535	7.87	Produces sparks if powdered	2, 8, 14, 2	Fe^{2+}, Fe^{3+}
Chromium	1860	7.19	Little reaction	2, 8, 13, 1	Cr^{2+}, Cr^{3+}
Sodium	98	0.97	Burns very brightly	2, 8, 1	Na^+

(a) The properties of iron and chromium are typical of transition metals.
The properties of magnesium and sodium are typical of Group 1 and 2 metals.
Suggest three differences between the two types of metal.
(3 marks)

(b) Give two further characteristic properties that distinguish transition metals from other metals.
(2 marks)

(c) Explain what causes the characteristic properties of the transition metals.
(1 mark)

CHEMISTRY 3I — ELEMENTS, ACIDS AND WATER

Acids and Alkalis

Theories about what makes an acid an acid, and a base a base, have <u>evolved</u> a bit over the years.

Arrhenius said acids *release hydrogen ions* in water

1) A guy called Arrhenius studied acids and bases in water. His theory was that when mixed with <u>water</u>, all acids release <u>hydrogen ions</u>, H⁺ (a H⁺ ion is a proton).

   Example:

   $$HCl_{(g)} + water \rightarrow H^+_{(aq)} + Cl^-_{(aq)}$$
   $$H_2SO_{4(l)} + water \rightarrow 2H^+_{(aq)} + SO_4^{2-}_{(aq)}$$

   But HCl <u>doesn't</u> release hydrogen ions <u>until</u> it meets water — so hydrogen chloride gas isn't an acid.

2) He also said that <u>alkalis</u> form OH⁻ ions (<u>hydroxide</u> ions) when in <u>water</u>.

   Example:

   $$\text{ammonia: } NH_{3(g)} + H_2O_{(l)} \rightarrow NH_4^+{}_{(aq)} + OH^-_{(aq)}$$

   Not all bases <u>dissolve</u> in water, but those that do are called <u>alkalis</u>.

The idea *only* worked for acids and bases that *dissolved in water*

Arrhenius' idea worked pretty well, <u>but</u> it only worked for acids and bases that dissolved in <u>water</u>. However, <u>ammonia gas</u> can react as a base even when it isn't dissolved in water, which was one reason why these ideas weren't immediately accepted. (A hypothesis is always less likely to be accepted when there are lots of <u>exceptions</u> which the hypothesis can't explain.)

Also, back in the 1880s when Arrhenius first suggested that molecules ionise in water, many scientists didn't think it was <u>possible</u>. <u>Charged subatomic particles</u> hadn't been <u>discovered yet</u>, so the idea of charged ions seemed <u>strange</u>. Scientists couldn't imagine how Cl⁻ could be different from Cl₂ gas.

Acids and Alkalis

Arrhenius had made a good start, but his theory couldn't explain <u>all</u> of the known facts. However, other scientists who followed him were able to use his ideas and <u>improve</u> on them.

Lowry and Brønsted said acids are proton donors

1) <u>Lowry and Brønsted</u> (working separately) made things a bit more general. They came up with definitions that work for both <u>soluble</u> and <u>insoluble</u> bases:

> <u>Acids</u> release H^+ ions — i.e. they're <u>proton donors</u>.
> <u>Bases</u> accept H^+ ions — i.e. they're <u>proton acceptors</u>.

In fact, it'd be more accurate to say that acids have their proton <u>taken away</u> from them.

2) These ideas were <u>readily accepted</u> because they explained the behaviour of acids and bases in solvents other than water.

3) Also, they were an <u>adaptation</u> of an idea which <u>already kind of worked</u>. When Arrhenius came up with his idea it was <u>totally new</u>, so people took more convincing.

Protons are hydrated in water

Anyway... for a substance to act as an acid or as a base, you <u>usually</u> need <u>water</u>. This is what happens...

In acidic solutions:

The acid molecules <u>dissociate</u>, releasing lots of <u>H^+ ions</u>. These H^+ ions (protons) become <u>hydrated</u> (surrounded by water molecules). The protons are now given the fancy name '<u>hydrated protons</u>' and can be represented by '<u>$H^+(aq)$</u>'. And it's these hydrated protons that make acids acidic, if you like.

In basic solutions:

Water molecules can <u>dissociate</u> into H^+ and OH^- ions, although they almost never do in pure water. But some base molecules, like ammonia (NH_3), can <u>take hydrogen ions</u> from water, causing more molecules to dissociate, and leaving an excess of OH^- ions behind. Other bases, like potassium hydroxide (KOH), <u>release hydroxide ions</u> straight into the solution.

This is an example of how theories gradually develop into facts

It's another example of how scientific knowledge progresses — lots of people contributing ideas to fit the <u>available evidence</u>. Some ideas are better than others, but usually the rubbish ones are quickly forgotten and you don't have to learn about those (e.g. acidic behaviour being due to magic pixies).

Acids and Alkalis

Acids can be *strong* or *weak*

1) Strong acids (e.g. sulfuric, hydrochloric and nitric) ionise almost completely in water. This means almost every hydrogen atom is released to become a hydrated proton (so there are loads of H⁺(aq) ions).

2) Weak acids (e.g. ethanoic, citric, carbonic) ionise only very slightly — only some of the hydrogen atoms in the compound are released — so only small numbers of H⁺(aq) ions are formed.

For example,

$$\text{Strong acid: } HCl + \text{water} \longrightarrow H^+ + Cl^-$$

$$\text{Weak acid: } H_2CO_3 + \text{water} \rightleftharpoons H^+ + HCO_3^-$$

Note the 'reversible reaction' symbol for a weak acid.

3) The pH of an acid or alkali is a measure of the concentration of H⁺(aq) ions in a solution. Strong acids typically have a pH of about 1 or 2, while the pH of a weak acid might be 4, 5 or 6.

4) The pH of an acid or alkali can be measured with a pH meter or with universal indicator paper (or can be estimated by seeing how fast a sample reacts with, say, magnesium).

5) There are strong and weak alkalis too. The hydroxides of sodium and potassium, KOH and NaOH, are strong (typically pH 13 or 14), while ammonia solution is a weak alkali (pH 9-10).

Don't confuse *strong* acids with *concentrated* acids

1) Acid strength (i.e. strong or weak) tells you what proportion of the acid molecules ionise in water.

2) The concentration of an acid is different. Concentration measures how many moles of acid molecules there are in a litre (1 dm³) of water. Concentration is basically how watered down your acid is.

3) Note that concentration describes the total number of acid molecules — not the number of molecules that release hydrogen ions.

4) The more moles of acid molecules per dm³, the more concentrated the acid is.

5) So you can have a dilute but strong acid, or a concentrated but weak acid.

Warm-Up and Exam Questions

Give these questions your best shot. It'll help boost your confidence for the exam.

Warm-Up Questions

1) When sulfuric acid, H_2SO_4, dissolves in water, what ions are found in the solution?
2) According to the ideas of Lowry and Brønsted, what is the definition of an acid?
3) Citric acid is an example of a weak acid. What is a weak acid?
4) Write the equation for the ionisation of ethanoic acid, CH_3COOH.
5) What is the difference between a strong acid and a concentrated acid?

Exam Questions

1 Ammonia dissolves in water to give a weak alkali.

(a) In the 1880s, Arrhenius proposed that when molecules are dissolved in water they can form ions. Copy and complete the ionic equation below to show how ammonia can dissolve in water to form a hydroxide ion.

NH_3 (g) + _____ (l) → _____ (aq) + OH^- (aq)

(2 marks)

(b) Arrhenius's ideas were not widely accepted at first. One reason was that ammonia can act as a base even when it is not dissolved in water. Explain how the ideas of Lowry and Brønsted in the 1920s showed why ammonia gas acts as a base.

(2 marks)

(c) Ammonia solution is a weak alkali. How are weak alkalis different from strong alkalis?

(2 marks)

2 In 1887 Arrhenius proposed new definitions of acids and alkalis. He used these definitions to explain the reactions between acids and alkalis.

(a) (i) What ion did Arrhenius suggest alkalis formed when they dissolved in water?

(1 mark)

   (ii) What ion did Arrhenius suggest acids formed when they dissolved in water?

(1 mark)

(b) Give one limitation of Arrhenius' theory.

(1 mark)

(c) Explain why scientists were reluctant to accept Arrhenius' ideas.

(1 mark)

Lowry and Brønsted broadened the definition of acids and bases.

(d) How did Lowry and Brønsted define acids and bases?

(1 mark)

(e) Give one reason why the Lowry and Brønsted theory was readily accepted.

(1 mark)

Concentration

A rather dull and boring page here. But at least there are some calculations on it.

Concentration *is a measure of how* crowded *things are*

The concentration of a solution can be measured in moles per dm^3 (i.e. moles per litre).
So 1 mole of stuff in 1 dm^3 of solution has a concentration of 1 mole per dm^3 (or 1 mol/dm^3).

The more solute you dissolve in a given volume, the more crowded the solute molecules are and the more concentrated the solution.

1 litre
= 1000 cm^3
= 1 dm^3

Concentration can also be measured in grams per dm^3. So 56 grams of stuff dissolved in 1 dm^3 of solution has a concentration of 56 grams per dm^3.

There's a calculation you can do to convert moles per dm^3 to grams per dm^3 (see next page). In the exam, look out for which one the question's asking for.

Concentration *= no. of moles ÷ volume*

Here's a nice formula triangle for you to learn:

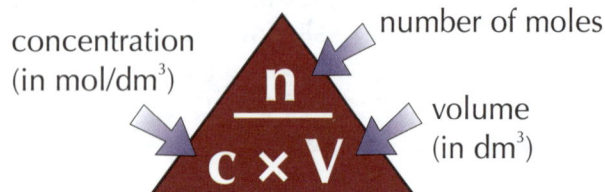

concentration (in mol/dm^3) — $\frac{n}{c \times V}$ — number of moles, volume (in dm^3)

One dm^3 is a litre.

concentration = no. of moles ÷ volume

Example 1:

What's the concentration of a solution with 2 moles of salt in 500 cm^3?

Answer: Easy — you've got the number of moles and the volume, so just use the formula...

Concentration = $\frac{2}{0.5}$ = 4 moles per dm^3

Convert the volume to litres (i.e. dm^3) first by dividing by 1000.

Example 2:

3 molar is sometimes written '3 M'.

How many moles of sodium chloride are in 250 cm^3 of a 3 molar solution of sodium chloride?

Answer: Well, 3 molar just means it's got 3 moles per dm^3. So using the formula...

Number of moles = concentration × volume = 3 × 0.25 = 0.75 moles

CHEMISTRY 3I — ELEMENTS, ACIDS AND WATER

Concentration

Converting *moles per dm³* to *grams per dm³* (and vice versa)

They might ask you to find out a concentration in grams per dm³. If they do, don't panic — you just need another formula triangle:

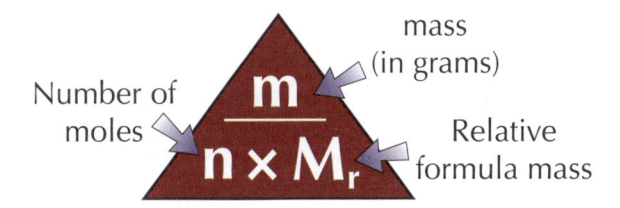

Formula triangle: $\dfrac{m}{n \times M_r}$ — m = mass (in grams), n = Number of moles, M_r = Relative formula mass

number of moles = mass ÷ relative formula mass

Example 1:

You have a solution of sulfuric acid of 0.04 mol/dm³. What is the concentration of this solution in GRAMS per dm³?

Step 1: Work out the relative formula mass for the solute
(you should be given the relative atomic masses, e.g. H = 1, S = 32, O = 16):
So, H_2SO_4 = (1 × 2) + 32 + (16 × 4) = 98

Step 2: Convert the concentration in moles into concentration in grams.
So, in 1 dm³: mass in grams = moles × relative formula mass = 0.04 × 98 = 3.92 g

So the concentration in g/dm³ = 3.92 g/dm³

Example 2:

The concentration of a solution of sulfuric acid is 19.6 grams/dm³. What is it in MOLES per dm³?

Step 1: The relative formula mass of H_2SO_4 = 98

Step 2: moles = mass in grams ÷ relative formula mass = 19.6 ÷ 98 = 0.2 moles

So the concentration in mol/dm³ = 0.2 mol/dm³

If you remember the formula triangles, the rest will follow

High concentration's like a whole rugby team in a mini. Or everyone in Britain on the Isle of Wight.
Low concentration's like a guy stranded on a desert island, or a small fish in a big lake. Poetic, no?

Indicators

You can test for H⁺ and OH⁻ ions — that is, acids and alkalis — by using indicators.

An *indicator* is just a *dye* that changes *colour*

The dye in an acid/base indicator changes colour depending on whether it's above or below a certain pH. Common indicators are:

1) Litmus

Testing for H^+(aq) and OH^-(aq) ions can be done using red or blue litmus indicator.

- Blue litmus turns red if lots of H^+(aq) ions are present — i.e. if the solution is an acid.
- Red litmus turns blue if lots of OH^-(aq) ions are present — i.e. if the solution is an alkali.

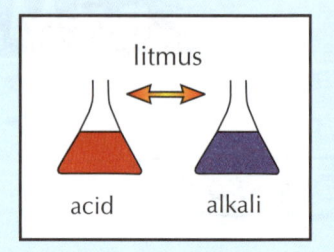

2) Methyl orange

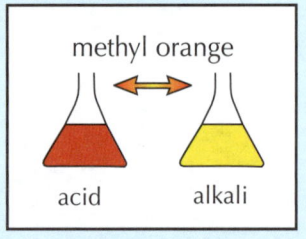

Methyl orange is yellow in alkalis but red in acids.

3) Phenolphthalein

Phenolphthalein is pink in alkalis but colourless in acids.

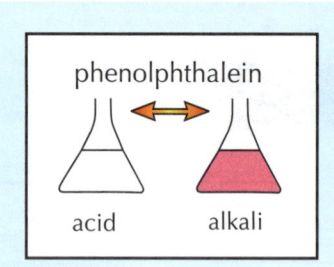

Universal indicator is useful for estimating pH

Universal indicator is a very useful combination of dyes which gives the colours shown below. It's very good for estimating the pH of a solution.

pH 1 2 3 4 5 6 7 8 9 10 11 12 13 14

CHEMISTRY 3I — ELEMENTS, ACIDS AND WATER

Titrations

Titrations have a bad reputation — but they're not as difficult as they're sometimes made out to be.

Titrations are used to find out concentrations

Titrations allow you to find out exactly how much acid is needed to neutralise a quantity of alkali (or vice versa). Here's how you do a titration...

1) Using a pipette and pipette filler, add some alkali (usually about 25 cm^3) to a conical flask, along with two or three drops of indicator.

2) Fill a burette with the acid. Make sure you do this BELOW EYE LEVEL — you don't want to be looking up if some acid spills over.

    You can also do titrations the other way round — adding alkali to acid.

3) Using the burette, add the acid to the alkali a bit at a time — giving the conical flask a regular swirl.

4) Go especially slowly when you think the end-point (colour change) is about to be reached.

5) The indicator changes colour when all the alkali has been neutralised. The indicator used depends on the strengths of the acid and the alkali.

   - Phenolphthalein is used for a weak acid and strong alkali
   - Methyl orange is used for a strong acid and weak alkali
   - If both the acid and alkali are strong any acid-base indicator can be used.

6) Record the volume of acid used to neutralise the alkali.

7) It's best to repeat this process a few times, making sure you get (pretty much) the same answer each time — this makes for more reliable results.

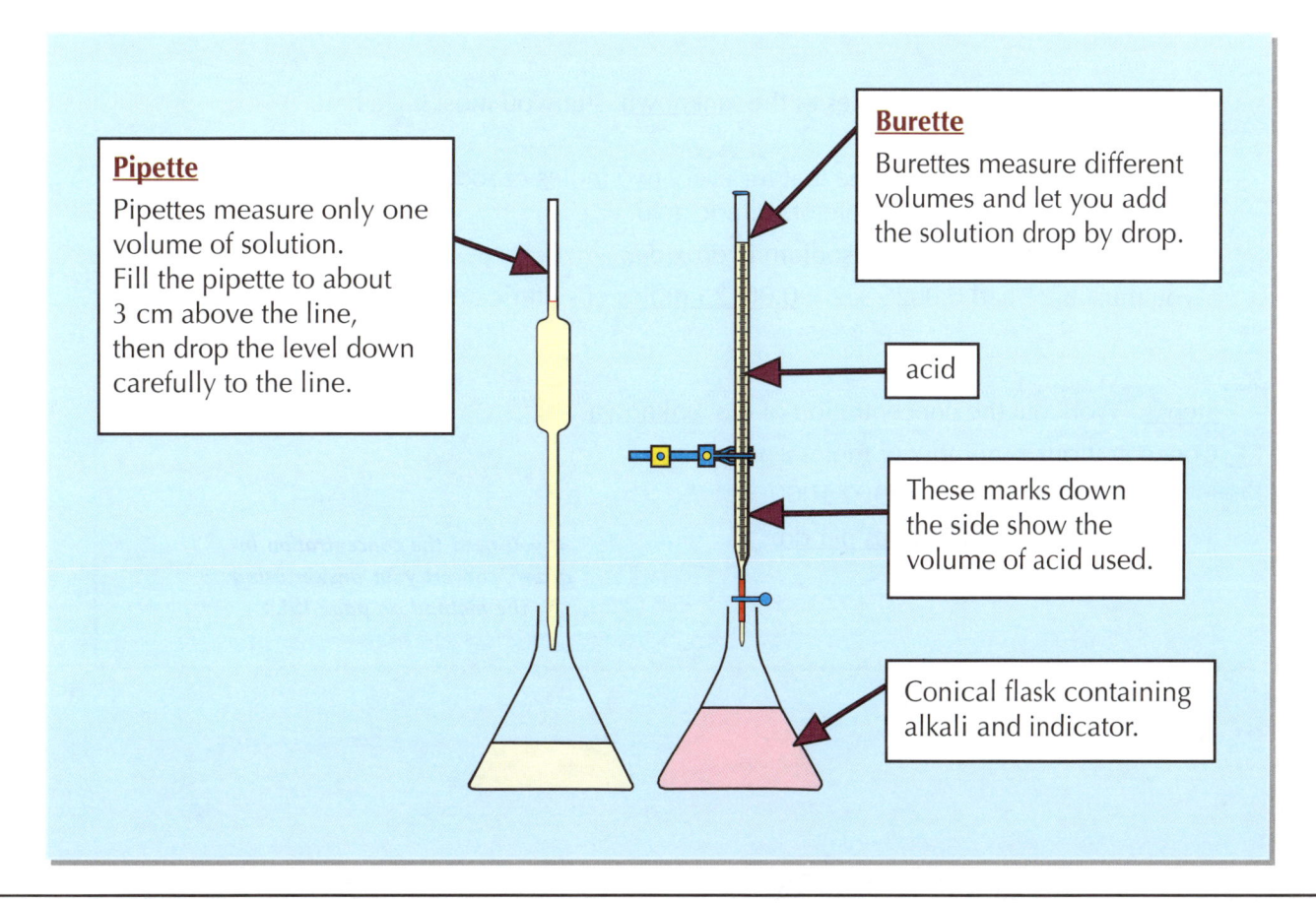

Pipette
Pipettes measure only one volume of solution.
Fill the pipette to about 3 cm above the line, then drop the level down carefully to the line.

Burette
Burettes measure different volumes and let you add the solution drop by drop.

acid

These marks down the side show the volume of acid used.

Conical flask containing alkali and indicator.

CHEMISTRY 31 — ELEMENTS, ACIDS AND WATER

Titration Calculations

Titrations are often done in order to find out the <u>concentration</u> of a mystery solution of an acid or alkali. If you can find out the <u>volume</u> needed to neutralise a known solution, then all you need to do is slot all the numbers into a handy formula. The example below should make everything clear.

The *calculation* — work out the *numbers of moles*

Here goes... basically, you're trying to find the <u>number of moles</u> of each substance.
A <u>formula triangle</u> is pretty handy here, I reckon.
(And it's the same one as on page 150, conveniently.)

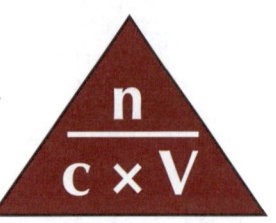

$$\frac{n}{c \times V}$$

Example:

Suppose you start off with <u>25 cm³</u> of sodium hydroxide in your flask, and you know that its concentration is <u>0.1 moles per dm³</u>.
You then find from your titration that it takes <u>30 cm³</u> of sulfuric acid (of an unknown concentration) to neutralise the sodium hydroxide.
Find the <u>concentration</u> of the acid.

<u>Step 1</u>: Work out how many <u>moles</u> of the 'known' substance you have:
number of moles = concentration × volume = 0.1 × (25 / 1000) = <u>0.0025 moles</u>

<u>Step 2</u>: Write down the <u>equation</u> for the reaction:
$2NaOH + H_2SO_4 \longrightarrow Na_2SO_4 + 2H_2O$

...and work out how many <u>moles</u> of the '<u>unknown</u>' stuff you must have had:

Using the equation, you can see that for every <u>two moles</u> of sodium hydroxide you had, there was just <u>one mole</u> of sulfuric acid.
So if you had <u>0.0025 moles</u> of sodium hydroxide...
...you must have had 0.0025 ÷ 2 = <u>0.00125 moles</u> of sulfuric acid.

<u>Step 3</u>: Work out the concentration of the '<u>unknown</u>' stuff.
Concentration = number of moles ÷ volume
= 0.00125 ÷ (30 / 1000)
= <u>0.0417 moles per dm³</u>

If you need the concentration in g/dm³, convert your answer using the method on page 151.

Warm-Up and Exam Questions

Come on now, don't look at me like that — it's a while since you had two pages of questions to do at once.

Warm-Up Questions

1) A solution has a volume of 0.15 litres. Convert this volume into cm³.
2) How many moles of hydrochloric acid are there in 25 cm³ of a 0.1 mol/dm³ solution?
3) A solution of sodium carbonate, Na_2CO_3, has a concentration of 2.65 g/dm³. What is the concentration of this solution in mol/dm³?
4) In an acid-base titration, what is the end-point?

Exam Questions

1   Paul works for a soft drinks manufacturer and is investigating the use of phosphoric acid, H_3PO_4, as a flavouring agent.

   (a) Paul prepares a solution of phosphoric acid by dissolving 4.9 g of the acid in 250 cm³ of water.

      (i) What is the concentration of the acid solution in g/dm³?

(1 mark)

      (ii) What is the concentration of the acid solution in mol/dm³?
Relative atomic masses: H = 1, P = 31, O = 16.

(2 marks)

   (b) Paul wants to prepare a phosphoric acid solution with a concentration of 0.1 mol/dm³. What mass of phosphoric acid should he dissolve in 1 dm³ of water?

(1 mark)

2   You are asked to find the concentration of a bottle of hydrochloric acid solution. Describe how you could use a titration method to find the concentration of the acid if you had a solution of sodium hydroxide of known concentration. Include names of special equipment needed for this procedure.

(5 marks)

3   In a titration, 27.5 cm³ of a solution of 0.1 mol/dm³ sodium hydroxide was required to neutralise 25 cm³ of a solution of hydrochloric acid.

   (a) Calculate the number of moles of sodium hydroxide used in the titration.

(2 marks)

   (b) Use the equation for the reaction shown below to work out the number of moles of hydrochloric acid used in the titration:

HCl (aq) + NaOH (aq) → NaCl (aq) + H_2O (l)

(1 mark)

   (c) Calculate the concentration of the hydrochloric acid solution.

(2 marks)

CHEMISTRY 31 — ELEMENTS, ACIDS AND WATER

Exam Questions

4. In a titration, 30.3 cm³ of a solution of 1.0 mol/dm³ sodium hydroxide was required to neutralise 25 cm³ of a solution of sulfuric acid.
   (a) Calculate the number of moles of sodium hydroxide used in the titration.
   (2 marks)
   (b) Work out the number of moles of sulfuric acid used in the titration.
   The equation is: $2NaOH\ (aq) + H_2SO_4\ (aq) \rightarrow Na_2SO_4\ (aq) + 2H_2O\ (l)$
   (1 mark)
   (c) Calculate the concentration of the sulfuric acid solution.
   (2 marks)

5. Jonah is concerned about the amount of acid in soft drinks. He decides to use a titration method to find the acid content of his favourite lemonade. He uses a solution of 0.1 mol/dm³ sodium hydroxide in titrations with 25 cm³ samples of the lemonade. His results are shown in the table.

	Initial burette reading (cm³)	Final burette reading (cm³)	Vol. of NaOH needed (cm³)
1	0.0	9.4	9.4
2	9.4	18.4	9.0
3	18.4	27.4	9.0

   Jonah calculates that the average volume of 0.1 mol/dm³ NaOH needed is 9.0 cm³.
   (a) The first titration value was not included in calculating the average. Why not?
   (1 mark)
   (b) The equation for the reaction in the titration can be written:
   $HA + NaOH \rightarrow NaA + H_2O$, where HA is the acid present in the lemonade.
   Calculate the concentration of acid HA present in the lemonade.
   (3 marks)
   (c) The calculated acid concentration in (b) is relatively high. However, this isn't a cause for too much concern. Use ideas about the properties of different acids in solution to explain why the high concentration isn't dangerous.
   (2 marks)

Water

Without water, there'd be no swimming, no cups of tea, no power showers — a nightmare. Plus you wouldn't even exist — you need water to live.

The water cycle means water is endlessly recycled

This stuff about the water cycle probably won't come as a complete surprise...

1) The Sun causes evaporation of water from the sea.

2) The water vapour is then carried upwards as the warm air rises.

3) As the water vapour rises it cools — due to the general cooling of the lower part of the atmosphere at higher altitudes.

4) This fall in temperature means the water condenses to form clouds.

5) When the condensed droplets get too big they fall as rain.

6) Then the water runs back to the sea.

7) As it does this, at some stage it's going to come into contact with the rocks on (or underneath) the ground — meaning that water in different places will dissolve different minerals.

8) Then the cycle starts over again.

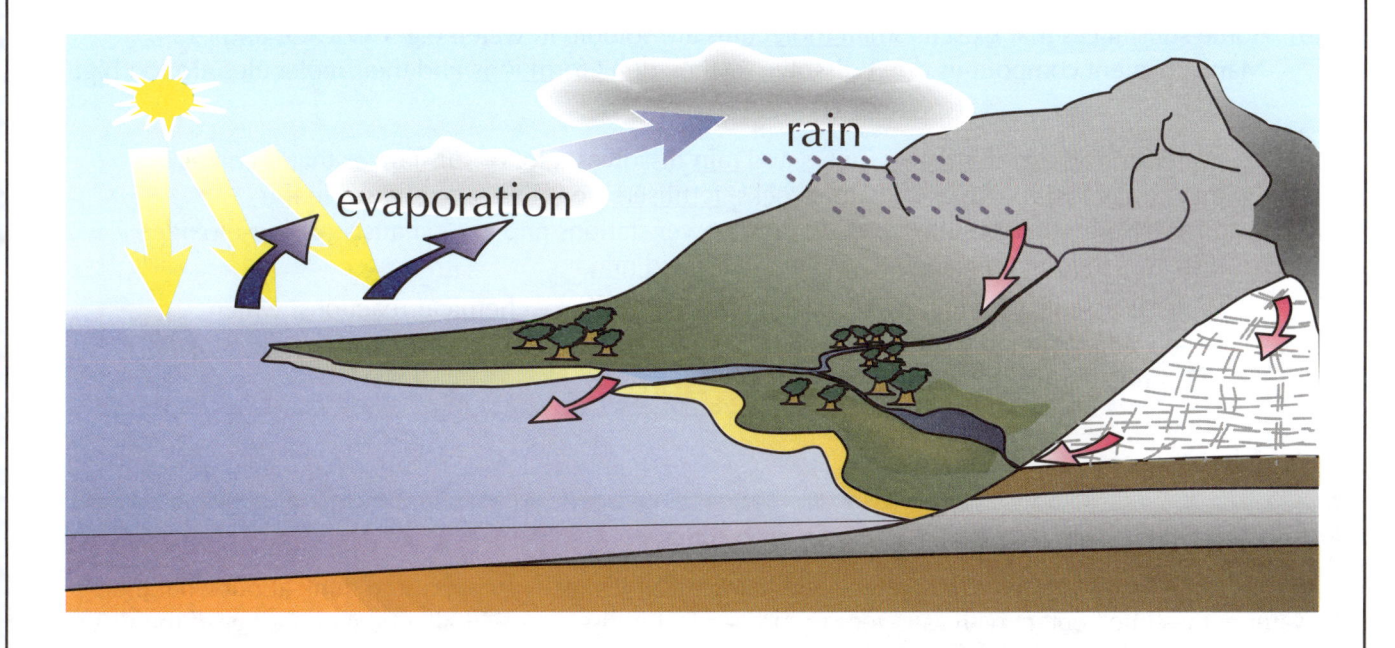

CHEMISTRY 31 — ELEMENTS, ACIDS AND WATER

Water

Water doesn't just dissolve minerals from the ground — in fact, it's known as the universal solvent.

Water's a solvent — it dissolves many other chemicals

So many substances dissolve in water that sometimes it's called the universal solvent.

1) Water dissolves most ionic compounds. Water molecules start to surround the ions and disrupt the ionic bonding, so the solid structure of the ionic compound gradually falls apart.

2) Water molecules are polar — they've got a positive hydrogen side and a negative oxygen side.

3) The slightly negative side attracts the positive ions and the slightly positive side attracts the negative ions.

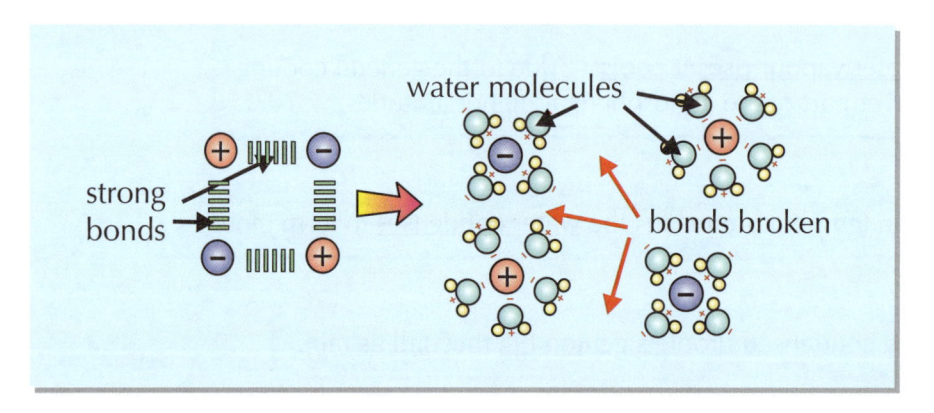

4) The following ionic compounds dissolve in water — LEARN them:

> a) Salts of SODIUM (Na), POTASSIUM (K) or AMMONIUM (NH_4). ALL of these dissolve.
> b) NITRATES (NO_3). ALL of these dissolve. *Plus there are one or two others, but you don't need to know about them.*
> c) CHLORIDES (Cl), except for silver and lead.
> d) SULFATES (SO_4), except for barium and lead. Calcium sulfate is only slightly soluble.

5) Some substances that exist as small molecules are soluble in water, e.g. CO_2, SO_2 and Cl_2. Many covalent compounds don't dissolve — they don't form ions and their molecules are too big.

> Water in the form of streams, rivers and rain dissolves a lot of substances that it comes into contact with — e.g. salts from rocks, fertilisers from fields, and gases in the atmosphere, such as sulfur dioxide from power stations and car exhausts. Sulfur dioxide dissolves to form an acid, which can fall as acid rain.
>
> Water is essential for life. Life is a complicated bunch of chemical reactions, which largely take place in solution in water. Many important biological chemicals like sugars, salts and amino acids dissolve in water.

Round and round and round it goes

You've more than likely seen the water cycle before. But it's really important to think about what the water comes into contact with as it goes round — what it dissolves will affect the properties of the water. You'll have to learn the rules for which ionic compounds dissolve, I'm afraid. No easy shortcuts.

Water Quality

It's easy to take water for granted... turn on the tap, and there it is — nice, clean water. The water you drink has been round the block a few times though — so there's some fancy chemistry needed to make it drinkable.

Drinking water needs to be good quality

Water is essential for life, but it must be free of poisonous salts (for example, phosphates and nitrates) and harmful microorganisms. Microorganisms in drinking water can cause diseases such as cholera and dysentery.

Most of our drinking water comes from reservoirs. Water flows into reservoirs from rivers and ground-water — water companies choose to build reservoirs where there's a good supply of clean water. Government agencies keep a close eye on pollution in reservoirs, rivers and ground-water.

Water from reservoirs is treated at the water treatment works

1) The water passes though a mesh screen to remove big bits like twigs.

2) Next, it's treated with ozone or chlorine to kill microorganisms.

3) Chemicals are added to make solids and microorganisms stick together and fall to the bottom. Sometimes iron is added to remove dissolved phosphates. Bacteria are used to remove nitrates.

4) The water is filtered through gravel beds to remove all the solids. Nasty tastes and odours can also be removed by passing the water through "activated carbon" filters or with "carbon slurry".

5) The pH is corrected if the water is too acidic or too alkaline.

6) Water is chlorinated to kill off any harmful microorganisms left.

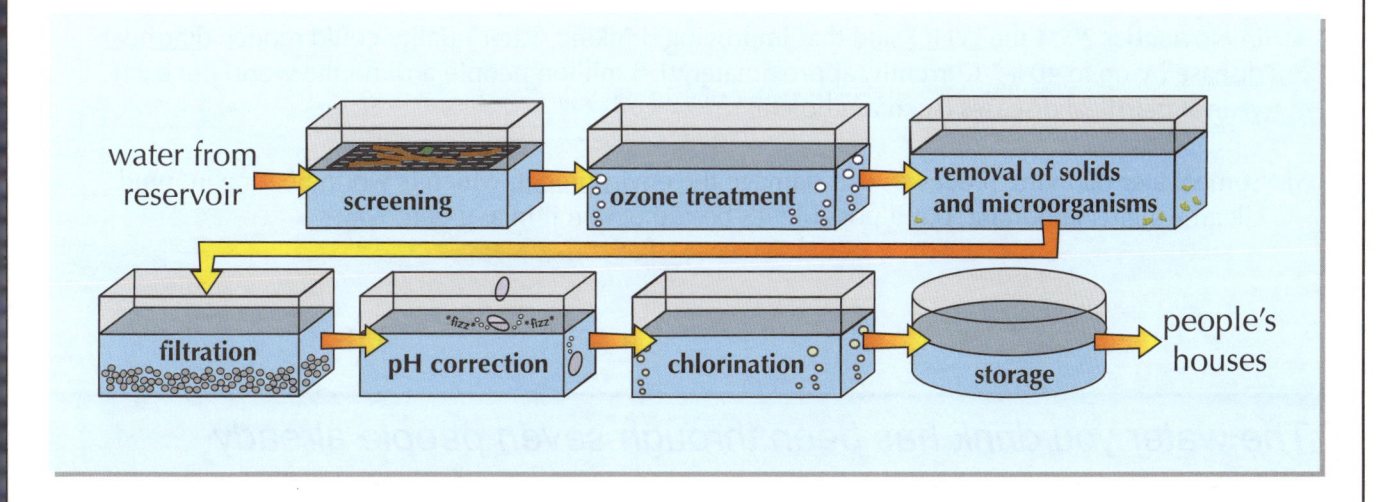

CHEMISTRY 31 — ELEMENTS, ACIDS AND WATER

Water Quality

The only way to get totally pure water is by distillation. So how come they don't do that...?

Water quality is constantly monitored

To monitor water quality, water companies take samples of water — from the water entering the treatment works right though to the taps in consumers' houses.

> Some people still aren't satisfied. They buy filters that contain carbon or silver to remove substances from their tap water. Carbon in the filters removes the chlorine taste and silver is supposed to kill bugs.
>
> Some people in hard water areas buy water softeners which contain ion exchange resins (see page 165 for more on this).

Totally pure water with nothing dissolved in it can be produced by distillation — boiling water to make steam and condensing the steam. But this process is too expensive to use for producing tap water — bags of energy would be needed to boil all the water we use (which wouldn't be great for the environment either). Distilled water is used in chemistry labs though.

You'd use pure water to make a solution of (say) KBr, because you wouldn't want any other ions mucking it up.

Clean water is essential for life

1) Not everyone has clean water. The World Health Organisation (WHO) and the United Nations estimated in 1995 that a billion people in the world don't have access to clean drinking water.

2) In many developing countries it's very expensive to get clean water. Some people in developing countries live in isolated rural areas, and have to walk miles to get any water at all.

3) It's a fact that the biggest increases in life expectancy in most countries' histories (including the UK's) are linked with the ability to supply clean water — not with medical advances or anything like that. Clean water is that vital.

4) In November 2004 the WHO said that improving drinking water quality could reduce diarrheal disease by up to 40%. Currently, approximately 1.8 million people around the world die each year of diarrheal diseases (such as cholera).

5) Some water purifying processes can damage the environment, which is worth bearing in mind. Clean water is important, but if possible it's best to obtain it in a 'green' way.

The water you drink has been through seven people already

Well, it's possible. It's also possible that the water you're drinking used to be part of the Atlantic Ocean. Or it could have been drunk by Alexander the Great. Or been part of an Alpine glacier. It gets about a bit, does water. And remember... tap water isn't pure — but it's drinkable, and that's the main thing.

Warm-Up and Exam Questions

Warm-Up Questions

1) By what process does water in the oceans become water vapour in the atmosphere?
2) What property of water molecules makes water a good solvent for ionic compounds?
3) Why is drinking water treated by filtration?
4) Why is drinking water treated with chlorine?
5) How can totally pure water be produced?

Exam Questions

1   (a) The diagram shows a simple form of the water cycle. Write down three words to fill in the blanks (1), (2) and (3) in the diagram.

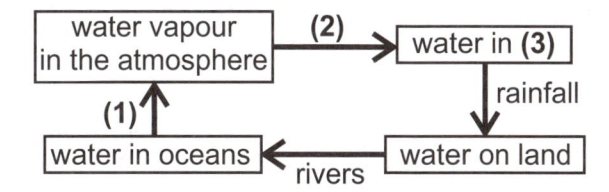

water vapour in the atmosphere —(2)→ water in (3)
(1) ↑ ↓ rainfall
water in oceans ←rivers— water on land

(3 marks)

(b) Rainwater is relatively pure, but seawater contains large amounts of dissolved substances. Explain how these dissolved substances enter the water.

(2 marks)

2   Kate is investigating the solubility of potassium nitrate in water.

(a) She finds that potassium nitrate dissolves readily in water. What does this suggest about the type of bonding found in potassium nitrate?

(1 mark)

(b) Kate then investigated how the solubility of potassium nitrate in water is affected by temperature. She recorded her results in a table:

Temperature (°C)	20	30	40	50	60
Solubility (g/100g water)	30	45	65	85	110

What is the relationship between the temperature and the solubility?

(1 mark)

CHEMISTRY 3I — ELEMENTS, ACIDS AND WATER

Solubility

Something is soluble if it dissolves — like sugar when you put it in tea (hurrah).
Something is insoluble if it doesn't dissolve — like sand when you put it in tea (boo, hiss).

All gases are soluble — to some extent, anyway

1) "Chlorine water" is (unsurprisingly) a solution of chlorine gas in water. It's used as bleach in the paper and textile industries, and also to sterilise water supplies (it kills bacteria).

2) The amount of gas that dissolves depends on the pressure of the gas above it — the higher the pressure, the more gas there is dissolving.

> Fizzy drinks initially contain a lot of carbon dioxide dissolved in water (carbonated water). But when you take the cap off, the pressure's released and a lot of the carbon dioxide fizzes out of solution.

3) But... gases become less soluble as the temperature of the solvent increases, which is exactly the opposite of solids (see the next page).

> Aquatic life needs dissolved oxygen, but oxygen levels in rivers can be lowered by pollution and a rise in temperature (caused by warm water discharged from towns and industry).

Solubility — learn the proper definitions

> The solubility of a substance in a given solvent is the number of grams of the solute (usually a solid) that dissolve in 100 g of the solvent (the liquid) at a particular temperature.

E.g. at room temperature (20 °C), about 36 g of sodium chloride (NaCl) will dissolve in 100 g of water.

> The solubility of (solid) solutes usually increases with temperature.

E.g. at 60 °C, about 37 g of sodium chloride (NaCl) will dissolve in 100 g of water.

> A saturated solution is one that cannot hold any more solid at that temperature — and you have to be able to see solid on the bottom to be certain that it's saturated.

Solubility

Solubility curves are useful for investigating how much solid can dissolve in a particular solution.

Solubility curves show when a solution is saturated

1) A solubility curve plots the mass of solute dissolved in a saturated solution at various temperatures.

2) The solubility of most solids increases as the temperature increases.

3) This means that cooling a saturated solution will usually cause some solid to crystallise out — that means it separates from the solution.

4) The mass of crystals formed by cooling a solution a certain amount can be calculated from a solubility curve...

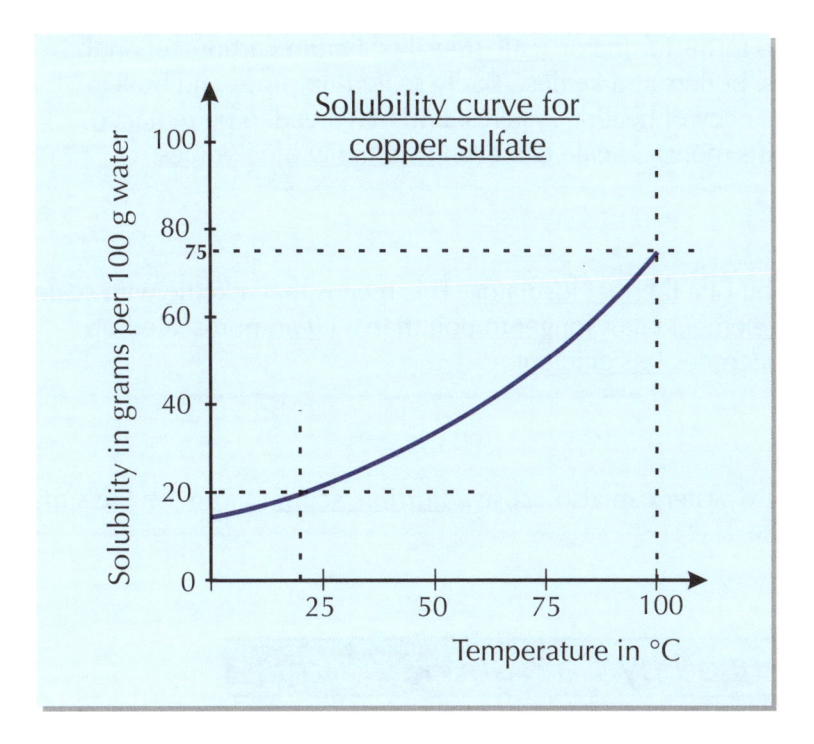

Solubility curve for copper sulfate

Draw lines perpendicular to both axes through the temperatures in the question, then subtract the smaller mass from the larger — that difference will precipitate out on cooling.
This graph is for 100 g of water — so if you had 1000 g of water instead, you'd just multiply your answer by 10. Simple.

Example:

What mass of solid copper sulfate will crystallise out when a saturated solution containing 100 g of water is cooled from 100 °C to 20 °C?

Answer: 75 g − 20 g = **55 g**

CHEMISTRY 31 — ELEMENTS, ACIDS AND WATER

Hard Water

The water in your part of the country might be hard or soft — it depends on the rocks rainwater passes through on its way to you. With soft water, you get a nice lather with soap. Not so with hard water...

Hard water makes scum and scale

1) Hard water won't easily form a lather with soap (non-soap detergents aren't affected) — you get a nasty scum instead. So to get a decent lather you need to use more soap. The problem is the 'hardness minerals' (see below) in the hard water reacting with the soap.

2) Hard water also forms furring or scale (mostly calcium carbonate) on the insides of pipes, boilers and kettles. Badly scaled-up pipes and boilers reduce the efficiency of heating systems, and may need to be replaced — all of which costs money. Scale can even eventually block pipes.

3) Scale is also a bit of a thermal insulator. This means that a kettle with scale on the heating element takes longer to boil than a clean non-scaled-up kettle — so it becomes less efficient.

4) Worst of all, hard water can also cause a horrible scum to form on the surface of tea.

Hardness is caused by Ca^{2+} and Mg^{2+} ions

1) Most hard water is hard because it contains lots of calcium and magnesium ions. You get hard water in certain areas because of the type of rocks there. Hardness often comes from limestone, chalk and gypsum.

2) For instance, rain falling on some types of rocks can dissolve magnesium sulfate (which is soluble), and calcium sulfate (which is also soluble, though only a bit).

3) Other calcium and magnesium salts come from a reaction. When carbon dioxide from the air dissolves in rainwater, you get carbonic acid ($CO_2 + H_2O \rightarrow H_2CO_3$) — so rainwater is slightly acidic. Then if there's calcium carbonate ($CaCO_3$) in the rocks, calcium hydrogencarbonate is formed ($H_2CO_3 + CaCO_3 \rightarrow Ca(HCO_3)_2$), which is soluble. It's similar with rocks containing $MgCO_3$.

Hard Water

Hard water *isn't all bad*

1) Ca^{2+} ions are good for healthy teeth and bones.

2) And scale inside pipes forms a protective coating. It stops poisonous metal ions, e.g. Pb^{2+} and Cu^{2+} (from lead and copper pipes) getting into drinking water. It also protects iron pipes from rust.

Remove **hardness** by removing **dissolved Ca^{2+} and Mg^{2+}** ions

1) By adding sodium carbonate.
   The carbonate ions join onto the calcium or magnesium ions and make an insoluble precipitate.

   $$\text{e.g.} \quad Ca^{2+}_{(aq)} + CO_3^{2-}_{(aq)} \rightarrow CaCO_{3(s)}$$

2) By 'ion exchange columns'. Sometimes a water supply is fed through an ion exchange column to remove the hardness. These clever bits of chemistry have lots of sodium ions (or hydrogen ions) and 'exchange' them for calcium or magnesium ions in the water that runs through them.

   $$\text{e.g.} \quad Na_2Resin_{(s)} + Ca^{2+}_{(aq)} \rightarrow CaResin_{(s)} + 2Na^+_{(aq)}$$

   ('Resin' is a huge insoluble resin molecule.)

3) Scale is mainly just calcium carbonate, and can be dissolved by acid. Most descaling products that you buy to clean your kettle out are some kind of acid.

And if the water's really hard, you can chip your teeth...

Hard water — good thing or bad thing... Well, it provides minerals that are good for health, but it creates an awful lot of unnecessary expense. In hard water areas, you need more soap to get a lather, it takes longer (and therefore more electricity) to boil water (as heating elements get furred up), and you need to get your pipes replaced more often. It's a bit of a drag. But you still need to learn it.

Warm-Up and Exam Questions

Almost done with this section. Just a few more questions to get stuck into.

Warm-Up Questions

1) What is the relationship between water temperature and the solubility of gases in the water?
2) What is the relationship between water temperature and the solubility of solids in the water?
3) What is a saturated solution?
4) What is hard water?

Exam Questions

1   Charlie works for a food company and investigated the solubility of a sweetener, compound X, in water. The solubility curve for compound X is shown on the graph.

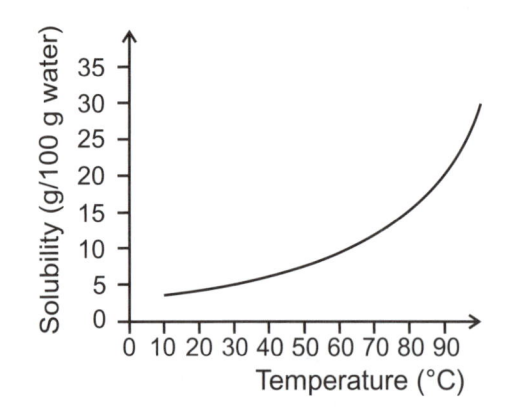

    (a) Why does Charlie not record any data for temperatures above 100 °C?

(1 mark)

    (b) What is the maximum mass of X that can dissolve in 100 g of water at 25 °C?

(1 mark)

    (c) Charlie has a beaker containing 250 g of water at 80 °C. What is the maximum mass of compound X that Charlie will be able to dissolve in this water?

(2 marks)

    (d) What mass of solid compound X will crystallise out when a saturated solution of compound X in 100 g of water is cooled from 90 °C to 10 °C?

(2 marks)

2   Hard water in many areas is caused by dissolved Ca^{2+} ions.
    (a) Give two disadvantages of living in a hard water area.

(2 marks)

    (b) Give two advantages of living in a hard water area.

(2 marks)

Revision Summary for Chemistry 3(i)

Bit of a mixed bag — one minute you're pondering the periodic table, the next you're worrying about how many millions of people are without clean drinking water. The one thing that's constant and unchanging is the need to learn it all for the exam you've got coming up. So test yourself on these little beauties.

1) Before 1800, how were elements classified?
2) Give two reasons why Newlands' Octaves were criticised.
3) Why did Mendeleev leave gaps in his Table of Elements?
4) How many electrons can fit into energy level 2? How many in energy level 3?
5) What is shielding?
6) Explain why Group 7 elements get less reactive as you go down the group from fluorine to iodine.
7) As you go down Group I, what's the trend in: a) reactivity, b) density, c) melting point?
8) Write down the balanced equation for the reaction between sodium and water.
9) Describe the physical properties of: a) chlorine, b) bromine, c) iodine.
10) Do halogens do covalent bonding, ionic bonding, or both?
11)* Write down the balanced equation for the reaction between iron and chlorine gas.
12) Will the following reactions occur: a) iodine with lithium chloride, b) chlorine with lithium bromide?
13) Describe the physical properties of a typical transition metal.
14) Give an industrial use for transition metals.
15) Write down the electron configuration of: a) titanium, b) cobalt, c) zinc.
16) Briefly write down Arrhenius's theory about acids and bases.
17) Why weren't scientists willing to accept the ideas of Arrhenius at first?
18) What is the Brønsted/Lowry definition of an acid? Why were their ideas more readily accepted?
19) What's the difference between a weak acid and a strong acid?
20)* Name a suitable indicator you could use in the titration of potassium hydroxide into ethanoic acid.
21)* In a titration, 49 cm^3 of hydrochloric acid was required to neutralise 25 cm^3 of sodium hydroxide with a concentration of 0.2 moles per dm^3. Calculate the concentration of the hydrochloric acid in: a) mol/dm^3 b) g/dm^3
22)* Calculate the concentration of the solution formed when 7.5 g of calcium hydroxide, Ca(OH)$_2$, is dissolved in: a) 1 dm^3 of water, b) 100 cm^3 of water.
23) Explain why water vapour condenses and falls as rain.
24) Sea water contains dissolved minerals. Where do these come from?
25)* Which of the following will dissolve in water? a) Lead nitrate, b) PbCl, c) ammonium chloride, d) potassium sulfate, e) AgSO$_4$, f) silver chloride, g) CuSO$_4$, h) barium sulfate, i) Ba(NO$_3$)$_2$.
26) What is a saturated solution?
27)* The graph shows the solubility of lead nitrate in 100 g of water.
   a) How much lead nitrate will dissolve in 100 g of water at 40 °C?
   b) At what temperature will 70 g of lead nitrate dissolve in 100 g of water?
   c) What mass of solid lead nitrate will crystallise when a saturated solution containing 100 g of water is cooled from 60 °C to 40 °C?
28) Why does a bottle of lemonade fizz up when you open it?
29) What are the main ions that cause water hardness?
30) Give two methods of removing hardness from water.
31) How are microorganisms removed from drinking water?
32) Tap water is not pure water. Why don't we make sure that all our drinking water is pure water?
33) Give an example of the social and economic consequences of poor water quality.

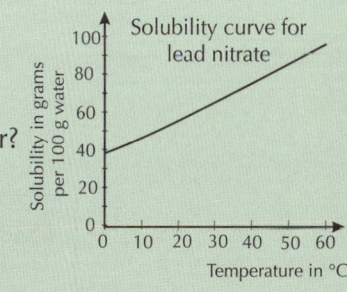

*Answers on page 244-245.

Energy

Whenever chemical reactions occur, there are changes in energy. This is kind of interesting if you think of the number of chemical reactions that are involved in everyday life.

Reactions are **exothermic** or **endothermic**

See page 172 for more info.

An EXOTHERMIC reaction is one which gives out energy to the surroundings, usually in the form of heat and usually shown by a rise in temperature.

E.g. fuels burning or neutralisation reactions.

An ENDOTHERMIC reaction is one which takes in energy from the surroundings, usually in the form of heat and usually shown by a fall in temperature.

E.g. photosynthesis.

Energy transfer can be **measured**

1) You can measure the amount of energy produced by a chemical reaction (in solution) by taking the temperature of the reagents (making sure they're the same), mixing them in a polystyrene cup and measuring the temperature of the solution at the end of the reaction. Easy.

2) The biggest problem with energy measurements is the amount of energy lost to the surroundings.

3) You can reduce it a bit by putting the polystyrene cup into a beaker of cotton wool to give more insulation, and putting a lid on the cup to reduce energy lost by evaporation.

4) This method works for reactions of solids with water (e.g. dissolving ammonium nitrate in water) as well as with neutralisation reactions.

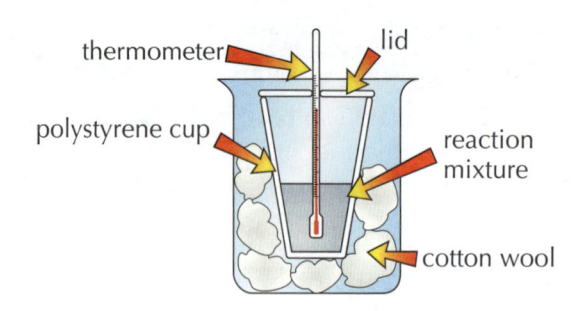

Example:
1) Place 25 cm³ of dilute hydrochloric acid in a polystyrene cup, and record the temperature of the acid.
2) Put 25 cm³ of dilute sodium hydroxide in a measuring cylinder and record its temperature.
3) Add the alkali to the acid and stir.
4) Take the temperature of the mixture every 30 seconds, and record the highest temperature it reaches.

Energy

*Energy must always be **supplied** to **break bonds**...*
*...and energy is always **released** when **bonds form***

1) During a chemical reaction, old bonds are broken and new bonds are formed.

2) Energy must be supplied to break existing bonds — so bond breaking is an endothermic process. Energy is released when new bonds are formed — so bond formation is an exothermic process.

BOND BREAKING – ENDOTHERMIC

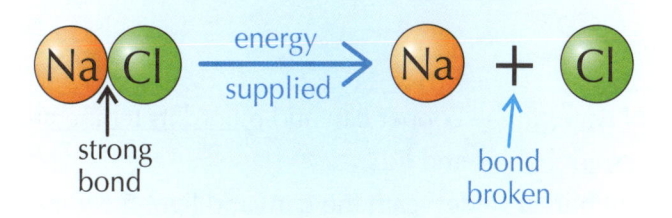

Na–Cl →(energy supplied)→ Na + Cl
(strong bond) (bond broken)

BOND FORMING – EXOTHERMIC

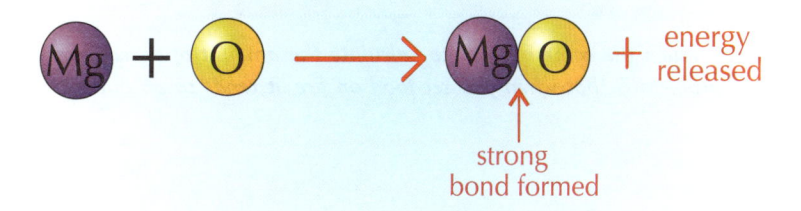

Mg + O → MgO + energy released
(strong bond formed)

3) In an endothermic reaction, the energy required to break old bonds is greater than the energy released when new bonds are formed.

4) In an exothermic reaction, the energy released in bond formation is greater than the energy used in breaking old bonds.

Save energy — break fewer bonds...

You can get cooling packs that use an endothermic reaction to draw heat from an injury. The pack contains two compartments with different chemicals in. When you use it, you snap the partition and the chemicals mix and react, taking in heat — pretty cool, I reckon (no pun intended).

CHEMISTRY 3II — ENERGY AND CHEMICAL TESTS

Energy and Fuels

We burn fuels, and they release energy — so this is an exothermic process.
Just how exothermic you can find by calorimetry. Bet you can't wait...

Fuel energy is calculated using calorimetry

To measure the amount of energy produced when a fuel is burnt, you can simply burn the fuel and use the flame to heat up some water. Of course, this has to have a fancy chemistry name — calorimetry. Calorimetry uses a metal container, usually made of copper because copper conducts heat so well.

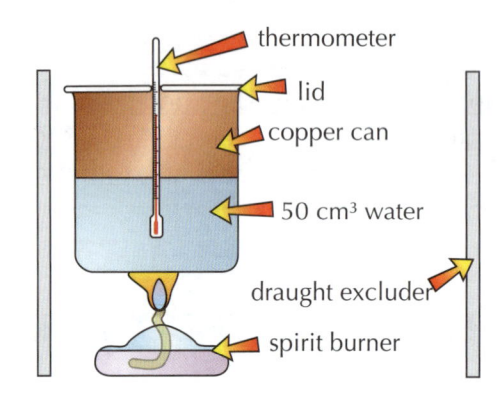

Diagram labels: thermometer, lid, copper can, 50 cm³ water, draught excluder, spirit burner

Method:
1) Put 50 g of water in the copper can and record its temperature.
2) Weigh the spirit burner and lid.
3) Put the spirit burner underneath the can, and light the wick. Heat the water, stirring constantly, until the temperature reaches about 50 °C.
4) Put out the flame using the burner lid, and measure the final temperature of the water.
5) Weigh the spirit burner and lid again.

You can use pretty much the same method to calculate the amount of energy produced by foods. The only problem is that when you set food on fire, it tends to go out after a bit.

Example: to work out the energy per gram of methylated spirit (meths):
Mass of spirit burner + lid before heating = 68.75 g
Mass of spirit burner + lid after heating = 67.85 g   ➡ Mass of meths burnt = 0.90 g
Temperature of water in copper can before heating = 21.5 °C
Temperature of water in copper can after heating = 52.5 °C   ➡ Temperature rise of 50 g of water due to heating = 31.0 °C

So 0.90 g of fuel produces enough energy to heat up 50 g of water by 31 °C.
It takes 4.2 joules of energy to heat up 1 g of water by 1 °C. ⬅ You'll be told this in the exam.
Therefore, the energy produced in this experiment = 4.2 × 50 × 31 = 6510 joules.
So 0.9 g of meths produces 6510 joules of energy...
... meaning 1 g of meths produces 6510/0.9 = 7233 J or 7.233 kJ

Energy's wasted heating the can, air, etc. — so this figure will often be much lower than the actual energy content.

Energy and Fuels

Different fuels produce different amounts of energy

This table shows some common fuels.

Fuel	Energy (kJ/g)
Hydrogen	143
Methane (natural gas)	56
Butane	50
Petrol	49
Meths	30

Fuels provide energy — but there are consequences

- Fuels release energy which we use in loads of ways — e.g. to generate electricity, to heat our houses, and to power cars, lorries, trains, planes, etc. So, hurrah for fuels.

- Burning fuels has various effects on the environment. Burning fossil fuels releases CO_2, a greenhouse gas.

- This causes global warming and other types of climate change. It'll be expensive to slow down these effects, and to put things right. Developing alternative energy sources (e.g. tidal power) costs money.

- The price of crude oil has a big economic effect. We use a lot of fuels made from crude oil (e.g. petrol and diesel). When the price of oil goes up, they get more expensive — everything that's transported by lorry, train or plane gets more expensive too. The price of oil is linked to the supply (the less there is, the dearer it gets), and there isn't a bottomless supply of oil. Same goes for natural gas, and coal.

Energy from fuels — it's a burning issue...

Alrighty. A bit of method, a few sums and some social 'n' environmental gubbins to round it off. Fuel never seems so important as when you're running out of it — power cuts and petrol shortages get folk more than a tad ticked off. Crude oil will run out one day for sure, which is a bit of a scary thought.

Bond Energies

You already know what's meant by exothermic and endothermic — now things get a bit more technical.

Energy level diagrams show if it's exo- or endothermic

In exothermic reactions, ΔH is –ve

1) This shows an exothermic reaction — the products are at a lower energy than the reactants. The difference in height represents the energy given out in the reaction (per mole). ΔH is negative here.

2) The initial rise in the line represents the energy needed to break the old bonds. This is the activation energy.

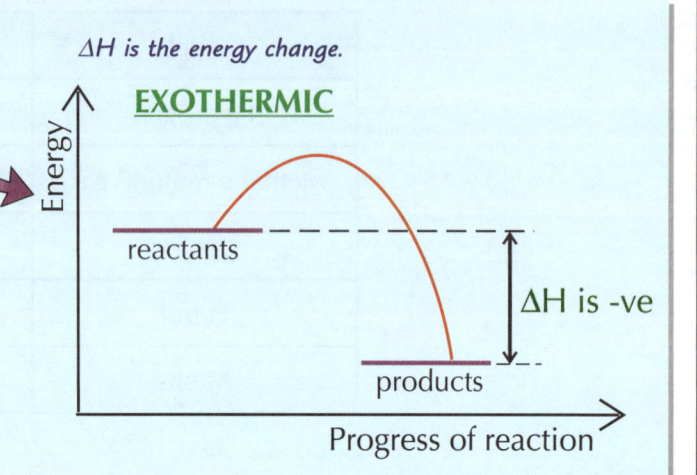

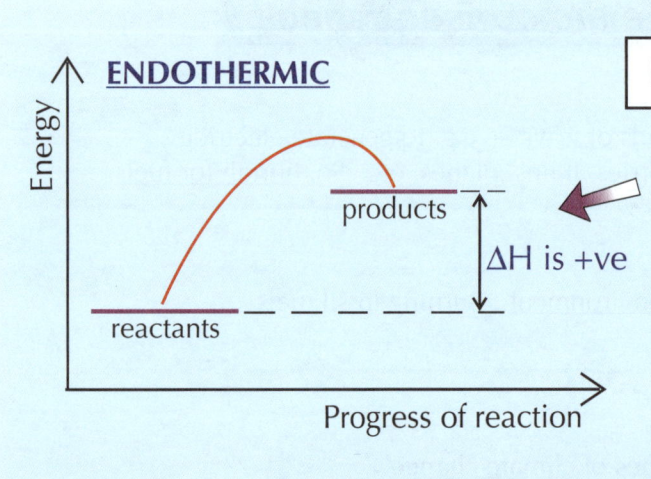

ΔH is the energy change.

EXOTHERMIC — graph showing reactants at higher energy, curve rising to peak then falling to products at lower energy, with ΔH is -ve marked between reactants and products levels. Axes: Energy (vertical), Progress of reaction (horizontal).

ENDOTHERMIC — graph showing reactants at lower energy, curve rising to peak then falling to products at higher energy, with ΔH is +ve marked. Axes: Energy (vertical), Progress of reaction (horizontal).

In endothermic reactions, ΔH is +ve

1) This shows an endothermic reaction because the products are at a higher energy than the reactants, so ΔH is positive.

2) The difference in height represents the energy taken in during the reaction.

The activation energy is lowered by catalysts

1) The activation energy represents the minimum energy needed by reacting particles for the reaction to occur.

2) A catalyst makes reactions happen easier (and therefore quicker) by reducing the initial energy needed.

3) This is represented by the lower curve on the diagram showing a lower activation energy.

4) The overall energy change for the reaction, ΔH, remains the same though.

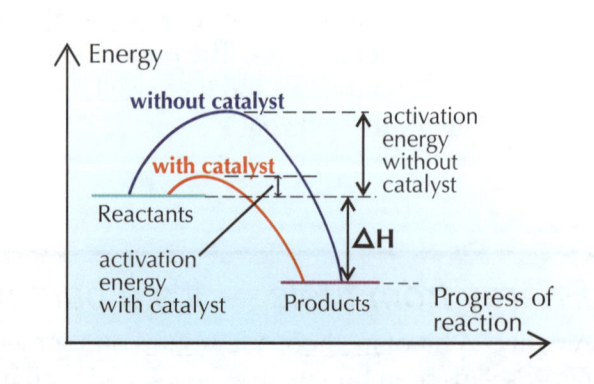

Graph showing two curves — "without catalyst" (higher peak) and "with catalyst" (lower peak) — between Reactants and Products levels, with activation energy without catalyst, activation energy with catalyst, and ΔH labelled. Axes: Energy (vertical), Progress of reaction (horizontal).

Bond Energies

You need to be able to work out ΔH for a particular reaction.

Bond energy calculations need to be practised

1) Every chemical bond has a particular bond energy associated with it.

2) This bond energy varies slightly depending on the compound the bond occurs in — but don't worry, you'll be given any you need to use in the exam.

3) You can use these known bond energies to calculate the overall energy change for a reaction.

You need to practise a few of these, but the basic idea is really very simple...

Example: The formation of HCl

Using known bond energies you can calculate the energy change for this reaction:

$$H_2 + Cl_2 \rightarrow 2HCl$$

The bond energies you need are:
- H—H: +436 kJ/mol
- Cl—Cl: +242 kJ/mol
- H—Cl: +431 kJ/mol

1) Breaking one mole of H—H and one mole of Cl—Cl bonds requires:
   436 + 242 = 678 kJ
2) Forming two moles of H—Cl bonds releases 2 × 431 = 862 kJ.
3) Overall more energy is released than is used to form the products:
   862 − 678 = 184 kJ/mol released.
4) Since this is energy released, if you wanted to show ΔH you'd need to put a negative sign in front of it to indicate that it's an exothermic reaction, like this:

$$\Delta H = -184 \text{ kJ/mol}$$

You're given the bond energies, but you must know how to use them

I admit — it's a bit like maths, this. But think how many times you've heard energy efficiency mentioned over the last few years. Well, this kind of calculation is used in working out whether we're using resources efficiently or not. So even if it's not exciting, it's useful at least.

CHEMISTRY 3ⁱⁱ — ENERGY AND CHEMICAL TESTS

Energy and Food

You (and me as well, I'm told) are just a mass of chemical reactions. You take in fuel (food), and convert the energy it contains. That's what you do. Among other things.

Food energy is often measured in calories and kilocalories

1) Back on p.170, the calorimetry calculation for the amount of energy in a fuel gives the answer in joules. The joule is the standard unit of energy used by all scientists, and it replaced an older unit of energy called the calorie.

   1 calorie = amount of energy needed to raise the temp of 1 g of water by 1 °C. 1 calorie = 4.2 joules.

2) The dietary information on food labels is in kilocalories (kilo- means 1000, remember). Confusingly, on food labels they don't usually write it as "kilocalorie" or "kcal". That would be far too straightforward. They usually write it as Calorie, with a capital C.

   1 Calorie (big-C) = amount of energy needed to raise the temp of 1 KILOGRAM of water by 1 °C.
   1 Calorie = 4200 joules.

You get your energy from food

As with all fuels, different foods produce different amounts of energy.

1) The composition of the food determines how much energy it produces. Foods with high proportions of fats and oils produce relatively large amounts of energy.

2) Carbohydrates produce some energy, but much less than fats and oils.

3) Proteins contain about as much energy as carbohydrates, but we don't tend to use it for energy in our bodies.

4) The table below shows the difference in energy content between a chocolate bar and a chicken breast.

	Chocolate (per 100 g)	Chicken breast (per 100 g)
Energy	525 kcal	164 kcal
Protein	7.6 g	27 g
Carbohydrate	56.1 g	–
Fat	30.1 g	6.2 g
Sodium	–	0.3 g

Energy and Food

Taking in more fuel than you use means the **excess** is **stored**

1) Your body needs energy to perform all your <u>daily activities</u> — including tasks you do without thinking, e.g. breathing, heart beating, etc. Chemical reactions in your cells that go on <u>all the time</u> need energy.

2) The energy in food is <u>released</u> by the process of <u>respiration</u>, where glucose reacts with oxygen to produce carbon dioxide, water and energy. This goes on in your cells <u>all the time</u>.

glucose + oxygen → carbon dioxide + water + ENERGY

3) When the food you eat contains <u>more energy</u> than your body needs, the excess food gets <u>stored</u> by the body as <u>fat</u>. Continually taking on more energy than you need will eventually make you <u>obese</u>.

4) When the food you eat contains <u>less energy</u> than your body needs, your body <u>uses up</u> some of its <u>fat stores</u>.
<u>Calorie-controlled diets</u> are designed to give the body <u>slightly less energy</u> than it needs each day, e.g. a person who uses up 2000 kcal a day could eat 1700 kcal a day and gradually lose fat.

5) Most calorie-controlled diets are <u>low fat</u> diets. Calorie-controlled diets usually avoid <u>sugar</u>, because it's high in energy and it <u>stimulates the appetite</u>. Some weight loss diets recommend "<u>slow release</u>" carbohydrates such as wholemeal bread and oats because they <u>fill you up for longer</u> than white bread or sugary carbohydrates, making you <u>less likely</u> to scoff <u>snacks</u> between meals.

All very "fashion and lifestyle" if you ask me...
Weight loss is nothing more than energy in/energy out at the end of the day, so there are two ways to go at it — <u>eat less energy-rich food</u>, or <u>do more exercise</u> to use up more energy. Or (gasp) do <u>both</u>. Learn which types of food are energy rich, and don't forget that calories and Calories are different.

Warm-Up and Exam Questions

Bond energies can seem quite a strange idea at first. Hopefully these questions will get you used to it.

Warm-Up Questions

1) What word is used to describe a reaction which gives out heat?
2) An endothermic reaction happens when ammonium nitrate is dissolved in water. Predict how the temperature of the solution will change during the reaction.
3) Describe the type of energy change that happens when new chemical bonds form.
4) Which symbol is used to represent the energy change per mole in a reaction?
5) The specific heat capacity of water is 4.2 J/g/°C. What does this mean?

Exam Questions

1   When methane burns in air it produces carbon dioxide and water, as shown in the diagram:

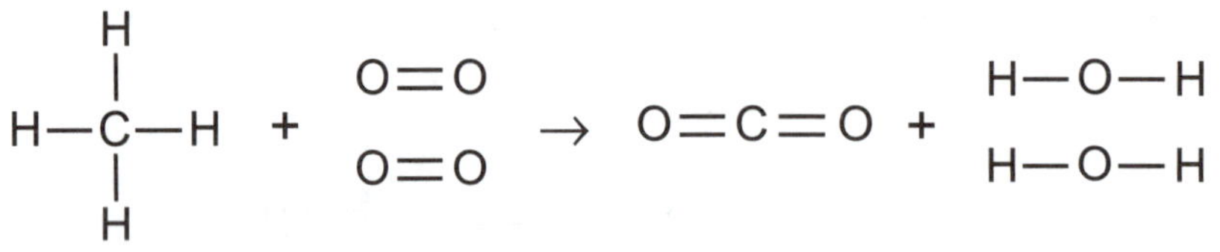

$$H-\underset{\underset{H}{|}}{\overset{\overset{H}{|}}{C}}-H \;+\; \begin{matrix}O=O\\O=O\end{matrix} \;\rightarrow\; O=C=O \;+\; \begin{matrix}H-O-H\\H-O-H\end{matrix}$$

The bond energies for each bond in the above molecules are given below.

| Bond energies (kJ/mol): C–H +414   O=O +494   C=O +800   O–H +459 |

(a) How could you tell just by observing the reaction that it is exothermic?
(1 mark)

(b) (i) Which two types of bond are broken during the reaction?
(1 mark)

   (ii) Which of these bonds needs the most energy before it will break? Suggest why its bond energy is higher.
(1 mark)

(c) Calculate an energy value (in kJ/mol) for:
   (i) the total bonds broken.
(1 mark)

   (ii) the total bonds formed.
(1 mark)

   (iii) the difference between the bonds formed and the bonds broken.
(1 mark)

(d) Use the values from part (c) to explain why the reaction is exothermic.
(1 mark)

Exam Questions

2. An energy level diagram for the decomposition of sodium hydrogencarbonate is shown.

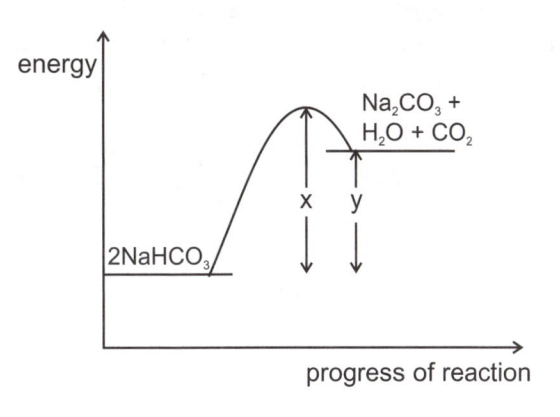

   (a) Complete the diagram by naming x and y.
   (2 marks)

   (b) Is this an exothermic or an endothermic reaction? Give a reason for your choice.
   (2 marks)

   (c) Why doesn't the compound decompose at room temperature?
   (1 mark)

3. The amount of energy produced by two different fuels was compared. 1 g of each fuel was burnt and the heat produced was used to increase the temperature of 100 cm³ of water. The temperature rise for fuel A was 21 °C and for fuel B it was 32 °C. (The specific heat capacity of water is 4.2 J/g/K.)

   (a) Why must the same volume of water be used each time?
   (1 mark)

   (b) Calculate the heat energy transferred to the water from Fuel A, if the water weighs 100 g.
   (2 marks)

   (c) Complete the diagrams to compare the energy changes caused by the two fuels.
   (2 marks)

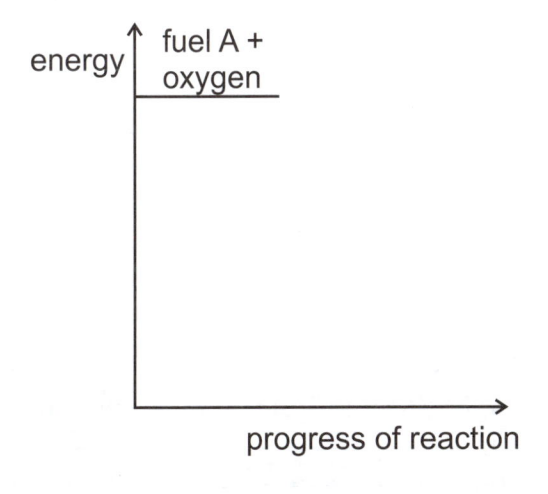

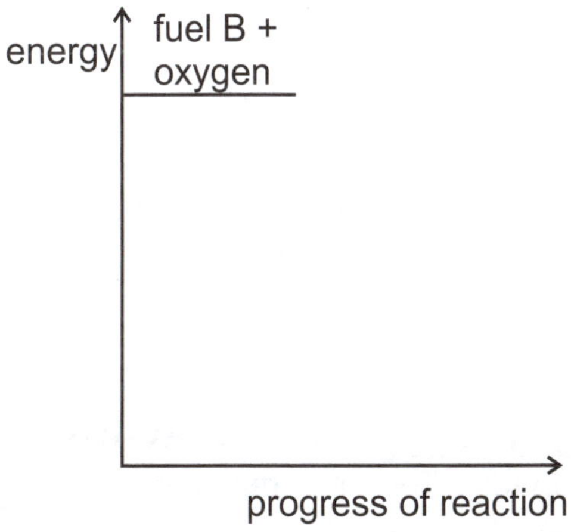

Tests for Cations

Forensic science involves a lot of chemical tests, which is what these next pages are about. Before you start reading, you have to pretend you have a mystery substance. You don't know what it is, but you need to find out — just like that bloke off the telly who investigates murders.

First off, some tests for cations (positive ions — such as Cu^{2+} or Ca^{2+}).

Add *sodium hydroxide* and look for a *coloured precipitate*

This is the first test for positive ions you need to know about. It's a bit complicated, so concentrate...

1) Many metal hydroxides are insoluble and precipitate out of solution when formed. Some of these hydroxides have a characteristic colour.

2) So in this test you add a few drops of sodium hydroxide solution to a solution of your mystery compound — all in the hope of forming an insoluble hydroxide.

3) If you get a coloured insoluble hydroxide you can then tell which metal was in the compound. *Usually, anyway... the result for NH_4^+ is a bit different.*

CALCIUM (Ca^{2+}) gives a **WHITE** precipitate. The ionic reaction is:

$$Ca^{2+}(aq) + 2OH^-(aq) \rightarrow Ca(OH)_2(s)$$

COPPER(II) (Cu^{2+}) gives a **BLUE** precipitate. The ionic reaction is:

$$Cu^{2+}(aq) + 2OH^-(aq) \rightarrow Cu(OH)_2(s)$$

IRON(II) (Fe^{2+}) gives a **SLUDGY GREEN** precipitate. The ionic reaction is:

$$Fe^{2+}(aq) + 2OH^-(aq) \rightarrow Fe(OH)_2(s)$$

IRON(III) (Fe^{3+}) gives a **RED-BROWN** precipitate. The ionic reaction is:

$$Fe^{3+}(aq) + 3OH^-(aq) \rightarrow Fe(OH)_3(s)$$

ALUMINIUM (Al^{3+}) first gives a **WHITE** precipitate, then redissolves in excess NaOH to give a colourless solution. The ionic reactions are:

$$Al^{3+}(aq) + 3OH^-(aq) \rightarrow Al(OH)_3(s)$$
$$\text{then } Al(OH)_3(s) + OH^-(aq) \rightarrow Al(OH)_4^-(s)$$

MAGNESIUM (Mg^{2+}) gives a **WHITE** precipitate. The ionic reaction is.

$$Mg^{2+}(aq) + 2OH^-(aq) \rightarrow Mg(OH)_2(s)$$

CHEMISTRY 3II — ENERGY AND CHEMICAL TESTS

Tests for Cations

There are more tests for cations that involve spotting colours, but these are a bit more exciting, as you get to use fire — and the colours are more exciting as well.

Flame tests identify metal ions

Compounds of some metals burn with a characteristic colour (as you see every November 5th). So you can test for various metal ions by heating your substance and seeing whether it burns with a distinctive colour flame.

Lithium, Li^+, burns with a crimson-red flame.

Sodium, Na^+, burns with an yellow-orange flame.

Potassium, K^+, burns with a lilac flame.

Calcium, Ca^{2+}, burns with a brick-red flame.

Barium, Ba^{2+}, burns with a green flame.

"Ammonium compound + NaOH" gives off (stinky) ammonia

1) Ammonia (NH_3) is smelly — it reeks of cat wee. This is a good way to tell if there's ammonia about, usually — the smell's quite distinctive.
2) Another way is to use damp red litmus paper — ammonia turns it blue.
3) You can use this fact to test for ammonium ions (NH_4^+) using sodium hydroxide. Add sodium hydroxide to a solution of your mystery substance — ammonia given off means there are ammonium ions in your mystery substance. No nasty ammonia smell means no NH_4^+.

Tip: waft the smell towards your nose. Don't take big snorts — ammonia's a bit poisonous.

The Ammonia Mystery — smells like my cat did it...

Remember... your cation is your metal ion, and cations are positive — they'd be attracted to a cathode (which is negative, remember). Now these tests assume that your mystery substance is ionic, which of course it might not be. But you might be able to tell — ionic substances tend to be crystalline solids with a high melting point. So, if it's a gas, a volatile liquid (you might be able to smell it) or a soft solid, no need to bother with these tests. See p.184-185 for testing for organic (carbon-chain) compounds.

CHEMISTRY 3II — ENERGY AND CHEMICAL TESTS

Tests for Anions

So now maybe you know what the positive part of your mystery substance is.
Now it's time to test for the negative bit — or anion.

Testing for carbonates (CO_3^{2-}) — check for CO_2

First thing's first — the test for carbon dioxide (CO_2).

1) You can test to see if a gas is carbon dioxide by bubbling it through limewater. If it is carbon dioxide, the limewater turns milky:
2) You can use this to test for carbonates, since carbonates react with dilute acids to form carbon dioxide.

$$\text{Acid + Carbonate} \rightarrow \text{Salt + Water + Carbon dioxide}$$

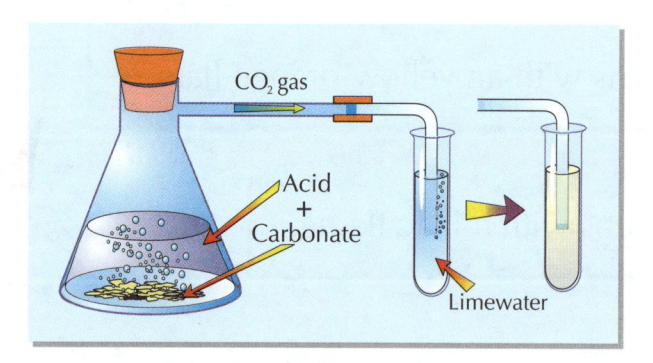

And some carbonates change colour when they decompose

Sometimes, a colour change during a reaction can give you clues to the identity of a substance.

1) Method: put one spatula of carbonate into an test tube and heat strongly, then allow to cool.
2) Copper carbonate turns from green to black and it stays black when cool.

$$CuCO_3(s, \text{green}) \rightarrow CuO(s, \text{black}) + CO_2(g)$$

3) Zinc carbonate turns from white to yellow, but when it cools down it turns back to white.

$$ZnCO_3(s, \text{white}) \rightarrow ZnO(s, \text{yellow when hot, white when cold}) + CO_2(g)$$

It's all about colour changes then...

So the first test tells you if there's a carbonate present, and then the tests involving colour changes let you know which carbonate you've got. Simple, just make sure you remember the different colours.

Tests for Anions

Test for **sulfates** (SO_4^{2-}) and **halides** (Cl^-, Br^-, I^-)

You can test for certain ions by seeing if a precipitate is formed after these reactions...

Sulfate ions, SO_4^{2-}

1) To test for a sulfate ion (SO_4^{2-}), add dilute HCl, followed by barium chloride solution, $BaCl_2$.
2) A white precipitate of barium sulfate means the original compound was a sulfate.

$$Ba^{2+}(aq) + SO_4^{2-}(aq) \longrightarrow BaSO_4(s)$$

Chloride, bromide or iodide ions, Cl^-, Br^-, I^-

To test for chloride, bromide or iodide ions, add dilute nitric acid (HNO_3), followed by silver nitrate solution ($AgNO_3$).

A chloride gives a white precipitate of silver chloride. $Ag^+(aq) + Cl^-(aq) \longrightarrow AgCl(s)$
A bromide gives a cream precipitate of silver bromide. $Ag^+(aq) + Br^-(aq) \longrightarrow AgBr(s)$
An iodide gives a yellow precipitate of silver iodide. $Ag^+(aq) + I^-(aq) \longrightarrow AgI(s)$

The test for **nitrates** (NO_3^-) produces **ammonia**

1) Mix some of your mystery compound with a little aluminium powder.

2) Then add a few drops of sodium hydroxide solution and heat. If you started off with a nitrate, it'll be reduced to ammonia.

3) As always, test for ammonia using your nose or, better, damp red litmus paper (which will turn blue).

Don't just guess that your substance contains any old anion...

So you might have to do loads of different chemical tests to find out all the information about your mystery substance. It's a bit like detective work — eliminating suspects, narrowing down possibilities, and so on. It's the kind of stuff exam questions are made of, by the way, so be warned. They might give you the results from several chemical tests, and you have to say what the substance is. See p.188.

Warm-Up and Exam Questions

Lots of tests to remember on the last four pages. Try these questions to test your memory.

Warm-Up Questions

1) What metal ions would produce:
   a) a lilac flame when burnt?
   b) a green flame when burnt?
2) What colour is the precipitate formed when sodium hydroxide is added to a solution of copper(II) ions?
3) How would you test for ammonia gas?
4) A unknown compound is reacted with hydrochloric acid. The gas produced turns limewater cloudy. What type of anion is present in the unknown compound?

Exam Questions

1. Kelly carried out flame tests on compounds of four different metal ions. Copy and complete the table below showing her results.

Flame colour	Metal ion
green	
	K^+
orange-yellow	
	Ca^{2+}

(4 marks)

2. You are provided with a solution of a halide salt. Describe how you would test this solution to identify whether the solution is of a chloride, bromide or iodide.

(4 marks)

3. A bottle of a chemical solution is labelled 'iron(II) sulfate'.
   (a) Describe a chemical test to confirm that the solution contains iron(II) ions.

   (2 marks)

   (b) Describe a chemical test to confirm that the solution contains sulfate ions.

   (2 marks)

CHEMISTRY 3II — ENERGY AND CHEMICAL TESTS

Exam Questions

4. William conducted a series of tests on several solutions of ionic compounds to identify the positive ions. Complete the table by writing the correct symbol for the positive ion that William has identified in each case.
The first one has been done for you.

TEST	OBSERVATION	ION
sodium hydroxide solution	reddish-brown precipitate	Fe^{3+}
sodium hydroxide solution	white precipitate that redissolves with excess sodium hydroxide	
sodium hydroxide solution	no precipitate, but when heated a strong-smelling gas is released	
sodium hydroxide solution	blue precipitate	
sodium hydroxide solution and then flame test	white precipitate with sodium hydroxide and brick-red flame	

(4 marks)

5. The table below shows the results of a series of chemical tests conducted on two unknown compounds, X and Y.

TEST	OBSERVATION	
	COMPOUND X	COMPOUND Y
sodium hydroxide solution	white precipitate	no precipitate
hydrochloric acid & barium chloride solution	no precipitate	no precipitate
flame test	brick-red flame	lilac flame
aluminium powder & NaOH solution (any gas released on heating is tested with damp red litmus)	litmus paper stays red	litmus paper turns blue
nitric acid & silver nitrate solution	white precipitate	no precipitate

(a) What is the chemical name of compound X?

(2 marks)

(b) What is the chemical name of compound Y?

(2 marks)

Tests for Organic Compounds

The previous pages were about testing <u>inorganic</u> compounds (things not built around a chain of carbon atoms). But your mystery substance might just as easily be <u>organic</u>. In that case, here's what you do...

Organic compounds burn when heated

1) Organic compounds burn in air, with a <u>yellowy-orange and/or blue flame</u>.

2) The greater the proportion of carbon in the compound, the more <u>yellow</u> and smoky the flame is.

3) When there's <u>plenty of air</u> available, burning a hydrocarbon produces <u>carbon dioxide</u> and <u>water</u>.

A hydrocarbon is an organic compound containing only carbon and hydrogen, remember.

4) If the amount of air is reduced, then <u>carbon monoxide</u> (a poisonous gas), and <u>carbon</u> (soot) can also be produced.

5) <u>Solid</u> organic compounds will <u>char</u> — in other words, their surface will get <u>scorched with black marks</u> of <u>carbon</u>.

Compounds with C=C bonds decolourise bromine water

The test for C=C double bonds is a <u>piece of cake</u> (though not literally).

1) If your organic compound is <u>unsaturated</u> (i.e. it has <u>double</u> or <u>triple</u> bonds between carbon atoms), it'll <u>decolourise bromine water</u>.

2) If your organic compound is <u>saturated</u> (i.e. there are <u>no</u> double or triple bonds), the bromine water will stay <u>brown</u>.

...so this one's unsaturated.

3) You can do this test on <u>margarine</u>, which has C=C bonds. Shake 1 cm³ of bromine water with a small amount of <u>melted margarine</u>, and the bromine water decolourises.

Tests for Organic Compounds

You can do more than just tell if an organic compound is saturated or unsaturated — you can even work out its empirical formula with a few simple(ish) calculations.

Find the **empirical formula** of an organic compound by burning it

An empirical formula shows the ratios of all the elements in a substance (see also page 88).

It's possible to work out the empirical formula of an organic compound by burning a known mass of it completely in oxygen, and measuring the masses of all the products.

With a hydrocarbon, all the carbon ends up in CO_2 and all the hydrogen ends up in water. So...

Step 1 Find the mass of each element in the compound.
- To find the mass of carbon in the compound, multiply the mass of CO_2 produced by the proportion of C in CO_2.
- To find the mass of hydrogen in the compound, multiply the mass of H_2O produced by the proportion of H in H_2O.

> Using relative atomic masses, the proportion of C in CO_2 is $12 \div 44 = 0.2727...$
> And the proportion of H in H_2O is $2 \div 18 = 0.1111...$

Step 2 Divide these masses of C and H by the atomic masses of C and H (to find the no. of moles).

Step 3 Divide both answers by the smallest one to get the simplest ratio of atoms of each element.

Example:

> 0.4 g of an organic hydrocarbon is burnt completely in oxygen. 1.1 g of carbon dioxide and 0.9 g of water are formed. What is the compound's empirical formula?

- Step 1 — Find the mass of carbon in the compound: $1.1 \times (12 \div 44) = \underline{0.3 \text{ g}}$
  Do the same for hydrogen: $0.9 \times (2 \div 18) = \underline{0.1 \text{ g}}$

- Step 2 — The relative atomic mass of carbon is 12, so: $0.3 \div 12 = \underline{0.025 \text{ mol}}$
  The relative atomic mass of hydrogen is 1, so: $0.1 \div 1 = \underline{0.1 \text{ mol}}$

- Step 3 — Divide the biggest answer by the smallest one to get the ratio of carbon to hydrogen:
  The simplest whole number ratio of atoms of each element is $0.1 \div 0.025 = \underline{4}$
  (meaning there is 1 carbon to 4 hydrogens).

- This gives an empirical formula for this compound of $\underline{CH_4}$.

A bit of practice and you'll soon be breezing through these

Finding an empirical formula involves an awful lot of sums. Sure, they're simple sums taken one by one, but it'd be all too easy to get confused, do them in the wrong order, and end up with completely the wrong answer. Learn the three steps and follow them — mass, then moles, then ratio.

Instrumental Methods

Nowadays you can turn to machines to do the donkey work of identifying substances, if need be.

Machines can also analyse unknown substances

1) Machines are useful for medical purposes, police forensic work, environmental analysis, drugs testing, analysis of products in industry, and so on.

2) Rapid advances in electronics and computing have made more advanced analysis possible.

Advantages of using machines

'Lab methods' means doing tests like the ones earlier in the section.

- Can be operated by technicians. Lab methods need trained chemists to do everything.
- More accurate than lab methods, and can detect even the tiniest amounts of substances.
- Much faster than lab methods, and tests can be automated.

Disadvantages of using machines

- It's very expensive to buy, run and maintain the machines.

Atomic absorption spectroscopy identifies metals

1) Atomic absorption spectroscopy is a bit like a flame test machine, and it's used to identify metals.

2) The patterns of light absorbed by the metals in the sample are analysed.

3) Each metal present in the sample produces a different pattern.

4) It's much faster and much more reliable than anything that can be done with the human eye.

5) The steel industry uses atomic absorption spectroscopy to check the composition of the steels. (Each kind of steel has to have the right composition to make it suitable for its particular use.)

6) This only takes minutes, compared to days with the lab method.

Instrumental Methods

Other techniques identify *elements* or *compounds*

1) Infrared (IR) spectroscopy

This identifies which frequencies of infrared radiation are absorbed — the pattern of absorbance is unique for every compound. This 'fingerprint' allows identification of individual compounds.

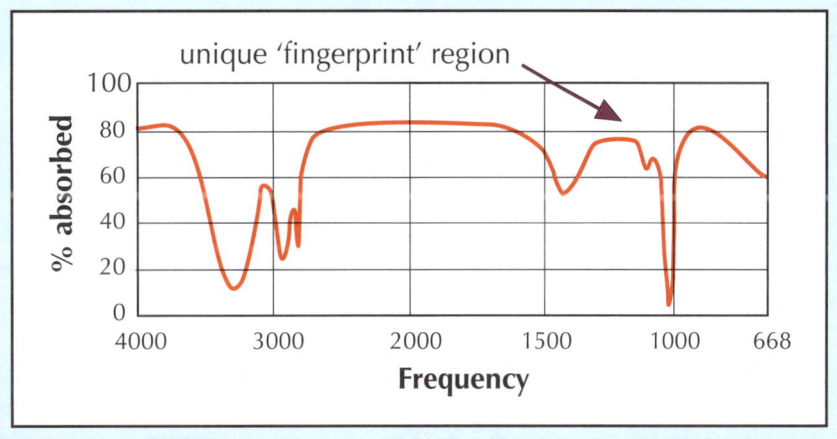

2) Ultraviolet (UV) spectroscopy

This is similar to infrared spectroscopy, but with ultraviolet light instead of infrared.

3) Nuclear magnetic resonance (NMR) spectroscopy

This method is used for organic compounds. It shows what atoms the hydrogen atoms are connected to. This helps find the structure of the molecule, by telling you if there are –OH groups, –NH_2 groups, etc.

4) Gas-liquid chromatography

This uses a similar principle to paper chromatography. It's used to identify gases and liquids.

5) Mass spectrometry

This method can be used for both elements and compounds. It tells you the mass of each molecule or particle. For elements, this tells you exactly what element you've got, and for larger molecules the mass is a good clue.

Identifying Unknown Substances

In the exam, you might have to apply your knowledge, which is kind of scary. It means thinking. Eeek. Most likely, you'll have to interpret information that the examiners provide. Just keep your head.

Using chemical tests

Time for a walk-through of a typical question that could come up in the exam. It uses the identification tests from pages 178-181 — if you don't know those thoroughly, go back and learn 'em.

- Compound A is a bluey-green crystalline solid that dissolves in water to give a blue solution.

- A flame test was carried out on compound A, and a bright green colour was produced.

- The following tests were then carried out on separate samples of the solution of compound A, and the results for each test are recorded in the table. From the information given, identify compound A.

1) Add a few drops of sodium hydroxide	A blue precipitate is formed
2) Add 5 cm³ of hydrochloric acid	No change
3) Add 2 cm³ dilute hydrochloric acid followed by 2 cm³ of barium chloride	No change
4) Add a little aluminium powder, a few drops of sodium hydroxide solution and warm.	A blue precipitate is formed, but no bubbles of gas.
5) Add 2 cm³ dilute nitric acid followed by 2 cm³ of silver nitrate	A white precipitate is formed

OK, it's a crystalline solid, so it's ionic. You can identify it in two parts — first identify the cation by looking at the tests that tell you something about the cation, then do the same for the anion.

Cation: The flame test result tells you the cation can't be lithium, sodium, potassium, calcium or barium. Test 1 shows that it's copper, because there's a blue precipitate of copper hydroxide.

Anion: Test 2 indicates it's not a carbonate because there were no bubbles of gas. Test 3 shows it's not a sulfate — there's no white precipitate. Test 4 is the test for nitrates — no ammonia means no nitrate. (The blue precipitate is formed because NaOH has been added to a solution of copper ions — like in Test 1.) Test 5 tells you that a chloride ion is there because of the white precipitate of silver chloride.

Compound A is therefore COPPER CHLORIDE.

If you aren't part of the solution, you're part of the precipitate...

In the exam they may well give you the results of a bunch of tests and ask you to identify a substance. So learning one or two tests might not help much — you need them all, see.

CHEMISTRY 3$_{II}$ — ENERGY AND CHEMICAL TESTS

Identifying Unknown Substances

Using *instrumental analysis*

You might have to interpret results from an instrumental analysis...

A local health authority received reports that some bottles of wine were contaminated. Scientists isolated a compound from the wine and analysed the substance using IR and mass spectrometry. The IR spectrum is as shown:

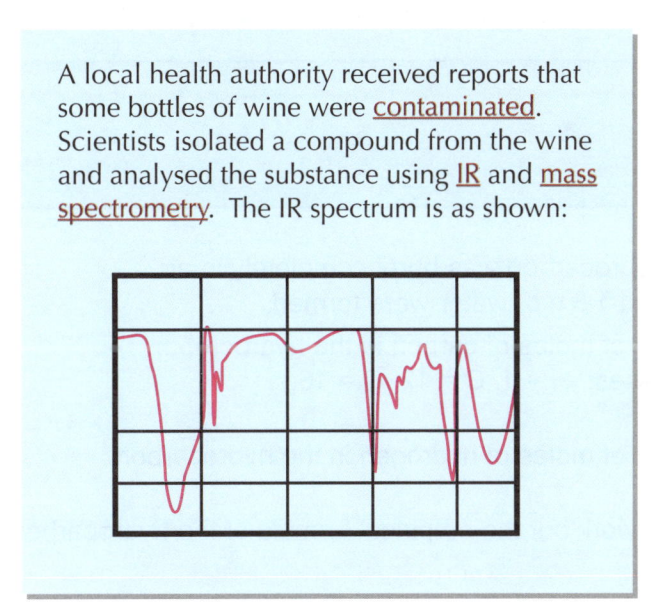

A forensic scientist compared the IR spectrum of the unknown with IR spectra of methanol (CH_3OH), ethanol (C_2H_5OH) and propanol (C_3H_7OH) (below). What conclusions could the scientist draw?

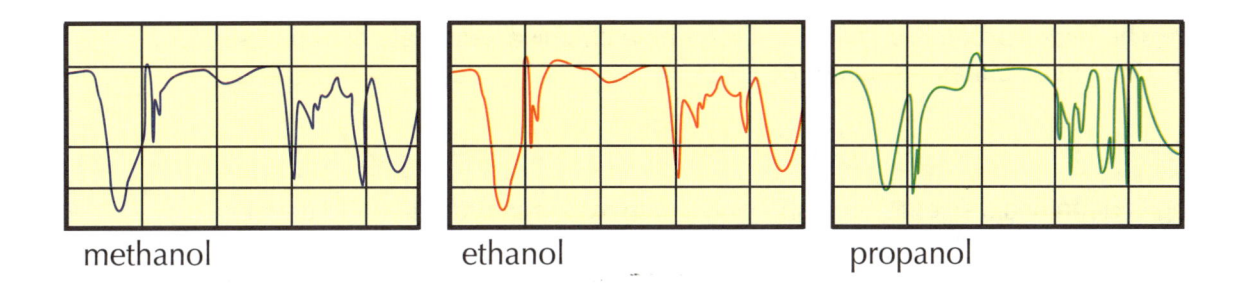

methanol   ethanol   propanol

The scientist could say the substance isn't propanol because the IR spectra are very different. (Those for methanol and ethanol are similar, so it's tricky to decide between these — more evidence would be good.)

The mass spectrum showed that the relative molecular mass (M_r) of the unknown compound was 32.

The M_r of methanol (CH_3OH) is $(1 \times 12) + (4 \times 1) + (1 \times 16) = 32$, and the M_r of ethanol (C_2H_5OH) is $(2 \times 12) + (6 \times 1) + (1 \times 16) = 46$. So the contamination was due to METHANOL.

Warm-Up and Exam Questions

Time to test your knowledge again — first a warm-up, and then some very realistic exam questions.

Warm-Up Questions

1) An organic solid is heated strongly. How would the appearance of its surface change?
2) Suggest an instrumental method that could be used to identify a solid non-metal element.

Exam Questions

1. A sample of an organic hydrocarbon was burnt completely in air. 4.4 g of carbon dioxide and 1.8 g of water were formed.
    (a) Calculate the number of moles of carbon in the hydrocarbon.
       (Relative atomic masses: H = 1, C = 12, O = 16.)
       (2 marks)
    (b) Calculate the number of moles of hydrogen in the hydrocarbon.
       (2 marks)
    (c) Use your answers to work out the empirical formula of the hydrocarbon.
       (1 mark)

2. An organic hydrocarbon was burnt completely in air. 1.1 g of carbon dioxide and 0.675 g of water were formed.
    (a) Calculate the empirical formula of the hydrocarbon. Show all your working out.
       (Relative atomic masses: H = 1, C = 12, O = 16)
       (3 marks)
    (b) The hydrocarbon is an alkane. Describe a chemical test that could be used to demonstrate that it is saturated.
       (2 marks)

3. Meg is a materials scientist and she works with metals in order to try to develop new catalysts. She frequently uses instrumental methods to test the quality and composition of metal samples.
    (a) One of the techniques that Meg uses to test her samples is atomic absorption spectroscopy. Which of the following best describes how this technique works?
       A Ultraviolet light is used to excite electrons in the metallic 'sea' of free electrons. The amount of energy absorbed by these electrons is different for each metal.
       B The metal sample is vaporised and a type of gas chromatography is used to identify the different metals in the sample.
       C The patterns of light absorbed by the metals in a sample are analysed — each metal produces its own characteristic pattern.
       (1 mark)
    (b) Give two advantages of using modern machine-based instrumental methods compared to older, lab-based methods.
       (2 marks)

CHEMISTRY 3II — ENERGY AND CHEMICAL TESTS

Revision Summary for Chemistry 3(ii)

Whenever anything at all happens, energy is either taken in or released. So it's amazingly important. If that doesn't inspire you to learn the stuff about it, the fact that you're likely to get exam questions on it should. There are bag loads of chemical tests in this section, and they all need learning I'm afraid.

1) An acid and an alkali were mixed in a polystyrene cup, as shown below. The acid and alkali were each at 20 °C before they were mixed. After they were mixed, the temperature of the solution reached 24 °C.
   a) State whether this reaction is exothermic or endothermic.
   b) Explain why the cotton wool is used.

   20 cm³ of dilute sulfuric acid + 20 cm³ of dilute sodium hydroxide — cotton wool

2) Is energy released when bonds are formed or when bonds are broken?
3) The apparatus below is used to measure how much energy is released when pentane is burnt. It takes 4.2 joules of energy to heat 1 g of water by 1 °C.
   a)* Using the following data, calculate the amount of energy per gram of pentane.

Mass of empty copper can	64 g
Mass of copper can + water	116 g
Initial temperature of water	17 °C
Final temperature of water	47 °C
Mass of spirit burner + pentane before burning	97.72 g
Mass of spirit burner + pentane after burning	97.37 g

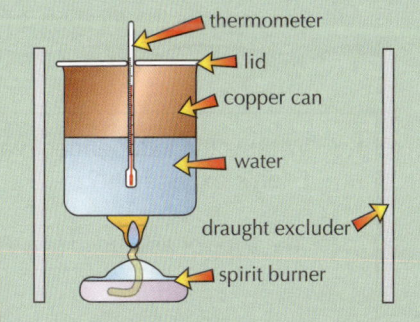

   b) A data book says that pentane has 49 kJ/g of energy. Why is the amount you calculated different?
4) Explain why the price of bananas might rise if we keep burning so much fuel.
5) a) Draw energy level diagrams for exothermic and endothermic reactions.
   b) Explain how bond breaking and forming relate to these diagrams.
6) What is the activation energy for a reaction? Mark it on your exothermic energy level diagram from Q5.
7) How does a catalyst affect: a) activation energy, b) overall energy change for a reaction?
8)* a) Calculate the energy change for the following reaction: $2H_2 + O_2 \rightarrow 2H_2O$
   You need these bond energies: H–H: +436 kJ/mol, O=O: +496 kJ/mol, O–H: +463 kJ/mol
   Hint: There are 2 O–H bonds in each molecule of water.
   b) Is this an exothermic or endothermic reaction?
9)* A tin of beans contains 655 kJ of energy. How many calories does it contain? How many kcal is this?
10) Give a reason why your body uses energy all the time, not just when you exercise.
11) What happens if the food you eat contains more energy than you need?
12) Explain how you can test for the following ions. Give ionic equations where appropriate.
    a) Li^+, b) K^+, c) Ba^{2+}, d) Ca^{2+}, e) Fe^{2+}, f) Al^{3+}, g) NH_4^+, h) SO_4^{2-}, i) Cl^-, j) I^-, k) NO_3^-
13) How would you distinguish between solutions of: a) magnesium sulfate and aluminium sulfate,
    b) sodium bromide and sodium iodide,   c) copper nitrate and copper sulfate?
14) Describe what you would notice when you heated: a) copper carbonate,   b) zinc carbonate.
    What is produced when these compounds react with a dilute acid?
15) Explain how you could distinguish between butane and butene.
16) What's an empirical formula?
17)* An organic hydrocarbon is burnt completely in oxygen. 4.4 g of carbon dioxide and 1.8 g of water are formed. What is the compound's empirical formula?
18) Give three advantages of instrumental analysis over traditional lab methods.
19) What lab test is atomic absorption spectroscopy a bit like? Why does the steel industry use it?

Answers on page 246.

Answering Experiment Questions (i)

Science is all (well... a lot) about <u>doing experiments</u> carefully, and <u>interpreting results</u>.
And so that's what they're going to test you on when you do your exam. Among other things.

Read the question *carefully*

Expect at least some questions to describe experiments — a bit like the one below.

> Q3 Ellen has three different bottles of citric acid: A, B and C.
> The citric acid in each bottle is of a different concentration.
>
> Ellen also has another quantity of citric acid, in the form of kitchen descaler.
>
> Ellen wants to know if any of her three acids are the same concentration as the kitchen descaler. She plans to titrate each of the four citric acid solutions against a solution of sodium hydroxide of a known concentration, as shown.
>
> She repeats the titration 3 times for each acid.
>
> *Burette containing acid*
>
> *Sodium hydroxide*

> 1. What is the independent variable in Ellen's experiment?
>
>   *The type of acid used (e.g. A, B or C).*
>
> 2. What is the dependent variable?
>
>   *The quantity of acid required to neutralise the sodium hydroxide.*
>
> 3. Give two variables that must be kept the same to make it a fair test.
>
>   1. *The amount of NaOH.*
>   2. *The type and amount of indicator used.*
>
> 4. Give one other precaution that Ellen should take to ensure her results are reliable.
>
>   *Wash and dry the equipment each time (to ensure no contamination).*

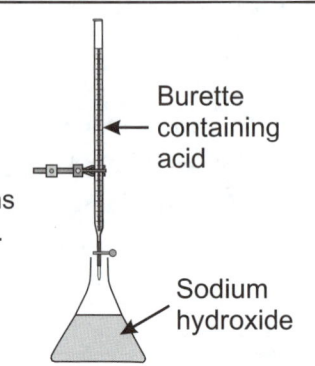

The <u>independent variable</u> is the <u>thing the experimenter changes</u> — to see what effect the change has.

Quite often, experiments involve recording what happens over <u>time</u>, e.g. rate of reaction experiments. In these cases, <u>time</u> is always the <u>independent</u> variable — the experimenter isn't 'changing the time' exactly, but they do want to see what happens <u>as the time changes</u>.

The <u>dependent variable</u> is the <u>thing the experimenter measures</u> (every time they change the independent variable).

To make it a <u>fair test</u>, you've got to keep <u>all</u> the other variables the same (you're <u>only changing</u> the <u>independent variable</u>). That way you know that the <u>only thing</u> affecting the dependent variable is the <u>independent variable</u>.

If your experiment is being done in a <u>lab</u>, this should be fairly easy (though not always — e.g. you might have to keep temperature constant, which could be tricky). But it's <u>trickier</u> still when you don't have much control over the conditions at all — e.g. if your experiment has to be done <u>outside</u> (where temperature, humidity, etc. can vary considerably).

Anything that might affect the results needs to be kept constant, so look at the apparatus, think what Ellen's going to be doing — and you should be able to come up with answers fairly easily.

If the equipment isn't <u>clean</u>, that will definitely affect the results. And if the flask's not <u>dry</u>, the extra water would dilute the sodium hydroxide slightly (which would affect the results). A temperature change could also be a problem (though probably a small one) — things expand as they get hotter, so Ellen could get a false reading from the burette if the temperature in the lab changes a lot between tests.

Exam Skills

Answering Experiment Questions (ii)

5. Why did Ellen repeat the titration 3 times for each acid?

   To check for anomalous results and make the results more reliable.

   > Sometimes you get <u>unusual results</u> — <u>repeating</u> an experiment gives you a better idea what the <u>correct result</u> should be.

6. The table below shows the amount of acid required in each titration.

	1st result (cm³)	2nd result (cm³)	3rd result (cm³)	Mean (cm³)
Kitchen descaler	24.1	23.9	23.7	
Acid A	23.9	23.5	24.0	23.8
Acid B	33.3	33.7	(38.6)	33.5
Acid C	23.7	23.9	24.1	23.9

   > When an experiment is <u>repeated</u>, the results will usually be <u>slightly different</u> each time.
   > To get a single <u>representative</u> value, you'd usually find the <u>mean</u> (average) of all the results.
   > The more times the experiment is <u>repeated</u> the <u>more reliable</u> this average will be.
   > To find the mean:
   >
   > **Add together all the data values and DIVIDE by the total number of values in the sample.**
   >
   > The <u>range</u> is how <u>spread out</u> the data is. You just work out the <u>difference</u> between the <u>highest</u> and <u>lowest</u> numbers.

   a) Calculate the mean amount of kitchen descaler required to neutralise the NaOH.

   Mean = (24.1 + 23.9 + 23.7) ÷ 3 = 23.9 cm³

   b) What is the range of the quantities of kitchen descaler required?

   24.1 − 23.7 = 0.4 cm³

7. One of the results in the table is anomalous. Circle the result and suggest why it may have occurred.

   The reading may not have been taken correctly, or the wrong quantity of NaOH may have been used.

   > If one result doesn't seem to fit in — it's wildly out compared with the others — then it's called an <u>anomalous</u> result. You should usually <u>ignore</u> an anomalous result (or even better — investigate it and try to work out what happened). Here, it's been <u>ignored</u> when the mean was worked out.
   > This one's a <u>random error</u> — one that only happens occasionally.
   >
   > If you make the same mistake every time, it's a <u>systematic error</u>.
   > For example, if you measured the volume of a liquid using the <u>top</u> of the meniscus rather than the <u>bottom</u>, all your readings would be a little on the large side.
   >
   > *This reading should be 24.5 cm³*

8. Using these results, which acid can you conclude is <u>not</u> the same concentration as the kitchen descaler?

   Acid B

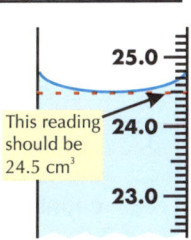

   > You have to be careful here — both Acids A and C could be the same concentration, since all experiments have a "<u>margin of error</u>" — meaning results are never absolutely spot on.
   > So you can say that Acid B has a different concentration — but Acids A and C <u>could</u> be the same.

You can believe me — I'm a scientist...

This is a question all about making results <u>trustworthy</u> (a not-very-scientific way of saying <u>reliable</u>, <u>accurate</u> and <u>precise</u> — see next page). So you need to make the experiment fair, and you need to double-check results to make sure nothing weird happened. It's the same for all scientists.

EXAM SKILLS

Answering Experiment Questions (iii)

Use *sensible measurements* for your *variables*

Charley has four bottles of acid labelled A to D, which he has been told are of different concentrations.

He does a titration experiment to find out what volume of each acid is needed to neutralise 25 cm^3 of alkali. He measures 25 cm^3 of the alkali into a flask, with some indicator solution, and sets up a burette filled with 50 cm^3 of acid A. He gradually adds acid to the alkali, and when the indicator shows that the alkali is almost neutralised, he adds the acid very slowly, drop by drop. He stops when the alkali has been neutralised, and writes down the volume of acid that was needed. He repeats this experiment for the other three acids.

Before starting, Charley did a trial run, adding each acid very quickly, so he knows that between 15 cm^3 and 25 cm^3 of the acids are needed to neutralise 25 cm^3 of the alkali.

---

1. What kind of variable is the volume of acid needed?

   A   A continuous variable ✓

   B   A categoric variable

   C   An ordered variable

   D   A discrete variable

2. Charley should initially add the acid...

   A   0.01 cm^3 at a time.

   B   10 cm^3 at a time.

   C   1 cm^3 at a time. ✓

   D   5 cm^3 at a time.

3. The burette used to measure the volume of acid should be capable of measuring...

   A   to the nearest 0.1 cm^3. ✓

   B   to the nearest cm^3.

   C   to the nearest 10 cm^3.

   D   to the nearest 0.5 cm^3.

Continuous data is numerical data that can take any value in a range — e.g. length, volume, temperature, time.

Note: You can't measure the exact value of continuous data. Say you measure a height as 5.6 cm to the nearest mm. It's not exact — you get a more precise value if you measure to the nearest 0.1 mm or 0.01 mm, etc.

Categoric variables are variables that can't be related to size or quantity — they're types (categories) of things. E.g. names of metals or types of fertiliser.

Ordered variables are things like small, medium and large lumps, or warm, very warm, and hot.

Discrete data is the type that can be counted in chunks, where there's no in-between value. E.g. number of people is discrete not continuous because you can't have half a person.

It's important to use sensible values for variables.

It's no good adding loads of acid at once, as you might shoot past the neutralisation point. But on the other hand, adding it in tiny amounts like 0.01 cm^3 could take ages.

A burette measuring only in whole cm^3 or more, would not be sensitive enough — when the alkali is nearly neutralised, Charley adds acid drop by drop, so he needs to measure to the nearest 0.1 cm^3 to get precise results.

The sensitivity of an instrument is the smallest change it can detect. E.g. some balances measure to the nearest gram, but really sensitive ones measure to the nearest hundredth of a gram. For measuring tiny changes — like from 2.00 g to 1.92 g — a sensitive balance is needed.

You also have to think about the precision and accuracy of your results.

Measurements (of the same thing) that are very precise will be close together. Really accurate measurements are those that have an average value that's really close to the true answer. So it's possible for results to be precise but not very accurate, e.g. a fancy piece of lab equipment might give results that are precise, but if it's not calibrated properly those results won't be accurate.

Answering Experiment Questions (iv)

Once you've collected all your data together, you need to **analyse** it to find any **relationships** between the variables. The easiest way to do this is to draw a **graph**, then describe what you see...

Graphs are used to show relationships

Melissa did an experiment on rate of reaction, mixing magnesium and dilute hydrochloric acid. She measured how much mass was 'lost' from the flask of reactants as a gas was given off. These were her results.

Time (s)	10	20	30	40	50	60	70	80	90	100
Loss in mass (g)	0.02	0.05	0.15	0.18	0.19	0.21	0.23	0.15	0.23	0.23

1. a) Eight of the points are plotted below. Plot the remaining two points on the graph.
   b) Draw the line or curve which best fits the points.

To plot the points, use a **sharp** pencil and make a **neat** little cross.

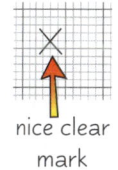

nice clear mark

smudged unclear marks

If your points lie roughly in a line, draw a line of best fit. If your points make a curve, draw a smooth curve. Whatever else you do, **don't** just join the dots.

(Graph: Loss of mass (g) vs time (s), with anomalous result at 80 s marked)

When you're drawing your curve (or line), make it go as close to as many points as possible. It doesn't have to go **through** them — you want a **smooth** curve (or a **straight** line) not a wiggly one. In this case, the curve has to go through the **origin** (0, 0) as you know there'd be no gas given off if you hadn't mixed the reactants together yet.

You might have some **anomalous results** — usually when you've done something daft, like reading a scale wrongly. You can **ignore** these anomalous results when you're drawing your curve (or line).

2. Explain what your graph shows about how the rate of reaction changes with time.

   The curve is steep for the first 30 s, showing that the reaction is quickest at first, but as the reactants are gradually used up, the reaction slows down and the curve flattens off.

3. Sketch a graph to show the results you would expect to see if Melissa repeated the experiment using more concentrated acid, but keeping everything else the same.

You'd expect that, with more concentrated acid, the reaction would go **faster** — so the curve would be steeper at the beginning, and reach its highest value sooner. But there's the same mass of the other reactant (magnesium) as before, so the **same total amount** of gas will be given off — the final loss in mass will be the **same** as before.

EXAM SKILLS

Answering Experiment Questions (v)

Not all experiments can be carefully controlled in a laboratory. Some have to be done in the real world.

Relationships do NOT always tell you the cause

Most car bodies are made from strong steel panels, but engineers are looking for innovative materials which will improve efficiency and safety. 'Alucars' has released a new car with body panels made of aluminium. The bar chart below shows how many accidents there were involving cars with aluminium bodies, and how many involving cars with steel bodies, in one year.

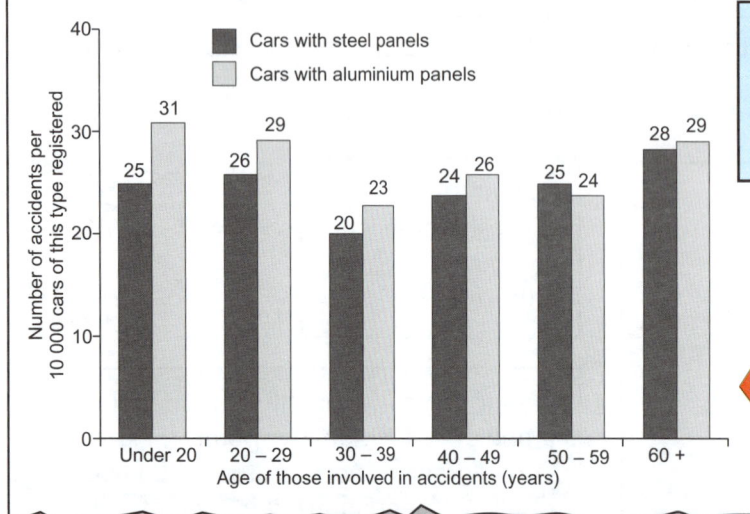

Bar chart: Number of accidents per 10 000 cars of this type registered vs Age of those involved in accidents (years).
- Under 20: steel 25, aluminium 31
- 20–29: steel 26, aluminium 29
- 30–39: steel 20, aluminium 23
- 40–49: steel 24, aluminium 26
- 50–59: steel 25, aluminium 24
- 60+: steel 28, aluminium 29

In large studies done outside a lab it's really difficult to keep all the variables the same and to make sure the control group are kept in the same conditions.

In this study the control group are the people in 'normal' cars, with steel panels.

This is a bar chart. It contains a key to tell you what colour bars relate to which group.

---

1. There are approximately 5000 aluminium cars registered in the county of Wessex. Use the bar chart to estimate how many under-20s will be involved in accidents in one year, in aluminium-panelled cars.

   31 ÷ 2 = 15.5 ≈ 16 people.

   They're asking you the number of injuries you'd expect for 5000 cars — the graph tells you injuries per 10 000 cars. Don't get caught out, read the question carefully. (And don't write something daft with half a person in it.)

2. What conclusion can you draw from the results?

   There are proportionately more accidents involving cars with aluminium bodies than cars with steel bodies.

   When describing the data and drawing conclusions it's really important that you don't say that having an aluminium-panelled car causes accidents. The graph only shows that there's a positive relationship between the two.

   In studies like these where you can't control everything, it's possible a third variable is causing the relationship. E.g. aluminium-bodied cars would be lighter than steel-bodied cars, so they might appeal to people who like driving fast, and driving faster causes more accidents.

3. Suggest how the accident data may have been collected.

   e.g. from police records.

   Use your common sense here.

   Try to suggest a method to get reliable results. For example, it's very unlikely that the data would have been collected by a telephone survey or an internet search.

A relationship doesn't necessarily mean cause and effect

Just looking at numbers (like here) doesn't mean you can say that one variable changing causes the other to change too. 'Ice cream sales' and 'cases of heatstroke' probably rise and fall together — but you can't say that ice cream causes heatstroke. (They'd more likely both be caused by a heatwave.)

Practice Exam

Once you've been through all the questions in this book, you should feel pretty confident about the exam. As final preparation, here is a **practice exam** to really get you set for the real thing. The total time allowed for each paper is 45 minutes. The paper is designed to give you the best possible preparation for the differing question styles of the actual AQA exams. You can then work out your overall mark and get an idea of how your revision is going.

CGP Practice Exam Paper: AQA GCSE Chemistry

General Certificate of Secondary Education

AQA GCSE Chemistry
(Written Paper)

Unit Chemistry 1
Higher Tier

Time allowed: 45 minutes.

Centre name
Centre number
Candidate number
Surname
Other names
Candidate signature

Instructions to candidates
- Write your name and other details in the spaces above.
- Answer all questions in the spaces provided.
- Do all rough work on this question paper.
- Write your answers in black or blue ink or ball-point pen.

Information for candidates
- The marks available are given in brackets at the end of each question or part-question.
- In calculations show clearly how you worked out your answers.
- You may use a calculator.
- There are 8 questions in this paper.
- The maximum mark for this paper is 45.

Advice to candidates
- Work steadily through the paper.
- Don't spend too long on one question.
- If you have time at the end, go back and check your answers.

For examiner's use

Q	Attempt N°			Q	Attempt N°		
	1	2	3		1	2	3
1				5			
2				6			
3				7			
4				8			
				Total 45			

Answer **all** questions in the spaces provided.

1 The diagram shows how a student extracted copper from copper ore by heating the ore with carbon in a crucible. The copper ore is mainly copper carbonate.

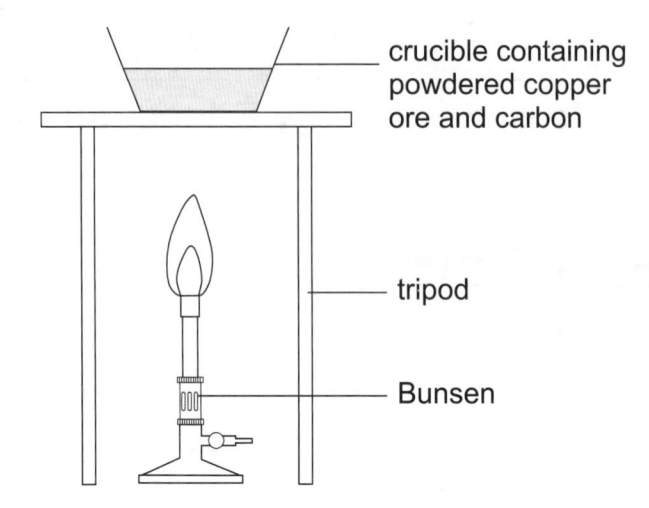

a) Suggest one safety precaution the student should take when doing this experiment.

....

....
(1 mark)

b) What is an ore?

....
(1 mark)

c) Two reactions happen during the experiment.
Complete the two balanced symbol equations below.

Reaction A

copper carbonate → copper oxide + carbon dioxide

$CuCO_3$ → .... + CO_2

Reaction B

copper oxide + carbon → copper + carbon dioxide

.... + C → $2Cu + CO_2$

(2 marks)

d) What type of reaction is Reaction A?

....
(1 mark)

e) In Reaction A, if 4 g of copper carbonate produces 2.6 g of copper oxide, how much carbon dioxide is produced?

....

.... g of carbon dioxide.
(1 mark)

Question 1 continues on the next page

Turn over▶

f) In Reaction B, carbon reduces the copper oxide to copper.
Explain why carbon is able to do this.

....

....
(1 mark)

g) Copper can be used to make electrical wires.
Explain, in terms of atoms, why copper can be drawn out into wires.

....

....

....
(2 marks)

2 A student did an experiment to study the greenhouse effect.
He assembled the equipment as shown in the diagram.

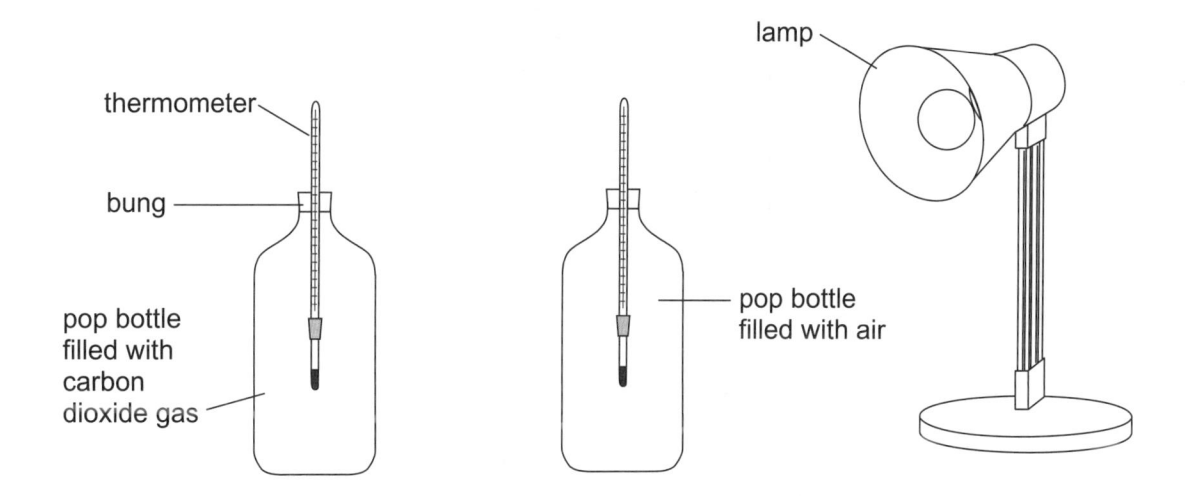

The student recorded the temperature of each bottle every 5 minutes for 25 minutes, and obtained the following results.

Time (min)	Temperature (°C)	
	Bottle filled with air	Bottle filled with carbon dioxide
0	20	20
5	23	24
10	25	27
15	27	29
20	28	30
25	29	31

Question 2 continues on the next page

Turn over▶

The graph shows how the temperature of the bottle filled with air increased during the experiment.

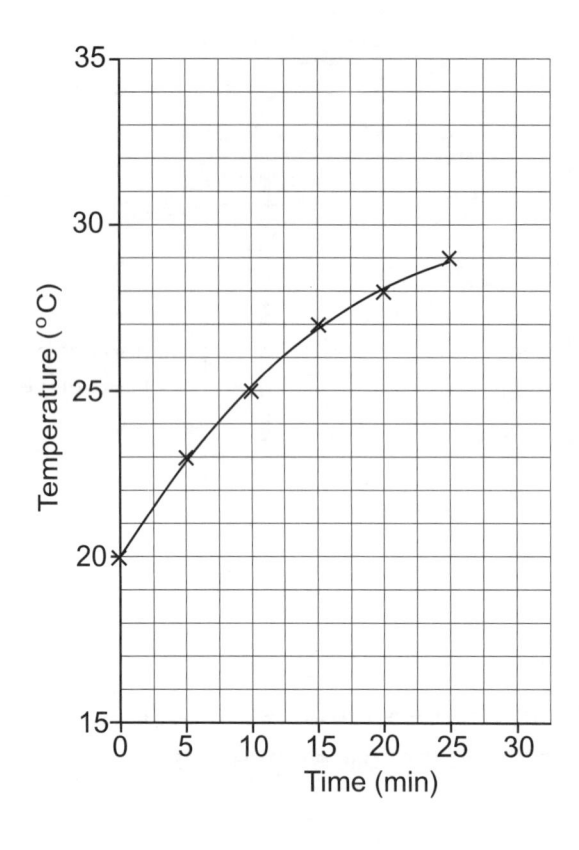

a) Plot the points for the temperature of the bottle filled with carbon dioxide on the same axes. Draw a curve of best fit through your points.

(2 marks)

b) Based on the graph, suggest a valid conclusion that the student could draw from his experiment.

....

....
(1 mark)

c) Suggest one thing the student should have done to ensure that the test was fair.

....

....
(1 mark)

3 Biodiesel is a diesel fuel replacement often made from vegetable oils.
When burnt, it produces carbon dioxide, sulfur dioxide and particulate matter.

a) Briefly describe the environmental problems caused by each of these pollutants.

....

....

....

....

....

....
(3 marks)

b) Burning biodiesel produces less sulfur and particulate matter pollution than burning ordinary diesel. Describe one other advantage of biodiesel over ordinary diesel.

....

....
(1 mark)

Turn over ▶

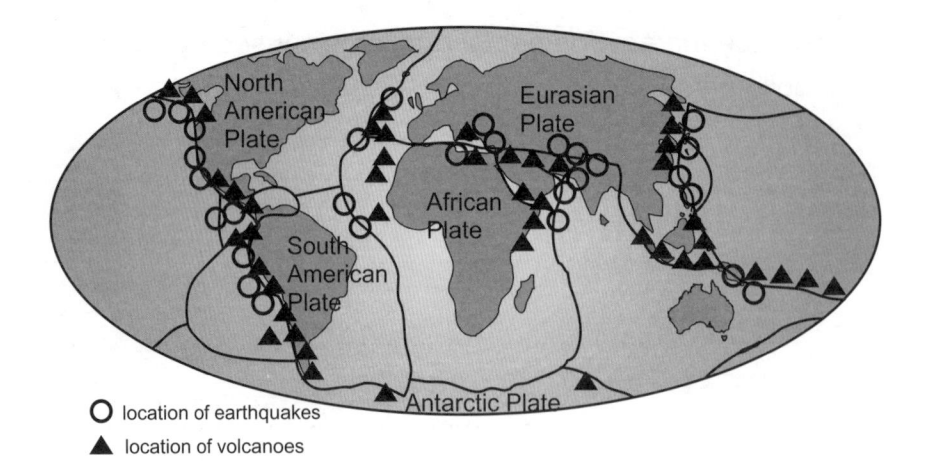

4 The map below shows the distribution of some recent volcanoes and earthquakes. It also shows plate boundaries.

a) Describe the distribution of volcanoes in relation to the plate boundaries.

....

....
(1 mark)

b) Explain why the majority of earthquakes occur at plate boundaries.

....

....
(1 mark)

c) Can scientists accurately predict when earthquakes and volcanoes will occur? Explain your answer.

....

....

....
(2 marks)

5 The symbol equation shows the reaction of ethene with steam.

$$C_2H_4 + H_2O \rightarrow C_2H_5OH$$

a) Phosphoric acid is used as a catalyst in this reaction.
What is a catalyst?

....

....
(1 mark)

b) Name the product with the formula C_2H_5OH.

....
(1 mark)

c) Briefly describe the commercial uses of the product with the formula C_2H_5OH.

....

....

....

....

....
(3 marks)

d) Explain why using ethene to produce C_2H_5OH could become very expensive.

....

....

....
(2 marks)

Turn over

6 The diagrams show the arrangement of atoms in pure iron and steel.

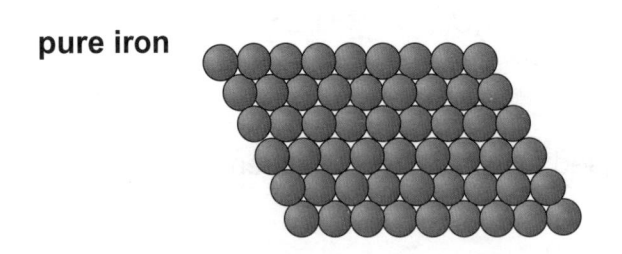

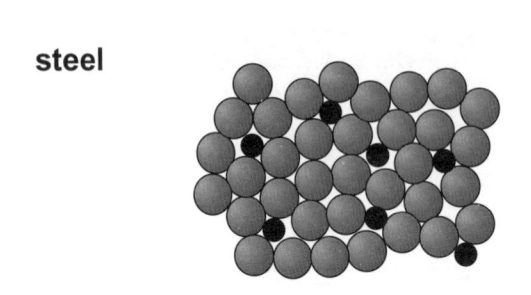

pure iron

steel

a) Explain why steel is harder than iron.

....

....

....

....
(2 marks)

b) Look at the graph below.

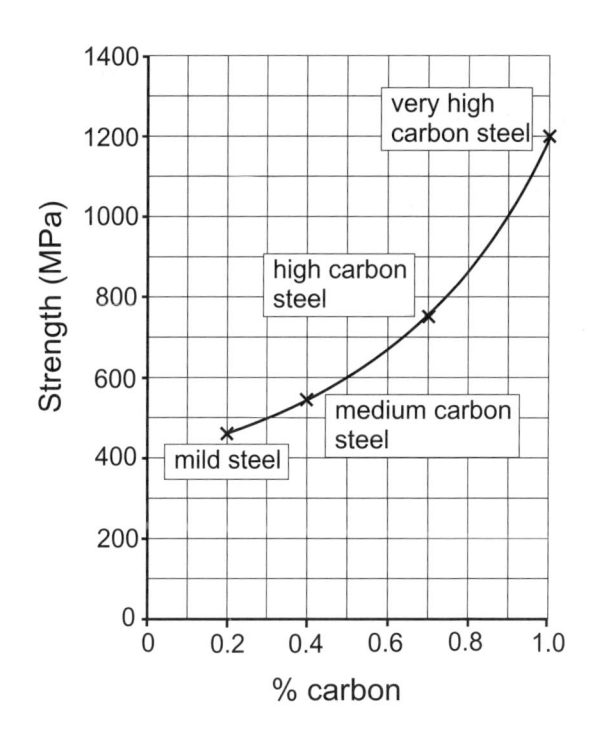

i) Which type of steel shown on the graph would be the easiest to shape?

....
(1 mark)

ii) Suggest an appropriate use for very high carbon steel.

....

....
(1 mark)

c) Iron is alloyed with manganese and silicon to make a smart alloy, which can be used to make dental braces. This alloy is a shape memory alloy.

i) What is a shape memory alloy?

....
(1 mark)

ii) Give one disadvantage of using smart alloys.

....

....
(1 mark)

Turn over►

7 A large supermarket chain is deciding whether to use wild salmon or farmed salmon in its own-brand recipes. They send samples of each type of salmon to be tested for nutritional value, and for the presence of chemical contaminants. The following results are obtained.

NUTRIENTS	Wild Salmon (per 100 g)	Farmed Salmon (per 100 g)
Protein	22 g	17 g
Total Fat	11 g	29 g
Saturated Fat	3 g	5 g
CONTAMINANTS		
Canthaxanthin (artificial colour)	0 mg	0.9 mg
Cypremethrin (pesticide)	0 mg	0.02 mg
PCBs (chemical pollutants)	0.0005 mg	0.005 mg

a) **i)** Which salmon would be the healthiest choice? ....
(1 mark)

ii) Give **two** reasons for your answer.

1. ....

....

2. ....

....
(2 marks)

b) Suggest what method of chemical analysis could have been used to identify the artificial colour in the salmon.

....
(1 mark)

c) Explain, in terms of carbon bonds, the difference between saturated and unsaturated fats.

....

....
(1 mark)

8 The pie charts below show the composition of Earth's atmosphere how we think it was 4 billion years ago, and how it is at the present time.

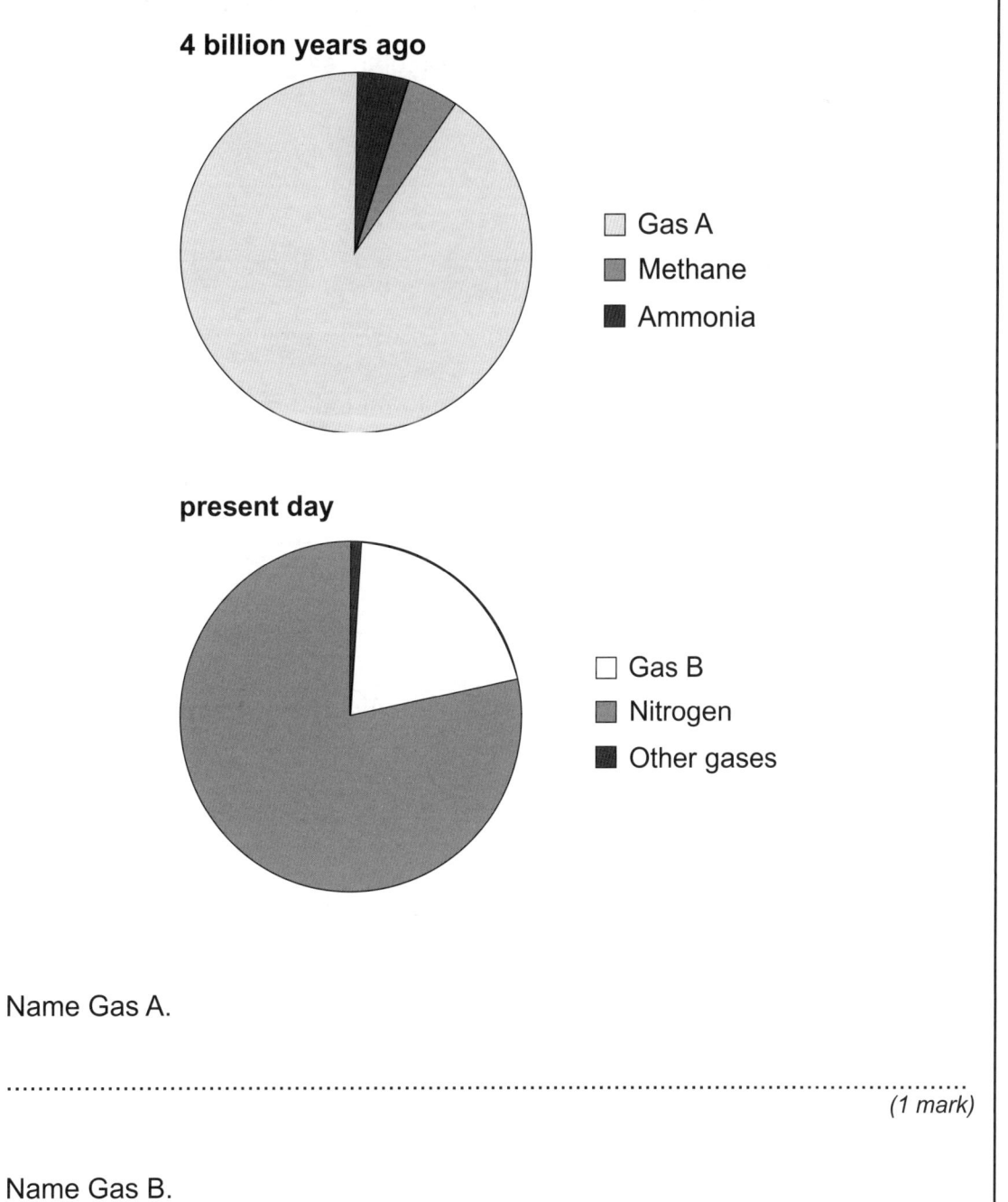

4 billion years ago

- ☐ Gas A
- ■ Methane
- ■ Ammonia

present day

- ☐ Gas B
- ■ Nitrogen
- ■ Other gases

a) Name Gas A.

....
(1 mark)

b) Name Gas B.

....
(1 mark)

Question 8 continues on the next page

Turn over▶

c) In the present day, Gas A makes up only a very tiny percentage of the atmosphere.

4 billion years ago, Gas B was not present in the atmosphere at all.

Describe and explain how the levels of these gases in the atmosphere have changed over the last 4 billion years.

....

....

....

....

....

....

....

(4 marks)

6

END OF TEST

General Certificate of Secondary Education

AQA GCSE Chemistry

Unit Chemistry 2
Higher Tier

Time allowed: 45 minutes.

Centre name
Centre number
Candidate number

Surname
Other names
Candidate signature

Instructions to candidates
- Write your name and other details in the spaces above.
- Answer all questions in the spaces provided.
- Do all rough work on this question paper.
- Write your answers in black or blue ink or ball-point pen.

Information for candidates
- The marks available are given in brackets at the end of each question or part-question.
- In calculations show clearly how you worked out your answers.
- You may use a calculator.
- There are 7 questions in this paper.
- The maximum mark for this paper is 45.

Advice to candidates
- Work steadily through the paper.
- Don't spend too long on one question.
- If you have time at the end, go back and check your answers.

For examiner's use							
Q	Attempt Nº			Q	Attempt Nº		
	1	2	3		1	2	3
1				5			
2				6			
3				7			
4							
				Total 45			

Answer **all** questions in the spaces provided.

1 Two students, David and Joanna, are investigating the speed at which hydrogen peroxide decomposes. David mixes a solution of hydrogen peroxide with a catalyst and records the volume of oxygen produced every 50 seconds, using the apparatus shown below.

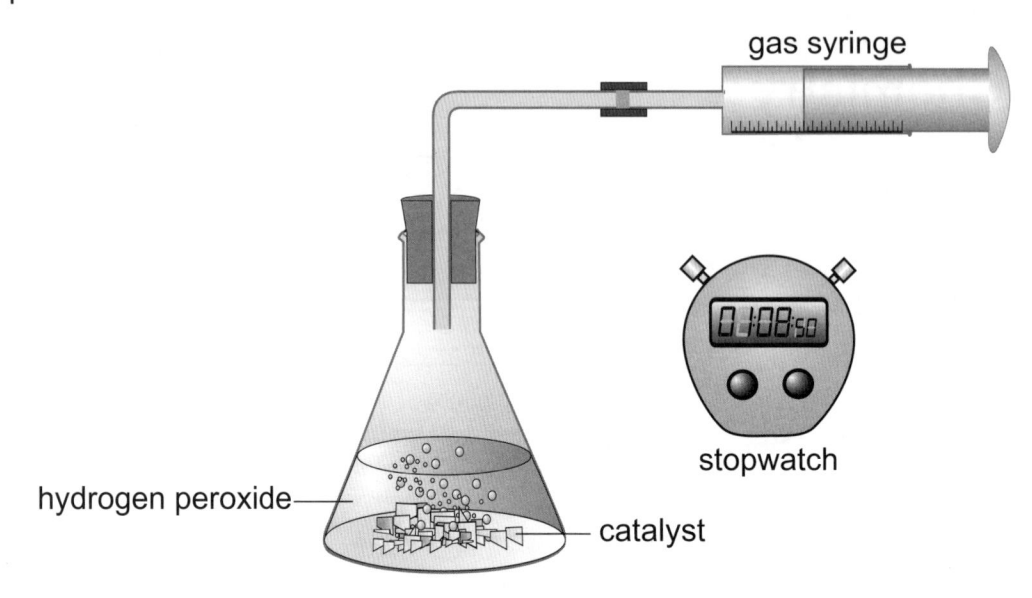

The results are shown in the table below.

Time (s)	0	50	100	150	200	250	300	350
Volume O_2 (cm³)	0	110	210	290	340	370	385	385

a) Plot the points on the graph. Connect the points by drawing a smooth curve.

Volume O_2 (cm³)

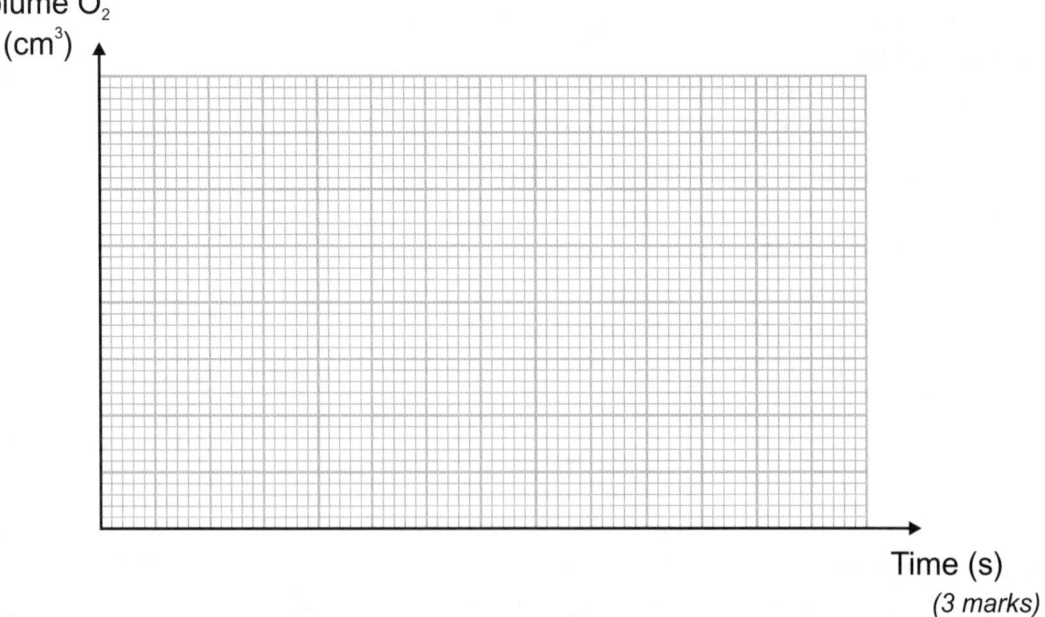

Time (s)

(3 marks)

Joanna uses the same apparatus and amount of hydrogen peroxide as David, but adds a different catalyst to the mixture.

b) After 350 seconds, Joanna has only collected 200 cm³ of oxygen. Sketch a graph on the same axes as David's results to show how you would expect her reaction to have progressed.

(2 marks)

c) When David and Joanna are clearing away the apparatus, they find that the reaction flasks are warm. What does this tell you about the nature of the reaction?

....
(1 mark)

Turn over➤

2 Read the information in the box and answer the questions that follow.

> Ammonium nitrate (NH_4NO_3) is a soluble salt.
>
> It can be produced by reacting an acid with an alkali in an aqueous solution.
>
> Relative atomic masses: hydrogen = 1, nitrogen = 14, oxygen = 16.

a) Name the acid and alkali that can be used to make ammonium nitrate.

....

....
(1 mark)

b) Describe how a solid sample of ammonium nitrate can be obtained from the solution produced.

....

....
(1 mark)

c) Calculate the relative formula mass of ammonium nitrate.

....

....
(2 marks)

d) Calculate the percentage of nitrogen in ammonium nitrate.

....

....
(1 mark)

e) Give a use of ammonium nitrate.

....
(1 mark)

Turn over▶

3 The Haber process is an industrial method of producing ammonia (NH_3).

a) The word equation for the reaction that occurs in the Haber process is:

nitrogen + hydrogen ⇌ ammonia

i) Write a balanced symbol equation, including state symbols, for the reaction.

....
(2 marks)

ii) Calculate the maximum theoretical yield of ammonia when 280 g of nitrogen is reacted with 60 g of hydrogen.

....

....
(1 mark)

iii) Calculate the percentage yield of ammonia, if the actual yield is 58.5 g.

....

....
(1 mark)

b) When the reaction is carried out in a closed system, it progresses to equilibrium. What is meant by the term 'equilibrium'?

....

....
(1 mark)

c) The decomposition of ammonia is endothermic.
Explain the effect of an increase in temperature on:

i) the yield of ammonia.

....

....

....
(1 mark)

ii) the rate of the reaction.

....

....

....
(1 mark)

Turn over▶

4 Silver is a metallic element that occurs naturally as two isotopes, Ag-107 and Ag-109.

a) The relative atomic mass of silver is 108.
Explain, as fully as you can, what is meant by the term 'relative atomic mass'.

....

....

....
(2 marks)

b) All metallic elements have a similar structure that is determined by the way in which the atoms bond. Draw a labelled diagram to represent the bonding within silver.

(1 mark)

c) How does the structure of silver explain the following properties?

i) High thermal and electrical conductivity.

....

....
(1 mark)

ii) Ability to be bent and shaped.

....

....
(1 mark)

d) Silver nanoparticles have been found to have an antibacterial action. What are nanoparticles?

....
(1 mark)

Turn over▶

5   Tiffany is doing an experiment to investigate the electrolysis of sodium chloride solution. She measures the rate of the reaction by estimating the number of bubbles formed at the anode over a certain time.

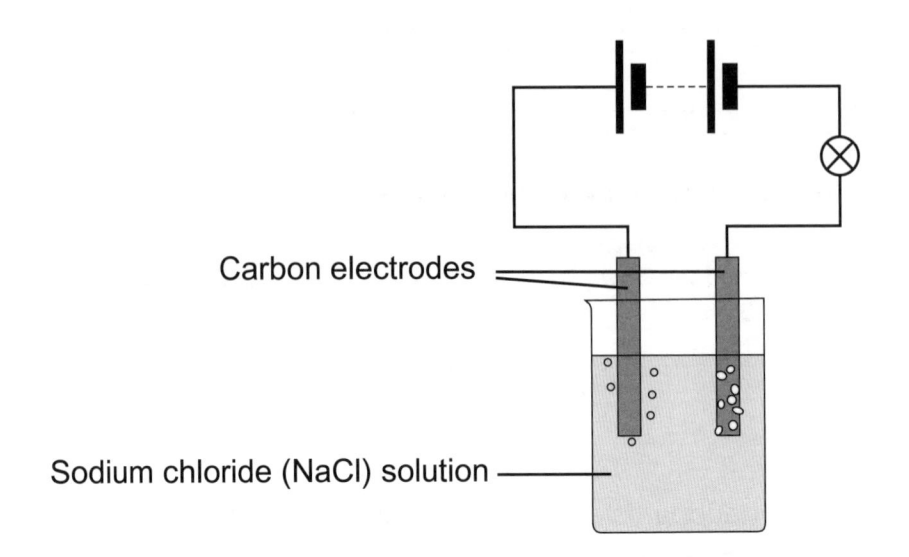

a) The reaction at each electrode can be described by a half equation. Complete the half equations for the reaction occurring at each electrode.

anode   .... Cl^- → Cl_2 + ...

cathode   .... H^+ + ... → H_2

(2 marks)

b) The sodium chloride solution used in this experiment has a known molar concentration. Give the units for molar concentration.

(1 mark)

c) Tiffany has 250 cm³ of sodium chloride (NaCl) solution and 250 cm³ of sodium hydroxide (NaOH) solution. Both solutions have the same molar concentration. How does the mass of sodium in the two solutions compare?

(1 mark)

6 Oven cleaners often contain an aqueous solution of sodium hydroxide (NaOH). The sodium hydroxide reacts with dirt and grease inside the oven to produce water-soluble salts that can be easily removed.

a) Suggest a value for the pH of sodium hydroxide.
Give a reason for your answer.

....
(1 mark)

b) Describe an industrial method that is often used to make sodium hydroxide solution.

....

....
(1 mark)

c) Sodium hydroxide solution must be carefully disposed of because it is corrosive. It can be neutralised by the addition of aqueous hydrochloric acid. Complete the balanced symbol equation, including state symbols, for this reaction.

NaOH(......) + HCl(......) → ....(......) + ...(......)
(2 marks)

d) Calculate the mass of hydrochloric acid needed to neutralise 1 g of sodium hydroxide.

....

....

....

mass of hydrochloric acid = ... g
(3 marks)

Turn over ▶

7 Sulfuric acid is made on an industrial scale using a series of reactions called the Contact process. The information below describes the steps involved in the process.

1. Sulfur is burned in air at a temperature of 350 °C to produce sulfur dioxide:
$$S(s) + O_2(g) \rightarrow SO_2(g).$$

2. Sulfur dioxide is converted to sulfur trioxide.
The reaction is carried out at 450 °C, using a catalyst:
$$2SO_2(g) + O_2(g) \rightleftharpoons 2SO_3(g).$$

3. Sulfur trioxide is dissolved in sulfuric acid to make a chemical called oleum:
$$SO_3(g) + H_2SO_4(l) \rightarrow H_2S_2O_7(l).$$

4. Water is added to the oleum to make concentrated sulfuric acid:
$$H_2S_2O_7(l) + H_2O(l) \rightarrow 2H_2SO_4(l).$$

Stage 2 of the process, the formation of sulfur trioxide, is exothermic.
The energy produced is used to heat more sulfur dioxide and oxygen in stage 1.

a) Explain why recycling energy in this way is important.

....

....
(1 mark)

b) Explain why there is no net energy transfer from the stage 2 reaction at equilibrium.

....

....

....

....
(2 marks)

c) At stage 2, changing the pressure affects the relative amounts of each substance present at equilibrium. State the effect on the yield of sulfur trioxide of **increasing** the pressure. Explain your answer.

....

....
(2 marks)

d) Stages 1 and 2 are both carried out at atmospheric pressure using 1 mole of oxygen. Explain why the **volume** of oxygen gas would not be the same in the two reactions.

....

....
(1 mark)

The table below shows the reactants and products at each stage of the process, and their relative masses.

Stage	Reactants	Relative mass of reactants	Useful product	Relative mass of useful product
1	$S + O_2$	64	SO_2	64
2	$2SO_2 + O_2$	160	$2SO_3$	160
3	$SO_3 + H_2SO_4$		$H_2S_2O_7$	
4	$H_2S_2O_7 + H_2O$		$2H_2SO_4$	

e) Complete the missing entries in the table using the following information.

Relative atomic mass: sulfur = 32, oxygen = 16, hydrogen = 1
(2 marks)

f) What is the overall atom economy of the Contact process?

....
(1 mark)

END OF TEST

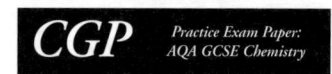

General Certificate of Secondary Education

AQA GCSE Chemistry

Unit Chemistry 3

Higher Tier

Time allowed: 45 minutes.

Centre name				
Centre number				
Candidate number				

Surname
Other names
Candidate signature

Instructions to candidates
- Write your name and other details in the spaces above.
- Answer all questions in the spaces provided.
- Do all rough work on this question paper.
- Write your answers in black or blue ink or ball-point pen.

Information for candidates
- The marks available are given in brackets at the end of each question or part-question.
- In calculations show clearly how you worked out your answers.
- You may use a calculator.
- There are 6 questions in this paper.
- The maximum mark for this paper is 45.

Advice to candidates
- Work steadily through the paper.
- Don't spend too long on one question.
- If you have time at the end, go back and check your answers.

For examiner's use

Q	Attempt Nº			Q	Attempt Nº		
	1	2	3		1	2	3
1				5			
2				6			
3							
4							
				Total 45			

Answer **all** questions in the spaces provided.

1 The nutritional information for two brands of crisps is shown below.

MINI KRINGLES

Energy/100 g: 2099 kJ
Contents/100 g: Protein 4.5 g
Carbohydrates 57 g
Fat 28 g
Fibre 3.3 g
Salt 0.9 g

SALT & QUAKE
Energy/100 g: 2260 kJ

Contents/100 g:
Protein 6.5 g
Carbohydrates 50 g
Fat 35 g
Fibre 4 g
Salt 2.4 g

a) Explain why the energy and contents values are expressed per 100 g of crisps.

....

....
(1 mark)

b) What is likely to be responsible for the higher energy value in the 'Salt & Quake' crisps? Explain your answer.

....

....
(1 mark)

c) Salt is also known by the chemical name sodium chloride. Describe what you would see if a flame test was carried out using sodium chloride.

....
(1 mark)

Question 1 continues on the next page

Turn over ▶

Beth wanted to carry out an experiment to compare the energy values for each type of crisp. Her idea was to burn some crisps on a tin lid and observe the temperature increase of 100 g of water. Her preliminary experiment, using 1 g of 'Mini Kringles', gave only a 5 °C increase in temperature. She modified the experiment to double this to 10 °C.

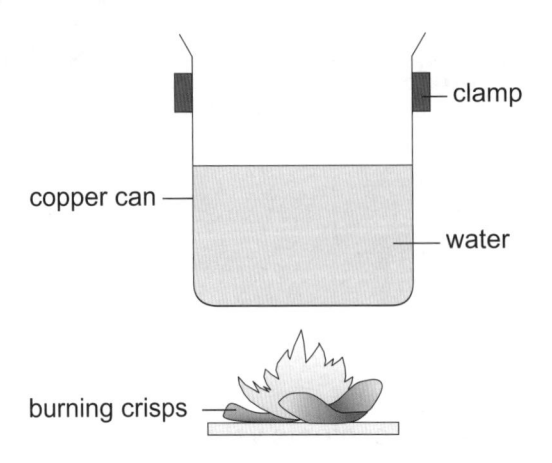

d) Suggest two ways in which Beth could have doubled the temperature rise.

....

....
(2 marks)

e) Why was a copper can used rather than a glass beaker?

....
(1 mark)

f) Calculate the heat energy produced by burning 1 g of 'Mini Kringles' in the preliminary experiment. Heat capacity for water = 4.2 J/g/°C. Assume that all the heat produced is absorbed by the water in the can.

....

....
(1 mark)

g) Suggest why the value obtained is much less than the value on the packet.

....

....
(2 marks)

2 Suggest tests that could be used to distinguish between the following pairs of compounds in solution. You should describe the tests and results expected for each solution.

Solution A	Solution B	Description of test	Observations	
			Solution A	Solution B
Iron(II) chloride	Iron(III) chloride			
Sodium chloride	Sodium iodide			
Ammonium chloride	Sodium chloride			

(6 marks)

3   Limewater is a saturated solution of calcium hydroxide. It is a weak alkali.
    The concentration of limewater can be determined by titration with 0.05M
    hydrochloric acid using a suitable indicator.

    In an experiment, 8.8 cm³ of hydrochloric acid was needed to neutralise 10 cm³ of
    limewater.

    $$2HCl(aq) + Ca(OH)_2(aq) \rightarrow CaCl_2(aq) + 2H_2O(l)$$

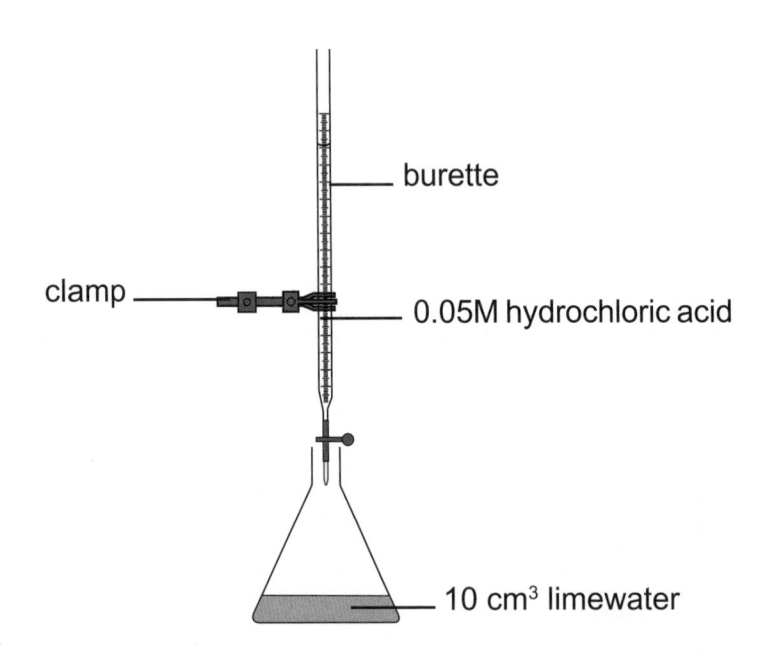

    [Diagram of titration apparatus showing burette containing 0.05M hydrochloric acid, held by clamp, above a conical flask containing 10 cm³ limewater]

    a) What does it mean if a solution is saturated?

    ....
                                                                                                    (1 mark)

    b) Name a suitable indicator for the titration.

    ....
                                                                                                    (1 mark)

c) Limewater is a weak alkali. Explain what is meant by the term 'weak'.

....
(1 mark)

d) i) How many moles of hydrochloric acid reacted with the calcium hydroxide in the limewater in the titration?

....

....
(1 mark)

ii) How many moles of calcium hydroxide reacted with the acid?

....

....
(1 mark)

iii) Calculate the concentration of the calcium hydroxide in the limewater in mol/dm^3.

....

....
(1 mark)

iv) Calculate the concentration of the calcium hydroxide in the limewater in g/dm^3. The M_r for calcium hydroxide is 74.

....

....
(1 mark)

e) What changes could be made to the experiment to make the results more reliable?

....

....
(1 mark)

Turn over▶

4 Solubility data for potassium nitrate is given in the table below.

saturation temperature (°C)	solubility (g/100 g water)
26	40
33	50
45	75
56	100
65	122
74	148
84	175

a) The graph below shows the solubility of sodium chloride, NaCl, at various temperatures. Plot the data for potassium nitrate on the same graph.

(2 marks)

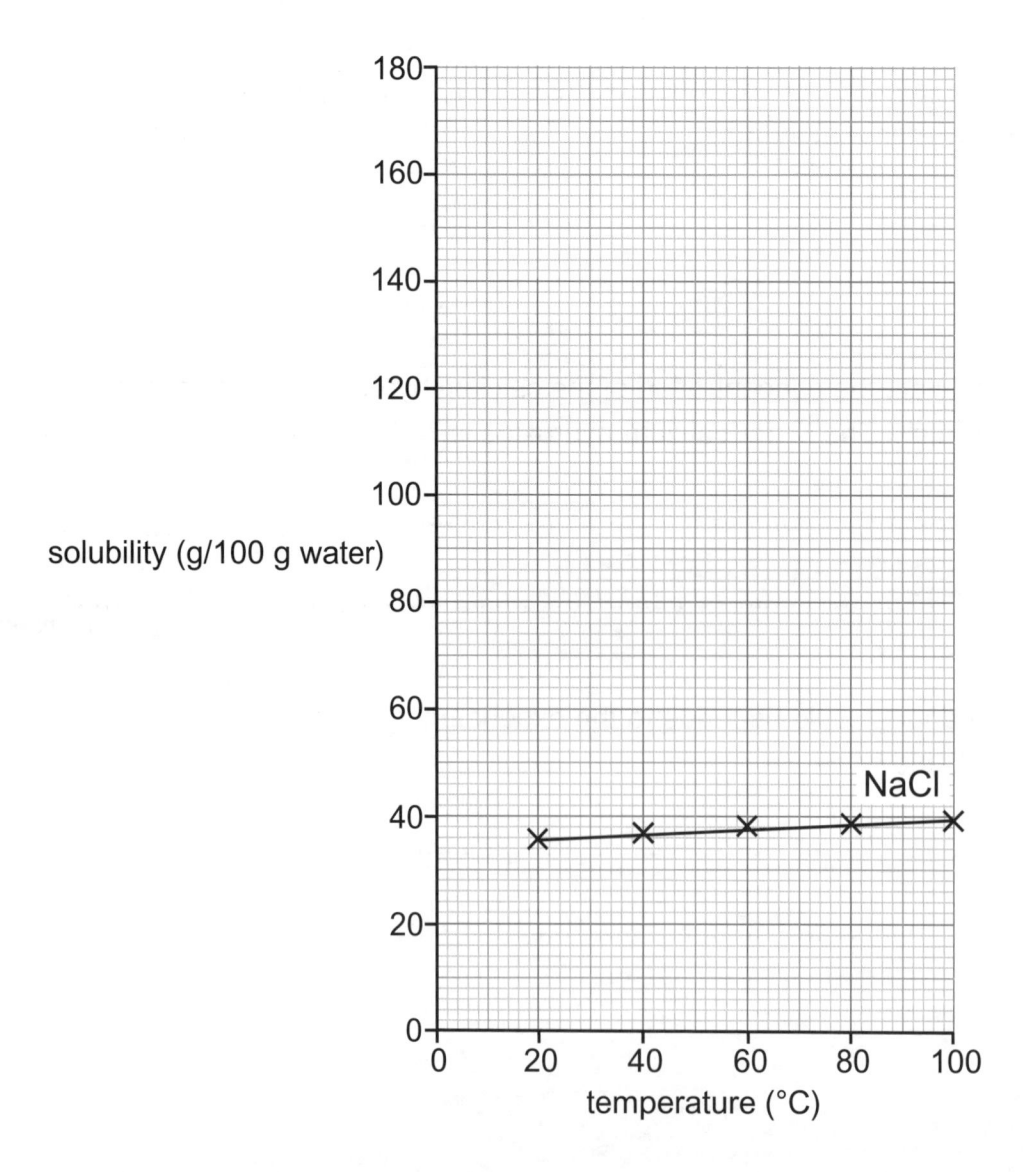

b) Describe how the solubilities of sodium chloride and potassium nitrate change as the temperature increases.

....

....
(1 mark)

c) If a saturated solution of potassium nitrate at 70 °C was cooled down to 30 °C, how much potassium nitrate would crystallise out? Show your working.

....

....
(3 marks)

d) Which of the two graphs below shows the solubility curve for a gas? Explain your answer.

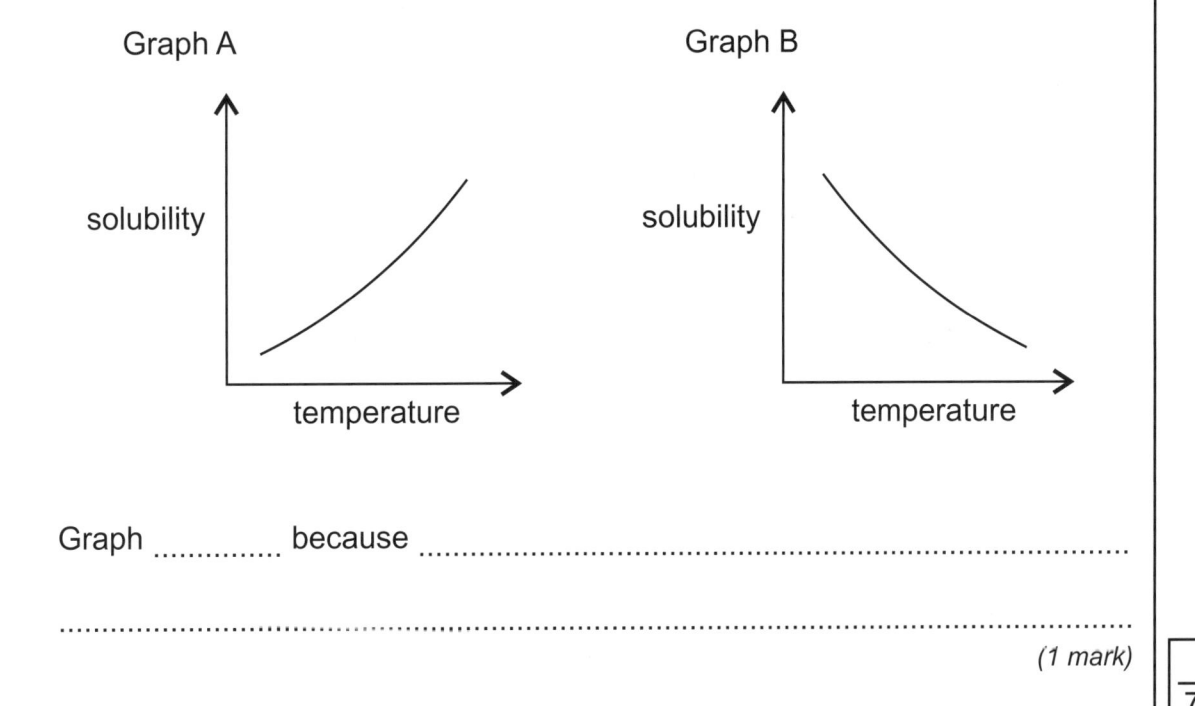

Graph A

Graph B

Graph .... because ....

....
(1 mark)

7

Turn over for the next question

Turn over ➤

5 Water becomes hard because it is a good solvent and can dissolve small amounts of calcium and magnesium salts when it passes over certain rocks. Water can be tested for hardness by taking samples and adding soap solution, 1 cm³ at a time, until it forms a good lather on shaking. The results for 5 cm³ samples of hard water and distilled water are shown in the table below.

Water	Volume of soap solution needed to form a good lather (cm³)		
	Test 1	Test 2	Test 3
Distilled	1	1	1
Hard	8	10	9

a) What is initially formed when soap solution is added to hard water?

....
(1 mark)

b) Explain how the test can be used to show the relative hardness of samples of water.

....

....
(1 mark)

c) Explain why the test was repeated three times on each water sample.

....

....
(1 mark)

d) The experiment outlined above is a fair test. Explain why the repeated results are quite variable even though the test is considered to be fair.

....

....
(1 mark)

e) Describe and explain two ways in which hardness caused by calcium and magnesium ions can be removed from water.

1. ....

....

2. ....

....
(4 marks)

f) Give one disadvantage of hard water.

....

....
(1 mark)

Turn over for the next question

Turn over ▶

6 Methane is the main component of natural gas and burns well in air.

a) Use the bond energies provided and the diagram of the bonds involved during combustion to calculate the energy change for the reaction.

Bond energy values kJ/mole:
- E(C-H) = + 413
- E(O=O) = + 498
- E(C=O) = + 805
- E(O-H) = + 464

$$CH_4 + 2O_2 \rightarrow CO_2 + 2H_2O$$

....

....

....

Energy change = ... kJ/mol

(4 marks)

b) Is the reaction above exothermic or endothermic? Explain your answer in terms of bond energies.

....

....

(2 marks)

END OF TEST

Answers

Page 18-19
Warm-Up Questions

An element is a substance that consists of only one type of atom. For example: Air contains the elements oxygen and nitrogen; Metals: iron, aluminium, etc.

$C_6H_{12}O_6 + 6O_2 \rightarrow 6CO_2 + 6H_2O$

(s) — solid, (l) — liquid, (g) — gas, (aq) — dissolved in water.

Any three of, e.g. as a building material / making glass / making cement / making slaked lime.

Any one of, e.g. destroys habitats / uses land / causes noise / causes pollution / leads to unsightly tips.

Cement is limestone that has been heated with clay. Mortar is cement mixed with sand and water.

Exam Questions

1 C *(1 mark)*
2 B *(1 mark)*
3 C *(1 mark)*
4 (a) In a compound, different types of atoms are bonded together chemically. In a mixture they are not. *(1 mark)*
  (b) e.g. carbon dioxide / methane *(1 mark)*
  (c) $2Mg + O_2 \rightarrow 2MgO$ *(1 mark for correct products and reactants, 1 mark for correctly balancing the equation)*
5 (a) sulfuric acid + ammonia → ammonium sulfate *(1 mark)*
  (b) $H_2SO_4 + 2NH_3 \rightarrow (NH_4)_2SO_4$ *(1 mark for correct products and reactants, 1 mark for correctly balancing the equation)*
  (c) 15 *(1 mark)*
  There are eight atoms of hydrogen, one atom of sulfur, four atoms of oxygen, and two atoms of nitrogen.
6 (a) $CaCO_3 \rightarrow CaO + CO_2$ *(1 mark)*
  (b) (i) calcium hydroxide *(1 mark)*, $Ca(OH)_2$ *(1 mark)*
      (ii) e.g. neutralising acidic soils *(1 mark)*
7 (a) Powdered limestone is heated in a kiln with powdered clay. *(1 mark for limestone and clay, 1 mark for heating in a kiln)*
  (b) Limestone is heated with sand and sodium carbonate. *(1 mark for heating, 1 mark for sodium carbonate and sand)*

Page 26-27
Warm-Up Questions

Any three of, hard / strong / good electrical conductors / good conductors of heat / malleable / ductile / flexible.

metallic bonding

E.g. haematite, bauxite, chalcopyrite

Copper extracted by reduction with carbon is impure and doesn't conduct electricity well enough. Electrolysis produces very pure copper which is a much better conductor.

Any one of, e.g. zinc / iron / tin / copper.

Exam Questions

1 B *(1 mark)*
2 (a) E.g. electrical wires, plumbing *(2 marks)*
  (b) Any one of, e.g. the supply of copper-rich ores is limited / demand for copper is growing *(1 mark)*.
  (c) (i) E.g. other methods need a lot of energy / other methods release sulfur dioxide gas, which causes acid rain. *(1 mark)*
      (ii) E.g. using bacteria is slower than other methods. *(1 mark)*
3 (a) Any two of, e.g. useful products can be made / provides jobs / brings money into the local area *(1 mark each)*.
  (b) Any two of, e.g. causes noise / scars landscape / loss of habitats / abandoned mine shafts can be dangerous *(1 mark each)*.
4 (a) E.g. potassium, sodium, calcium, magnesium, aluminium (any metal above carbon in the reactivity series). *(1 mark)*
  (b) (i) removal of oxygen (accept gain of electrons) *(1 mark)*
      (ii) zinc oxide + carbon → zinc + carbon dioxide *(1 mark)*
  (c) $Fe_2O_3(s) + 3CO(g) \rightarrow 2Fe(s) + 3CO_2(g)$ *(1 mark for correct products and reactants, 1 mark for correctly balancing the equation, 1 mark for correct state symbols)*
  (d) C *(1 mark)*
      Zinc is more reactive than copper, so zinc will displace copper.
5 (a) The outer electrons of each atom can move freely, creating a sea of free electrons *(1 mark)*. These can carry electric current through the material *(1 mark)*.
  (b) The free electrons can conduct heat *(1 mark)*.

Page 32
Warm-Up Questions

1 Carbon
2 A mixture of metals, or a mixture of a metal and a non-metal, e.g. bronze — sculpture, medals / cupronickel — coins / solder — joining wires.
3 A smart alloy is a metal alloy that has a shape memory property.
4 E.g. Metal fatigue is worse in smart alloys. Smart alloys are quite expensive.
5 The surface of aluminium is covered in a protective layer of aluminium oxide that stops corrosion of the metal underneath.
6 When metals are put under repeated stresses and strains they become more prone to breaking.

Exam Questions

1 D *(1 mark)*
2 B *(1 mark)*
3 A — 2 *(1 mark)*
  B — 3 *(1 mark)*
  C — 4 *(1 mark)*
  D — 1 *(1 mark)*

Page 41-42
Warm-Up Questions

1. Any three of, e.g. Refinery gas / petrol / naphtha / kerosene / diesel / oil / bitumen.
2. Compounds made from carbon and hydrogen only.
3. Saturated hydrocarbons with the general formula C_nH_{2n+2}.
4. Any three of, e.g. transport / electricity generation / making plastics / heating / making medicines / making paints and dyes.
5. Sulfur dioxide produced from burning fossil fuels mixes with clouds and forms dilute sulfuric acid. This then falls as acid rain.
6. Global dimming is the reduction in the amount of sunlight reaching the Earth's surface. It is caused by particles of soot and ash released when fossil fuels are burnt that reflect light back into space.

Exam Questions

1. A *(1 mark)*
2. (a) (i) There should be an M in the bottom box *(1 mark)*.
    (ii) There should be a B in the top box *(1 mark)*.
    Fractions with bigger molecules have a higher boiling point, so condense at the higher temperatures at the bottom of the column. Fractions with smaller molecules have a lower boiling point, so don't condense until they reach the top of the column.
   (b) Any one of, e.g. jet fuel, domestic heating, paint solvent *(1 mark)*.
   (c) The explanation should contain three of the following points:
      the fractions have different boiling points
      the crude oil is heated
      the fractions boil
      fractions condense at different heights in the fractionating column
      fractions are tapped off where they condense
      (1 mark per point; maximum 3 marks)
3. C *(1 mark)*
4. (a) E.g. Carbon dioxide is thought to cause global warming. Sulfur dioxide causes acid rain. Particulate matter causes global dimming. *(1 mark per point; maximum 3 marks)*
   (b) E.g. Engines need to be converted. Ethanol is not widely available. *(1 mark for any correct point)*
5. (a) (i) methane and CO_2 *(1 mark)*
    (ii) By microorganisms digesting waste *(1 mark)*. It can be burnt to heat water/generate electricity *(1 mark)*.
    (iii) Advantage: any one of, e.g. cheap / carbon neutral / renewable / uses waste products *(1 mark)*.
        Disadvantage: e.g. production is slow in cold weather *(1 mark)*.
   (b) (i) by electrolysing water *(1 mark)*
    (ii) It's highly explosive, so it has to be kept in very secure containers *(1 mark)*.
    (iii) Any one of, e.g. you would need a specially designed, expensive engine / hydrogen isn't widely and cheaply available / large, strong gas containers are heavy and would increase fuel consumption *(1 mark)*.

Page 43
Revision Summary for Chemistry 1a

3. Calcium
4. 2 sodium atoms, 1 carbon atom and 3 oxygen atoms
5. a) b) c) d)
   a) Could be water and carbon dioxide.
   b) Could be argon (or any other noble gas) and hydrogen/oxygen/nitrogen (or any other diatomic gaseous element).
   c) Could be hydrogen/oxygen/nitrogen (or any other diatomic gaseous element).
   d) Could be carbon dioxide (water molecules are bent).
7. a) $CaCO_3 + 2HCl \rightarrow CaCl_2 + H_2O + CO_2$
   b) $Ca + 2H_2O \rightarrow Ca(OH)_2 + H_2$
25. Propane — the fuel needs to be a gas at -10 °C to work in a camping stove.

Page 49
Warm-Up Questions

1. Long-chain hydrocarbons are cracked to make more useful products / because there's more demand for short-chain fractions
2. High temperature and a catalyst.
3. They contain carbon-carbon double bonds meaning they have the potential to form more bonds by splitting the double bonds.
4. Ethene is reacted with steam using phosphoric acid as a catalyst at 300 °C and 70 atmospheres pressure.
5. Ethene is pressurised in the presence of a catalyst.

Exam Questions

1. (a) $n \begin{pmatrix} H \\ C=C \\ H & CH_3 \end{pmatrix} \longrightarrow \begin{pmatrix} H & H \\ -C-C- \\ H & CH_3 \end{pmatrix}_n$ *(1 mark)*
   (b) *(1 mark)*
2. (a) ethanol *(1 mark)*
   (b) phosphoric acid *(1 mark)*.

Page 56
Warm-Up Questions

1. The fruits or seeds are crushed. The oil is separated from the crushed plant material (by a centrifuge or using solvents). The oil is then distilled to refine it.
2. An emulsion is a mixture of oil and water.
3. A nickel catalyst, at about 60 °C.
4. Any three from: preservatives; colourings; flavourings; emulsifiers; stabilisers; sweeteners.

Exam Questions

1. A — 1 *(1 mark)*
   B — 2 *(1 mark)*
   C — 4 *(1 mark)*
   D — 3 *(1 mark)*

2. (a) vegetable oils *(1 mark)*
   (b) (i) Biodiesel comes from recently grown plants which took in carbon dioxide from the air when they were alive *(1 mark)*. This is released again when the biodiesel is burnt, so the net increase in carbon dioxide in the atmosphere is nil *(1 mark)*.
   (ii) Any two from, e.g. produces less sulfur dioxide than diesel or petrol / doesn't release as many particulates as diesel or petrol / it's biodegradable / it's less toxic than regular diesel / it's made from a renewable resource *(1 mark each)*.
   (c) E.g. it's more expensive than ordinary diesel / we're unable to make enough biodiesel to replace regular diesel *(2 marks)*.

3. A — 4 *(1 mark)*
   B — 1 *(1 mark)*
   C — 3 *(1 mark)*
   D — 2 *(1 mark)*

Page 62-63
Warm-Up Questions

1. A (theoretical) single land mass / supercontinent made from the all present continents joined together.
2. volcano / mountain chain
3. *Earthquakes occur at plate boundaries but they aren't a geological feature.*
4. Any one of, e.g. bulging of the ground near the volcano / mini-earthquakes.
5. The ozone layer blocked harmful rays from the sun which enabled complex organisms to survive.
6. Argon is used in filament lamps. Neon is used in electric discharge tubes (neon lights). Helium is used in party balloons and airships.

Exam Questions

1. B *(1 mark)*
2. (a) Any two of, there is a jigsaw fit between the continents / identical fossils of the same age have been found in rocks in different continents, which suggests the continents were joined once upon a time / certain rock layers of similar ages on different continents show similarity / there are various living creatures found in both America and Africa that couldn't have crossed the Atlantic Ocean. *(1 mark each)*.
   (b) This theory wasn't accepted because: any one of, e.g. he wasn't a geologist / proposed forces required would stop the Earth's rotation *(1 mark)*.
3. C *(1 mark)*
4. (a) The diagram should be labelled:
   A – crust *(1 mark)*
   B – mantle *(1 mark)*
   C – core *(1 mark)*
   (b) nickel *(1 mark)*, iron *(1 mark)*
5. (a) There have been large variations in temperature and CO_2 concentration over the last 250 000 years *(1 mark)*. There is a positive correlation between CO_2 concentration and temperature *(1 mark)*.
   The question's worth two marks, so you have to make two points.
   (b) The X should be drawn at 25 000 years ago *(1 mark)*.
6. A — 3 *(1 mark)*
   B — 2 *(1 mark)*
   C — 4 *(1 mark)*
   D — 1 *(1 mark)*

Page 64
Revision Summary for Chemistry 1b

24 b) 2 cm   c) 3.5 years
25 a) 2%   b) H_2O

Page 71
Warm-Up Questions

1. protons and electrons
2. Mass number is the sum of the number of protons and the number of neutrons in an atom. Atomic number is the number of protons (or electrons) in an atom.
3. neutron
4. isotopes
5. (a) 2
   (b) 8

Exam Questions

1. B *(1 mark)*
2. B and C *(2 marks)*
3. (a) 11 *(1 mark)*
   (b) Group 1 *(1 mark)*, because it has one electron in its outer shell / because it's got 11 electrons, so it's sodium which is in Group 1. *(1 mark)*.

Page 75
Warm-Up Questions

1. A high boiling point
2. When giant ionic solids are dissolved the ions separate and are free to move in the solution. These free-moving charged particles allow the solution to carry electric current.
3. cations
4. anions
5. $Al(OH)_3$

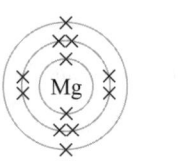

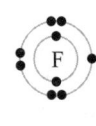

Exam Questions

1 (a) [diagram of Mg and F electron shells] *(1 mark)* *(1 mark)*

(b) Mg^{2+} *(1 mark)* and F^- *(1 mark)*

(c) MgF_2 *(1 mark)*

(d) The positively charged magnesium ions are attracted to the negatively charged fluoride ions *(1 mark)*.

(e) (i) There are strong forces of attraction between the ions *(1 mark)* so a large amount of energy is needed to melt the compound *(1 mark)*.

(ii) When the magnesium fluoride is molten the ions can move about and carry charge (i.e. conduct a current) through the liquid *(1 mark)*.

2 (a)

	Potassium atom, K	Potassium ion, K⁺	Chlorine atom, Cl	Chloride ion, Cl⁻
Number of electrons	19	18	17	18
Electron arrangement	2, 8, 8, 1	2, 8, 8	2, 8, 7	2, 8, 8

(1 mark for each correct column, maximum 3 marks)

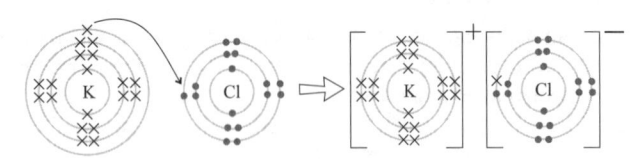

(b) [diagram of K and Cl electron transfer]

(2 marks — 1 mark for correct electron arrangements, 1 mark for correct arrow and charges on ions)

Page 84-85
Warm-Up Questions

1 In a covalent bond, the atoms share electrons. In an ionic bond, one of the atoms donates electrons to the other atom.

2 Diamond is very hard and graphite is fairly soft.
Graphite conducts electricity and diamond doesn't.
Diamond is clear/transparent and graphite is opaque.
Diamond is colourless and graphite is black.

3 E.g. silicon dioxide/silica

4 Because the intermolecular forces between the chlorine molecules are very weak.

Exam Questions

1 [diagram of O=C=O]

(1 mark for double bonds shown correctly, 1 mark for remaining electrons shown correctly)

2 (a) (i) giant covalent *(1 mark)*

(ii) giant covalent *(1 mark)*

(iii) simple covalent *(1 mark)*

(b) It doesn't contain any free electrons or ions to carry the charge *(1 mark)*.

(c) It contains free electrons able to carry the charge *(1 mark)*.

(d) All of the atoms in silicon dioxide and in graphite are held together by strong covalent bonds *(1 mark)*. In bromine, each molecule is held together with a strong covalent bond but the forces between these molecules are weak *(1 mark)*.

In order to melt, a substance has to overcome the forces holding its particles tightly together in the rigid structure of a solid. If the forces between the particles are weak, this is easy to do and doesn't take much energy at all. But if the forces are really strong, like in a giant covalent structure, you have to provide loads of heat to give the particles enough energy to break free.

3 (a) (i) nm *(1 mark)*

(ii) surface area *(1 mark)*, volume *(1 mark)*

(b) The CNTs provided strength *(1 mark)* and lightness/low density *(1 mark)*.

(c) Any one of, e.g. in computers / in sensors / as catalysts *(1 mark)*.

4 In carbon nanotubes with a structure like that in the diagram, each carbon atom only forms three bonds *(1 mark)*. This leaves each atom with a spare electron *(1 mark)*, and if a current is applied these electrons are free to move and carry the charge, so the tube conducts *(1 mark)*.

Page 88

1) a) 30.0% b) 88.9% c) 65.3%

2) CH_4

Page 89

1) 21.4 g

Page 92-93
Warm-Up Questions

1 Mass number

2 The relative atomic mass

3 The relative formula mass

4 One mole of atoms or molecules of any substance will have a mass in grams equal to the relative formula mass for that substance.

5 One mole of O_2 weighs $16 \times 2 = 32$ g.

6 Moles = volume (l) × molarity
= 0.5 × 0.5
= 0.25 moles

Exam Questions

(a) (i) Relative atomic mass *(1 mark)*.
 (ii) Boron-11 has one more neutron in its nucleus than boron-10 *(1 mark)*.
 (iii) Boron-11 must be the most abundant *(1 mark)*. The A_r value takes into account the relative abundance of each isotope, and in the case of boron it is closer to 11 than to 10 *(1 mark)*.
(b) (i) M_r of $BF_3 = 11 + (19 \times 3) = 68$ *(1 mark)*
 (ii) M_r of $B(OH)_3 = 11 + (17 \times 3) = 62$ *(1 mark)*

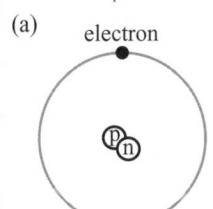

(a) electron

(1 mark for showing the correct particles in the nucleus, 1 mark for showing the single orbiting electron correctly).

(b) (i) $M_r = (2 \times 2) + 16 = 20$ *(1 mark)*
 (ii) Because the mass of water molecules containing deuterium (20) is greater than the mass of ordinary water molecules (18) *(1 mark)*.

(a) % mass of N in $CO(NH_2)_2 = [(A_r \times \text{no. of atoms}) \div M_r] \times 100$
$= [(14 \times 2) \div (12 + 16 + 32)] \times 100$
$= 47\%$
(1 mark for correct working, 1 mark for correct answer)

% mass of N in $KNO_3 = [14 \div (39 + 14 + 48)] \times 100$
$= 14\%$
(1 mark for correct working, 1 mark for correct answer)

% mass of N in $NH_4NO_3 = [(14 \times 2) \div (28 + 4 + 48)] \times 100$
$= 35\%$
(1 mark for correct working, 1 mark for correct answer)

Calculations are often worth more than one mark. It can be tempting just to scribble down enough working out to get you to the answer. But it's worth bearing in mind that if you get the final answer wrong, you could still get some marks for the working. So if you put down each step clearly it could pay off.

(b) Urea *(1 mark)*. It contains the greatest percentage mass of nitrogen, so would provide more nitrogen for plant growth per kg spread on the soil *(1 mark)*.

(a) $100 - 60 = 40\%$ *(1 mark)*
(b) 40 g of sulfur combine with 60 g of oxygen.
S = 40   O = 60
40 ÷ 32   60 ÷ 16
= 1.25   = 3.75
1.25 ÷ 1.25 = 1   3.75 ÷ 1.25 = 3
Therefore, the formula of the oxide is SO_3
(2 marks — 1 mark for correct working)

5 (a) 100g .... reacts to give ...   56 g
 1 g .... reacts to give ... $56 \div 100 = 0.56$ g
 2 g .... reacts to give ... $0.56 \times 2 = 1.12$ g *(1 mark)*
(b) E.g. When transferring the $CaCO_3$ from the weighing apparatus to the test tube, or the CaO from the test tube to the weighing apparatus some of the solid may be left behind *(1 mark)*.

Page 98
Warm-Up Questions

1 Waste by-products decrease the atom economy of a reaction.
2 100%.
3 Because they use up resources very quickly and produce a lot of waste. This might be polluting and it has to be disposed of (e.g. in landfill sites or in the sea).
4 The raw materials would cost a lot and the waste would be expensive to dispose of. There would also be less product to sell.
5 Percentage yield $= (4 \div 5) \times 100$
$= 80\%$

Exam Questions

1 M_r of ethanol $= (12 \times 2) + 6 + 16 = 46$
M_r of ethene $= (12 \times 2) + 4 = 28$ *(1 mark)*
Atom economy $= (28 \div 46) \times 100$ *(1 mark)*
$= 61 \%$ *(1 mark)*

2 (a) From the equation, 4 moles of CuO $\rightarrow$ 4 moles of Cu
so 1 mole CuO $\rightarrow$ 1 mole Cu *(1 mark)*
$63.5 + 16 = 79.5$ g CuO $\rightarrow$ 63.5 g Cu *(1 mark)*
1 g CuO $\rightarrow$ $63.5 \div 79.5 = 0.8$ g (1 d.p.)
4 g CuO $\rightarrow$ $0.8 \times 4 = 3.2$ g *(1 mark)*

(b) Percentage yield $= (2.8 \div 3.2) \times 100$ *(1 mark)*
$= 87.5\%$ *(1 mark)*

(c) Any three of:
There may have been an incomplete reaction — some copper oxide was not reduced *(1 mark)*.
There may have been unexpected reactions (which produced different products) due to impurities in the reactants *(1 mark)*.
Some of the copper may have been left behind when it was scraped out into the beaker *(1 mark)*.
Some of the copper may have been left on the filter paper *(1 mark)*.

Page 99
Revision Summary for Chemistry 2i

15 (a) A: metal, B: giant molecular, C: ionic
 (b)(i) A, (ii) B, (iii) C
18 (a) $CaCO_3 + 2HCl \rightarrow CaCl_2 + H_2O + CO_2$
 (b) $H_2SO_4 + 2KOH \rightarrow K_2SO_4 + 2H_2O$
20 (a) 40 (b) 108 (c) 44 (d) 84 (e) 106 (f) 81 (g) 56 (h) 17
21 (a) (i) 12.0% (ii) 27.3% (iii) 75.0%
 (b) (i) 74.2% (ii) 70.0% (iii) 52.9%
22 $MgSO_4$
23 80.3 g
25 0.46 moles

Page 107
Warm-Up Questions

1. Increase the temperature (of the acid).
   Use smaller pieces of/powdered magnesium.
   Increase the acid concentration.
2. It would increase the time taken (i.e. reduce the rate of reaction).
3. By keeping the milk cool/storing it in a fridge.
4. The corrosion of iron is a reaction that happens very slowly. Explosions are very fast reactions. (Other answers possible.)
5. Measure the volume of gas given off by collecting it in a gas syringe/monitor the mass of a reaction flask from which the gas escapes.

Exam Questions

1. (a) Any two of, the concentration of sodium thiosulfate/ hydrochloric acid / the person judging when the black cross is obscured / the black cross used (size, darkness etc.) *(1 mark each)*.

   Judging when a cross is completely obscured is quite subjective — two people might not agree on exactly when it happens. You can try to limit this problem by using the same person each time, but you can't remove the problem completely.
   The person might have changed their mind slightly by the time they do the next experiment — or be looking at it from a different angle, be a bit more bored, etc.

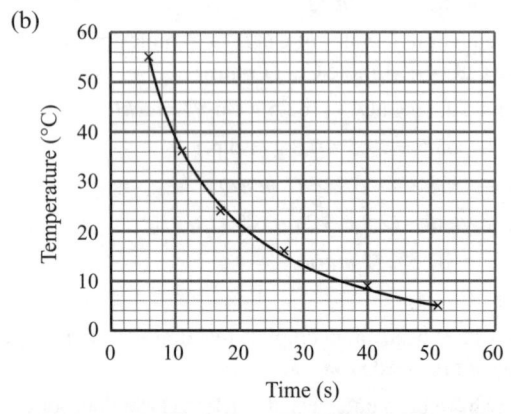

   (b) [Graph: Temperature (°C) vs Time (s), curve decreasing from ~55°C at 5s to ~5°C at 50s]
   (1 mark for all points plotted correctly, 1 mark for best-fit curve)

   (c) As the temperature increases the time decreases, meaning that the reaction is happening faster *(1 mark)*. An increase in temperature causes an increase in the rate of a reaction because the particles have more energy *(1 mark)*.

   (d) Each of the reactions would happen more slowly *(1 mark)*, although they would still vary with temperature in the same way *(1 mark)*.

2. (a) A gas/carbon dioxide is produced and leaves the flask *(1 mark)*.

   (b) The same amount and concentration of acid was used each time, with excess marble *(1 mark)*.

   (c) (i) E.g. The marble chips were smaller/the temperature was higher *(1 mark)*.

   (ii) E.g. Smaller chips give an increased surface area, increasing the rate/a higher temperature means the particles have more energy, increasing the rate *(1 mark)*.

   (d) The concentration of the acid is greatest at this point, before it starts being converted into products *(1 mark)*.

Page 112
Warm-Up Questions

1. They must collide with enough energy.
2. Heat the reaction mixture.
3. The particles are squashed more closely together and so collide more often.
4. A catalyst is a substance which changes the speed of a reaction, without being changed or used up in the reaction.
5. The activation energy is the minimum amount of energy needed for the reaction to happen.

Exam Questions

1. (a) Heating makes the hydrogen peroxide particles move faster *(1 mark)*, so they collide more often *(1 mark)* and with greater energy *(1 mark)*.

   (b) The surface area of the catalyst is increased *(1 mark)*, giving the particles a greater area that they can stick to and react *(1 mark)*.

   (c) By increasing the hydrogen peroxide concentration *(1 mark)*

2. (a) This gives the catalyst a greater surface area *(1 mark)*.

   (b) This reduces the amount of energy needed for heating *(1 mark)*, meaning that the energy costs are reduced and the product is cheaper to make (and using less energy is also better for the environment) *(1 mark)*.

   (c) Any two of, they can be very expensive to buy / they may need to be removed from the product and cleaned, which could be costly and wastes time / they can be poisoned by impurities and need replacing *(1 mark each)*.

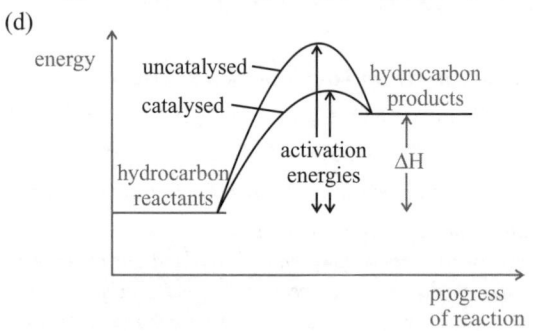

   (d) [Energy profile diagram showing uncatalysed and catalysed curves from hydrocarbon reactants to hydrocarbon products, with activation energies and ΔH labelled]

   (1 mark for showing two curves of the correct shape that peak above the 'products' energy level. 1 mark for showing that the catalysed activation energy is lower. 1 mark for showing both the activation energies clearly.)

241

Page 118
Warm-Up Questions

1) exothermic
2) The temperature will decrease.
3) Add a catalyst.
4) They are the same.
5) It increases the amount/concentration/yield of products / shifts the position of equilibrium to the right.
6) iron/Fe
7) They are recycled and used to produce more product.

Exam Questions

1 (a) Because the CO_2 gas that's produced would escape if the system wasn't closed. This would cause the equilibrium to shift *(1 mark)*.
 (b) Increasing the temperature *(1 mark)* and reducing the pressure *(1 mark)*.
2 (a) (i) crude oil/methane/water *(1 mark)*
   (ii) air *(1 mark)*
 (b) $3H_2(g) + N_2(g) \rightleftharpoons 2NH_3(g)$
   (1 mark for correct formula, 1 mark if correctly balanced, 1 mark for correct state symbols).
 (c) E.g. fertilisers/explosives *(1 mark)*.
 (d) A high temperature reduces the equilibrium yield but increases the rate of the reaction *(1 mark)*. If the temperature was any lower, the product would be formed too slowly *(1 mark)*.
   Remember, it's better to get a yield of 10% after 20 seconds than a yield of 20% after 60 seconds.

Revision Summary for Chemistry 2ii (page 119)

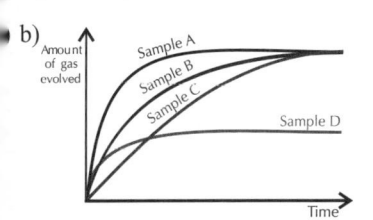

b) [Graph: Amount of gas evolved vs Time, showing Sample A, Sample B, Sample C, Sample D curves]

Page 125-126
Warm-Up Questions

1) Neutralisation.
2) A salt and hydrogen gas.
3) Copper nitrate and water.
4) Add the insoluble base to an acid until all the acid is neutralised and the excess base can be seen on the bottom of the flask. Then filter out the excess base and evaporate off the water to leave a pure, dry sample.
5) Iron is less reactive than aluminium, so it would not displace the aluminium from the salt.

Exam Questions

1 (a) A — red
   B — pH 7
   D — pH 8/9
   E — purple
   (2 marks if all correct, 1 mark for 2 or 3 correct)
 (b) C *(1 mark)*
 (c) E *(1 mark)*
 (d) B *(1 mark)*
 (e) A *(1 mark)*

   With questions like this, always have a guess if you're not sure. Remember, the examiners can't take marks off you (even for a really silly answer) and if you're stuck between two possibilities you're much more likely to get a mark if you go for one of them than if you put nothing at all.

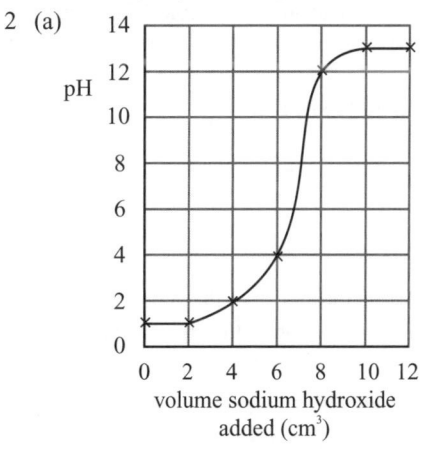

2 (a) [Graph: pH vs volume sodium hydroxide added (cm^3), S-shaped titration curve from pH 1 rising to pH ~13]

   (1 mark for points plotted correctly, 1 mark for best fit curve)
 (b) 7 cm^3 (also accept 6 or 8, depending on best fit curve at pH 7) *(1 mark)*.
 (c) Because the starting pH is pH 1 *(1 mark)*.
   This is the kind of question that can somehow trip you up, even if it seems obvious once you know the answer. So it's lucky you've come across it now rather than in the exam, isn't it? The pH before any alkali is added has to be the pH of the acid, and a pH of 1 means a very strong acid. See? Obvious.
 (d) sodium sulfate *(1 mark)*
3 (a) sodium chloride *(1 mark)*
 (b) potassium hydroxide and ammonia *(1 mark)*
 (c) zinc oxide *(1 mark)*
 (d) (i) $Mg + 2HCl \rightarrow MgCl_2 + H_2$ *(1 mark)*
   (ii) $NH_3 + HCl \rightarrow NH_4Cl$ *(1 mark)*
   (iii) $ZnO + 2HCl \rightarrow ZnCl_2 + H_2O$ *(1 mark)*
   (iv) $KOH + HCl \rightarrow KCl + H_2O$ *(1 mark)*
4 (a) It must be insoluble *(1 mark)*.
 (b) silver nitrate + hydrochloric acid → silver chloride + nitric acid *(1 mark)*.
 (c) First, filter the solution to remove the salt which has precipitated out *(1 mark)*. Then wash the insoluble salt (with distilled water) *(1 mark)* and then leave it to dry/dry it in an oven *(1 mark)*.

ANSWERS

Page 130-131
Warm-Up Questions

1) It must be molten or dissolved in water.
2) At the cathode/negative electrode.
3) hydrogen, chlorine and sodium hydroxide
4) hydrogen and oxygen
5) It makes the copper a better (electrical) conductor.

Exam Questions

1. (a) The bulb lit up because there was a flow of electrons around the circuit *(1 mark)*.
   (b) At the anode/positive electrode *(1 mark)*.
   (c) The positive lead ions move to the negative cathode where they gain electrons to give lead atoms *(1 mark)*. The lead metal is denser than the lead bromide so it sinks to the bottom *(1 mark)*.
   (d) (i) $Pb^{2+} + 2e^- \rightarrow Pb$ *(1 mark)*
   (ii) $2Br^- \rightarrow Br_2 + 2e^-$ *(1 mark)*

2. (a) (i) hydrogen *(1 mark)*
   (ii) H^+ *(1 mark)*
   (b) (i) chlorine *(1 mark)*
   (ii) The negative chloride ions move to the anode and give up their electrons *(1 mark)* to form chlorine gas molecules, Cl_2 *(1 mark)*.

3. (a) $2H^+$ *(1 mark)* $+ 2e^-$ *(1 mark)* $\rightarrow H_2$
   (b) $2Cl^-$ *(1 mark)* $- 2e^- \rightarrow Cl_2$ *(1 mark)*
   (c) (i) Any one of, e.g. Haber process/making ammonia / making margarine *(1 mark)*.
   (ii) Any one of, e.g. making disinfectants / killing bacteria / making bleach / making plastics / making hydrochloric acid / making insecticides *(1 mark)*.
   (d) sodium *(1 mark)* and chlorine *(1 mark)*

4. (a) When solid, potassium bromide has no free ions/charge carriers and so cannot conduct electricity *(1 mark)*.
   (b) (i) the positive *(1 mark)*
   The bromide ion has a negative charge, so it will be attracted to the positive electrode.
   (ii) oxidised *(1 mark)*
   The bromide ions have lost electrons — this is oxidation.

Revision Summary for Chemistry 2iii (page 132)

9. a) i) magnesium chloride: $2HCl + Mg \rightarrow MgCl_2 + H_2$
   ii) aluminium chloride: $6HCl + 2Al \rightarrow 2AlCl_3 + 3H_2$
   iii) zinc chloride: $2HCl + Zn \rightarrow ZnCl_2 + H_2$
   b) i) magnesium sulfate: $H_2SO_4 + Mg \rightarrow MgSO_4 + H_2$
   ii) aluminium sulfate: $3H_2SO_4 + 2Al \rightarrow Al_2(SO_4)_3 + 3H_2$
   iii) zinc sulfate: $H_2SO_4 + Zn \rightarrow ZnSO_4 + H_2$

11. a) e.g. Hydrochloric acid and copper(II) oxide
    $2HCl + CuO \rightarrow CuCl_2 + H_2O$
    b) e.g. Nitric acid and calcium oxide
    $2HNO_3 + CaO \rightarrow Ca(NO_3)_2 + H_2O$
    c) e.g. Sulfuric acid and zinc oxide
    $H_2SO_4 + ZnO \rightarrow ZnSO_4 + H_2O$
    d) e.g. Nitric acid and magnesium oxide
    $2HNO_3 + MgO \rightarrow Mg(NO_3)_2 + H_2O$
    e) e.g. Sulfuric acid and sodium hydroxide
    $H_2SO_4 + 2NaOH \rightarrow Na_2SO_4 + 2H_2O$
    f) e.g. Hydrochloric acid and potassium hydroxide
    $HCl + KOH \rightarrow KCl + H_2O$

Page 141-142
Warm-Up Questions

1) it increases
2) The elements go from gas to liquid to solid (at room temperature).
3) hydrogen
4) E.g. silver bromide, zinc chloride (any metal halide).

Exam Questions

1. D *(1 mark)*
2. (a) Fluorine — gas *(1 mark)*
   Chlorine — gas *(1 mark)*
   Bromine — liquid *(1 mark)*
   Iodine — solid *(1 mark)*
   (b) Arrow should be pointing upwards. *(1 mark)*
   (c) (i) displacement *(1 mark)*
   Chlorine is displacing iodine.
   (ii) iodine/I/I_2 *(1 mark)*
3. A — 2 *(1 mark)*
   B — 3 *(1 mark)*
   C — 1 *(1 mark)*
   D — 4 *(1 mark)*

(a) Chlorine reacts with metals to form (giant) ionic compounds/ Cl⁻ ions *(1 mark)*. Chlorine reacts with non-metals to form molecular compounds with covalent bonding/by sharing electrons *(1 mark)*.

(b) (i) From colourless to orange/brown *(1 mark)*

    (ii) chlorine + potassium bromide → bromine + potassium chloride *(1 mark)*

    (iii) Chlorine has a stronger attraction for electrons *(1 mark)* because the outer shell is closer to the nucleus/less shielded from the nucleus *(1 mark)*.

Atoms react by gaining or losing electrons. Bromine is less able to attract an extra electron as its outer shell is further from the nucleus than chlorine's.

Page 145
Warm-Up Questions

1) 18

2) Any three of, e.g. more than one ion (with different charges) / coloured compounds / make useful catalysts / good conductors of heat/electricity / dense / strong / shiny / hard / have high melting points.

Exam Questions

1 (a) C and E *(1 mark each)*.

C is scandium and E is nickel, if you're interested.

  (b) (i) Any two of, e.g. iron has a higher melting point / iron is stronger / iron is harder / iron is denser / *(1 mark each)*.

    (ii) Any one of, e.g. iron is less reactive / iron forms more than one ion (Fe^{2+}, Fe^{3+}) *(1 mark)*.

  (c) (i) Cu^{2+} / copper(II) *(1 mark)*

    (ii) It is coloured/blue *(1 mark)*.

2 (a) Transition metals have higher melting points than group 1 and 2 metals / transition metals have higher densities than group 1 and 2 metals / transition metals can form ions with different charges / transition metals react less vigorously when heated in air than group 1 and 2 metals
(3 marks available — 1 mark for each correct point).

Questions like this are easy marks — all you're asked to do is find information from the table — the answers are right there in front of you.

(b) E.g. catalytic properties (as metals or compounds) *(1 mark)*, transition metal compounds are usually coloured *(1 mark)*.

(c) The properties are due to the overlap between the third and fourth energy levels, which affects the way the electron shells fill *(1 mark)*.

Page 149
Warm-Up Questions

1) H^+ and SO_4^{2-}

2) A proton donor.

3) An acid that only partially ionises in solution.

4) $CH_3COOH \rightleftharpoons H^+ + CH_3COO^-$

5) A strong acid is one that almost completely ionises in water. A concentrated acid is one with a large number of molecules (or ions) in a particular unit volume of it.

Exam Questions

1 (a) $NH_3(g) + H_2O(l)$ *(1 mark)* → $NH_4^+(aq)$ *(1 mark)* + $OH^-(aq)$

  (b) Ammonia is a proton acceptor *(1 mark)* — it doesn't need to be in solution to do this *(1 mark)*.

  (c) Weak alkalis only partially ionise when dissolved in water *(1 mark)*. Strong alkalis (almost) completely ionise when dissolved in water *(1 mark)*.

2 (a) (i) OH^- ions/$OH^-(aq)$ ions/hydroxide ions/hydroxyl ions *(1 mark)*

    (ii) H^+ ions/$H^+(aq)$ ions/hydrogen ions *(1 mark)*

  (b) Arrhenius' theory was limited to acids and bases that dissolved in water *(1 mark)*.

  (c) Scientists were reluctant to accept Arrhenius' theory because ideas about ions were new and they didn't understand how they could be formed. / The theory had limitations, and a hypothesis is less likely to be accepted when there are lots of exceptions that it can't explain *(1 mark)*.

  (d) Acids were defined as proton donors and bases were defined as proton acceptors *(1 mark)*.

  (e) The theory could explain reactions of acids and bases in different solvents / in the absence of a solvent (e.g. HCl(g) and $NH_3(g)$) *(1 mark)*.

Pages 155–156
Warm-Up Questions

1) $0.15 \times 1000 = 150$ cm³

2) $n = c \times V = 0.1 \times (25/1000) = 0.0025$ mol

3) $M_r = (2 \times 23) + 12 + (3 \times 16) = 106$
Concentration $= 2.65 \div 106 = 0.025$ mol/dm³

4) The point at which the indicator changes colour/the solution is just neutralised.

Exam Questions

1. (a) (i) $4.9 \times (1000/250) = 19.6$ g/dm^3 *(1 mark)*
   (ii) $M_r = (3 \times 1) + 31 + (4 \times 16) = 98$ *(1 mark)*
   Concentration $= 19.6 \div 98 = 0.2$ mol/dm^3 *(1 mark)*
   (b) Mass $= n \times M_r$
   mass $= 0.1 \times 98 = 9.8$ g *(1 mark)*

2. Measure 25 cm^3 of the hydrochloric acid using a pipette and place the acid in a conical flask *(1 mark)*. Add a few drops of indicator/methyl orange/phenolphthalein *(1 mark)*. Fill a burette with the sodium hydroxide solution *(1 mark)*. Add the sodium hydroxide slowly until the indicator changes colour *(1 mark)*. Repeat the experiment and find the average volume required *(1 mark)*. Use this volume to calculate the number of moles of each reactant used in the titration and use this to calculate the concentration of the hydrochloric acid *(1 mark)*.

   (Any five for a maximum of 5 marks — note that it is acceptable to have the sodium hydroxide in the conical flask and add the acid.)

3. (a) $n = c \times V$ *(1 mark)*
   $n = 0.1 \times (27.5/1000) = 0.00275$ mol *(1 mark)*
   (b) HCl and NaOH react in a 1:1 ratio, so number of moles of HCl $= 0.00275$ mol *(1 mark)*
   (c) $c = n \div V$ *(1 mark)*
   $V = 25/1000 = 0.025$
   $c = 0.00275 \div 0.025 = 0.11$ mol/dm^3 *(1 mark)*

4. (a) $n = c \times V$ *(1 mark)*
   $n = 1.0 \times (30.3/1000) = 0.0303$ mol *(1 mark)*
   (b) H_2SO_4 and NaOH react in a 1:2 ratio, so number of moles of H_2SO_4
   $= 0.0303 \div 2 = 0.01515$ mol *(1 mark)*
   (c) $c = n \div V$ *(1 mark)*
   $V = 25/1000 = 0.025$
   $c = 0.01515 \div 0.025 = 0.606$ mol/dm^3 *(1 mark)*

5. (a) Any one of, e.g. it was an anomalous result/an outlier / the first titration is often a 'rough' titration and its result is not accurate *(1 mark)*.
   (b) Moles of NaOH $= c \times V$
   $= 0.1 \times (9.0/1000) = 0.0009$ mol *(1 mark)*
   HA and NaOH react in a 1:1 ratio, so moles of HA $= 0.0009$ moles *(1 mark)*
   Concentration of HA $= n \div V$
   $= 0.0009 \div 0.025 = 0.036$ mol/dm^3 *(1 mark)*
   (c) The acid used in lemonade is a weak acid (e.g. citric acid) *(1 mark)*. There will actually be very few free H^+ ions in the lemonade/the acid will be only partially ionised *(1 mark)*.

Page 161
Warm-Up Questions

1) By evaporation.
2) Water molecules are polar.
3) To remove solids.
4) To kill microorganisms.
5) By distillation (boiling water and condensing the steam).

Exam Questions

1. (a) 1 — evaporation *(1 mark)*
   2 — condensation *(1 mark)*
   3 — clouds *(1 mark)*
   (b) Rainwater falls onto land where it dissolves soluble substances, e.g. from rocks/fertilisers/waste *(1 mark)* and it then runs back to the sea (in rivers) *(1 mark)*.

2. (a) It suggests that it is ionic bonding *(1 mark)*.
   (b) As the temperature increases, so does the solubility *(1 mark)*.

Page 166
Warm-Up Questions

1) The higher the temperature, the lower the solubility of gases.
2) Usually the higher the temperature, the greater the solubility of solids.
3) A saturated solution is one that cannot dissolve any more solid at that temperature.
4) Water that doesn't form a lather with soap / Water that forms scale on the inside of pipes / Water that contains a lot of calcium and magnesium ions.

Exam Questions

1. (a) Because above this temperature the water becomes a gas — 100 °C is the boiling point of water *(1 mark)*.
   And, fairly obviously, you can't dissolve a solid in a gas...
   (b) 5 g (accept answers between 4 g and 6 g) *(1 mark)*
   (c) Solubility is 15 g per 100 g of water at 80 °C *(1 mark)*
   250 g of water will dissolve $(250 \div 100) \times 15$ g $= 37.5$ g *(1 mark)* (Accept answers between 35 g and 40 g)
   (d) At 90 °C, 20 g dissolved. At 10 °C, 4 g dissolved *(1 mark)*.
   $20 - 4 = 16$ g will crystallise out *(1 mark)*.
   (Accept answers between 14 g and 18 g.)

2. (a) Any two of, e.g. Forms scum with soap. / Requires more soap for cleaning. / Forms limescale on heating systems/kettles, etc. / May block pipes. *(1 mark each)*.
   (b) Calcium ions are good for healthy teeth and bones. Scale can form a protective coating inside metal pipes to stop them from corroding. *(1 mark each)*

Revision Summary for Chemistry 3i (page 167)

11. $2Fe\ (s) + 3Cl_2\ (g) \rightarrow 2FeCl_3\ (s)$
20. Phenolphthalein.
21. a) No. of moles NaOH $= 0.2 \times (25 \div 1000) = 0.005$
    HCl + NaOH $\rightarrow$ NaCl + H_2O, so no. of moles HCl $= 0.005$
    Concentration HCl (moles per dm^3)
    $= 0.005 \div (49 \div 1000) = 0.102$ moles per dm^3
    b) M_r HCl $= 1 + 35.5 = 36.5$
    mass $=$ number of moles $\times M_r$
    $= 0.102 \times 36.5 = 3.72$ grams per dm^3

245

2 a) M_r Ca(OH)$_2$ = 40 + (2 × 16) + (2 × 1) = 74
No. of moles Ca(OH)$_2$ = mass ÷ M_r = 7.5 ÷ 74 = 0.101 mol
Concentration (moles per dm^3) = moles ÷ volume
= 0.101 ÷ 1 = 0.101 moles per dm^3

b) Concentration (moles per dm^3) = moles ÷ volume
= 0.101 ÷ (100 ÷ 1000) = 1.01 moles per dm^3

5 a), c), d), e), g) and i) will all dissolve in water.
b), f) and h) will not dissolve in water.

7 a) 75 g   b) 35 °C   c) 95 g – 75 g = 20 g

Pages 176-177
Warm-Up Questions

1) exothermic
2) The temperature will decrease.
3) Energy is given out — it's exothermic.
4) ΔH
5) This is the amount of energy needed to raise the temperature of 1 g of water by 1 °C.

Exam Questions

1 (a) The methane burns / gives out heat/light *(1 mark)*.
  (b) (i) C—H and O=O *(1 mark)*
      (ii) O=O, because it is a double bond *(1 mark)*.
  (c) (i) (4 × 414) + (2 × 494) = 2644 kJ/mol *(1 mark)*
      (ii) (2 × 800) + (4 × 459) = 3436 kJ/mol *(1 mark)*
      (iii) 3436 – 2644 = 792 kJ/mole *(1 mark)*
  (d) The energy released when the new bonds are formed is greater than the energy needed to break the original bonds, so overall energy is given out *(1 mark)*.

2 (a) x = activation energy *(1 mark)*. y = ΔH *(1 mark)*.
  (b) Endothermic *(1 mark)*, because the products have more energy than the reactants, so energy must be taken in during the reaction *(1 mark)*.
  (c) Because the activation energy is too high *(1 mark)*.

3 (a) To make it a fair test/so that the temperature rise is proportional to the amount of heat produced *(1 mark)*.
  (b) 100 × 4.2 × 21 *(1 mark)* = 8820 J/8.82 kJ *(1 mark — units needed)*.
  This gives you the energy transferred (in J) and normally you would then have to divide this by the mass of fuel burned (in g) to find the heat energy transferred per gram of fuel. But in this case only 1 g of fuel was burned anyway. So you're done.
  (c) [energy diagrams for fuel A + oxygen and fuel B + oxygen, showing products lower than reactants, with fuel B products lower than fuel A]

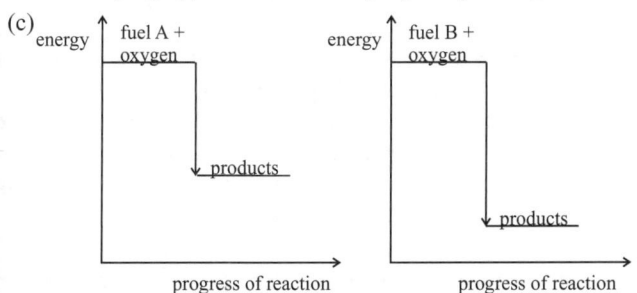

(1 mark for showing products lower than reactants, 1 mark if products are shown at a lower level for fuel B than for A.)

Pages 182-183
Warm-Up Questions

1) a) K$^+$
   b) Ba^{2+}
2) Blue.
3) Use damp red litmus paper — it will turn blue. (Or smell it.)
4) carbonate

Exam Questions

1
Flame colour	Metal ion
green	Ba^{2+}
lilac	K$^+$
orange-yellow	Na$^+$
(brick-)red	Ca^{2+}

(1 mark each)

2 Add nitric acid and then silver nitrate solution *(1 mark)*.
A white precipitate indicates chloride ions *(1 mark)*.
A cream precipitate indicates bromide ions *(1 mark)*.
A yellow precipitate indicates iodide ions *(1 mark)*.

3 (a) Add sodium hydroxide solution *(1 mark)*. A (sludgy) green precipitate indicates iron(II) ions *(1 mark)*.
  (b) Add dilute hydrochloric acid and then barium chloride solution *(1 mark)*. A white precipitate indicates sulfate ions *(1 mark)*.

4 Al^{3+} *(1 mark)*
  NH$_4^+$ *(1 mark)*
  Cu^{2+} *(1 mark)*
  Ca^{2+} *(1 mark)*

5 (a) Calcium(II) chloride, CaCl$_2$
     (1 mark for calcium, 1 mark for chloride).
  (b) Potassium nitrate, KNO$_3$
     (1 mark for potassium, 1 mark for nitrate).

Page 190
Warm-Up Questions

1) The surface would char/blacken.
2) e.g. mass spectrometry

Answers

Exam Questions

1. (a) Proportion of C in $CO_2 = 12 \div 44 \approx 0.27$
   mass of C in compound $= 4.4 \times 0.27 \approx 1.2$ g *(1 mark)*
   moles of C $= 1.2 \div 12 = 0.1$ mol *(1 mark)*
   (b) Proportion of H in $H_2O = 2 \div 18 \approx 0.11$
   mass of H in compound $= 1.8 \times 0.11 \approx 0.2$ g *(1 mark)*
   moles of H $= 0.2 \div 1 = 0.2$ mol *(1 mark)*
   (c) Ratio of C:H $= 0.1:0.2 = 1:2$
   So the empirical formula is CH_2 *(1 mark)*.

2. (a) Mass of C in compound $= 1.1 \times (12 \div 44) = 0.3$ g
   Moles of C $= 0.3 \div 12 = 0.025$ mol *(1 mark)*
   Mass of H in compound $= 0.675 \times (2 \div 18) = 0.075$ g
   Moles of H $= 0.075 \div 1 = 0.075$ mol *(1 mark)*
   Ratio C:H $= 0.025:0.075 = 1:3$
   So empirical formula is CH_3 *(1 mark)*.
   (b) Shake with bromine water *(1 mark)*. The bromine water will not decolourise / will stay coloured/brown/orange *(1 mark)*.

3. (a) C *(1 mark)*
   (b) Any two of, e.g. they're much quicker / they're more accurate / they can be carried out by technicians — you don't have to pay trained chemists to do everything / the tests can be automated / even very tiny amounts of chemical can be detected and analysed *(1 mark for each correct answer, maximum 2 marks)*.

Revision Summary for Chemistry 3ii (page 191)

3. a) Mass of water heated $= 116$ g $- 64$ g $= 52$ g
   Temperature rise of water $= 47$ °C $- 17$ °C $= 30$ °C
   Mass of pentane burnt $= 97.72$ g $- 97.37$ g $= 0.35$ g

   So 0.35 g of pentane provides enough energy to heat up 52 g of water by 30 °C.

   It takes 4.2 joules of energy to heat up 1 g of water by 1 °C.

   Therefore, the energy produced in this experiment is
   $4.2 \times 52 \times 30 = 6552$ joules.

   So, 0.35 g of pentane produces 6552 joules of energy...
   ... meaning 1 g of pentane produces 6552/0.35
   $= 18\,720$ J or 18.720 kJ

8. a) Bonds broken: 2 moles of H–H bonds $= 2 \times 436 = 872$ kJ
   1 mole of O=O bonds $= 496$ kJ
   Total energy needed to break bonds $= 872 + 496 = 1368$ kJ

   Bonds made: 2 moles of (2 × O–H bonds) $= 2 \times 2 \times 463$
   $= 1852$ kJ

   Overall more energy is released than is used,
   so $1852 - 1368 = 484$ kJ/mol is released.
   b) This is an exothermic reaction.

9. 4.2 J = 1 calorie, 655 kJ = 655 000 J
   $655\,000 \div 4.2 = 156\,000$ calories $= 156$ kcal

17. Mass of carbon $= 4.4 \times (12 \div 44) = 1.2$ g
    Mass of hydrogen $= 1.8 \times (2 \div 18) = 0.2$ g
    No. moles carbon $= 1.2 \div 12 = 0.1$ moles
    No. moles hydrogen $= 0.2 \div 1 = 0.2$ moles
    $0.2 \div 0.1 = 2$ (so there's 1 carbon to every 2 hydrogens)
    Empirical formula $= CH_2$

Exam Paper — Chemistry Unit 1

1. a) *Any one of,* e.g. wear safety goggles / use a heatproof mat under the apparatus / wear a lab coat *(1 mark)*.
   b) An ore is a mineral/rock that contains enough of a metal to make it worth extracting *(1 mark)*.
   c) $CuCO_3 \rightarrow$ **CuO** $+ CO_2$,
   2CuO $+ C \rightarrow 2Cu + CO_2$
   (1 mark for CuO, 1 mark for correctly balancing the equations)
   d) Thermal decomposition *(1 mark)*
   The copper carbonate is being broken down into new products.
   e) 4 g $-$ 2.6 g $= 1.4$ g *(1 mark)*
   The mass of the reactants always equals the mass of the product because atoms aren't gained or lost in chemical reactions.
   f) Copper is less reactive than carbon, so the carbon reacts with the oxygen in copper oxide *(1 mark)*.
   g) The atoms are arranged in layers *(1 mark)* which can slide over each other *(1 mark)*.

2. a) All points accurately plotted *(1 mark)*. Smooth curve of best fit drawn (no double lines, no straight lines between points) *(1 mark)*.

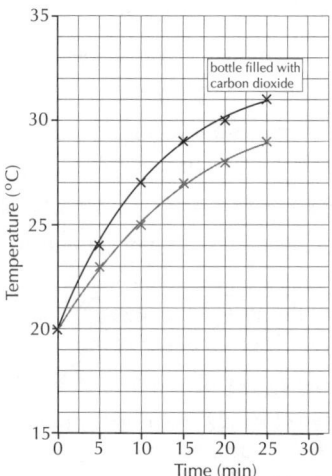

   b) The temperature of the carbon dioxide increased more (and more quickly) than the temperature of the air *(1 mark)*.
   The line showing the temperature of the carbon dioxide reaches a higher point on the graph.
   c) E.g. he should have made sure the bottles were the same distance away from the lamp *(1 mark)*.
   This would ensure that the bottles were receiving the same amount of heat from the lamp.

3. a) Carbon dioxide — adds to the greenhouse effect, leading to global warming/climate change *(1 mark)*.
   Sulfur dioxide — causes acid rain, which can harm trees and water life and erode buildings *(1 mark)*.
   Particulate matter — stays in the air and may prevent some of the Sun's light reaching Earth's surface (global dimming) / has been linked to various health problems in humans (including narrowing of the arteries) *(1 mark)*.
   b) Biodiesel is made from a renewable resource so it won't run out / the carbon released from burning biodiesel was recently in the atmosphere, so it makes a smaller contribution to the greenhouse effect *(1 mark)*.

a) Most of the volcanoes are found on or near plate boundaries *(1 mark)*.
b) It is usually only at the boundaries that large bodies of rock move past/rub against each other, causing earthquakes *(1 mark)*.
c) No *(1 mark)*, earthquakes are sudden movements / there are very few clues to tell scientists when a volcano or earthquake is likely to happen *(1 mark)*.

a) A substance that speeds up a reaction, without being changed or used up as part of the reaction. *(1 mark)*.
b) ethanol *(1 mark)*
c) *Any three of,* e.g. used as a fuel in cars and spirit lamps / present in alcoholic drinks / used as a solvent in many industries / used in some perfumes and paints / used in antibacterial wipes for hospitals and the catering industry *(3 marks)*.
d) Ethene is usually produced from crude oil, which is a non-renewable resource *(1 mark)*. As stocks run low, crude oil products will become increasingly expensive *(1 mark)*.

a) Steel contains elements which have different sized atoms *(1 mark)*. This makes it more difficult for the layers to slide over each other / the atoms to slide past each other *(1 mark)*.
b) i) mild steel *(1 mark)*
   It has the lowest strength out of the alloys shown on the graph.
   ii) E.g. for making cutting tools, such as drills *(1 mark)*
   This steel has the greatest strength, which is a property needed in tools.
c) i) An alloy that returns to its original shape after being deformed and raised above a certain temperature. *(1 mark)*.
   ii) Smart alloys are more expensive than, e.g. steel or aluminium / they suffer more from metal fatigue *(1 mark)*.

a) i) Wild salmon is the healthier choice *(1 mark)*.
   ii) *Any two of,* because it has more protein / because it has less fat / because it has less saturated fat / because it contains fewer contaminants *(2 marks)*.
b) chromatography *(1 mark)*
c) Unsaturated fats contain some double carbon-carbon bonds and saturated fats contain only single carbon-carbon bonds *(1 mark)*.

a) carbon dioxide *(1 mark)*
b) oxygen *(1 mark)*
c) In the early atmosphere there was a lot of carbon dioxide released from active volcanoes *(1 mark)*. As the Earth cooled, the oceans formed, dissolving a lot of carbon dioxide *(1 mark)*. Green plants evolved, which removed more carbon dioxide *(1 mark)* and added oxygen to the air *(1 mark)* by photosynthesis.

Exam Paper — Chemistry Unit 2

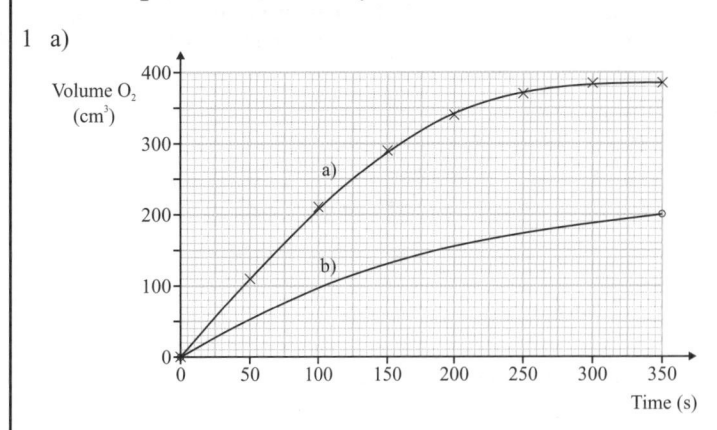

1 a) *(1 mark for sensible scales on axes, 1 mark for correctly plotted points, 1 mark for smooth curve through the points)*

   b) See diagram in part a). The line should be a smooth curve with a shallower gradient than the original graph *(1 mark)* and should pass through the origin and the point (350, 200). *(1 mark)*

   Make sure you use all the information in the question. You've been given a data point, so your graph has to go through that point.

   c) It is exothermic. *(1 mark)*

2 a) Ammonia and nitric acid *(1 mark)*
   b) By evaporating the liquid from the solution, allowing the salt to crystallise. *(1 mark)*
   c) $14 + (1 \times 4) + 14 + (16 \times 3) = 80$ *(2 marks for correct answer, otherwise 1 mark for correct substitution)*
   d) $[(14 + 14) \div 80] \times 100 = 35\%$ *(1 mark)*
   e) E.g. as a fertiliser *(1 mark)*

3 a) i) $N_2(g) + 3H_2(g) \rightleftharpoons 2NH_3(g)$ *(1 mark for correct substances with state symbols, 1 mark for correct balancing)*
      ii) $280 + 60 = 340$ g *(1 mark)*
      iii) $(58.5 \div 340) \times 100 = 17\%$ *(1 mark)*
   b) The point at which the forward and reverse reactions occur at exactly the same rate. *(1 mark)*
   c) i) Increasing the temperature decreases the yield of ammonia because the endothermic reaction is favoured. *(1 mark)*
      ii) Increasing the temperature increases the rate of the reaction because it increases the speed of the reacting particles, so that they collide more frequently and energetically. *(1 mark)*

4 a) The relative atomic mass of an element is the mass of one atom of that element compared with an atom of carbon-12. *(1 mark)* It is an average value for the isotopes of that element. *(1 mark)*

b) E.g.

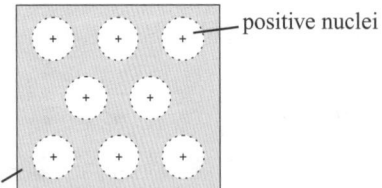

[diagram: square with 7 circled '+' symbols labelled "positive nuclei", with shaded background labelled "delocalised electrons"]

(1 mark)

The question asks for a <u>labelled</u> diagram, so if you don't label it, you don't get the mark.

c) i) The delocalised electrons within silver are able to move and conduct heat and electricity across the metal. *(1 mark)*

ii) The layers of atoms within silver are able to slide over each other. *(1 mark)*

d) Structures that are 1-100 nm in size. *(1 mark)*

5 a) $2Cl^- \rightarrow Cl_2 + 2e^-$ *(1 mark)*
$2H^+ + 2e^- \rightarrow H_2$ *(1 mark)*

b) moles per cubic decimetre (mol/dm³) or moles per litre (mol/l) *(1 mark)*

c) The two solutions contain the same mass of sodium. *(1 mark)*

6 a) Value given must be greater than 7 (actual value between 13 and 14) because it contains hydroxide (OH⁻) ions. *(1 mark)*

b) E.g. The electrolysis of sodium chloride solution. *(1 mark)*

c) $NaOH(aq) + HCl(aq) \rightarrow NaCl(aq) + H_2O(l)$ *(1 mark for correct substances, 1 mark for state symbols)*

d) Calculate the mass of 1 mole of, NaOH: 23 + 16 + 1 = 40 g, HCl: 1 + 35.5 = 36.5 g
The equation shows that 1 mole of HCl neutralises 1 mole of NaOH, so the ratio is 36.5 g : 40 g
Divide both sides by 40 to get the ratio 1 g of NaOH : 0.9125 g of HCl, so 0.9125 g of HCl are needed.
(3 marks for correct answer, otherwise 1 mark for calculating molar masses and 1 mark for setting up a ratio)

7 a) Because it saves money and energy, which is important for sustainable development. *(1 mark)*

b) Because if the forward reaction is exothermic, the backward reaction must be endothermic by the same amount. *(1 mark)* At equilibrium the two reactions occur at the same rate, so the amount of energy taken in and given out is equal. *(1 mark)*

Be careful with questions like this — there's no energy transfer because the forward and reverse reactions are happening <u>at the same rate</u>. They haven't stopped.

c) It will increase the yield of sulfur trioxide *(1 mark)*, because increasing the pressure favours the reaction that produces the least number of molecules, i.e. the forward reaction *(1 mark)*.

d) Because the reactions are carried out at different temperatures. *(1 mark)*

e)

(1 mark for each correctly completed row)

f) 100% *(1 mark)*

Exam Paper — Chemistry Unit 3

1 a) E.g. so that a comparison can easily be made between different products / because different products may contain different amounts of crisps *(1 mark)*.

b) The higher fat content, because fat has a higher energy content than carbohydrate or protein *(1 mark)*.

c) A yellow/orange flame *(1 mark)*.

d) Halve the volume of water/reduce the volume to 50 g *(1 mark)*. Double the mass of crisps burnt/increase the mass of crisps burnt to 2 g *(1 mark)*.

e) It is a better conductor of heat than a glass beaker *(1 mark)*.

f) Heat produced by 1 g of crisps = 100 × 4.2 × 5 = 2100 J *(1 mark)*

g) Any two of, e.g. a lot of heat is lost to the surroundings / not all the crisps would be burnt / incomplete combustion would reduce the amount of heat produced *(2 marks)*

Notice that this question is worth 2 marks — even though the questions don't always say how many points they want you to write, the number of marks is usually a big clue.

Solution A	Solution B	Description of test	Observations	
			Solution A	Solution B
Iron(II) chloride	Iron(III) chloride	Add sodium hydroxide (NaOH) solution	Dirty green precipitate	Rust red precipitate
Sodium chloride	Sodium iodide	Add dilute nitric acid (HNO$_3$) followed by silver nitrate (AgNO$_3$) solution	White precipitate	Yellow precipitate
Ammonium chloride	Sodium chloride	1. Add sodium hydroxide (NaOH) solution 2. Carry out a flame test	1. Smell of ammonia or gas turns red litmus blue. 2. No flame colour	1. No gas detected. 2. Yellow/orange colour flame

(1 mark for each test, 1 mark for each set of observations.)

a) A solution in which no more solute/solid can dissolve *(1 mark)*.
b) Indicator — methyl orange *(1 mark)*.
c) It only partially ionises in water *(1 mark)*.
d) i) $(8.8 \div 1000) \times 0.05 = 0.00044$ *(1 mark)*
   ii) $0.00044 \div 2 = 0.00022$ *(1 mark)*

   From the equation you can see that there are two molecules of HCl to every one of Ca(OH)$_2$. This means that you can just divide your answer to part i) by two.

   iii) $0.00022 \times (1000 \div 10) = 0.022$ mol/dm^3 *(1 mark)*
   iv) $0.022 \times 74 = 1.63$ g/dm^3 *(1 mark)*
e) E.g. repeat the titration *(1 mark)*.

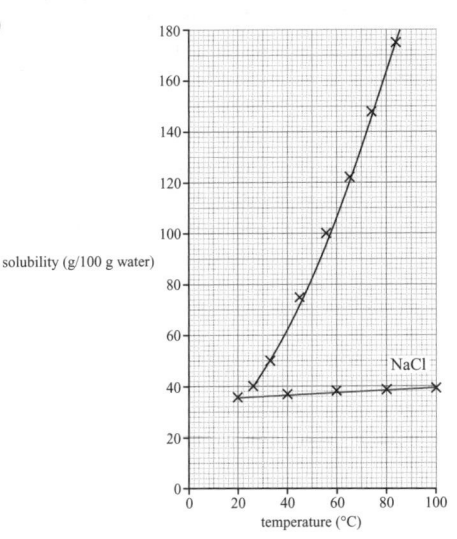

a) [Graph of solubility (g/100 g water) vs temperature (°C), showing NaCl curve nearly flat around 40, and another steeply rising curve reaching ~180 at 100 °C]

(1 mark for points correctly plotted, 1 mark for curve of best fit.)

b) The solubility increases as the temperature increases *(1 mark)*.
c) At 70 °C, 136 g (accept 134-138 g) could be dissolved *(1 mark)*.

   At 30 °C, 46 g (accept 44-48 g) could be dissolved *(1 mark)*.

   So when the solution is cooled from 70 °C to 30 °C, 136 – 46 = 90 g will crystallise out *(1 mark for a value correctly calculated from the above data)*.

   This question is pretty much just a case of reading off the graph, so make sure you're familiar with this so that you don't lose easy marks.

d) Graph B because gases show a decrease in solubility with increasing temperature *(1 mark)*.

5 a) A scum/dirty white precipitate *(1 mark)*.
b) The more soap needed for a good lather, the harder the water *(1 mark)*.
c) So that an average can be calculated from the results / to get a more reliable estimate of the true value *(1 mark)*.
d) The results are variable because deciding when a good lather has formed requires a judgement which may not be consistent *(1 mark)*.
e) Adding sodium carbonate *(1 mark)* — the calcium and magnesium ions are precipitated out of solution as insoluble carbonates *(1 mark)*.

   Using an ion exchange column *(1 mark)* — the calcium and magnesium ions are replaced by sodium ions, making the water soft *(1 mark)*.
f) Using hard water can increase costs as more soap will be needed to make a lather. / Scale can build up in kettles and heating systems, reducing their efficiency *(1 mark)*.

6 a) Bonds broken $(4 \times 413) + (2 \times 498) = +2648$ *(1 mark)*
   Bonds formed $(2 \times 805) + (4 \times 464) = -3466$ *(1 mark)*
   Total change $+2648 - 3466 = -818$ (kJ/mole) or 818 kJ released *(1 mark)*
   Energy change $= -818$ kJ/mole *(1 mark)*
b) Exothermic *(1 mark)*. The energy released from forming new bonds is greater than the energy needed to break existing bonds *(1 mark)*.

Index

A

accuracy 194
acid gas scrubbers 38
acid rain 15, 31, 37, 38, 120, 158
acidic soils 15, 120
acidic solutions 147
acids 120-124, 146-148, 152, 165
activated carbon filters 159
activation energy 109, 110, 172
air 13
alkali metals 68, 137, 138
alkalis 120, 122, 146-148, 152
alkanes 34, 35, 44
alkenes 44-48
alloys 28-31
alternative energy sources 171
alternative fuels 37, 40
aluminium 22, 30, 178
aluminium chloride 121, 140
aluminium sulphate 121
ammonia 77, 117, 123, 128, 146, 147
ammonium carbonates 123
ammonium hydroxides 123
ammonium nitrate 123
ammonium salts 123, 158
anions 74, 127, 180-181, 188
anode 127-129
anomalous results 193, 195
aqueous 14
Arrhenius 146
atmosphere 60, 61
atmospheric change 61
atom economy 94, 95
atomic number 65, 67, 68, 133, 135
atomic structure 1, 2, 10, 65-70
atoms 1, 2, 10, 12, 65, 69
averages 5

B

balancing equations 14
bar chart 196
bases 120, 123, 146, 147
bauxite 22
bias 5
biodegradable 48
biodiesel 52
biogas 40
bond energies 172-173
brine 128
bromine 139, 140

bromine water 184
Brønsted 147
bronze 29
buckminsterfullerene 82
burettes 153
burning 184, 185
burning fuels 113
burning splint test 121
butane 34
butene 45
by-products 95

C

C–C bond 34
C=C double bond 45, 53, 184
calcium carbonate 15, 114, 164
calcium hydrogencarbonate 164
calcium hydroxide 12, 120, 122
calcium ions 124, 165
calcium sulfate 122
calculating masses in reactions 89
calories 174
calorimetry 170
cancer 4
carbon 79, 82, 160, 184
carbon-12 67, 86, 90
carbon-14 67
carbon dioxide 38, 39, 52, 60, 61, 162, 180, 184
carbon monoxide 38
carbon slurry 159
carbon tetrachloride 139
carbonated water 162
carbonates 60, 123
carbonic acid 164
catalyst poisoning 111
catalysts 44, 106, 109-111, 116, 117, 144, 172
catalytic converters 38
categoric variables 194
cathode 127, 129
cations 74, 127, 178, 188
cement 16, 17
centrifuge 50
CFCs 61
chalcopyrite 22
chalk 164
chemical bonds 12
chemical tests 188
chloride (Cl–) ions 127
chlorides 123, 158
chlorination 159
chlorine 76, 139, 140, 159
chlorine water 162
cholera 159, 160
cholesterol 53

chromatography 55
clean water 159, 160
climate change 8, 9, 31, 39, 171
closed system 115
cold fusion 3
collision theory 108, 109
colourings (food) 54
combustion 113
comets 61
compounds 12, 66
concentrated acids 148
concentration 104-106, 108, 148, 150, 151, 153
conclusions 196
concrete 16, 17
condensation 157
conductors 81
continents 57
continuous data 194
control group 196
controlled experiments 3
convection currents 59
cooling packs 169
copper 22, 23, 121, 129, 178
copper carbonate 123
copper chloride 122
copper nitrate 123
copper oxide 122
copper sulfate 124
corrosion 30, 31
covalent bonding 76, 77-79, 80
cracking hydrocarbons 44, 110
crude oil 33-37, 44, 46, 48, 171
crystallisation 163
cupronickel 29

D

ΔH 110
data 5
decomposition 44, 106
deforestation 61
dependent variable 103, 192
developing countries 160
diamond 78
diesel 33, 52
dietary information 174
diets 175
discrete data 194
disinfectants 128
displacement 124
dissolving 157, 158, 162, 163
distillation 50, 160
double bonds 45, 53, 184
drinking water 124, 159, 160
drugs testing 186

dynamic equilibrium 115, 117
dysentery 159

E

earthquake 59
Earth's structure 59
economic factors 7
electricity 38, 127, 171
electrolysis 23, 25, 30, 127, 128, 129
electrolyte 127
electron arrangement 69, 74, 136
electrons 10, 12, 65, 67-69, 72, 76, 81, 127, 133, 136
electron shells 69, 70, 72, 74, 136, 144
elements 10, 11, 66, 68, 133
empirical formulas 88, 185
emulsifiers 54
emulsions 51
endothermic reactions 114, 116, 168, 172
energy 113, 168-171, 174
energy levels 69, 136
energy transfer 113, 168
E-numbers 54
environment 7, 16, 160, 171
environmental analysis 186
environmental problems 37-40
equilibrium 97, 115, 117
ethane 34
ethanol 40, 46
ethene 44-46
ethics 6
evaporation 123, 157
evidence 1-5
exothermic reactions 113, 116, 168, 170, 172, 173
experimental mass 88
experiments 2-4, 192, 196
explosion 100
extraction of metals 25

F

fair tests 3, 192
fats 174
filters 123, 159, 160
filtration 97
finite resource 37
fizzing 138
flame tests 179, 186

Index

flavourings 54
fluorine 139
food 174, 175
food additives 54, 55
forensic science 178, 186
fossil fuels 33, 38, 39, 60, 61
fossils 57
fractional distillation 33, 44
fractionating column 33
free electrons (in metals) 81
fuels 36, 38, 44, 170, 171, 174
fullerenes 82

G

gases 13, 14, 80, 102, 103, 106, 162
gas syringe 102, 103, 106
gelatin 54
giant covalent structures 78, 79, 81
giant ionic structures 73
glass 16, 17
global dimming 31, 37, 39
global warming 37, 171
graphite 79
graphs 103, 104, 195
greenhouse gases 61, 171
ground-water 159
Group 1 11, 74, 137, 138, 143
Group 2 74
Group 6 74
Group 7 11, 74, 139, 140
gypsum 164

H

Haber process 95, 110, 117, 128
haematite 22
half-equations 127
halogens 68, 139, 140
hardness minerals 164
hard water 124, 164, 165
heart disease 53
heat (in reactions) 113, 114
high density lipoproteins (HDLs) 53
H^+ ions 120, 146, 147
hydration 147
hydrocarbons 33, 35, 44, 184
hydrochloric acid 120-122, 124
hydrogen 40, 76, 121, 127, 129, 138, 165
hydrogenated vegetable oil 128
hydrogenation 53

hydrogen chloride 76, 105, 139
hydrogen gas 40
hydrogen peroxide 106
hydroxides 122, 123, 138, 146-148
hypotheses 1, 2, 8, 146

I

impurities 97
independent variable 103, 192
indicators 120, 124, 152
indigestion 120
inert gases 61
insecticides 128
insoluble 162
insoluble bases 147
insoluble hydroxide 178
insoluble precipitate 165
instrumental methods 186, 187, 189
insulation 168
inter-molecular forces 80
interpreting data 9, 188, 192, 193
iodine 139, 140
ion exchange columns 165
ion exchange resins 160
ionic bonding 72-74, 81, 138, 139, 158
ionic compounds 138, 158
ionisation 148
ions 72-74, 143, 165
iron 22, 28, 140
iron catalyst 117
iron (II) 178
iron (III) 178
iron(III) bromide 140
IR spectroscopy 189
isotopes 67, 86

J

joules 174

K

keys (bar charts) 196

L

landfill site 31, 48
lattice 73
lead chloride 123, 124
lead nitrate 124
lead sulfate 123
life expectancy 160
lime 120

limestone 15, 16, 17, 38, 164
limewater 180
line of best fit 195
lithium 137, 138
litmus paper 128, 152
low density lipoproteins (LDLs) 53
Lowry 147
Lowry and Brønsted 147

M

magnesium chloride 121
magnesium ions 124
magnesium nitrate 122
magnesium oxide 120, 122
magnesium sulphate 121
malleable 81
manganese(IV) oxide catalyst 106
marble 17
marble chips/acid reaction 103
margarine 53, 128, 184
margin of error 193
mass number 65, 67, 86
mass spectroscopy 189
mean 193
measuring reaction rates 101-106
medical tests 186
Mendeleev, Dimitri 134
metal carbonate 123
metal halides 140
metal hydroxides 123, 178
metallic bonds 21, 81
metallic structures 81
metal oxides 122
metals 20-24, 28, 29, 143, 186
methane 34, 77
methyl orange 152, 153
microorganisms 48, 159
minerals 157
mining 22
mixtures 13
molar mass 91
molecular substances 80
molecular engineering 83
moles 90, 91, 148, 150, 151, 154, 185
money 7
monounsaturated fats 53
morals 7
mortar 16

N

nanomaterials 82, 83
neutral 120
neutralisation 113, 120-124, 153, 154, 168
neutrons 10, 65, 67, 86
Newlands' law of octaves 133
nitinol 83
nitrates 121, 123, 158, 159
nitric acid 121, 123
nitrogen 60
nitrogen oxides 121
noble gases 61, 68
nuclear energy 36
nuclear magnetic resonance (NMR) spectroscopy 187
nucleus 10, 65
numerical data 194

O

oceans 60
oil spills 37
olive oil 50
ordered variables 194
ores 22
organic compounds 184, 185
organisms 60
outer shell 68, 76
oxidation reactions 113
oxides 122, 123
oxygen 60, 77
ozone layer 60, 61

P

paraffin 44
percentage mass calculations 87
percentage yield 96-97
periodic table 11, 20, 68, 133-136, 143
petrol 44
pH 120, 148, 152, 159
Phenolphthalein 152, 153
phosphates 159
photosynthesis 60
pipettes 153
plant oils 50, 52, 53
plants 60
plastics 48
plate tectonics 57, 58
pollution 38, 52, 159, 162
polymerisation 47
polymers 47, 48
polythene bags 47
polyunsaturated fats 53
population 3
position of equilibrium 116
potassium 123, 138
potassium hydroxides 122, 123, 147
potassium nitrate 122

Index

potassium salts 158
precipitation reactions 101, 124, 178
predictions 1, 2
preservatives 54
pressure 100, 108, 116
pressure of gas 162
processed foods 54
propane 34
propene 45
properties of metals 20, 21
proteins 123
proton acceptors 147
proton donors 147
proton number 65, 67
protons 10, 65, 67, 86, 133, 147
pure water 160

Q

quicklime 15, 114

R

radioactive decay 59
rainwater 164
random error 193
range 193
rates of reaction 100, 103-106, 108, 109, 195
reactants 13, 94
reaction rate graphs 100
reactivity series 24, 25, 129
recycling 31, 48, 157
reduction 25
  with carbon 129
refinery gas 35
relationships 195, 196
relative atomic mass, A_r 86-88, 90, 133, 185
relative formula mass, M_r 86-91, 94, 151
reliability 3, 4, 192, 193, 196
renewable fuels 52
renewable resources 46
reservoirs 159
respiration 175
results 5, 193
reversible reactions 97, 115-116
rubidium 137
rusting 100, 165

S

safety glass 17
salt 73, 120-124, 128
samples 3
saturated 34, 53
saturated organic compound 184
saturated solution 162
scientists 1, 2
scum 164
sedimentary rock 60
sensitivity of instruments 194
shells 10, 65, 136
shielding 136
silica 79
silicon dioxide 79
silver chloride 123
simple covalent structures 80
slaked lime 15
smart alloys 29
smart materials 48, 83
soap 128
social factors 7
sodium 72, 121, 123, 138, 165
sodium carbonate 165
sodium chloride 72, 122, 127, 128, 150
sodium hydroxide 122, 123, 128, 154, 178
sodium salts 158
sodium thiosulfate 105
solar power 36
solubility 158, 162, 163
solubility curves 163
soluble bases 147
soluble salts 123
solutes 162, 163
solutions 158, 162, 163
solvents 158
spandex fibre 48
speed of a reaction 101
squeaky pop 121, 138
stabilisers 54
stainless steel 28
state symbols 14
steel 28
steel industry 186
sterilising 162
strong acids 148
subatomic particles 10
sulfates 123, 158, 181
sulfur 105
sulfur dioxide 17, 38, 158
sulfuric acid 12, 38, 121, 122, 151, 154
supercontinent 57
surface area 100, 103, 109, 110
sustainable development 111
sweeteners 54
symbols 11
systematic error 193

T

tectonic plates 59
temperature
  reaction rate 100, 103, 106,
  collision theory 108-110,
  energy transfer 114, 116, 168
tests for anions 180, 181
tests for cations 178, 179
theories 2
thermal decomposition 44, 114
titanium 30
titrations 153, 154, 192-194
trans fats 53
transferring liquids 97
transition metals 20, 143, 144

U

ultraviolet (UV) spectroscopy 187
Universal Indicator 120, 148, 152
unsaturated 45, 53, 184

V

validity 4, 8
variables 3, 4, 192, 194, 196
vegetable oils 50, 52
viscous hydrocarbons 35
volatile hydrocarbons 35
volcanoes 59-61
volume
  reaction rates 102
  reversible reactions 116
  concentration 150

W

water 77, 138, 146, 147, 157-160, 162-164
water cycle 157
water quality 159, 160
water softeners 160
water treatment works 159
water vapour 60, 157
weak acids 148
Wegener's theory 57
wind power 36
World Health Organisation (WHO) 160

Z

zinc chloride 121
zinc oxide 122
zinc sulfate 122
zinc sulphate 121